RICK LANCASTER

PLANTERS

PERSPECTIVE

A DAILY

THRU-THE-BIBLE

DEVOTIONAL

OLD TESTAMENT

VOLUME ONE

PLANTERS PERSPECTIVE
OLD TESTAMENT: VOLUME ONE
By Rick Lancaster

Format and Layout Copyright © 2008 by LAMP PoST Inc.

Print Version and Electronic Version Copyright © 2008 by Rick Lancaster.

All rights reserved.

Scripture quotations are taken from the Holy Bible, New Living Translation, copyright ©1996 by Tyndale Charitable Trust. All rights reserved.

No part of this book (whether in printed or ebook format, or any other published derivation) may be reproduced in any form without written permission of the publisher or copyright owner except for review purposes. Unauthorized duplication is a violation of applicable laws.

LAMP PoST Inc. assumes no responsibility for any errors or inaccuracies that may appear in this book.

www.lamppostpubs.com

God's Word promises that all who seek the LORD will find Him.

This book is dedicated to those that hunger and thirst for more of God. It is my prayer that these devotionals will be used by the Holy Spirit to plant seeds of truth in the hearts of God's people.

It is my further prayer that these humble offerings will spark a love for God's Word that will draw you ever closer to Him.

CONTENTS

JANUARY

January 1 — Genesis 2:18 13
Read: Genesis 1:1-2:25

January 2 — Genesis 3:1 14
Read: Genesis 3:1-4:26

January 3 — Genesis 6:8 15
Read: Genesis 5:1-7:24

January 4 — Genesis 9:21 16
Read: Genesis 8:1-10:32

January 5 — Genesis 12:1 17
Read: Genesis 11:1-13:4

January 6 — Genesis 15:6 18
Read: Genesis 13:5-15:21

January 7 — Genesis 16:3 19
Read: Genesis 16:1-18:15

January 8 — Genesis 18:27 20
Read: Genesis 18:16-19:38

January 9 — Genesis 21:22 21
Read: Genesis 20:1-22:24

January 10 — Genesis 23:5-6 22
Read: Genesis 23:1-24:51

January 11 — Genesis 25:21 23
Read: Genesis 24:52-26:16

January 12 — Genesis 26:22 24
Read: Genesis 26:17-27:46

January 13 — Genesis 28:15 25
Read: Genesis 28:1-29:35

January 14 — Genesis 31:7 26
Read: Genesis 30:1-31:16

January 15 — Genesis 32:10 27
Read: Genesis 31:17-32:12

January 16 — Genesis 33:10 28
Read: Genesis 32:13-34:31

January 17 — Genesis 36:31 29
Read: Genesis 35:1-36:43

January 18 — Genesis 37:4 30
Read: Genesis 37:1-38:30

January 19 — Genesis 40:23 31
Read: Genesis 39:1-41:16

January 20 — Genesis 42:5 32
Read: Genesis 41:17 – 42:17

January 21 — Genesis 43:18 33
Read: Genesis 42:18-43:34

January 22 — Genesis 45:8 34
Read: Genesis 44:1-45:28

January 23 — Genesis 46:2 35
Read: Genesis 46:1-47:31

January 24 — Genesis 48:15 36
Read: Genesis 48:1-49:33

January 25 — Genesis 50:19 37
Read: Genesis 50:1-Exodus 2:10

January 26 — Exodus 2:23 38
Read: Exodus 2:11-3:22

January 27 — Exodus 4:18 39
Read: Exodus 4:1-5:21

January 28 — Exodus 7:22 40
Read: Exodus 5:22-7:25

January 29 — Exodus 9:16 41
Read: Exodus 8:1-9:35

January 30 — Exodus 12:6 42
Read: Exodus 10:1-12:13

January 31 — Exodus 13:3 43
Read: Exodus 12:14-13:16

FEBRUARY

February 1 — Exodus 13:17 45
Read: Exodus 13:17-15:18

February 2 — Exodus 16:7 46
Read: Exodus 15:19-17:7

February 3 — Exodus 18:17 47
Read: Exodus 17:8-19:15

February 4 — Exodus 20:6 48
Read: Exodus 19:16-21:21

February 5 — Exodus 23:4 49
Read: Exodus 21:22-23:13

February 6 — Exodus 25:22 50
Read: Exodus 23:14-25:40

February 7 — Exodus 26:30 51
Read: Exodus 26:1-27:21

February 8 — Exodus 28:1 52
Read: Exodus 28:1-43

February 9 — Exodus 29:1 53
Read: Exodus 29:1-30:10

February 10 — Exodus 30:19 54
Read: Exodus 30:11-31:18

February 11 — Exodus 32:1 55
Read: Exodus 32:1-33:23

February 12 — Exodus 34:29 56
Read: Exodus 34:1-35:9

February 13 — Exodus 35:26 57
Read: Exodus 35:10-36:38

February 14 — Exodus 38:8 58
Read: Exodus 37:1-38:31

February 15 — Exodus 39:32 59
Read: Exodus 39:1-40:38

February 16 — Leviticus 1:2 60
Read: Leviticus 1:1-3:17

February 17 — Leviticus 4:2 61
Read: Leviticus 4:1-5:19

February 18 — Leviticus 7:7 62
Read: Leviticus 6:1-7:27

February 19 — Leviticus 9:6 63
Read: Leviticus 7:28-9:6

February 20 — Leviticus 10:11 64
Read: Leviticus 9:7-10:20

February 21 — Leviticus 11:4 65
Read: Leviticus 11:1-12:8

February 22 — Leviticus 13:41 66
Read: Leviticus 13:1-59

February 23 — Leviticus 14:34 67
Read: Leviticus 14:1-57

February 24 — Leviticus 15:31 68
Read: Leviticus 15:1-16:28

February 25 — Leviticus 17:7 69
Read: Leviticus 16:29-18:30

February 26 — Leviticus 20:8 70
Read: Leviticus 19:1-20:21

February 27 — Leviticus 21:6 71
Read: Leviticus 20:22-22:16

February 28 — Leviticus 23:22 72
Read: Leviticus 22:17-23:44

February 29 — Leviticus 24:2 73
Read: Leviticus 24:1-25:46

MARCH

March 1 — Leviticus 25:28 75
Read: Leviticus 24:1-25:46

March 2 — Leviticus 26:3 76
Read: Leviticus 25:47-27:13

March 3 — Leviticus 27:30 77
Read: Leviticus 27:14-Numbers 1:54

March 4 — Numbers 3:12 78
Read: Numbers 2:1-3:51

March 5 — Numbers 4:2 79
Read: Numbers 4:1-5:31

March 6 — Numbers 6:4 80
Read: Numbers 6:1-7:89

March 7 — Numbers 8:2 81
Read: Numbers 8:1-9:23

March 8 — Numbers 11:11 82
Read: Numbers 10:1-11:23

March 9 — Numbers 12:1 83
Read: Numbers 11:24-13:33

March 10 — Numbers 14:33 84
Read: Numbers 14:1-15:16

March 11 — Numbers 16:9 85
Read: Numbers 15:17-16:40

March 12 — Numbers 18:7 86
Read: Numbers 16:41-18:32

March 13 — Numbers 20:12 87
Read: Numbers 19:1-20:29

March 14 — Numbers 21:8 88
Read: Numbers 21:1-22:20

March 15 — Numbers 23:8 89
Read: Numbers 22:21-23:30

March 16 — Numbers 25:3 90
Read: Numbers 24:1-25:18

March 17 — Numbers 26:51 91
Read: Numbers 26:1-51

March 18 — Numbers 27:7 92
Read: Numbers 26:52-28:15

March 19 — Numbers 29:40 93
Read: Numbers 28:16-29:40

March 20 — Numbers 31:16 94
Read: Numbers 30:1-31:54

March 21 — Numbers 32:19 95
Read: Numbers 32:1-33:39

March 22 — Numbers 34:2 96
Read: Numbers 33:40-35:34

March 23 — Deuteronomy 1:2 97
Read: Numbers 36:1-Deuteronomy 1:46

March 24 — Deuteronomy 3:22 98
Read: Deuteronomy 2:1-3:29

March 25 — Deuteronomy 4:12 99
Read: Deuteronomy 4:1-49

March 26 — Deuteronomy 6:6 100
Read: Deuteronomy 5:1-6:25

March 27 — Deuteronomy 7:7 101
Read: Deuteronomy 7:1-8:20

March 28 — Deuteronomy 10:12-13 102
Read: Deuteronomy 9:1-10:22

March 29 — Deuteronomy 11:2 103
Read: Deuteronomy 11:1-12:32

March 30 — Deuteronomy 14:2 104
Read: Deuteronomy 13:1-15:23

March 31 — Deuteronomy 17:19 105
Read: Deuteronomy 16:1-17:20

PLANTERS PERSPECTIVE / *A Devotional*

APRIL

April 1 — Deuteronomy 19:8-9 107
Read: Deuteronomy 18:1-20:20

April 2 — Deuteronomy 21:17 108
Read: Deuteronomy 21:1-22:30

April 3 — Deuteronomy 24:5 109
Read: Deuteronomy 23:1-25:19

April 4 — Deuteronomy 26:19 110
Read: Deuteronomy 26:1-27:26

April 5 — Deuteronomy 28:2 111
Read: Deuteronomy 28:1-68

April 6 — Deuteronomy 30:8 112
Read: Deuteronomy 29:1-30:20

April 7 — Deuteronomy 32:6 113
Read: Deuteronomy 31:1-32:27

April 8 — Deuteronomy 32:47 114
Read: Deuteronomy 32:28-52

April 9 — Deuteronomy 33:11 115
Read: Deuteronomy 33:1-29

April 10 — Joshua 1:8 116
Read: Deuteronomy 34:1-Joshua 2:24

April 11 — Joshua 4:24 117
Read: Joshua 3:1-4:24

April 12 — Joshua 7:11 118
Read: Joshua 5:1-7:15

April 13 — Joshua 8:2 119
Read: Joshua 7:16-9:2

April 14 — Joshua 9:14 120
Read: Joshua 9:3-10:43

April 15 — Joshua 11:15 121
Read: Joshua 11:1-12:24

April 16 — Joshua 14:12 122
Read: Joshua 13:1-14:15

April 17 — Joshua 15:63 123
Read: Joshua 16:1-18:28

April 18 — Joshua 18:3 124
Read: Joshua 16:1-18:28

April 19 — Joshua 20:3 125
Read: Joshua 19:1-20:9

April 20 — Joshua 21:44 126
Read: Joshua 21:1-22:20

April 21 — Joshua 23:14 127
Read: Joshua 22:21-23:16

April 22 — Joshua 24:15 128
Read: Joshua 24:1-33

April 23 — Judges 2:2 129
Read: Judges 1:1-2:9

April 24 — Judges 3:1-2 130
Read: Judges 2:10-3:31

April 25 — Judges 4:9 131
Read: Judges 4:1-5:31

April 26 — Judges 6:14 132
Read: Judges 6:1-40

April 27 — Judges 7:2 133
Read: Judges 7:1-8:17

April 28 — Judges 8:27 134
Read: Judges 8:18 – 9:21

April 29 — Judges 9:23 135
Read: Judges 9:22-10:18

April 30 — Judges 11:31 136
Read: Judges 11:1-12:15

MAY

May 1 — Judges 13:8 138
Read: Judges 13:1-14:20

May 2 — Judges 15:10 139
Read: Judges 15:1-16:31

May 3 — Judges 17:6 140
Read: Judges 17:1-18:31

May 4 — Judges 19:1 141
Read: Judges 19:1-20:48

May 5 — Ruth 1:16 142
Read: Judges 21:1-Ruth 1:22

May 6 — Ruth 4:16 143
Read: Ruth 2:1-4:22

May 7 — 1 Samuel 2:17 144
Read: 1 Samuel 1:1-2:21

May 8 — 1 Samuel 3:10 145
Read: 1 Samuel 2:22-4:22

May 9 — 1 Samuel 6:6 146
Read: 1 Samuel 5:1-7:17

May 10 — 1 Samuel 8:20 147
Read: 1 Samuel 8:1-9:27

May 11 — 1 Samuel 10:1 148
Read: 1 Samuel 10:1-11:15

May 12 — 1 Samuel 12:23 149
Read: 1 Samuel 12:1-13:23

May 13 — 1 Samuel 14:6 150
Read: 1 Samuel 14:1-52

May 14 — 1 Samuel 15:22 151
Read: 1 Samuel 15:1-16:23

May 15 — 1 Samuel 17:37 152
Read: 1 Samuel 17:1-18:4

May 16 — 1 Samuel 18:9 153
Read: 1 Samuel 18:5-19:24

May 17 — 1 Samuel 21:13 154
Read: 1 Samuel 20:1-21:15

May 18 — 1 Samuel 22:2 155
Read: 1 Samuel 22:1-23:29

May 19 — 1 Samuel 24:5 156
Read: 1 Samuel 24:1-25:44

May 20 — 1 Samuel 26:9 157
Read: 1 Samuel 26:1-28:25

May 21 — 1 Samuel 30:6 158
Read: 1 Samuel 29:1-31:13

May 22 — 2 Samuel 1:16 159
Read: 2 Samuel 1:1-2:11

May 23 — 2 Samuel 3:36 160
Read: 2 Samuel 2:12-3:39

May 24 — 2 Samuel 5:2 161
Read: 2 Samuel 4:1-6:23

May 25 — 2 Samuel 8:15 162
Read: 2 Samuel 7:1-8:18

May 26 — 2 Samuel 9:1 163
Read: 2 Samuel 9:1-11:27

May 27 — 2 Samuel 12:28 164
Read: 2 Samuel 12:1-31

May 28 — 2 Samuel 13:15 165
Read: 2 Samuel 13:1-39

May 29 — 2 Samuel 14:1 166
Read: 2 Samuel 14:1-15:22

May 30 — 2 Samuel 16:10 167
Read: 2 Samuel 15:23-16:23

May 31 — 2 Samuel 17:14 168
Read: 2 Samuel 17:1-29

JUNE

June 1 — 2 Samuel 19:2 170
Read: 2 Samuel 18:1-19:10

June 2 — 2 Samuel 19:41 171
Read: 2 Samuel 19:11-20:13

June 3 — 2 Samuel 21:17 172
Read: 2 Samuel 20:14-21:22

June 4 — 2 Samuel 23:8 173
Read: 2 Samuel 22:1-23:23

June 5 — 2 Samuel 24:15 174
Read: 2 Samuel 23:24-24:25

June 6 — 1 Kings 1:5 175
Read: 1 Kings 1-53

June 7 — 1 Kings 2:3 176
Read: 1 Kings 2:1-3:2

June 8 — 1 Kings 3:28 177
Read: 1 Kings 3:3-4:34

June 9 — 1 Kings 6:12-13 178
Read: 1 Kings 5:1-6:38

June 10 — 1 Kings 7:51 179
Read: 1 Kings 7:1-51

June 11 — 1 Kings 8:11 180
Read: 1 Kings 8:1-66

June 12 — 1 Kings 9:4-5 181
Read: 1 Kings 9:1-10:29

June 13 — 1 Kings 12:15 182
Read: 1 Kings 11:1-12:19

June 14 — 1 Kings 13:7 183
Read: 1 Kings 12:20-13:34

June 15 — 1 Kings 14:7 184
Read: 1 Kings 14:1-15:24

June 16 — 1 Kings 17:16 185
Read: 1 Kings 15:25-17:24

June 17 — 1 Kings 18:21 186
Read: 1 Kings 18:1-46

June 18 — 1 Kings 19:10 187
Read: 1 Kings 19:1-21

June 19 — 1 Kings 20:28 188
Read: 1 Kings 20:1-21:29

June 20 — 1 Kings 22:14 189
Read: 1 Kings 22:1-53

June 21 — 2 Kings 1:6 190
Read: 2 Kings 1:1-2:25

June 22 — 2 Kings 4:8 191
Read: 2 Kings 3:1-4:17

June 23 — 2 Kings 5:13 192
Read: 2 Kings 4:18-5:27

June 24 — 2 Kings 6:16 193
Read: 2 Kings 6:1-7:20

June 25 — 2 Kings 8:5 194
Read: 2 Kings 8:1-9:13

June 26 — 2 Kings 10:27 195
Read: 2 Kings 9:14-10:31

June 27 — 2 Kings 12:2 196
Read: 2 Kings 10:32-12:21

June 28 — 2 Kings 13:23 197
Read: 2 Kings 13:1-14:29

June 29 — 2 Kings 16:10 198
Read: 2 Kings 15:1-16:20

June 30 — 2 Kings 17:7 199
Read: 2 Kings 17:1-18:12

JULY

July 1 — 2 Kings 18:22 201
Read: 2 Kings 18:13-19:37

July 2 — 2 Kings 20:3 202
Read: 2 Kings 20:1-22:2

July 3 — 2 Kings 23:3 203
Read: 2 Kings 22:3-23:30

July 4 — 2 Kings 25:5 204
Read: 2 Kings 23:31-25:30

July 5 — 1 Chronicles 1:10 205
Read: 1 Chronicles 1:1-2:17

July 6 — 1 Chronicles 3:4 206
Read: 1 Chronicles 2:18-4:4

July 7 — 1 Chronicles 4:10 207
Read: 1 Chronicles 4:5 – 5:17

July 8 — 1 Chronicles 5:25 208
Read: 1 Chronicles 5:18-6:81

July 9 — 1 Chronicles 7:33 209
Read: 1 Chronicles 7:1-8:40

July 10 — 1 Chronicles 10:13-14 210
Read: 1 Chronicles 9:1-10:14

July 11 — 1 Chronicles 11:2 211
Read: 1 Chronicles 11:1-12:18

July 12 — 1 Chronicles 12:40 212
Read: 1 Chronicles 12:19-14:17

July 13 — 1 Chronicles 15:14 213
Read: 1 Chronicles 15:1-16:36

July 14 — 1 Chronicles 17:6 214
Read: 1 Chronicles 16:37-18:17

July 15 — 1 Chronicles 21:1 215
Read: 1 Chronicles 19:1-21:30

July 16 — 1 Chronicles 23:1 216
Read: 1 Chronicles 22:1-23:32

July 17 — 1 Chronicles 24:5 217
Read: 1 Chronicles 24:1-26:11

July 18 — 1 Chronicles 27:24 218
Read: 1 Chronicles 26:12-27:34

July 19 — 1 Chronicles 28:5 219
Read: 1 Chronicles 28:1-29:30

July 20 — 2 Chronicles 1:1 220
Read: 2 Chronicles 1:1-3:17

July 21 — 2 Chronicles 5:11 221
Read: 2 Chronicles 4:1-6:11

July 22 — 2 Chronicles 7:14 222
Read: 2 Chronicles 6:12-8:10

July 23 — 2 Chronicles 10:15 223
Read: 2 Chronicles 8:11-10:19

July 24 — 2 Chronicles 12:8 224
Read: 2 Chronicles 11:1-13:22

July 25 — 2 Chronicles 16:7 225
Read: 2 Chronicles 14:1-16:14

July 26 — 2 Chronicles 17:10 226
Read: 2 Chronicles 17:1-18:34

July 27 — 2 Chronicles 20:33 227
Read: 2 Chronicles 19:1-20:37

July 28 — 2 Chronicles 22:4 228
Read: 2 Chronicles 22:1-23:21

July 29 — 2 Chronicles 24:20 229
Read: 2 Chronicles 24:1-25:28

July 30 — 2 Chronicles 26:16 230
Read: 2 Chronicles 26:1-28:27

July 31 — 2 Chronicles 29:3 231
Read: 2 Chronicles 29:1-36

AUGUST

August 1 — 2 Chronicles 30:9 233
Read: 2 Chronicles 30:1-31:21

August 2 — 2 Chronicles 33:10 234
Read: 2 Chronicles 32:1-33:13

August 3 — 2 Chronicles 34:33 235
Read: 2 Chronicles 33:14-34:33

August 4 — 2 Chronicles 36:14 236
Read: 2 Chronicles 35:1-36:23

August 5 — Ezra 1:2 237
Read: Ezra 1:1-2:70

August 6 — Ezra 3:3 238
Read: Ezra 3:1-4:23

August 7 — Ezra 5:5 239
Read: Ezra 4:24-6:22

August 8 — Ezra 7:10 240
Read: Ezra 7:1-8:20

August 9 — Ezra 9:2 241
Read: Ezra 8:21-9:15

August 10 — Ezra 10:4 242
Read: Ezra 10:1-44

August 11 Nehemiah 3:1 243
Read: Nehemiah 1:1-3:14

August 12 — Nehemiah 5:9 244
Read: Nehemiah 3:15-5:13

August 13 — Nehemiah 6:9 245
Read: Nehemiah 5:14-7:73a

August 14 — Nehemiah 8:17 246
Read: Nehemiah 7:73b-9:21

August 15 — Nehemiah 10:32 247
Read: Nehemiah 9:22-10:39

August 16 — Nehemiah 11:2 248
Read: Nehemiah 11:1-12:26

August 17 — Nehemiah 12:30 249
Read: Nehemiah 12:27-13:31

August 18 — Esther 1:22 250
Read: Esther 1:1-3:15

August 19 — Esther 6:1 251
Read: Esther 4:1-7:10

August 20 — Esther 8:8......................252
Read: Esther 8:1-10:3

August 21 — Job 1:10 253
Read: Job 1:1-3:26

August 22 — Job 5:8..........................254
Read: Job 4:1-7:21

August 23 — Job 9:4..........................255
Read: Job 8:1-11:20

August 24 — Job 13:3 256
Read: Job 12:1-15:35

August 25 — Job 16:9........................257
Read: Job 16:1-19:29

August 26 — Job 21:34 258
Read: Job 20:1-22:30

August 27 — Job 23:13 259
Read: Job 23:1-27:23

August 28 — Job 30:20 260
Read: Job 28:1-30:31

August 29 — Job 33:14 261
Read: Job 31:1-33:33

August 30 — Job 36:5 262
Read: Job 34:1-36:33

August 31 — Job 38:2........................263
Read: Job 37:1-39:30

SEPTEMBER

September 1 — Job 40:2 265
Read: Job 40:1-42:17

September 2 — Ecclesiastes 2:24 266
Read: Ecclesiastes 1:1-3:22

September 3 — Ecclesiastes 4:12 267
Read: Ecclesiastes 4:1-6:12

September 4 — Ecclesiastes 8:15........ 268
Read: Ecclesiastes 7:1-9:18

September 5 — Ecclesiastes 12:11.........269
Read: Ecclesiastes 10:1-12:14

September 6 — Song of Songs 2:2 270
Read: Song of Songs 1:1-4:16

September 7 — Song of Songs 8:6 271
Read: Song of Songs 5:1-8:14

September 8 — Isaiah 2:17.................272
Read: Isaiah 1:1-2:22

September 9 — Isaiah 3:12.................273
Read: Isaiah 3:1-5:30

September 10 — Isaiah 6:8 274
Read: Isaiah 6:1-7:25

September 11 — Isaiah 9:1..................275
Read: Isaiah 8:1-9:21

September 12 — Isaiah 10:15 276
Read: Isaiah 10:1-11:16

September 13 — Isaiah 14:26 277
Read: Isaiah 12:1-14:32

September 14 — Isaiah 17:7 278
Read: Isaiah 15:1-18:7

September 15 — Isaiah 19:13 279
Read: Isaiah 19:1-21:17

September 16 — Isaiah 22:13 280
Read: Isaiah 22:1-24:23

September 17 — Isaiah 26:12 281
Read: Isaiah 25:1-28:13

September 18 — Isaiah 30:10..............282
Read: Isaiah 28:14-30:11

September 19 — Isaiah 31:7 283
Read: Isaiah 30:12-33:9

September 20 — Isaiah 35:3............... 284
Read: Isaiah 33:10-36:22

September 21 — Isaiah 37:4 285
Read: Isaiah 37:1-38:22

September 22 — Isaiah 41:4 286
Read: Isaiah 39:1-41:16

September 23 — Isaiah 42:20 287
Read: Isaiah 41:17-43:13

September 24 — Isaiah 44:20............ 288
Read: Isaiah 43:14-45:10

September 25 — Isaiah 47:6............... 289
Read: Isaiah 45:11-48:11

September 26 — Isaiah 49:4 290
Read: Isaiah 48:12-50:11

September 27 — Isaiah 53:6............... 291
Read: Isaiah 51:1-53:12

September 28 — Isaiah 55:8 292
Read: Isaiah 54:1-57:14

September 29 — Isaiah 59:1 293
Read: Isaiah 57:15-59:21

September 30 — Isaiah 62:1 294
Read: Isaiah 60:1-62:5

OCTOBER

October 1 — Isaiah 64:4......................296
Read: Isaiah 62:6-65:25

October 2 — Isaiah 66:1......................297
Read: Isaiah 66:1-24

October 3 — Jeremiah 1:5 298
Read: Jeremiah 1:1-2:30

October 4 — Jeremiah 3:15 299
Read: Jeremiah 2:31-4:18

October 5 — Jeremiah 5:25 300
Read: Jeremiah 4:19-6:15

October 6 — Jeremiah 7:27 301
Read: Jeremiah 6:16-8:7

October 7 — Jeremiah 8:11 302
Read: Jeremiah 8:8-9:26

October 8 — Jeremiah 10:21 303
Read: Jeremiah 10:1-11:23

October 9 — Jeremiah 12:5 304
Read: Jeremiah 12:1-14:10

October 10 — Jeremiah 16:13 305
Read: Jeremiah 14:11-16:15

October 11 — Jeremiah 17:8 306
Read: Jeremiah 16:16-18:23

October 12 — Jeremiah 20:9 307
Read: Jeremiah 19:1-21:14

October 13 — Jeremiah 22:4 308
Read: Jeremiah 22:1-23:20

October 14 — Jeremiah 23:29 309
Read: Jeremiah 23:21-25:38

October 15 — Jeremiah 27:13 310
Read: Jeremiah 26:1-27:22

October 16 — Jeremiah 29:7 311
Read: Jeremiah 28:1-29:32

October 17 — Jeremiah 31:18 312
Read: Jeremiah 30:1-31:26

October 18 — Jeremiah 32:17 313
Read: Jeremiah 31:27-32:44

October 19 — Jeremiah 34:16 314
Read: Jeremiah 33:1-34:22

October 20 — Jeremiah 36:24 315
Read: Jeremiah 35:1-36:32

October 21 — Jeremiah 38:15 316
Read: Jeremiah 37:1-38:28

October 22 — Jeremiah 39:18 317
Read: Jeremiah 39:1-41:18

October 23 — Jeremiah 42:6 318
Read: Jeremiah 42:1-44:23

October 24 — Jeremiah 45:5 319
Read: Jeremiah 44:24-47:7

October 25 — Jeremiah 49:11 320
Read: Jeremiah 48:1-49:22

October 26 — Jeremiah 50:6 321
Read: Jeremiah 49:23-50:46

October 27 — Jeremiah 51:17 322
Read: Jeremiah 51:1-53

October 28 — Jeremiah 52:10 323
Read: Jeremiah 51:54-52:34

October 29 — Lamentations 2:14 324
Read: Lamentations 1:1-2:22

October 30 — Lamentations 3:25 325
Read: Lamentations 3:1-66

October 31 — Lamentations 5:19 326
Read: Lamentations 4:1-5:22

NOVEMBER

November 1 — Ezekiel 2:5 328
Read: Ezekiel 1:1-3:15

November 2 — Ezekiel 3:18 329
Read: Ezekiel 3:16-6:14

November 3 — Ezekiel 9:11 330
Read: Ezekiel 7:1-9:11

November 4 — Ezekiel 11:5 331
Read: Ezekiel 10:1-11:25

November 5 — Ezekiel 12:2 332
Read: Ezekiel 12:1-14:11

November 6 — Ezekiel 15:2 333
Read: Ezekiel 14:12-16:41

November 7 — Ezekiel 17:18 334
Read: Ezekiel 16:42-17:24

November 8 — Ezekiel 18:24 335
Read: Ezekiel 18:1-19:14

November 9 — Ezekiel 20:39 336
Read: Ezekiel 20:1-49

November 10 — Ezekiel 22:30 337
Read: Ezekiel 21:1-22:31

November 11 — Ezekiel 23:35 338
Read: Ezekiel 23:1-49

November 12 — Ezekiel 26:12 339
Read: Ezekiel 24:1-26:21

November 13 — Ezekiel 28:3 340
Read: Ezekiel 27:1-28:26

November 14 — Ezekiel 29:20 341
Read: Ezekiel 29:1-30:26

November 15 — Ezekiel 32:17 342
Read: Ezekiel 31:1-32:32

November 16 — Ezekiel 33:8 343
Read: Ezekiel 33:1-34:31

November 17 — Ezekiel 36:26 344
Read: Ezekiel 35:1-36:38

November 18 — Ezekiel 37:12 345
Read: Ezekiel 37:1-38:23

November 19 — Ezekiel 39:18 346
Read: Ezekiel 39:1-40:27

November 20 — Ezekiel 41:22 347
Read: Ezekiel 40:28-41:26

November 21 — Ezekiel 42:14 348
Read: Ezekiel 42:1-43:27

November 22 — Ezekiel 44:8 349
Read: Ezekiel 44:1-45:12

November 23 — Ezekiel 45:17 350
Read: Ezekiel 45:13-46:24

November 24 — Ezekiel 48:11 351
Read: Ezekiel 47:1-48:35

November 25 — Daniel 1:8 352
Read: Daniel 1:1-2:23

November 26 — Daniel 2:30 353
Read: Daniel 2:24-3:30

November 27 — Daniel 4:30 354
Read: Daniel 4:1-37

November 28 — Daniel 5:17 355
Read: Daniel 5:1-31

November 29 — Daniel 6:4 356
Read: Daniel 6:1-28

November 30 — Daniel 7:10 357
Read: Daniel 7:1-28

DECEMBER

December 1 — Daniel 8:12 359
Read: Daniel 8:1-27

December 2 — Daniel 10:12 360
Read: Daniel 9:1-11:1

December 3 — Daniel 11:32 361
Read: Daniel 11:2-35

December 4 — Daniel 12:3 362
Read: Daniel 11:36-12:13

December 5 — Hosea 3:1 363
Read: Hosea 1:1-3:5

December 6 — Hosea 4:6 364
Read: Hosea 4:1-5:15

December 7 — Hosea 9:8 365
Read: Hosea 6:1-9:17

December 8 — Hosea 10:1 366
Read: Hosea 10:1-14:9

December 9 — Joel 1:9 367
Read: Joel 1:1-3:21

December 10 — Amos 1:1 368
Read: Amos 1:1-3:15

December 11 — Amos 4:6 369
Read: Amos 4:1-6:14

December 12 — Amos 8:11 370
Read: Amos 7:1-9:15

December 13 — Obadiah 4 371
Read: Obadiah 1-21

December 14 — Jonah 1:3 372
Read: Jonah 1:1-4:1

December 15 — Micah 1:5 373
Read: Micah 1:1-4:13

December 16 — Micah 6:3 374
Read: Micah 5:1-7:20

December 17 — Nahum 1:3 375
Read: Nahum 1:1-3:19

December 18 — Habakkuk 1:11 376
Read: Habakkuk 1:1-3:19

December 19 — Zephaniah 3:9 377
Read: Zephaniah 1:1-3:20

December 20 — Haggai 2:4 378
Read: Haggai 1:1-2:23

December 21 — Zechariah 1:3 379
Read: Zechariah 1:1-21

December 22 — Zechariah 3:2 380
Read: Zechariah 2:1-3:10

December 23 — Zechariah 4:10 381
Read: Zechariah 4:1-5:11

December 24 — Zechariah 7:13 382
Read: Zechariah 6:1-7:14

December 25 — Zechariah 8:6 383
Read: Zechariah 8:1-23

December 26 — Zechariah 9:12 384
Read: Zechariah 9:1-17

December 27 — Zechariah 10:2b 385
Read: Zechariah 10:1-11:17

December 28 — Zechariah 12:7 386
Read: Zechariah 12:1-13:9

December 29 — Zechariah 14:6-7 387
Read: Zechariah 14:1-21

December 30 — Malachi 2:5 388
Read: Malachi 1:1-2:17

December 31 — Malachi 3:16 389
Read: Malachi 3:1-4:6

PLANTERS PERSPECTIVE | *A Devotional*

JANUARY

JANUARY 1 || GENESIS 2:18

And the LORD God said, "It is not good for the man to be alone. I will make companion who will help him."

Read: Genesis 1:1-2:25

Within the very nature of people is the need for other people. One of the very worst things that you can do to someone is to isolate them from other people. People need other people.

This verse in context is speaking about the relationship between a man and a woman. And in this context, we need to understand that ministry is not a solo act. Your spouse and family are a part of that ministry, whether they like it or not. They do play a role. But I believe that it also speaks to other issues of life. I believe that this verse is one of the key texts to explain why we do many forms of ministry.

God created us with a need for companionship. And when we have that companionship, it meets many of our physical, emotional, and spiritual needs. Ministries are often developed because of a perceived need within the body that is not being met. Or ministries are developed that help people to better meet those relationship needs.

The greatest of those relationship needs is for God. God placed within every living being a need for God. The purpose of a church or a ministry is to help people to learn how to meet that need. And something that is so very important for us to understand is that we cannot meet that need for them. God created each of us to have a personal relationship with God. We cannot fill their need for God. Our role is to teach them how to meet God.

No one should need the church so that they can have an experience with God. The church should be the school that they can go to learn how to meet God. Church and ministries ought to be the places that people can go to learn how to fill their need for fellowship, to learn how to fill their need for accountability, to learn how to be in a relationship with God. And it is our responsibility as the church to model those things for them.

Churches and ministries exist to meet many of the basic human needs of life. But if we are not teaching people to do it for themselves, then we are trying to take the place of God in their lives and in the long run they will suffer as a result of it.

Jesus, help us to bring everyone to the cross. And Lord, teach us how to teach them how to get there.

JANUARY 2 || GENESIS 3:1

Now the serpent was the shrewdest of all the creatures the Lord God had made. "Really?" he asked the woman. "Did God really say you must not eat of any of the fruit in the garden?"

Read: Genesis 3:1-4:26

Genesis three might be the saddest book in the entire Bible. Man and woman stand in the perfect creation of God in perfect unity and fellowship with each other and God. Then in slithers the serpent to tempt them away from that perfection. It is not until the end of Revelation that we see this perfection and fellowship restored.

Revelation also identifies the serpent as none other than Satan himself. His first appearance in Scripture gives us a great picture of how he works in the world even today. Understanding his tactics can help us to withstand the temptations that he will send our way.

First, he appeared as a part of God's creation. God created the serpents along with the rest of the animals. Satan took the perfect creation of God and distorted it to his evil will. Satan still disguises himself within the harmless things of creation. Riches, wine, sex (to name but a few) are not evil, but Satan uses them to tempt us to do evil. We sometimes judge the thing as evil when it is what is behind the evil of that thing that we ought to be fighting.

Second, Satan begins with Eve by encouraging her to question what God said. And he did it by twisting what God said. He asked her if God had said that she couldn't eat 'any' of the fruit. Satan knew what God had said, but he wanted to get Eve to think about it. Satan knows the Scriptures better than anyone alive. If he can he will use them to get you thinking about the things that God has said and questioning them.

Satan also knew Eve's desires. He knew that she wanted to taste of the forbidden fruit. He knew that the seed of sin already resided within Eve and all he did was cause it to grow. All of us will be faced with the same kinds of temptations in our lives. We will be tempted to question what God has said and desire something that is forbidden to us. It is not the questions or the desire that is sin. It was not sin until Eve took the fruit and ate it. Having sinful desires does not make you a sinner; you have sinful desires because you are a sinner. The desire to sin is found within all mankind because we are all descended from Adam and Eve.

The difference between success and failure in our daily battle against the temptation to sin is found in our knowledge and faith in the Word of God. If you know what God says about something in your life, act like you know it. If God said don't eat of that forbidden fruit, then ignore all the slithering encouragements to question what God said. If you are not sure, the best move is to stay away from it until you can get clarification from God. Our only true defense against the temptations of Satan is a good knowledge of Scripture and the faith to do what it says. Jesus, be our strong tower!

Rick Lancaster / PLANTERS PERSPECTIVE

JANUARY 3 || GENESIS 6:8

But Noah found favor with the Lord.

Read: Genesis 5:1-7:24

Noah lived at a time when the whole world was set only on evil and wickedness all the time. God has looked down upon the earth and is disgusted by what he sees people doing to each other and against Him. As the Lord looks down He sees one light shining brightly out from the darkness that mankind has become, Noah. The text goes on to say that Noah was righteous and blameless.

To be righteous and blameless does not mean perfect. Genesis 9 records a sin that Noah committed. Noah lived his life in a way that kept him close to God. Noah desired to be right and blameless and lived his life to stay that way. And he did it in a world that was totally corrupted. We sometimes look at the world around us and believe that it's impossible to live a life that pleases God. It is difficult but not impossible. If Noah could do it, so can we. It is simply a matter of setting our mind and heart to follow God regardless of what the world around us is doing.

One of the fascinating things about the account of Noah is the ark. God decided to judge the world of its sin by destroying all life on the planet. But Noah had found favor with God. God was going to save Noah and his family from this impending disaster. God didn't supernaturally save Noah, He told Noah to build a really big boat.

In the favor that God gave to Noah, He also gave Noah a project. That project would last for over one hundred years. For over a century, Noah worked to build the ark so that his family would be safe and so that God could save some of the animals.

We live at a time when we might also believe that God might be looking down in disgust upon the world that he recreated after the flood. How many lights does He see shining out from the darkness of this world? Are you one of those lights? Do you live in this world in such a way that God would describe you as righteous and blameless? Are you trying to live a life that glorifies Him and draws others to Him? If you are then you also have found favor with Him.

With that favor comes a project. God would also have you build a big boat to save your family and as many others as possible. Of course I don't mean a real boat. God had Noah build a boat so that everyone around him knew that something different was coming. God wants you and your family and your church to be so different from the world that they notice and have to choose between truth and the lie. Too many believers and even a lot of churches don't act any differently than the world around them.

You don't have to be perfect to find favor in God's eyes. As we trust in Jesus for our salvation and walk the path that the Holy Spirit leads us down, we will come to know God's favor more fully. And as we do, we will also grow to see the project that he will have us working on to save as many as possible. Jesus, help us to build a really big boat.

PLANTERS PERSPECTIVE / *A Devotional*

JANUARY 4 || GENESIS 9:21

One day he became drunk on some wine he had made and lay naked in his tent.

Read: Genesis 8:1-10:32

One of the things that made the Bible more believable to me as I was first falling in love with it was the fact that it didn't hide the dark side of God's people. The Bible doesn't portray God's people as perfect. Only a few escape having one or more of their sins exposed and immortalized. For me as an average believer that means that my mistakes don't disqualify me as one of God's people.

In our text today we have one of God's greatest men Noah making a mistake. Noah is one of the most remarkable men in the Bible. He is one of the people listed in Hebrews 11 as a great man of faith. And yet, here he is drunk and passed out naked in his tent. How is that possible? How did it happen? What should we learn from Noah's failure?

There is a great lesson for all of us that desire to someday have the same kind of description that Noah earned; Noah walked with God. The simple truth is that it is easier to walk with God during those times when it hard to walk in the world. When Noah was described as walking with God, the world was a terribly evil and wicked place. The temptation and pressure on Noah's walk would have been terrible. And yet he stood up under that pressure and walked with God.

After the flood there was no such temptation or pressure. There was only his family and the animals from the ark. It was during this time of peace and comfort that Noah fell into the sin of drunkenness. Being naked in his tent is a picture of shame and disgrace. It is what God covered when He clothed Adam and Eve in Genesis 3.

As Christians, the time that we need to be the most careful is when things are going the best. When we are successful and comfortable, we need to watch out. When there is peace and ease, it is a time that we need to be on our guard. If you let your guard down and relax, the enemy will come and lead you down a path that will leave you spiritually passed out drunk and naked.

There is a saying that I am fond of using, 'There is plenty of time to rest when I am dead.' It is a cute saying to justify working too hard and wearing yourself out physically. But spiritually it is absolute truth. Until we stand before the Lord in heaven we cannot rest from seeking to draw nearer to Him spiritually. We can never rest and never let our guard down. If we do, we will find ourselves laid out and exposed for others to laugh at. Jesus, help us to never let a day go by that we are not walking closer to You.

Rick Lancaster | PLANTERS PERSPECTIVE

JANUARY 5 || GENESIS 12:1

Then the Lord **told Abram, "Leave your country, your relatives, and your father's house, and go to the land that I will show you.**

Read: Genesis 11:1-13:4

Here we have the amazing call of Abram. God speaks to Abram and tells him to pack his bags and take his family someplace that He will show them. Abram had no idea where he was going. Can you imagine if this had been you? The culture was totally different then but still it had to have been quite a thing to come to his wife and tell her that they were leaving with no idea where they were going.

Try to imagine yourself in Abram's place. What would you be thinking if God were to come to you and tell you to move to some place that was unfamiliar to you? Would you go? What would you tell your family and friends and boss and co-workers? Would you leave your country, your relatives, and your father's house? It seems like an odd question but the fact of the matter is that it is not that far-fetched.

God called Abram to leave and because Abram responded the way that he did God considered him righteous and blessed him super-abundantly. Abram believed God and obeyed him. Abram also made some pretty big mistakes which proves that God can use imperfect people like you and me just as he could Abram.

If God has called you to lead a family, ministry, or church than He is very likely to call you to leave at some point. Leaving is not just moving from one place to another. Leaving could also be a change in ministry or activity. It could mean a change in personal habits or behaviors. Whatever it might be, it probably is not going to make sense to anyone but you.

Here is a word of caution in that. God will not ask you to leave in a way that contradicts His Word. God will not ask you to leave your spouse or children. God will not ask you to do something that is unbiblical, illegal, unethical, or immoral. Seek good counsel and search the Word before you step out in an area that is questionable.

It didn't make sense for Abram to do what he was doing in response to God's call. No one understood why he was doing what he was doing. That's OK! It's hard but not so hard that God can't provide and protect. Stepping out of the boat requires that we believe God and that we keep our eyes focused on Him and not on ourselves or our circumstances. The most amazing things happen when we have stepped out in faith in response to God's call in our lives. Listen carefully for His voice and respond as Abram did by packing his bags and leading his family where God lead him. Jesus, give us ears to hear Your voice calling us out.

JANUARY 6 || GENESIS 15:6

And Abram believed the LORD, and the LORD declared him righteous because of his faith.

Read: Genesis 13:5-15:21

God told Abram that He was going to do something, to make Abram the father of a great nation. Abram's only responsibility at that time was to believe God. And because Abram believed God, it was counted to him as righteousness. There are times when all that God is asking us to do is believe Him. There are going to be times in all of our lives when the only thing that we can do is believe God. And that action will result in God counting us as righteous.

What an incredible thought! Sometimes all we have to do to please God and be righteous in His sight is believe Him. And there also comes with believing God something for us as well. When we believe God, we experience peace, joy, hope, and love. We have a confidence in our situation and circumstances that the world looks at and is astounded.

Noah believed God and it gave him the confidence and strength to work for 100 years building an ark. Even in the midst of what must have incredible criticism, ridicule, and persecution. Just by believing God we can cross through any wilderness or valley that may enter our lives.

Abraham believed God and it gave him the patience that he needed to wait for that promise to be fulfilled. And because Abram believed God, God used him in a supernatural way. Both he and Sarai were well past the age where they could have children. But because Abram believed God, they conceived and had a son.

God is the same today as He was then. He is still looking for people that will believe Him. And when He finds people that will believe Him, He will give them everything that they need for the day and will use them to do radical, supernatural things in the future.

Your church or ministry will only be as successful or effective as your ability to believe God. Do you want to be blessed in your life, in your ministry, and in your church? Then believe God! When God says that He is going to send a flood, believe Him! Noah waited 100 years to see what God said would come to pass. When God says that He is going to make you a father of a great nation, believe Him. Abram waited 15 years! What has God told you? How long have you been waiting to see it come to pass? Do you believe God?

If you do, God counts it as righteousness and is standing ready to provide you with everything that you need and He is preparing a miraculous, supernatural thing for you to be a part of. Lord, help us to believe you.

Rick Lancaster | PLANTERS PERSPECTIVE

JANUARY 7 || GENESIS 16:3

So Sarai, Abram's wife, took Hagar the Egyptian servant and gave her to Abram as a wife. (This happened ten years after Abram first arrived in the land of Canaan.)

Read: Genesis 16:1-18:15

Abram is 86 years old and Sarai is well into her seventies. Sarai is barren; meaning she is not able to have children. In that culture it was a great disgrace for a woman to be childless. It was looked down upon as a failure on the part of the woman. On top of that is the prophecy that Abram will be the father of many nations. It seems like an impossible thing to Sarai. Abram and Sarai take matters into their own hands.

This was a mistake! History has proven that. From this union between Abram and Hagar came Ishmael. The descendants of Ishmael have been Israel's greatest enemies throughout most of their history. The Muslim religion believes that it was through Ishmael that the Messiah would come and they believe that the Promised Land belongs to them and not to the Jews.

If they could have foreseen the hatred and violence that has come from that one poor choice, it is very unlikely that they would have done it. God had promised Abram a son through Sarai. The problem is that God wasn't moving fast enough for them. They were both getting old and their human minds could not comprehend a God that could bring a child out of a barren womb that was well past the age of bearing children.

God's Word is true; when He tells us something we must trust and believe that He can and will do it. There is nothing that is impossible for God. It doesn't matter that you don't understand how God is going to do something. If God wants your help to get His work done, He will tell you that. One of the biggest mistakes that we can make in our walk with the Lord is to believe that God needs our help with anything.

If you want to help God, ask Him what it is that He would like your help with. If He doesn't respond He is telling you to be patient and wait. If He does respond, do exactly what He says, and do it right away. Abram and Sarai are a perfect example that nothing is beyond God's power and ability. They are also examples of the problems you can create when you begin to believe that God needs your help to accomplish His plan.

It is a mistake to think God needs our help. God needs nothing; especially from us. All God wants is our obedience. If we start trying to help God, we tend to get in the way and then the consequences can be devastating. Let God be God and wait for Him to do what He said He was going to do. Jesus, help us to sit down, shut up, and wait for You to act.

JANUARY 8 || GENESIS 18:27

Then Abraham spoke again. "Since I have begun, let me go on and speak further to my Lord, even though I am but dust and ashes."

Read: Genesis 18:16-19:38

The Lord has spoken with Abraham and told him what His plan is for Sodom; God is going to judge it. Sodom's moral fabric had decayed to the point that God could no longer stand it. They had become so evil and wicked that God determined that it was time to utterly and completely destroy it so that it could not spread any further. God was treating Sodom like we would a cancer in the body.

Abraham intercedes on behalf of Sodom and asks the Lord a series of questions. One of the things that fascinate me about this exchange is that as Abraham is working his way down in the numbers of righteous people in Sodom that the Lord probably knew exactly how many righteous people there were in Sodom. He knew that only Lot and his wife and daughters would be saved from the city. The Lord did not rebuke Abraham for his boldness and persistence; He just patiently responded to each question.

It is the statement above that I believe helps to understand why the Lord allowed Abraham to keep asking these questions. Abraham understood that compared to the Lord that he was 'but dust and ashes'. He was a 'nobody' asking the creator of the universe to listen to him. Abraham was not just asking the Lord to listen to him but to do what he was asking. I believe that is the perfect picture of the attitude that Jesus wants us to have when we come to Him.

Jesus wants us to approach Him with everything in our lives. That is one of the reasons that He came to the earth as a man so that we would be able to relate to Him. There is nothing going on in our lives that he doesn't understand or sympathize with. Be persistent in your requests to the Lord. Don't stop asking until He gives you what you are asking for or until He tells you to stop asking. You should notice from the day's reading that the Lord did not tell Abraham to stop. He patiently waited until Abraham was finished. What a gracious God we serve.

Abraham approached the Lord with a right view of who he was in the presence of the Lord. We also need to have this same understanding of who we are in relation to God. God is God and we were created by Him to worship Him and serve Him. We are but dust and ashes in His presence. The fact that He will listen to us at all is an indication of His limitless grace; not of our position. God loves us so much that He will take the time to listen to us, even when we are whining and complaining and acting like dust and ashes. Abraham understood who he was and that gave him a reverential boldness with God. We can have this same boldness if we will also understand who we are. Jesus, help us, as dust and ashes, to view You as we should.

JANUARY 9 || GENESIS 21:22

About this time, Abimelech came with Phicol, his army commander, to visit Abraham. "It is clear that God helps you in everything you do," Abimelech said.

Read: Genesis 20:1-22:24

Abimelech is the ruler of the land that Abraham has camped out in. Abimelech comes to Abraham to make a treaty with him. He can see that God is blessing and protecting Abraham and so he wants to make sure that he and his family are not going to be harmed by Abraham and his family. Abimelech is a Gentile king; he does not worship God and yet he can see that Abraham is being blessed by Him.

What a beautiful testimony of the life of Abraham and a picture of why God blesses and protects those that are faithful to Him. Abraham's life was a living testimony of the power and grace of God. We know that because the people around Abraham could see that God was blessing him. They would know that it was God because Abraham was telling them that

Your life is meant to be just like that. God wants to use you to reveal Himself to the unbelieving world. Even if you never spoke a word to tell people about Jesus, they should see evidence in your life that he is real and that He is active in your life. And when people notice that your life is different than theirs, God wants you to give Him the glory when they ask you about it. They don't have to understand it; they don't even need to believe it but they should know it.

Jesus told us to let our light shine so that men would see our good works and glorify the Father in heaven. That is exactly what Abimelech is doing. He is glorifying God by coming to Abraham seeking a non-aggression treaty. However it is that Abraham and his family are living is speaking to this pagan king and causing him to want to be closer to Abraham.

Our lives should do the same thing. Our lives should be a magnet that draws people to God through the way that we live and the ways that God is blessing and protecting us. We need to let people see those areas of our lives so that they can be drawn to it and to us. God can use that to reveal Himself to them in a way that draws them to salvation. It is God's love that leads people to repentance. Let them see God's love as He pours it out into your life. And when they come to you and want to know what it is that you have, point them to Jesus. Jesus, thank you for your blessings and protection; please help us to use them to draw many to You.

JANUARY 10 || GENESIS 23:5-6

The Hittites replied to Abraham, "Certainly, for you are an honored prince among us. It will be a privilege to have you choose the finest of our tombs so you can bury her there."

Read: Genesis 23:1-24:51

Sarah, Abraham's beloved wife, has died while they were in the land of Canaan. This is the land that God has promised to give to Abraham's descendants. But for now, Abraham is a stranger in the land; it belongs to another people, the Hittites. Sarah had been an enormous part of the work that God had done with Abraham that it is hard to imagine his grief at her death. Abraham leaves her to go to the local Hittites to ask them to sell him a piece of land so that he can bury her.

The Hittites respond to Abraham in a remarkable way; they refer to him as a prince among them. It is this response that caught my attention. Abraham, as a foreigner among them, is treated with great respect. It is the great respect that these pagans had for Abraham that caused me to reflect on the meaning of respect.

We have all heard that respect must be earned. Respect can be earned in a number of ways. It can be earned simply based on position or title. It can be earned based on personal experience or abilities. Respect can also be earned based on reputation. The text doesn't explain how Abraham earned the respect of the Hittites, it just reveals that he did. In that fact Abraham's character is revealed.

To earn respect, one must be worthy of respect. It is seldom that someone can get respect when they are not worthy of it. Even if they can, they usually can't maintain it. Character matters and poor character will not get respect from anyone that matters. Abraham's character was such that it garnered him respect from the local leaders of the nation in which he was dwelling.

The Bible also teaches that we sow is what we reap. If we are respectful we will be respected. Often people try to reverse this and say that they will respect another once that person respects them. The problem with that theory is that it causes you to sow disrespect which can only produce more disrespect.

Abraham had so earned the respect of these Hittite leaders that they referred to him as a prince among them. This was probably one of the highest compliments that they could confer upon him. By being a person of character that is respectful and worthy of respect you will experience blessings even from the pagans living in the world around you. In this difficult time in Abraham's life, God used ungodly people to bless him because of his godly character. Who might God want to use to bless you? Are you a person that is worthy of respect? Are you a person that others would describe as respectful? Jesus, help us to treat others the way we would like to be treated.

Rick Lancaster | PLANTERS PERSPECTIVE

JANUARY 11 || GENESIS 25:21

Isaac pleaded with the Lord to give Rebekah a child because she was childless. So the Lord answered Isaac's prayer, and his wife became pregnant with twins.

Read: Genesis 24:52-26:16

It has been about twenty years since Isaac and Rebekah were married. It makes sense that they would be concerned about having children after that long. There is also the issue that God had promised Isaac's father Abraham that he would be the father of a nation of people that was so large that it was not possible to count them. Isaac was the next link in that chain. For that prophecy to come true, Isaac had to have children.

The word that struck me in this verse was 'pleaded'. Isaac pleaded with the Lord to give Rebekah a child. Aside from the fulfillment of prophecy I believe that there is something more to this request that Isaac makes of God. For most women the desire to have children is very strong. With that is the cultural stigma of that time that was attached to barren women that would have been very humiliating to Rebekah. Without children she was not complete. This would have likely made her unhappy. Isaac loved her and wanted her to be happy because his own happiness was linked to hers. I have a saying: HAPPY WIFE - HAPPY LIFE.

Isaac pleaded with God and God answered his prayer. There is a lesson in that for all of us. Most of us don't plead with God to intercede on our behalf in this life. Unless we are absolutely desperate we do not plead with God to change our lives or the lives of those around us. That shouldn't be the case; we should regularly be pleading with God in our prayer times.

Pleading is not about whining and complaining to God like a three year old wanting something that you shouldn't have. Pleading is about your heart being so touched by a matter that you feel as though it will break if God doesn't do something about the matter. Pleading with God is about being certain in your heart that there is no other option than for God to act and there is a sense of urgency and great need.

Isaac wanted Rebekah to be whole. All of us have people around us that need to be made whole. We live in a world that creates great needs within people. The greatest of these needs is Jesus Christ. Is your heart broken over the fact that your loved ones, neighbors, friends, or co-workers are lost and without God in their lives? Have you been pleading with God to do something about it? Do you know someone that is in great need physically, emotionally, or spiritually? Have you pleaded with God to provide for their needs? God might be trying to do a work in your heart that causes it to break over His people so that you will plead for them to the only person that can help them. Jesus, help us to be brokenhearted over the needs of Your people.

JANUARY 12 || GENESIS 26:22

Abandoning that one, he dug another well, and the local people finally left him alone. So Isaac called it "Room Enough," for he said, "At last the LORD has made room for us, and we will be able to thrive."

Read: Genesis 26:17-27:46

This is the third time that Isaac's men dig a well so that they can get water for their families and flocks. The two previous times, the local Philistines would come and claim the well and drive Isaac's men away from it. This third time, they did not. This time they allowed the men of Isaac to keep this well.

Fresh water is an absolute necessity. In Genesis 26, there is a famine in the land. That means water is especially scarce. These wells are of great value because they are providing life to the people and animals that so desperately need it.

If you are involved in planting a church or starting a ministry, there are a couple of great lessons in this text for you. First, as we begin a ministry or church, we are digging a well. There is a famine in the land and all around us people are dying. People are starving from a lack of God in their lives and they are dying without God. The well that we are digging will supply something that they need so desperately.

Twice Isaac was blocked after his men had done the work. And yet he persisted. He did because the need was so great. Just because our work is hindered or blocked by the Philistines around us, we shouldn't allow it to deter us from the work that God has given us. If you have to, move to a new location and start again. On the third attempt to provide water, Isaac was successful. Be persistent!

Twice the Philistines came in and took the fruit of what Isaac had done. It wasn't fair! It shouldn't have happened! And yet it did. Isaac didn't sit around moaning and complaining. He got to work to complete the work that was before Him. If you are successful at starting a church or ministry that provides life-giving water there will be people that will try to take it away from you.

And if they do, what should you do? Sue them? Fight them? No, you start digging. You move to a new location and you start digging. God blessed Isaac not because he had dug these wells, but because he had provided for the needs of the people. And while we can see no justice in this, we need to keep in mind that three wells ended being dug instead of one. Not only was Isaac and his family provided for but so were the families of many of the Philistines.

What might not seem fair or just to us may be a part of God's plan to bring life to more than just you and yours. No matter what happens you keep digging! Jesus, help us to persevere.

Rick Lancaster / PLANTERS PERSPECTIVE

JANUARY 13 || GENESIS 28:15

What's more, I will be with you, and I will protect you wherever you go. I will someday bring you safely back to this land. I will be with you constantly until I have finished giving you everything I have promised.

Read: Genesis 28:1-29:35

Jacob is on his way to Laban's home. He has recently stolen his brother Esau's blessing and Esau is so mad that he has said that he will kill Jacob as soon as Isaac dies. Rebekah sends Jacob to Laban's on the pretense that she doesn't want Jacob to marry a Canaanite woman. Laban is their relative and so she wants Jacob to find a wife among their own people.

On the way Jacob stops for the night and goes to sleep. He uses a rock as a pillow. You have got to believe that Jacob was thinking things were not going the way that he had expected. He got the rights of the firstborn from Esau for a bowl of stew and he got the blessing of the firstborn. He should be on top of the world. Instead, here he is out in the middle of the wilderness using a rock as a pillow.

God knows what we are thinking and what is bothering us. He shows Jacob a vision and speaks to Him. All of the words that God speaks to Jacob are encouraging and strengthening. God repeats the promise that He made to Abraham and Isaac that the land that Jacob was walking through would be theirs some day. Then God gives Jacob a very personal promise. God promises to take care of and protect Jacob until He has completed giving him everything that He had promised.

God promised to bring Jacob back to this land someday. Someday would end up being in twenty years. God promised to be with Him constantly. And as you read the accounts of those twenty years you can see that God was ever-present with Him and providing for him and protecting him.

Jacob took that rock that had been his pillow and turned it into a monument to the promises of God. In many respects that rock represents Jacob's struggles. Jacob has been struggling with the world. He will come back to this area and will struggle with God. God will strike Jacob's hip and leave him with a reminder that he had wrestled with God. Is there a pillow of stone that you have been sleeping on? There are times in all of our lives that we wrestle and struggle with the world around us.

God's promises are eternal and personal. He promised that He would never leave you nor forsake you; He is ever-present with you. Someday you will be able to take that thing that represents your struggle with the world and set it up as a monument to the power and promises of God. Until then, you just keep holding on to God's faithful promises. Jesus, give us the strength to hang on.

JANUARY 14 || GENESIS 31:7

but he has tricked me, breaking his wage agreement with me again and again. But God has not allowed him to do me any harm.

Read: Genesis 30:1-31:16

God has spoken to Jacob in a dream and told him that it is time for Him to return to his homeland. So Jacob has a conversation with his wives to let them know what he is thinking about doing. Jacob justifies why they should go quickly without telling Laban what is going on because Laban has not been very honest with Jacob and might try to stop him from leaving.

It is interesting that Jacob should have this happening to him since he has not been very honest in his own life. Twice the scriptures record how he deceived others for what he wanted. First, he traded his brother Esau his birthright for a bowl of stew. Then he deceived his father into giving Esau's blessing to him. Because of these two events Jacob had to flee for his life to his uncle Laban's home with nothing but the clothes on his back. While there God blessed Jacob and because of Jacob God blessed Laban also.

Laban didn't want Jacob to leave because he knew that he had been blessed because of Jacob. And even though Laban knew that he had been blessed by God because of Jacob, Laban still treated Jacob unfairly. Here it says that Laban had broken his wage agreement with Jacob again and again. Elsewhere it says that Laban lowered his wages ten times.

In the second half of our verse for the day Jacob tells his wives that God did not allow Laban to harm him. Even though Laban was being unfair to Jacob, God was still blessing him. Life is not fair! You have probably already noticed that. This world is engineered by our enemy to make things unfair. And as a Christian, you have a greater opportunity to experience the unfairness of this world. As a Christian, the Devil is determined to make our lives unfair. And if you have committed yourself to a ministry or a church that target that you are wearing is even larger.

That is why I appreciate this verse so much. Even in the midst of the unfairness of this world we can rest in the blessings and protection of God. God did not allow Laban to harm Jacob. That doesn't mean that Laban wasn't successful at being unfair; it just means that God worked through the unfairness and blessed Jacob anyways.

God can and will do that in our lives also. Jesus said that we will experience trials in this life. He also told us not to be worried about that because He has overcome the world. Jacob walked boldly through the persecution and unfairness because he knew that God had his back. Jacob didn't need to worry about the unfairness because he knew that God was in charge and was going to make it right. God is still in charge! Jesus, help us to walk through this life with the confident assurance that you are in charge.

Rick Lancaster / PLANTERS PERSPECTIVE

JANUARY 15 || GENESIS 32:10

I am not worthy of all the faithfulness and unfailing love you have shown to me, your servant. When I left home, I owned nothing except a walking stick, and now my household fills two camps!

Read: Genesis 31:17-32:12

Jacob is on his way home after twenty years at his uncle Laban's home. God has blessed Jacob tremendously in these twenty years. He has four wives and twelve children. He has flocks of sheep and goats and herds of cattle and camels. God has made him wealthy.

As he is returning home he sends messengers to his brother Esau to let him know that he is on his way. The messengers return saying that Esau is coming with four hundred of his men. God has also blessed Esau in the last twenty years. The news of Esau's coming with such a force sends Jacob to his knees to pray to God for his help.

Jacob's prayer is a great picture of how we can pray as well. He doesn't waste a lot of words getting to what he wants and reminds God of the promises that He had made to him. Jacob started this very simply by acknowledging who God was. Jacob was also reminding God that he was doing what God had told him to do; return to his father's home. Jacob knew God and knew that he could speak to Him boldly about the things that God had said to him.

It is the verse for today that caught my attention in this prayer. Jacob told God that he didn't deserve all that God had given to him. He knew that it was all from God and that without God he would still have nothing but a walking stick. Jacob was a wealthy man but he had not allowed his wealth to replace God in his life. All of us have stuff that God has given us. Even if all that we have is a walking stick we need to understand that it came from God. Everything we have was a gift from God. Jacob told God that he was not worthy of all that God had given him. It is because of God's grace that we have all that we have. There is a real risk when we have been blessed by God to forget that it came from God. Jacob didn't do that.

Jacob maintained a clear focus of who God was and what He had done for him. I think that is the message that this prayer has for us. By keeping our eyes on the Lord all the time we will not lose sight of Him no matter what happens in our lives. Whether we are in abundance or despair, keeping our eyes on the Lord assures a right approach to God and His blessings and protection.

In your family, ministry, or church there will be times of both plenty and little. If you will keep your eyes firmly focused on Jesus during all of those times you also will be able to walk boldly into the throne room of God and entreat Him for His help because it will be a natural thing for you to do. Jesus, help us to focus upon you rather than our circumstances or stuff.

JANUARY 16 || GENESIS 33:10

"No, please accept them," Jacob said, "for what a relief it is to see your friendly smile. It is like seeing the smile of God!"

Read: Genesis 32:13-34:31

As Jacob returns to the home of his father, Isaac, he is afraid that his brother, Esau, is still mad at him. He left because he was told that Esau intended to kill him after their father died. But God has told Jacob to return and so he does. In an attempt to appease his brother, Jacob prepares a gift for Esau.

Jacob's fears are confirmed when the messengers he sent ahead return reporting that Esau is coming with four hundred men. Jacob divides his caravan into two groups so that he might be able to save half of his stuff from Esau's anger.

Esau's greeting to Jacob was affectionate and emotional. Esau tells Jacob to keep the gifts that Jacob tried to give him because God had blessed him with abundance. But Jacob insists and says that he is very happy about the way that Esau has greeted him.

Jacob worried about how his brother was going to receive him, even after God had told him to return to his father's home. God had been doing a work in Esau's heart and Jacob had nothing to worry about. What Jacob feared was all in his mind.

When God has called us to do something, what do we have to fear? Nothing! If God is doing the leading then He is also doing the preparing. And while we only know our part, we must rest in the knowledge that He is working in all areas involving the work that He is doing.

We get way too caught up in the "What if's" in our minds. What if he doesn't respond well? What if he is still mad? What if it doesn't work out? What if I can't do it? What if I didn't hear God like I think I did?

If you are truly listening to God and seeking to please Him, then there is no part of your "What if" that He hasn't thought about and planned for. And ultimately it is going to come down to whether or not you trust God. You make your plans prayerfully and give them to God. Expect Him to do His part and you do your part. Then you must leave the results to God. He is responsible for the harvest, not you.

All of Jacob's fear, worries, and plans got him what? Nothing, because they were completely unfounded! What will all of your fears and worries get you? Nothing! Give it to God and go forward with confidence in His ability to take you through anything. Jesus, teach us to trust you with all our 'What if's'.

JANUARY 17 | | GENESIS 36:31

These are the kings who ruled in Edom before there were kings in Israel:

Read: Genesis 35:1-36:43

The reading for today focused mostly on Esau and his descendants. At first glance this is one of those sections of scripture that you can look at and wonder why I need to know any of this. But as always there is more to this reading than meets the eye of the casual observer. Esau was Jacob's fraternal twin brother, meaning they shared their mother's womb but were not identical twins.

God blessed Esau with wealth and property. He also blessed him with many sons. From these sons descended a great many people. Esau moved his family away from Canaan into what we will refer to in the book of Exodus as the wilderness. All throughout the history of the nation of Israel, you will find references to the descendants of Esau. And they will have both friendly and antagonistic roles in the history of the nation of Israel.

One of the most familiar of those descendants might be the Amalekites. The Amalekites seem to have caused Israel as much trouble as the Philistines and the Amalekites were relatives of the Israelites. Some others played important roles in the nation of Israel. Some of David's Mighty Men were descended from Esau.

Paul said to Timothy that all scripture is given by inspiration. That means that God breathed into those that were writing these books and inspired them to write every word. God didn't have these words written so that there would be a written record of people that lived thousands of years ago. He had them written down so that we would be able to mine out treasures of wisdom and knowledge of God, Jesus Christ, and the work of the Holy Spirit.

Paul also told Timothy that all scripture is useful. Our problem is that we don't know enough to make all scripture useful. When we come to a section of scripture like this we need to ask God to reveal to us what it is that He wrote this for and for the wisdom to understand why it applies to our lives. And you Bible teachers should not skip over sections or books like this; teach the whole word of God. Just because it is hard to understand doesn't mean you shouldn't teach it.

Jacob and Esau were brothers. There was a continual state of tension between them. It is difficult to imagine that Esau ever really got over the fact that Jacob stole his birthright and blessing. It is also not hard to imagine how that animosity over being displaced may have been passed down to future generations. Over time that animosity could have easily turned into a deep-felt hatred by the descendants of Esau toward the descendants of Jacob. That sets the stage for the next thousand years of history of the nation of Israel. Jesus, help us to see every word that You spoke as life-giving and priceless.

JANUARY 18 || GENESIS 37:4

But his brothers hated Joseph because of their father's partiality. They couldn't say a kind word to him.

Read: Genesis 37:1-38:30

Joseph was Jacob's eleventh son. He was born to him by his favorite wife Rachel. It was obvious to everyone that Jacob loved Joseph more than his other sons. This created incredible tension with at least ten of his brothers. From our verse for the day we are told that they couldn't say anything nice to him at all. There was a severe hatred that had developed by the brothers toward Joseph.

We all know the story; the brothers plotted to kill Joseph but instead sold him into slavery to some Ishmaelite traders going to Egypt. We also know that God works that out to the good of Joseph and to his family; including the brothers that wanted to kill him.

Every time we read this story we are appalled at the behavior of the brothers and feel that they should be punished. It seems that the only thing that they ultimately experienced was a bit of a guilty conscience. Those kinds of stories tend to bother us. We want to see justice and believe they should experience some penalty for what they did.

Have you ever thought how you might have behaved if you were in the same place as the brothers of Joseph? Do you think you would have handled it differently than they did? Those are great questions but we can't put ourselves in that situation so it is difficult to respond. However, we probably do find ourselves in similar situations on a fairly regular basis. There are usually people all around us that appear to be God's favorites. They are blessed beyond what seems reasonable and nothing ever goes wrong in their lives. That can very easily lead to feelings of jealousy and envy. The Bible teaches that God has no favorites but it is obvious that some people are experiencing greater blessings than others. Be careful, you can very quickly find yourself in the same place as Joseph's brothers.

Ministries and churches experience the same thing. As you look around and see other ministries and churches that are experiencing great success and growth while yours may not, it can lead to very wrong thinking and actions. Or if it is your ministry or church that is being blessed you might expect to experience some negative responses from those around you. Why God chooses to bless one and not another is God's sovereign will at work. We may not understand it but we have a choice in how we respond to it.

The best way to defeat hatred is to love. The way to defeat jealousy is to rejoice with those that are successful. Go to that person that God is blessing and give glory to God for what they are doing. Praise God for that ministry or church and what He is doing there; even if you don't agree with the way that it is done or the style it is done through.

You have to choose to fight against the natural tendency toward jealousy, envy, and hatred. Jesus, help us to rejoice with those that you have blessed more than us.

Rick Lancaster / PLANTERS PERSPECTIVE

JANUARY 19 || GENESIS 40:23

Pharaoh's cup-bearer, however, promptly forgot all about Joseph, never giving him another thought.

Read: Genesis 39:1-41:16

Pharaoh gets upset at his cup-bearer and baker and sends them to prison. They then both have dreams that they don't understand. God gives Joseph the ability to interpret their dreams so that they know what they mean. For the cup-bearer it is good news; for the baker it is bad news. Just as Joseph interpreted, the dreams came true and the cup-bearer was restored to his original position and the baker was impaled on a pole. The cup-bearer was so overjoyed to be out of prison and back in his normal life that he forgot all about the request of Joseph to be delivered from prison. It wasn't until two years later that the cup-bearer was reminded of what Joseph had done for him that he acted.

One of the characteristics about Joseph that are so important is that he was very patient. Joseph had been sold into slavery by his brothers and made a slave in Potiphar's house. He waited for the Lord to act on his behalf. He was then wrongfully accused by Potiphar's wife and thrown into prison. While in prison he waited for the Lord to act on his behalf. Here we see that Joseph makes a request of the Pharaoh's cup-bearer and then waits for the Lord to act upon his request.

There is a great lesson in patience for us in the story of Joseph. What was Joseph doing while he was waiting for the Lord to act on his behalf? He was busy staying busy. He wasn't sitting around on his hands; he was making good use of his time. Both Potiphar and the jailer saw the hand of God on Joseph's life and they elevated him to higher and higher positions within his circumstances. Joseph didn't just sit around moping and waiting for the prison doors to fly open; he made the best of the circumstances that he was in. Because he did that he was in a position to hear the cup-bearers dream and make the request of him for Pharaoh's mercy. If Joseph had not been actively waiting for the Lord to act, he would not have been in a position to hear the dream. The dream would have still come true and the cup-bearer would not have remembered Joseph in prison at all.

All of us will find ourselves in places where we are waiting for God to act on some thing in our lives. We need to follow Joseph's example and make the best of the circumstances the way that they are right now. If we do, God may bless us in our current circumstances to make the wait less burdensome. Also, by actively waiting we may without our knowledge be positioning ourselves for the help that we are looking for. God is always working in our lives and usually in ways that we can't see or understand until after the fact. While you wait for God stay busy doing whatever you can to stay busy. This will bring glory to God and may be how God will choose to deliver you. Jesus, help us to wait.

JANUARY 20 || GENESIS 42:5

So Jacob's sons arrived in Egypt along with others to buy food, for the famine had reached Canaan as well.

Read: Genesis 41:17 – 42:17

Jacob sends ten of his sons to Egypt to buy food because a famine is in the land of Canaan. Little does Jacob know but he is sending his ten sons to meet with his other son that they had sold into slavery that he thinks is dead. This is the second year of the famine that will last for another five years.

One of the questions that can get your mind all twisted up is: Did God cause the famine to happen so that Joseph's brothers would have to come to Egypt? Or did God know that the famine was going to happen and so He caused events to happen in Joseph's life so that he would be reunited with his family as a result of the famine? Scripture doesn't answer that question and so that means that we don't need to know the answer.

What we do need to take from that though is that God could do either one. It is kind of fascinating to think of questions like that because it gives you a picture of some of the things that God could do to carry out His will and plans in this world. There is nothing that is beyond the ability of God. If God wanted to change the weather patterns to cause a famine, that is no great feat for Him. If God wanted to arrange that Joseph was able to interpret dreams, that is nothing to Him.

However it happened, God was using circumstances to bring His plan to pass. He was reuniting the sons of Jacob and setting them up to grow into a great nation. While they are living in Egypt they grow to be well over one million people; all descendants of Jacob and his twelve sons.

As we go through life there are going to be famines. They will be of all kinds and causes. They can be material, physical, emotional, relational, or spiritual. Some of them we bring on ourselves. Others are imposed upon us by others. And some might even be brought on by God. Regardless how it happens God is still in control and has a plan that He is working out in your life and in the lives of everyone around you.

"Can God make a rock that is too big for Him to lift?" is a stupid question. "Can God rearrange the world and nature to cause His plan for my life to happen?" is a great question. These types of questions should remind us of the grace, mercy, and power of God. They should bring us back to His incredible love for us. And ultimately they should bring us back to the cross.

Any time we come to a question about God that His word doesn't answer then we need to go back to His character and nature; they will answer the question for us. Jesus, teach to let our questions draw us closer to You.

Rick Lancaster / PLANTERS PERSPECTIVE

JANUARY 21 || GENESIS 43:18

They were badly frightened when they saw where they were being taken. "It's because of the money returned to us in our sacks," they said. "He plans to pretend that we stole it. Then he will seize us as slaves and take our donkeys."

Read: Genesis 42:18-43:34

Joseph has been in Egypt for some time now. When he got there he was a young man, probably still in his teens. Now he is a full-grown man, probably dressed as an Egyptian. His brothers don't recognize him but he knows each one of them. It probably appears that they hadn't changed much at all. That is, except for Benjamin. When Joseph was sold into slavery Benjamin was but a boy. Now he would be an adult just a few years younger than Joseph.

It is hard to guess what all the brothers were feeling but we get a sense from the text that they were pretty worried about this trip to Egypt. They were expecting the worst and when Joseph told his manager to take them into his house for lunch they assumed that they were in deep trouble. There is a great sense of fear in this whole story of the famine.

The problem lies in their consciences. They carry a sense of guilt about what they did to Joseph. They know that they sold him into slavery and they believe that he is most likely still a slave somewhere or possibly dead. This guilty conscience has kept them in a state of fear since they sold Joseph into slavery.

They thought selling Joseph into slavery would make their lives better because it eliminated their problem. Joseph was never their problem. Their problem resided in the deepest parts of their hearts; they didn't really love or trust God. It seems that the closest the brothers get to God in this account is to believe that He is punishing them for what they did to their half-brother Joseph. Instead of making their lives better, it made their lives miserable.

Making a problem go away seldom solves the problem. This is true because the problem is usually not outside of you but in your heart. If you want to solve your problems, stop looking at the circumstances around you and trying to devise ways of selling them into slavery. Instead, open your heart to the Lord and allow Him to change the part of your heart that is causing you to feel the way that you are.

It was always God's plan to send Joseph to Egypt because that was how He intended to save them and countless thousands of others during the seven-year famine that was devastating the land. God used Joseph's brother's sin to get him to Egypt. But I believe that God wanted them repent of that sin and submit their hearts to Him. Instead they lived in fear and guilt and misery. Don't let guilt ruin your life. Lay it down at the foot of the cross and allow Christ's perfect blood to cleanse you. Allow His perfect love to cast out all fear from your heart so that you can live the life that He intended you to live. Jesus, help us to empty our hearts of everything but You.

JANUARY 22 || GENESIS 45:8

Yes, it was God who sent me here, not you! And he has made me a counselor to Pharaoh — manager of his entire household and ruler over all Egypt.

Read: Genesis 44:1-45:28

Joseph's brothers have come to buy grain because of the great famine in the land. God had warned Pharaoh in a dream that Joseph interpreted about the famine. Pharaoh then placed Joseph in charge of managing the country of Egypt so that they would survive the famine. This puts Joseph into a position that will allow him to help his family.

Joseph comes up with this elaborate plan to check to see if his brothers have changed since they sold him into slavery. And he can see from the way that they respond to his tests that in fact they have changed. In an incredible act of forgiveness and grace, Joseph tells his brothers that it wasn't them that sent him to Egypt but it was God. It was a part of God's plan.

Joseph understood clearly the idea of the providence of God. God has a plan; for us, for the world, for His church, for everything. And His plan will come to pass; nothing will prevent that. And even when something happens that seems to be out of the plan of God, God has the power to rearrange heaven and earth to cause His plan to come to pass.

Joseph knew, as well as his brothers, that God had promised to make them into a great nation. And so Joseph could see the providence of God at work when the famine began to affect not just Egypt but Canaan also. The famine was a part of God's plan. And God supernaturally arranged events in Joseph's life so that he would be in a position to save his family and thus participate in the plan of God.

Not once during the entire life of Joseph do you hear him complain about his circumstances. He knew that his circumstances, as hard as they might have been, had been arranged by God. And if God had allowed these things to happen to him that there was a reason for it.

There are times when building a church or a ministry is difficult. Things just don't seem to be going right as you do the things that you believe you should. Remember, Jesus said that He would build His church and that the gates of Hell would not prevail against it. That is God's plan! All you need to do is trust that God is rearranging heaven and earth to make it happen. And then you do like Joseph did. You look for just how it is that God is going to make this into a good thing. It may take a while, but patience and faithfulness will always result in seeing the mighty power of God at work. Jesus, help us to keep our hands to the plow and our eyes on you and our hearts trusting in your plan and not our own.

Rick Lancaster | PLANTERS PERSPECTIVE

JANUARY 23 || GENESIS 46:2

During the night God spoke to him in a vision. "Jacob! Jacob!" he called. "Here I am," Jacob replied.

Read: Genesis 46:1-47:31

Jacob's sons have returned from Egypt to get food and told him that they met Joseph there. He is stunned by the news and then his sons tell him that they have been invited to move to Egypt to escape the famine that is going to last for the next five years. So they pack up everything they own and start off to Egypt.

During the night, the Lord speaks to Jacob in a vision. At first you might wonder why the Lord would speak to Jacob as he is making this journey. But as you look at what the Lord says to him it starts to make sense. The Lord had promised the land of Canaan to Abraham and his descendants. Jacob may very well have been unsure about leaving Canaan to go to Egypt. He may have been questioning whether he was showing a lack of faith. He might have been concerned that something would happen in Egypt. There may have been all sorts of questions in his mind as he was making his way out of the Promised Land.

God knew what was going through Jacob's mind and so He gives him a vision to reassure Jacob that this is all a part of God's great plan for the nation of Israel. God goes on to tell Jacob that He is going to make them into a great nation while they are in Egypt and that He will bring them back. We know from the Exodus that there was an estimated 1 to 2 million people in the nation of Israel when they left Egypt. God kept His promise to Abraham, Isaac, and Jacob.

It was Jacob's reply in the verse above that I loved. When the Lord called to Jacob in the vision, he replied 'Here I am'. Part of the reason why God was able to do the things that He did in people's lives like Jacob is because they were waiting for Him to call them. I believe this was why men like Jacob heard the voice of God the way that they did; they were listening for it. Jacob was expecting to hear from God and he was waiting to hear from God.

God still speaks to His people. He especially wants to speak to those that have been called to shepherd His people. As leaders of families, ministries, and churches we need to be expecting God to speak to us; we need to be waiting for Him to call out to us. This involves preparation. We must prepare ourselves spiritually so that the lines of communication are clear. We start by opening a channel of communication through prayer. Next we continue to familiarize ourselves with God through His Word. We also need to be looking for things in our lives that will hinder our ability to hear from God; namely distractions and sins. Then we must believe that He is going to call. If we will do things like these, when the Lord does speak to us, we will answer immediately like Jacob did, 'Here I am Lord'. Jesus, teach to answer the phone from You on the first ring.

JANUARY 24 || GENESIS 48:15

Then he blessed Joseph and said, "May God, the God before whom my grandfather Abraham and my father, Isaac, walked, the God who has been my shepherd all my life."

Read: Genesis 48:1-49:33

Jacob is 147 years old and is about to die. Before he dies He blesses his sons and the sons of Joseph. As Jacob begins to bless Joseph he starts by pointing him to God. Jacob refers to God as the shepherd of his whole life. What a great picture of the kind of relationship that God wants to have with us. We would all have a greater relationship with God and a better life if we would all look at God as Jacob does here.

There are some powerful pictures that we can take from this image of God being our shepherd. If God is our shepherd, then we belong to Him. He has the authority and ability to do anything that He wants to with us and with our lives. He is also responsible for us and for our lives; He is responsible for taking care of us. He is also responsible for protecting us. If danger comes our way, it is the shepherd that will handle it; not the sheep. Psalm 23 is a great place to see what it means to us that God is our shepherd.

The one main difference between real sheep and people is that people can choose whether or not they accept the shepherd in their lives. Real sheep have no choice; they must accept the shepherd in their lives. As people we can choose not to accept the fact that Jesus is our shepherd. Our choice does not change the fact that He is our shepherd but it does affect the way that we interact with Him.

Jacob recognized and accepted the Lord as his shepherd. That is our first step; we need to accept the fact the Jesus is our Shepherd. This is different than accepting Him as Savoir. You can run to someone to save you from something but then decide not to do anything they tell you to do afterwards. That is a picture of a person that is saved but will not accept Jesus as shepherd of their life.

As leaders of families, ministries, and churches this is one of our two primary goals; get them into the sheepfold and help them to submit to the Shepherd. Getting them saved and into the sheepfold is great but they also need to act like they are a part of His flock. That is the only way that they can live the life that God intended for them.

It starts with you. Can you say as Jacob did that God is the shepherd of your whole life? Are there still some areas that you have not surrendered to Jesus? What areas of your life are you worrying and stressing over? Give them to the Shepherd! Too many of us think the Shepherd needs our help to run our lives. Oh, we wouldn't actually say that but we certainly act that way. We are sheep and we need to act that way because we have the perfect Shepherd watching over us. Jesus, teach us to follow You, the Good Shepherd.

Rick Lancaster / PLANTERS PERSPECTIVE

JANUARY 25 || GENESIS 50:19

But Joseph told them, "Don't be afraid of me. Am I God, to judge and punish you?"

Read: Genesis 50:1-Exodus 2:10

Here we come to the close of the book of Genesis. Jacob has recently died. They took his body back to Canaan to bury him with his father and grandfather. After they get back from this trip, Joseph's brothers start to worry. They think that Joseph is now going to take revenge upon them for what they did to him.

The brothers send word to Joseph telling him that their father had commanded Joseph to forgive them for what they did to him. It is not clear from the text whether Jacob had actually made that command or if the brothers made it up to try to protect them.

Joseph responds by pointing them back to God. He tells them that it is not his place to judge them for what they did to him. He also says that is the responsibility of God to punish them. Joseph also tells them that this thing that they had planned for evil, God used for good.

Joseph did not allow his brother's evil to affect him. He let it go. He lived today for what today was. He let yesterday stay where it is, in the past. And he let God worry about tomorrow and the future.

What Joseph's brothers did was wrong. And in most of our minds we believe that they should be punished. And in some respects they were punished. It was about twenty years from the time Joseph was sold into slavery to the time his brothers came to Egypt. During that time they had to watch their father mourn the loss of Joseph. It affected them very deeply. And then for the last seventeen years while being in Egypt, they have wondered if Joseph is going to take revenge upon them. Both of those are a form of bondage and result in suffering.

Our problem is that we judge the punishment. We look at the punishment that they receive and think that it is not enough or not the right kind of punishment. And I would ask you; Are you God? God is the righteous judge and the avenger. We must let Him handle those things for us.

Unfair things are going to happen to you in life, in the church, and in ministry. That will be the reality of this world until our Lord returns to take evil out of it forever. Knowing that we have got to let God be God and be satisfied to let Him deal with things in His own time and in His own way.

If you don't; you also will be in bondage. You will be in bondage to someone else's sin. You will be in bondage waiting for God to judge and punish them. If you truly trust God, then you will trust Him with that as well. Lord, teach us to let you deal with it.

PLANTERS PERSPECTIVE / *A Devotional*

JANUARY 26 || EXODUS 2:23

Years passed, and the king of Egypt died. But the Israelites still groaned beneath their burden of slavery. They cried out for help, and their pleas for deliverance rose up to God.

Read: Exodus 2:11-3:22

The Egyptians are treating the Israelites very harshly because they are afraid of them. Their population continues to increase no matter what the Egyptians try to do to stop it. This continues for a long time. At the time that Moses flees from Egypt to Midian he is about forty years old. That means that the Egyptians have been treating the Israelites harshly for at least that amount of time. Forty years of oppressive slavery is a long time to endure.

Our verse tells us that the Israelites groaned under this incredible burden of slavery. In their groaning they cry out for help. Their cries for help and deliverance rise up to God. The text goes on to say that God heard them and remembered His promises to Abraham, Isaac, and Jacob.

In our lives, marriages, families, ministries, or churches there are going to be times when we feel as though we are the Israelites making bricks without straw. We feel as though we are being whipped by our circumstances and it seems as though no rescue or deliverance is possible. It is not difficult to imagine that is exactly what the Israelites were feeling after at forty years of slavery.

There is a sense in the text that it is at this time that they cry out to God for help. For forty years they have been groaning under the heavy burden of slavery and only now they cry out to God. So often we make the same mistake of the Israelites; we wait until the situation is unbearable before we go to God and plead with Him to rescue us. We will see that these Israelites are a stubborn people. Before we jump to judge them we need to see that we are no different than they are; we can be just as stubborn.

Doesn't that sound foolish? It is foolishness for us to be stubborn about going to God and crying out to Him to rescue us. Usually He is the only one that can deliver us from many of the circumstances of our lives and yet we hesitate and sometimes even resist going to Him.

God wasn't busy running the universe and just picked up the message from the Israelites after forty years. The Israelites failed to make the call because they were so busy groaning about their burden. Stop groaning and start crying out to God. Deliverance may not come immediately but you can rest in one thing for sure, God hears immediately. God doesn't sleep or rest; He is always there to hear the cries of our heart. The Bible teaches that when we can't think of the words to pray that the Holy Spirit prays for us. Jesus, in the midst of our circumstances teach us to stop groaning and to start praying.

Rick Lancaster / PLANTERS PERSPECTIVE

JANUARY 27 || EXODUS 4:18

Then Moses went back home and talked it over with Jethro, his father-in-law. "With your permission," Moses said, "I would like to go back to Egypt to visit my family. I don't even know whether they are still alive." "Go with my blessing," Jethro replied.

Read: Exodus 4:1-5:21

Moses has just met with God and been told by God from the burning bush to go back to Egypt to lead the people of Israel out of Egypt and into the land that God promised them. Moses then goes and talks it over with Jethro, his father-in-law. I found that interesting. Why would Moses talk it over with Jethro and seek his permission to leave? Was it a lack of faith on Moses' part? I don't think so. I believe it was respect for Jethro that prompted Moses to do this.

Just because God had told Moses to go didn't mean that he could just walk away from everything else to go. Don't get me wrong, nothing should interfere with our obedience to God. However, God is not a God of chaos but of order. When He tells us to do something He wants us to do it well. When that something includes a change from one thing to another, God wants us to do it in such a way that He is glorified and honored. If Moses had just walked away from everything it would have been very disruptive to Jethro's household and would have had a negative effect on his relationship with his wife's family.

If Moses had done this poorly it may have closed the door to his relationship with Jethro. Because Moses didn't close that door, Jethro is there to help Moses as he is trying to lead the Israelites through the wilderness. The help that Jethro gives to Moses does more than just save him from leadership burnout but it also establishes the leadership system that they will need once they enter into the Promised Land.

Moses did not need Jethro's permission to do what God had told him to do. But by showing Jethro the respect that he did, God was glorified and God used that relationship to bless Moses and the Israelites later. We don't need anyone's permission to obey God. However, there are going to be circumstances that require us to go to someone else and seek their blessing or permission to do what God is directing us to.

There are going to be times when the only way that we can obey God is by getting someone's blessing or permission. This is not a 'necessary evil' as some might perceive it; it is a part of the process that God wants you to go through as He positions all the pieces to help you to accomplish the things that He is directing you to do. If we do it well God is glorified and His will is accomplished. If we resist it and fight this process, God must rearrange things to cause His will to be done and it will be much harder on us. God's instructions do not depend upon man's blessing but they often are found together. Jesus, help us to be humble enough to ask for a blessing on what God wants from us.

JANUARY 28 || EXODUS 7:22

But again the magicians of Egypt used their secret arts, and they, too, turned water into blood. So Pharaoh's heart remained hard and stubborn. He refused to listen to Moses and Aaron, just as the Lord had predicted.

Read: Exodus 5:22-7:25

God tells Moses and Aaron to go to Pharaoh and ask him to let the people of Israel go so that He can fulfill His promises to the people of Israel. It is not hard to imagine that the Pharaoh would be a little hesitant to let them all just leave. The Israelites represented a workforce of about 600,000 men and probably an equal number of women. Losing that many laborers out of any nation's workforce would have a tremendous impact on the society at large.

Moses does what God tells him to and Aaron points his staff at all the waters of Egypt. All water is turned into blood. Rather than believing that this is the hand of God at work, Pharaoh calls for his magicians and tells them to explain what happened. They show Pharaoh that they too can turn water into blood and so Pharaoh doesn't give in to God's request to let the Israelites go.

Pharaoh's magicians were somehow able to duplicate the miracle of turning water into blood. This should act as a warning to us about the abilities of the world. Just because something amazing happens it doesn't necessarily mean that it was God that made it happen. Our enemy is able to perform some astounding miracles as well. He can cause things to happen that are an attempt to get us to worship him instead of God.

The big difference between the works of magicians and the works of God is that the magicians bring glory to man, while God's miracles bring glory to God. Just because some tremendous miracle happens, it doesn't necessarily mean that it was God. Who is getting the glory? It could be a work of God because He is actively working in the world all around us. But we need to be careful not to be fooled by the works of our enemy who masquerades as an angel of light.

God calls us to be wise and not to be tricked by the works of the enemy. That means that we need to be testing to see if things are from God or from man or from our enemy. If God is getting the glory, then we should rejoice and give the glory to God also. If He is not getting the glory we should stay away from whatever it is and give God the glory anyway.

Our enemy's primary tactic is deception. His favorite approach is to hide a lie within the truth. He will create something that looks like it came from God but is formed out of a lie. God is holy and pure; He is light and there is no darkness in Him. His great works draw people to Himself. God doesn't use tricks; He uses power, grace, mercy, and love. Jesus, teach us to see through the tricks of the magicians of this world.

Rick Lancaster / PLANTERS PERSPECTIVE

JANUARY 29 || EXODUS 9:16

But I have let you live for this reason – that you might see my power and that my fame might spread throughout the earth.

Read: Exodus 8:1-9:35

God keeps sending Moses to Pharaoh to get him to let the people of Israel go. God intends to deliver them from their bondage but wants to send a message to the whole world as a result of what He is doing here in Egypt. The first thing that you notice about this message that God is sending to Pharaoh through Moses is that God is in control. Egypt is one of the most powerful nations in the world at this time. And the Egyptians considered their Pharaoh to be god on earth. This message from God to Pharaoh is to tell Pharaoh that there is only one God and Pharaoh is not it.

God tells Pharaoh not only that He is in control but that Pharaoh remains only because He has allowed it to be. God is telling Pharaoh that his very life is in God's hands and control. He then goes on to tell Pharaoh that He has allowed him to remain for a purpose. That purpose is so that God's power can be seen by the whole earth and so that His name can be proclaimed to the ends of the earth.

We live in a world that is filled with people that think they are gods, or at the very least kings. They might not use those words to describe themselves, but that is how they behave. They believe that they are in control of everything around them and that they are where they are because they deserve to be there or because they have earned the right to be there. And God allows them to stay there so that He can show His power and so that His name can be spread to the furthest parts of the earth. We also live in a world that is filled with things that hold people in bondage just as the Hebrews were in bondage in Egypt. Drugs, alcohol, pornography, sex, gambling, power, position, hatred, fear, and bitterness are just a few of the things that hold people.

God used Pharaoh to demonstrate His power and to proclaim His name. And God is still using the Pharaohs and 'gods' and 'kings' of this world to demonstrate His power and to proclaim His name. The reason your ministry or church exists is to be used by God to deliver His chosen people from the bondage of whatever their Egypt is. The reason that you are still on this earth and not in heaven with God is so that He can use you to demonstrate His power and proclaim His name through you.

Moses didn't volunteer to be the vessel that God used to deliver the Hebrews from Egypt; God picked him. You didn't volunteer either; God picked you. And just like Moses, if you will let Him, God will use you to deliver His people from bondage. And you will see incredible things being done in and through your life, ministry, and church. Jesus, help us to be clean vessels for your power and help us to proclaim Your name clearly to the world.

JANUARY 30 || EXODUS 12:6

Take special care of these lambs until the evening of the fourteenth day of this first month. Then each family in the community must slaughter its lamb.

Read: Exodus 10:1-12:13

God is about to keep His promise to the nation of Israel and deliver them from their bondage and bring them to a land of their own. To do that He is going to send one last plague to the nation of Egypt; He is going to send the Destroyer to kill the firstborn son of everyone in the land of Egypt. Here we see the institution of the Passover for the Israelites. The Passover lamb was slaughtered and its blood was smeared on the doorposts of the houses as a sign to God to pass over those houses. Some might say that God instituted the Passover to protect the Israelites from the angel of death. God didn't need the sign to tell Him who was an Israelite; He is God, He knows everything. The blood on the doorposts was to tell God who would follow Him. If an Israelite family did not smear the blood of the lamb on their doorposts they were no safer than the Egyptians.

The thing that struck me about this verse is that each family was to take special care of the lamb for four days. Tradition says that each family would bring this lamb into the house and it would be treated like one of the children. It would be bathed and fed and would probably play with the children. For four days this lamb would be a part of the family. It is not hard to imagine that even after such a short time that some amount of attachment would develop. This would be especially true if there were small children in the house.

As someone who has spent most of my life in the city it is very hard for me to imagine what it would be like to slaughter an animal. For that culture it would have been a fairly regular occurrence but I wonder what it would have been like to slaughter this animal that had been part of the family. It would almost seem to be like slaughtering a pet.

The Passover lamb is a picture of course of what Jesus would later do for all mankind with His sacrifice on the cross. The sacrificial lamb was Jesus. By having the Israelites take special care of this lamb before it is sacrificed they get a taste of what the Father would be feeling when He allowed Jesus to be sacrificed. It is just a taste; we could never really know the depth of the pain of the separation even for the brief time that God and Jesus were separated.

We do not have to annually take a lamb into our home and care for it because Jesus was the Lamb that saves us from spiritual death. But instead of bringing the lamb into our home we are to bring Jesus into our hearts. And there we are to care for Him; not just for four days but for our whole lives. Jesus, help us to bring you into our hearts and treat you with the love and respect that you deserve.

Rick Lancaster / PLANTERS PERSPECTIVE

JANUARY 31 || EXODUS 13:3

So Moses said to the people, "This is a day to remember forever — the day you left Egypt, the place of your slavery. For the LORD has brought you out by his mighty power. (Remember, you are not to use any yeast.)"

Read: Exodus 12:14-13:16

God has just delivered the Hebrews from 430 years of slavery and bondage. God has just saved them from the oppression of Pharaoh. Moses tells the people to remember this day. This day is special and the Hebrews are not to forget it. On this day God, using His mighty power, delivered them and God wants them to remember that. God works mighty miracles in all of our lives. The closer you get to God, the more you see His powerful hand at work in your life. And He wants us to remember those powerful acts that deliver us from the bondage of this world and its devices.

Unfortunately, we have a limited capacity to remember things. As much as we might want to remember all of the incredible things that God has done for us, we can't. God knows that! That is why we see in Scripture God creating festivals and having people set up memorials. Through setting up these events and monuments, God could help the people to obey Him by remembering His mighty works.

These celebrations and festivals and memorials also serve the purpose to remind the Israelites to teach their children about the mighty things that God has done in their lives. And as parents much of what our children learn about God will come from what we teach them. We must instill within our children the idea that if God did a mighty thing in my life that He can do mighty things in their lives as well. This is also our responsibility in our ministries and churches. We must share with those that God has entrusted into our care the mighty power of His hand. We must help them to see that because God has worked in our lives that he will also work in their lives.

We have a record of God's mighty works and the things that He did in the lives of ordinary people because the Holy Spirit inspired them to write those things down. Those words now inspire and teach us. Develop the habit of writing down in a diary or journal the things that God is doing in your life, ministry, and church. By writing these things down, you will be better able to remember the strength of the hand of the Lord in you life.

The nation of Israel has regular festivals and celebrations that they use to remember the work of God in their lives. Establish some celebrations of your own. Identify those significant events in your spiritual life and ask God to show you how to celebrate it. And then when others ask you why you celebrate this event, you share with them how the powerful hand of God worked in your life, ministry, or church. Jesus, help us to remember those miraculous movements of Your power.

FEBRUARY

FEBRUARY 1 || EXODUS 13:17

When Pharaoh finally let the people go, God did not lead them on the road that runs through Philistine territory, even though that was the shortest way from Egypt to the Promised Land. God said, "If the people are faced with a battle, they might change their minds and return to Egypt."

Read: Exodus 13:17-15:18

God miraculously brought the people of Israel out of Egypt. God is now leading them toward the land that He promised to their ancestors. Our verse for the day tells us that God is not going to take them the short way through Philistine territory but through the wilderness. Not only is it longer but there is no water or food in the wilderness.

It was the reason that God did this that caught my attention as I read this text today. God did it to avoid a fight with the Philistines. The Philistines will be one of the greatest enemies that the Israelites have in their history. God deliberately goes around their country so as to not engage in a battle with them. One might think from a verse like that, that God was concerned that He might not be able to protect them. That is not what is going on at all.

God is concerned about their feelings. God could if He so chose completely destroy the Philistines without the Israelites having to lift a hand. It is not an issue of power but of love. The Israelites were loved by God and He wanted to bless them. He knew that after all they had gone through that they were not ready to confront an enemy like the Philistines. He knew they needed some time to adjust to their new life before they were allowed to confront an enemy.

It is not long after this that the Amalekites attack the people of Israel. God allowed that attack to happen because the people were ready. God knows perfectly well when we are ready for the things that are going to happen in our lives. He is in complete control and if we will just follow where He leads He will keep us from the attacks and enemies that we are not ready for. If we are following Him then the attacks and enemies that come are ones that He will help us to deal with.

If you are following Jesus, the path that He leads you on is exactly the one that will take you where you need to be, even though it might not be the shortest route to where you are going and it may be lacking some of the things that you think you need. The route through Philistine territory was shorter and had food and water for the people to eat. If they had gone that way, the Israelites would have missed the miracles of the water from the rock and the manna. Don't take shortcuts on the journey that God is leading you on. You may miss some very cool miracles along the way. You may also have to face enemies that God has not prepared you to meet. If we follow God we can rest in the fact that He is going to provide and protect; He will give us everything we need and protect us from the enemies we are not ready for. Jesus, help us to stay right beside You.

FEBRUARY 2 || EXODUS 16:7

In the morning you will see the glorious presence of the Lord. He has heard your complaints, which are against the LORD and not against us.

Read: Exodus 15:19-17:7

The people come to Moses and complain to him that there is no food in the wilderness. They will complain throughout their journey to the Promised Land. Often you sense the frustration in Moses' voice as he talks with God about these unruly people. Often in their complaints they suggest it would be better for them to go back to Egypt rather than suffer in the wilderness. With all that God was doing for them and around them all they could see was their own discomfort. The most important thing for them was not what God wanted them to do and be but how they felt and what they had.

People are not much different today than they were 3,500 years ago. People still whine and complain about the slight discomforts of life and blame anyone but themselves for their circumstances. In the church, it is often the leaders that receive the blame when the sheep are uncomfortable. Moses had the right attitude about that in our verse for the day.

Moses told the people that they were complaining to God and not to him. He knew that the circumstances that the people were experiencing were not his responsibility; it was God's. This is so important for anyone the leads, whether it is a family, ministry, or church; God is responsible for providing for them and protecting them.

As leaders we have a role in that but ultimately the sheep are God's and He will provide for them and protect them as He wills. Sometimes that means that He is going to take them into the wilderness where there is no food or water. Sometimes they wander out into the wilderness on their own because they don't want to go where God is leading them. If you are in any place of leadership you are bound to get complaints. Don't take them personally. Moses had over a million people complaining; how many are complaining to you? The Bible teaches that we are to do all things without grumbling and complaining. When someone is grumbling and complaiing they are in sin and out of God's will. Don't join them by taking responsibility for something that is not yours.

God calls His leaders to do their part to protect and provide for the flock, but even the ability to do that comes from God. The next time someone comes to you and complains about something you have done, or worse, something that God has done, you encourage them to take it up with God. This assumes that you are following and obeying God yourself. If you have made a mistake, admit it and ask for forgiveness. After you have done that their complaints should then be redirected to God because you have been forgiven of the mistakes. We as leaders should respond to most complaints the way that Moses does with a clear understanding that they are complaining about God. With that kind of an attitude it will change the way that you respond to complaints. Jesus, help us to take what responsibility is ours and leave the rest with you.

Rick Lancaster / PLANTERS PERSPECTIVE

FEBRUARY 3 || EXODUS 18:17

"This is not good!" his father-in-law exclaimed.

Read: Exodus 17:8-19:15

Moses' father-in-law Jethro brings Moses' wife and sons out into the wilderness to join him. Jethro witnesses Moses' ministry to the people of Israel and is disturbed by what he sees. Moses is sitting before the people and helping them resolve all of the disputes that they have with one another. The people line up in the morning and stay in line all day long to present their cases to Moses. Jethro takes one look at this and tells Moses that what he is doing is not a good thing.

At first glance, you look at this and wonder what Jethro is talking about. Moses is representing God to the people. There are having disagreements and Moses is trying to minister to them by helping them to resolve these arguments. And on the surface that is a great thing that he is doing. The trap that Moses has fallen into is the same one that many in ministry fall into. Moses thinks he has to do it all!

Too many great Christian servants think the same way that Moses was thinking here. They think that they need to do everything. They might think that they are the only ones that can do it. They might believe that if they don't do it, it won't get done.

If that is the way that you think in your ministry or church, than I would say to you as Jethro said to Moses; this thing that you do is not good. Either you are going to burn out or your people are going to burn out. You must realize that you don't have to do everything. And you must learn to accept the fact that some things might not get done.

But a truth that many good people in ministry fail to apprehend is that there are people around you that God has been equipping to help you to minister. For Moses, there were literally hundreds of men all around him that were perfectly capable of helping him to minister to the flock around him. Around you also, while it may not be thousands, are people that are capable of helping you to minister. Many of them are just waiting to be invited. Some will need to be encouraged to help. Some of them might need some training or discipleship. A small investment in the people around you will reap incredible fruit for the Kingdom of God.

Don't be so arrogant as to think that you are the only one that can do it. And don't be so faithless as to believe that someone might do it better and see that as a threat to your 'position'. Your ministry or your church is not yours. It is God's! And He loves you and your flock more than you ever will. The best way to grow your ministry or church is to give it away. The more of it you give to capable men and women, the more God will bless you and your ministry or church. Jesus, help us to let go of the things that we can't do and give them to the ministers that you are preparing to do them.

FEBRUARY 4 || EXODUS 20:6

But I lavish my love on those who love me and obey my commands, even for a thousand generations.

Read: Exodus 19:16-21:21

Here nestled in the middle of the second commandment is this fantastic statement about the love of God. The second commandment tells us not to create a manufactured image of God. It also tells us not to bow down to any image, even if you do find an image of Jesus in your grandmother's meatloaf; thank God for it then eat it, don't bow down to it. God is so serious about this commandment that He takes three verses to express how He feels about this matter.

The reason that God gives that we shouldn't bow down to other gods is that he is a jealous God. God will not share our love with anything else. His love for us is limitless; it never ends. Because he loves us so much, He expects us to direct our love back to Him. When we don't, it upsets God because that was what we were created for, to love and worship God. When we direct our love to something else, God considers that idol worship. Of course this doesn't apply to the love that He has given us for others unless we allow that love for others to replace Him in our hearts.

God is so serious about this that He will punish those that choose to love something else other than Him. That should give us pause but it is our verse for the day that grabbed me today. God created us to worship Him and obey Him. Our verse tells us that if we will do that, God will lavish His love on us. It is the word 'lavish' that is so cool about this verse. To lavish is to give abundantly or without limits. This verse teaches us that if we will love God and obey His commands He will give us His love without any limitations.

When I lavish my love upon my wife I am doing everything that I can to make her life as great and blessed and joyous as I possibly can. The problem with me lavishing my love upon my wife is that I am limited; I can only do so much. Another problem is that I don't know enough to make her life all that it could be; my knowledge is limited.

God doesn't have those problems; He knows exactly how to make our lives as good as they can be and He also has unlimited resources and power to make whatever He desires come to pass. All I have to do to experience that lavishing of God's love is to love Him and to obey Him. Here's the amazing part about that, even the ability to love God and to obey Him are gifts that he gives us through the power of the Holy Spirit. God commands us to love and obey Him and then gives us the Holy Spirit so that we can because without the Holy Spirit we could only love ourselves.

Can you imagine what it might be like to experience the unlimited love of God being poured into your life? We can do more than imagine it; we can experience it. All we have to do is love Him and obey Him. Jesus, help us to experience the lavishing of God's unlimited love.

Rick Lancaster / PLANTERS PERSPECTIVE

FEBRUARY 5 || EXODUS 23:4

If you come upon your enemy's ox or donkey that has strayed away, take it back to its owner.

Read: Exodus 21:22-23:13

In today's reading God lays out regulations on the way that the people of Israel should govern their daily lives. These statutes cover virtually every aspect of their lives and were designed to set the people of Israel apart from all the nations around them. One of the things that we should keep in mind is that God is telling them to do these things because that is not how they are living when He gave them these directions. The Israelites were living based on the things that were normal in the nation of Egypt. In a very real sense the people of Israel were more like the Egyptians than anything else.

God gave these regulations to cause them to change their behavior to be totally different than everyone else around them. His purpose for doing that was so that he could use the nation of Israel to bless the whole world and through them to draw the whole world to God. This regulation in today's verse must have been one of the ones that had the Hebrews wondering and would certainly be one that set them apart from the rest of the world. God was telling the Hebrews to do nice things for their enemies. You have got to know that this must have taken quite a while to get used to.

Jesus told us to love our enemies and to pray for those who spitefully use us. This regulation that God gave to the people of Israel was reinforced by Jesus and is just as valid today as when it was given 3,500 years ago. God commands you to do things for your enemies that would be viewed as a blessing to them.

Your enemies expect you to behave as an enemy. You may not consider them to be enemies but they might consider you to be one. When you do something nice for them it causes them to wonder what is going on. If you see their dog wandering around, take it back home to them. If their trash can has been knocked over, pick it up. Practically every day brings opportunities to show the love of Christ and bless your enemies. There is nothing that can make an enemy a friend like the love of Christ.

You are to do this because God commands it not because they might start to like you. It might have absolutely no effect on them. They might remain your enemy for their entire lives. But if you obey this command, they are going to look pretty foolish to others calling you their enemy when you persist in doing nice things for them. And through it all, your kindness might be the thing that causes them to see Jesus.

There is no promise or blessing associated with this regulation; it is a simple command. We are to do it because God told us to. What God does with our acts of kindness are for Him to decide, including what he does with and for us. Jesus, help us to love you by loving our enemies.

FEBRUARY 6 || EXODUS 25:22

I will meet with you there and talk to you from above the atonement cover between the gold cherubim that hover over the Ark of the Covenant. From there I will give you my commands for the people of Israel.

Read: Exodus 23:14-25:40

It is not possible within the confines of a devotional to dig deep into the symbolism that is found in the Ark of the Covenant. It was here that God and man came together to meet. One of the many questions that remain to be answered for me is what happened to the Ark. The Ark was the center of Jewish religion. At some point in history it vanished and anyone that cares has their own opinion of what happened and where it is. Ultimately, it really isn't that important. If God wanted us to know where it was we would know. More importantly, the way that God wants us to worship Him is no longer focused around the temple or the Ark of the Covenant.

Jesus came to bring a new covenant that was written with His blood on the cross of Calvary. No longer do we need to bring sacrifices to pay for our sins; they are paid in full by Jesus. No longer do we need to have a High Priest to mediate between God and ourselves; we have the Holy Spirit within us.

God had always intended that His creation worship Him. His desire for humans is that this worship would be in the form of a relationship. God wants each of us to be in a personal relationship with Him. For the people of Israel, God did that through the tabernacle and its furnishings. This was how He created a relationship with them.

For us God chose a different method, He chose to send Jesus to fulfill the requirements of the temple once and for all and to pave the way for us to freely engage in a relationship with God. Some of my favorite verses in the Bible are the ones where people are described as having walked with God or as friends of God. One of the ways that Moses is described is as 'a friend of God'. It is my belief that this is exactly the way that God wants to relate to all of us. I believe that was what we were created for; to be friends of God.

It is not that God needed friends; He needs nothing outside of Himself. God created us because He wanted to. The way that we become friends of God is by learning who He is as best as we are able to do so and by listening to and obeying His commands. All of God's commands are meant to improve our relationship with Him and to teach others about God. Without God's commands it is not possible to know how to be God's friend.

That is such a key truth for us to embrace. We don't determine what it means to be a friend of God; He does and He does that through His commands. To receive the commands of God, we must meet with Him. To meet with Him we need to build a tabernacle in our heart for Him. Let the Holy Spirit build that tabernacle and then open the door to Jesus and let Him guide you to friendship with God. Jesus, take the keys of our heart and build yourself a beautiful temple.

Rick Lancaster / PLANTERS PERSPECTIVE

FEBRUARY 7 || EXODUS 26:30

Set up this Tabernacle according to the design you were shown on the mountain.

Read: Exodus 26:1-27:21

For several chapters here in the book of Exodus God has been describing to Moses how He would like the Israelites to build the Tabernacle. In some aspects there is great detail given but in some cases the instructions are relatively vague about just what it is to look like. It seems to me that while God had a specific design in mind, He left some of the details to the people that would use the creative abilities that He had given them. That is an important lesson for any leader; give your people the plan but let them use their God-given talents to work out some of the details.

In our verse for the day God tells Moses to set up the Tabernacle just he had seen it while he was on the mountain. Moses spent forty days (without food or drink) with the LORD on Mount Sinai. He did this not once but twice. During that time in intimate fellowship with God, the Lord taught Moses the Law of God and showed Moses many things. One of those things was the Tabernacle. Elsewhere in Scripture we are told that the Tabernacle on the earth was to be like the one in Heaven. God allowed Moses to see into heaven to see the Tabernacle.

Moses was given this incredible privilege for a reason. After seeing the heavenly Tabernacle, Moses would be better able to build the earthly Tabernacle. As I read through God's description I often wish that I could see what is being described. I marvel at people that can hear a description like this in Exodus and then go make it. I need to see what I am building before I can build it. In leadership we refer to this as vision.

One of the things that sets a true leader apart form others is an ethereal thing called vision. Vision is a leader's ability to see the task that they are working on already completed. They can see in their minds that the task can be completed and they can see what it will look like when it is done. If you are following a true leader that can create a real challenge for you because he can see it but you might not be able to. We might be working on one small piece of the project and have no idea what the whole thing looks like.

For the Tabernacle to be complete all the pieces had to be completed. All of the pieces were important. As we serve, especially in a large organization, we may not understand the vision. We might understand what the whole thing is going to look like when it is completed. That's okay, you don't need to understand. You just be faithful to complete your small piece and then trust God to use it to build for Himself a grand and beautiful Tabernacle. Jesus, teach us to work diligently on our small piece of Your Tabernacle.

FEBRUARY 8 || EXODUS 28:1

Your brother, Aaron, and his sons, Nadab, Abihu, Eleazar, and Ithamar, will be set apart from the common people. They will be my priests and will minister to me.

Read: Exodus 28:1-43

God tells Moses that his brother, Aaron, and Aaron's sons are now to take on a new responsibility. Aaron had played a key role in the delivering of the people of Israel from Egypt; he acted as Moses' mouthpiece before Pharaoh. Now he is going to be set apart to minister to the Lord. It is here that the priesthood is established within the nation of Israel.

There are a number of interesting things in this chapter and each of them is worthy of special attention. All of the objects have symbolic meaning and point to Jesus Christ. I would encourage you to study it on your own. One of the things that caught my attention in today's verse is the word 'common'. Aaron and his sons were set apart from the common people. The Hebrew word that is translated to common is 'ben' which is literally translated as 'son'. This simply means that Aaron and his sons were set apart from all the other men in the nation.

The chapter goes on to describe the garments and accessories that were made to signify this setting apart. It also says that these garments are to give them dignity and respect. Everyone that saw Aaron or his sons in these special garments knew that they had been set apart to minister to the Lord. These garments also identified them as the ones that were called to minister to the Lord.

The word 'minister' simply means to serve. Aaron and his sons were chosen specially to serve God in a special way. This did not make them special, just chosen. Unfortunately this is where some people stumble in their service to God. Just because you were chosen to serve, you are not any better than anyone else.

The term 'set apart' is often used of sacrifices and objects that are devoted to the Lord. These sacrifices and objects belong to the Lord and to Him alone. They can be used for no purpose other than the purpose that God has set them apart for. Too often we forget that when we think of those that are called to minister to the Lord. This is especially true of our own service to the Lord. If you have been called to serve the Lord, as all disciples of Jesus have, than you have been set apart to minister to Him. You are His and He can use you any way He chooses.

Today we don't wear elaborate garments to identify ourselves as set apart for God's use, but I do believe that it should be obvious to all those that look into our lives. We now wear the righteousness of Christ and carry the power of the Holy Spirit within us. This calling to be set apart does not make us better than others but it should make us different. Jesus, help us to walk as thought we are set apart.

Rick Lancaster | PLANTERS PERSPECTIVE

FEBRUARY 9 || EXODUS 29:1

This is the ceremony for the dedication of Aaron and his sons as priests: Take a young bull and two rams with no physical defect.

Read: Exodus 29:1-30:10

God instructs Moses in the ceremony to ordain Aaron and his sons as priests. It is described here as a dedication ceremony. Further on in this chapter God tells Moses that Aaron and his sons will be priests forever. This elaborate ceremony involved washing, dressing, anointing, and sacrifice. Each of those activities is a symbol of some greater thing that is taking place.

What struck me in this text was the word 'dedication' and how it applied to what was taking place. Aaron and his sons were being dedicated to the Lord for service as priests. Scripture seems to teach that once something or someone has been dedicated to the Lord that it cannot be un-dedicated. For the rest of its existence it is dedicated to the Lord.

As a pastor who has dedicated my life to the Lord, this means to me that my life is no longer mine. My life belongs to the Lord and He is free to do with it as He pleases. And that is true not just now but for the rest of my life. I may not always carry the worldly title of pastor but I will forever be dedicated to the Lord as a pastor.

I have met men that 'used to be pastors' and it causes me to wonder about their dedication. If they were truly dedicated to the Lord as pastors, then they are still pastors. Some of these men that I have met are men that God has used in the past and, I believe, wants to use in the future. These men, whether they know it or not, are currently in training to be better pastors than they were before.

There is no un-dedication ceremony. Once we are dedicated into the Lord's service we are dedicated for life. This is a source of strength and joy for me. Neither the circumstances of my life nor the wickedness of this world can change that. I can confidently go forward with my service to the Lord knowing that my dedication is to the Lord and therefore eternal.

For most of us we are dedicated to many titles. A wedding ceremony is dedicating two people as husband and wife. They are then forever dedicated to God and to each other in those roles. When we have children, we are dedicated to God as parents. Whatever such title you have walk confidently that the Lord will keep you in that thing as long as you will follow Him.

We should also note that even though the dedication is forever, our obedience to the Lord is required to maintain our position. Aaron's sons Nadab and Abihu were taken out of their positions (the Lord struck them dead) because they failed to respect God and obey Him. We can walk in confidence but our confidence must be in the Lord and not in our dedication ceremony. Jesus, dedicate our hearts to You.

FEBRUARY 10 || EXODUS 30:19

Aaron and his sons will wash their hands and feet there...

Read: Exodus 30:11-31:18

God speaks to Moses and tells him to make a washbasin for Aaron and his sons. This basin is to be used to wash their hands and feet before they minister before the Lord. God puts an exclamation on the requirement to be cleansed by saying that if they don't wash before they minister before the Lord they will be killed.

This washbasin was outside of the Tabernacle. Before Aaron and his sons entered into the tabernacle they were to wash themselves at this washbasin. The previous chapter of Exodus described the process that Moses was to institute to sanctify the priests that would minister before the Lord. That process made them holy and set apart for that service. And even though they had been set apart as holy, they still needed to wash before entering the Lord's presence.

Aaron and his sons were to cleanse their hands and feet. Just because they had been made holy, they still lived in a world that was not holy and so they needed to be cleansed of the unholiness that they come into contact with. They would wash their feet as a way of cleansing them from the places they may have been. They would wash their hands to cleanse them of the things they touched.

Jesus made a similar statement as He washed the feet of His disciples. As born-again believers of Jesus Christ we are washed by His blood and cleansed of our sins and unrighteousness. But we live in a world that is not clean. And we need to be cleansed of the dirt of this world on a regular basis. It would be great if once we accepted the cleansing of Jesus' blood that we would no longer be affected by the dirt of this world. But that is not the case. No matter how long you have walked with the Lord, your feet are still going to get dirty and need to be washed. And no matter how much your heart is turned to God, your hands are still going to get dirty and need to be cleansed of the things that you chose to touch. As long as we live, we will always need to be cleansed of the dirt that we pick up along the way.

This is especially true if we are ministering before the Lord. If you are involved in ministry or in a church, then you are ministering before the Lord. No matter how small your role might seem to you, when you do it you are entering into the Tabernacle and ministering before the Lord. And before we do it, we need to wash in the washbasin of God's grace and mercy and be cleansed. We need to ask God for His cleansing often. We need to ask the Lord to wash us clean of any sin or unrighteousness that we have picked up along our path. We need to confess our sins and receive the cleansing of the blood of Jesus. Jesus, help us to come before you to be cleansed before we go before you to minister.

Rick Lancaster / PLANTERS PERSPECTIVE

FEBRUARY 11 || EXODUS 32:1

When the people saw how long it was taking Moses to come back down the mountain, they gathered around Aaron. "Come on," they said, "make us some gods who can lead us. We don't know what happened to this fellow Moses, who brought us here from the land of Egypt."

Read: Exodus 32:1-33:23

Moses has been on the mountain with God for almost 40 days. All the people can see is that the mountain is covered by clouds so they have no idea what is going on up there. They have been forbidden from going too near the mountain or they will be killed. When Moses went up on the mountain to receive the Ten Commandments, he left Aaron and Hur in charge. The people get tired of waiting and so they go to Aaron and ask him to make them gods so that they can follow them back to Egypt. And Aaron responds by telling them to bring their jewelry so that he can make an idol for them to worship. Aaron failed to do one thing here, lead the people like Moses would have in this situation.

As the man selected to be 'in charge' in Moses' absence, Aaron should have responded the way that Moses would have responded. His thoughts should have been, 'What would Moses do in a situation like this.' Aaron's failure was in that he did not do what his leader had instructed him to do. Aaron was to keep things under control until Moses got back. He didn't do a very good job of that.

Aaron should have pointed them back to God. He should have reminded them that it wasn't Moses that led them out of Egypt but it was God. He should have reminded them that it was God that had performed all of the mighty miracles. And he should have told them to wait for God to tell them what to do next.

As a servant within a ministry or church you have a responsibility to the leader of that ministry to keep things going the way that they have told you to. If you are in submission to that leader as you should be then you have the belief that the Holy Spirit is leading him or her. If the Holy Spirit is leading them then any directions they give are to be obeyed as if they came from God (unless they contradict scripture of course). To not do so is to be in rebellion against God.

The leader's absence is not a time to change things to be the way you want them but an opportunity to prove to that leader that you trust God. Any ministry or church that you have even a tiny responsibility in or for deserves your faithful trust of those that God has placed in the leadership position. Ask yourself how your leader would make the next decision that you make. Jesus, help us to follow you by teaching us to follow the leaders that you have placed over us.

FEBRUARY 12 || EXODUS 34:29

When Moses came down the mountain carrying the stone tablets inscribed with the terms of the covenant, he wasn't aware that his face glowed because he had spoken to the LORD face to face.

Read: Exodus 34:1-35:9

Moses is just returning from having spent forty days on Mount Sinai alone with the LORD. This is the second time he has done this. He is carrying the second set of stone tablets that replaced the ones that he smashed after finding the nation of Israel dancing around the gold calf that Aaron made for the people to worship. This time his face is glowing. Something different happened on this trip that caused his face to glow.

In the previous chapter of Exodus we read that the thing that was different was that the LORD passed before Moses and He allowed Moses to get a glimpse of His glory. It was this glimpse of the glory of God that caused Moses' face to glow. However, I would suggest that was not all that was different about this event.

Moses was speaking to the LORD before God revealed His glory to him. Moses was begging the Lord to accompany them into the land that the LORD had given them. This was not a lack of faith in Moses; it was a revelation of his increased faith. Moses had previously spent forty days in the presence of God. None of us can truly appreciate what that might have been like; daily in the presence of Almighty God for almost six weeks.

Then, immediately after that huge spiritual experience Moses comes down the mountain to find God's Chosen people practicing the worst kinds of sins out in the open. It stirred within Moses a very natural human response; anger. In an instant Moses' mountaintop experience is shattered just like the stone tablets he smashed on the rocks at the base of Mount Sinai.

Moses went up that mountain differently than he had the first time. He realized how desperately they needed the presence of God with them as they entered the Promised Land. He realized that but for the presence of God; they were no different than the people that they were going to displace in the land. He also realized that he was no different than the rest of the people.

Much is made about getting into the presence of God. Books are written about how we climb the spiritual mountain to get into the presence of God. It is my belief that the trip is not upward but down. Moses was humbled before the LORD because he realized just how desperately he needed Him. Moses didn't know that his face glowed until others responded to him. He was not seeking the effects of being in the presence of God; he was simply seeking God with a desperate heart. God loves to reveal Himself to people that seek Him in this way. And after He does reveal His glory to you, others will know it and will either be afraid of it or be drawn to it. Don't seek the glow, seek to see His glory. Jesus, help us to have hearts that desperately seek You.

Rick Lancaster / PLANTERS PERSPECTIVE

FEBRUARY 13 || EXODUS 35:26

All the women who were willing used their skills to spin and weave the goat hair into cloth.

Read: Exodus 35:10-36:38

Moses over the last several chapters has described the Tabernacle and all of its furnishings. The Tabernacle is to be the place that God uses to focus the attention of the Israelites upon Him. Moses then told the people to make a contribution to the cause of building the Tabernacle. He gave them a list of the materials that were needed for the construction. Moses did not require them to donate to the construction. He did not institute a tax to provide for the construction of the Tabernacle. He asked for a donation from those that were willing.

The people responded by bringing everything that was needed. In fact, Moses had to tell the people to stop bringing materials because they had more than enough to complete the Tabernacle.

Moses also put out a call to all the craftsmen to come and assist with the construction of the Tabernacle. God had gifted a few with exceptional skill, but some He had given ordinary skills. The craftsmen also responded and worked to construct the Tabernacle.

In our text, women were also involved in the Tabernacle construction. God had also given them talents that were very useful to the project. But the thing that makes these women special is not their skills but their hearts. They had willing hearts! Their hearts had been stirred to help in this project to build a place where God would dwell.

God has given every person some sort of gift, skill, or ability. And those skills are useful in building, not the Tabernacle but something much grander, much greater, the Church. Every person, whether man or woman, has a place of service in building Jesus' church. Every person, whether highly skilled or with ordinary abilities, is necessary to build the Church in which the Savior of the world dwells.

But God doesn't want your skills, gifts, and abilities by themselves. First, He wants your heart. He wants you to bring the gifts, skills, and abilities that He gave to you with a willing heart. God is looking for people that want to help in the construction project of His Church because their hearts have been stirred to do so.

No one has to serve God; it is our choice. God can take a heart that is serving out of obedience and stir within it the desire to serve God. God is not glorified by a heart that serves because of selfish motives or out of compulsion. If you are serving God in any way, but especially in a leadership position, are you doing it because the Holy Spirit has stirred your heart? Are you helping to build the church of Jesus Christ because of your love for Him? If not, ask the Lord to change your heart. Jesus, stir our hearts to serve You out of a deep and abiding love for You.

FEBRUARY 14 || EXODUS 38:8

The bronze washbasin and its bronze pedestal were cast from bronze mirrors donated by the women who served at the entrance of the Tabernacle.

Read: Exodus 37:1-38:31

The Tabernacle is being constructed as it has been directed by the Lord to Moses. All of the materials have been donated by the people for the construction process. So much has been donated that the construction team had to tell Moses to tell the people to stop bringing stuff. One of the things that they made was a bronze washbasin. The purpose of the washbasin was that Aaron and his sons could wash themselves before they go in to the Tabernacle to serve before the Lord. The instruction to them was that every time they passed this washbasin they were to wash themselves of any dirt they may have picked up along the way.

The thing that I found interesting was what this bronze washbasin was made from. Apparently there was a group of women serving at the entrance to the Tabernacle. There is no indication what they were doing or how many there were; just that they were there. These women donated their bronze mirrors to the construction of the temple. The purpose of mirrors has not changed in the last 3,500 years. It is fascinating to me that God would use something that would be used to reveal beauty to create something that would be used to remove filth.

The fact that the washbasin was made from women's mirrors is a great picture for all of us and especially those that have been called to lead families, ministries and churches. God desires that we would be cleansed as we go about the daily tasks that have been assigned to us by God. Whatever you do today, at least that which is not sin, was assigned to you by God to do today. God wants you also to wash in the washbasin before you minister before Him to your family, ministry, or church, or anywhere else that you may find yourself today.

To do that you must look into the mirror of God's word, the Bible. The Bible was given to us so that we would be able to see what in our lives is filthy and not pleasing to God. But to look into that mirror and see clearly what we need to be cleansed of is not possible apart from the work of the Holy Spirit within us. As we look into the mirror of God's Word we need to ask the Holy Spirit to help us to see clearly what He sees. Otherwise we will only see what we want to see. Once we have seen that we need to be cleansed we must go to the washbasin and wash. Aaron and his sons had to wash every time they passed the washbasin. We also need to be washed that often. The difference for us is that the washbasin is with us always in the person of Jesus Christ. His work on the cross made a way for us to be cleansed of all the filth that we pick up during the day. We are washed by His blood through repentance and forgiveness. The picture that God is painting here for us is that we ought to be regularly being washed by that forgiveness through our repentance. Jesus, help us to get clean.

FEBRUARY 15 || EXODUS 39:32

And so at last the Tabernacle was finished. The Israelites had done everything just as the LORD had commanded Moses.

Read: Exodus 39:1-40:38

Scripture does not give any indication how long it took for the Tabernacle to be constructed but there is a sense in the text that it took quite a while. That is not hard to imagine since it was almost 3, 500 years ago and they were in the middle of the desert. There was not a lot of technology around for them to do a lot of the things that they were making.

The thing that struck me about this verse was that the Israelites had done everything just as the Lord had told Moses. Often when we think of the Israelites in this time of their history, we tend to think of them as being rebellious and stubborn. While that was certainly the case, they did also have times like this where they shined as great examples of how we are to follow God.

The Tabernacle was to be the temporary dwelling place of God as He traveled with the Israelites and carried them to the Promised Land as He had promised to their ancestors. The Israelites built the Tabernacle just as they had been told to. This is a good lesson for all of us that have been placed in the position of leading families, ministries, or churches. God is still building Tabernacles; except now they aren't physical structures, they are in people's hearts. And God wants those tabernacles built a certain way. We find those instructions for construction in the pages of His Word, the Bible.

Too often people, families, ministries, and churches get too wrapped up in the physical building of some structure to house the people that they are to be caring for. Homes, buildings, and facilities are tools to be used by God to lead people to the land that he has promised them. This world and everything in it belong to this world which is not our home. The Israelites were told to build a tabernacle that they were to carry with them as they traveled through the desert.

Until the Lord calls us home we also are walking in a desert. The tabernacle that we build in our heart is the most important thing that we need to build. The other structures that we build are just buildings. A building is not a church until God's people are inside of it. Once the people leave and the doors are locked it is just a building again; it is just another piece of the landscape of the desert.

As we build the various things that we need to so that we can minister to those that we are called to, let us never forget that the tabernacles of their hearts are more precious than anything else that we could build. Jesus, teach us to invest more into the tabernacles of hearts than we do in the brick and mortar of buildings.

PLANTERS PERSPECTIVE | *A Devotional*

FEBRUARY 16 || LEVITICUS 1:2

Give the following instructions to the Israelites: Whenever you present offerings to the LORD, you must bring animals from your flocks and herds.

Read: Leviticus 1:1-3:17

Some people have great difficulty reading or understanding the book of Leviticus. It seems to be filled with repetition and mundane instructions. It comes after all the action and adventure of Genesis and Exodus making it even more tedious. Often people that start reading through the Bible, then stumble and falter when they get to the book of Leviticus. Many struggle understanding how any of this book applies to their lives. If that describes you, you are not alone.

The book of Leviticus was written by Moses, probably at the foot of Mount Sinai or shortly after they left there. It was written for the tribe of Levi to instruct them on how to conduct worship within the Tabernacle and to teach the Hebrew people how to be set apart as holy to the LORD. It is within that context that this 'mundane' book has incredibly important lessons to teach us all about our relationship with God.

In today's verse we have the LORD instructing Moses to tell the Israelites in the correct way to make a sacrifice to him. The Israelites have just been delivered from bondage in Egypt for the last four hundred years. Generations of Israelites had been born and raised in the culture and ways of the Egyptians. All they knew about worshipping God was what they had learned from the culture that they had lived among. God didn't want His people to worship Him the way the Egyptian people worshipped their gods.

In this very first instruction, the LORD tells them to bring animals from their flocks and herds. The Lord is telling them that their sacrifice must cost them something. They were not to go out and catch a wild animal and bring it as an offering to the LORD. Their sacrifice had to come from the flocks and herds that they had been building up and investing into. For it to be an acceptable offering it had to be a sacrifice; it had to be of value to them personally.

Today, we don't go to the flocks and herds to bring an offering to the LORD. Our offerings come out of our day-planners and checkbooks. Instead of lambs, goats, and bulls the LORD wants our time, talents, and treasures as offerings to Him. But just like the Israelites grew up in a culture that did not know how to worship God, we have all grown up in a culture that worships different gods.

God created us to worship Him and Him alone, and to be in an intimate relationship with Him. Our first step to fulfilling that great purpose of our lives is to acknowledge that we don't know how to do it and that we need to be taught how. The book of Leviticus might still be difficult to read, but it and the rest of the Bible is there to teach you how to be what God created you to be; a child of Almighty God. Jesus, help us to see the beauty contained in every book, chapter, and word of the Bible.

Rick Lancaster / PLANTERS PERSPECTIVE

FEBRUARY 17 || LEVITICUS 4:2

Give the Israelites the following instructions for dealing with those who sin unintentionally by doing anything forbidden by the LORD's commands.

Read: Leviticus 4:1-5:19

At first glance the verse for today is a little confusing. God is instructing the Israelites to make an offering for sin that was committed unintentionally. The question that might be raised with this instruction is; if it was unintentional did they know they committed the sin. As you read further in the text for today you find that God expects this sacrifice after they become aware of their sin. This is comforting to me because it means that I don't have to worry if I have done anything contrary to God's laws until He reveals it to me.

People have come to me with that very concern. They are worried that they have done something against God and they don't know what it is. They are afraid that God is going to judge them because they have sinned in some way that they don't know about. I will usually encourage them to pray much like Job did for his children; asking God for forgiveness of sins that may have committed.

This viewpoint that God is going to judge us for sins that we are not aware of is contrary to the grace of God. God in His incredible love for us wants us to be in a right relationship with Him. He wants us to know where we have strayed away from His will and sinned against Him so that we can return to that right relationship. One of the primary responsibilities of the Holy Spirit is to convict us of our sin; that is make us aware that we have sinned against God.

If we have a desire to please God and obey His word as best as we are able, then we will know those areas that God wants us to repent of and get right in. He is not going to keep it a secret and pound us the first chance He gets. The fact that we are concerned that we might have sinned against God is an indication that our heart is turned toward God.

What God desires is that when we discover that we have sinned either intentionally or unintentionally that we repent immediately and do whatever it is that His Holy Spirit directs us to. Fortunately, we are not required to bring a goat or a bull to be slaughtered because of our sin but there may be another type of sacrifice or consequence that we need to bring to God as a result.

Unintentional sins are those that are committed by accident or in ignorance. To avoid these kinds of sins we need to make it a priority in our lives to get to know what God wants from us and learn what the things are that God wants us to avoid. We do that by making the Word of God a part of our everyday lives. We also do it by learning to hear the voice of God as He speaks to us in our daily activities. This will not completely eliminate unintentional sins but it will gradually reduce them until they are a rare occurrence. Jesus, help us to keep our hearts tender before God and our ears sensitive to His voice.

FEBRUARY 18 || LEVITICUS 7:7

For both the sin offering and the guilt offering, the meat of the sacrificed animal belongs to the priest in charge of the atonement ceremony.

Read: Leviticus 6:1-7:27

God gave to Moses to give to the Israelites very detailed instructions on how they were atone for sin. Different kinds of sins were atoned for with various types of sacrifices. These various sacrifices were intended to give the people a sense of the cost and damage that sinning against God causes. These sacrifices were intended to remind the people that sinning against God brings death. As always, the people couldn't pay the penalty of their sins themselves; they needed a substitute. The bulls and rams and other animals served as those substitutes. As Christians one of our foundational beliefs is that Jesus was the ultimate sacrifice for our sins; He was the final sacrifice that substituted for each of our sins.

One of the fascinating things that is seen in the sacrificial system of the Israelites was what was done with the sacrifices. Some sacrifices were burned up completely, while others only a small portion was burned up on the altar. Each different sacrifice had a different set of rules for performing the ritual. What happened with the meat that wasn't burned up also varied greatly.

The priests were the ones that performed almost all of the sacrificing. Some portions of the meat that was not burned up in the sacrifice were given to them as their food. In our verse for today we see that the meat from the sin and guilt offerings was given to the priests. I am sure that there is great symbolism in that but something very simple came out of it for me. By giving the meat to the priest, God was causing the priests to relate to the people that they were ministering for. As the priests ate the meat of the sacrifices they would be reminded of the sins and guilt of the people.

It is easy for people that minister to others to get to a place where they are hardened to the sins of those around them. The priests were fed from the sacrifices of the people that were coming to draw nearer to God. This should have reminded the priests of their own need to draw nearer to God. We, as those that are called to minister to our families, ministries, and churches need to be reminded of the same thing. One of the reasons why we exist is to help people deal with the sin in their lives, while at the same time dealing with the sin in our lives.

As we minister to those that we are called to we need to remember that we are ourselves sinners in need of forgiveness. We cannot disconnect ourselves from the flock as though they are sinners and we are not. The priests of Israel knew very well that their food came from the sins of the people. This ultimately led them to have a bit of a twisted view of the sins of the people. We must never forget the price that was paid to pay for those sins; Jesus' atoning death on the cross. Jesus, please help us to remember that our sins caused your sacrificial death.

Rick Lancaster / PLANTERS PERSPECTIVE

FEBRUARY 19 || LEVITICUS 9:6

Then Moses told them, "When you have followed these instructions from the LORD, the glorious presence of the LORD will appear to you."

Read: Leviticus 7:28-9:6

Moses had laid out for Aaron and his sons and the people of Israel all the instructions that were necessary for the people to worship God through their sacrifices. It was not really a complicated system, though there were a lot of details that they needed to remember. Moses then tells them that once they have followed these instructions that the Lord would appear to them. This is so important for all of us to see what God is saying in this text. It was only after the obedience of the priests and people that the Lord's presence would appear to them.

Too often we want it the other way around. We want God to appear to us and then we will obey Him. We think to ourselves and might even say out loud something like 'God, if you will do something, then I will do this thing'. That is not how it works. God is God and He can do whatever He wants to regardless of what we do, think, or say. He has chosen to operate in this world the way that we see it described in His word. Seldom will God operate on our wishes outside of our prior obedience.

We live in a world that desperately needs to experience the presence of God. And one of the primary tools that God will use to cause that to happen will be our obedience. As we do the things that he is leading and guiding us to do, it will result in His glorious presence being seen by those around us. God doesn't need us but He chooses to use us to reveal His presence to the whole world.

As the people chosen by God to lead our families, ministries, and churches we have the unique responsibility of obedience. Everyone is required to obey God but as leaders we have the greater requirement. Some would view that as a burden of responsibility. I see it as a tremendous opportunity. I have the privilege of showing the world Jesus Christ. That is not as huge a burden as some would imagine. God didn't ask me to reveal Christ to the more than six billion people living on this planet. He only expects me to reach out to the ones that are in 'my world'. My world consists of my family, my neighborhood, my workplace, my ministries, and my church.

It is my obedience to His instructions in the presence of those that live in 'my world' that God will reveal His glorious presence. My only responsibility is to obey His instructions. I don't need to concern myself with how or when God is going to reveal Himself to them; that is God's responsibility. There is no burden in that. In fact, there is great relief in the knowledge that all I have to do is what I am told to do by a God that loves me and them more than I can possibly imagine. I want the glorious presence of the Lord to appear to me and to those in 'my world' and so obedience is not a burden but a joy. Jesus, let my obedience be the key that opens 'my world' to Your glorious presence.

FEBRUARY 20 || LEVITICUS 10:11

And you must teach the Israelites all the decrees that the LORD has given them through Moses.

Read: Leviticus 9:7-10:20

God tells Aaron that he and his sons and their descendants are not to drink wine or other intoxicating drinks before going into the Tabernacle. This is because if they are intoxicated they will not be able to discern between holy and unholy things. The second reason given is the verse above that says they are to teach the people the laws that God gave them through Moses. It was the responsibility of the priest to teach the laws to the children of Israel and they couldn't do that while they are under any influence other than that of the spirit of God. Not much has changed in the 3,500 years since this command was given to Aaron. God still wants those that are acting in the role of the priests to keep themselves clean and pure. And the children of God still need to be taught who God is and how to worship Him.

If you are in any role within a family, ministry, or church you are in a role of the priest or are assisting the person who is fulfilling that role. And as such a person, you should be keeping yourself from anything that would intoxicate you. This includes drugs and alcohol, of course. But it can also include attitudes like pride, envy, selfishness, and covetousness. They will intoxicate you as much as alcohol will. They will affect your ability to discern holy from unholy and clean from unclean.

We have the holy responsibility of leading the people of God into a closer relationship with Him. To lead the people to God we must have clean hands and a pure heart. There is an ongoing debate over whether or not it is OK for Christians to have a beer or a glass of wine. And I am not going to add to that debate today but I will say that if we are going to minister to God's people that there should be nothing in our bodies or heart that would hinder that work.

Aaron was commanded to teach the people ALL the statutes that God had given to Moses. The Bible is our source of information to learn about God. The statutes that He gave to the Israelites helped them to discover who He is and how He wanted their relationship to operate. Many of the statutes that God gave to Moses were for the Israelites only, especially here in Leviticus as we are looking at the sacrifices. While the literal application of these statutes applies only to the nation of Israel, they are pictures of the Christian's relationship with God.

We need to teach all the statutes of the Bible. To do that we need to be excellent students of God's Word. We need to be able to discern what is to be taken literally and what is to be taken figuratively. But every word has something for the Christian that is seeking to grow in their relationship with the Almighty God of the Universe. Jesus, help us to keep our minds clear and focused on you and your truths.

FEBRUARY 21 || LEVITICUS 11:4

You may not, however, eat the animals named here because they either have split hooves or chew the cud, but not both. The camel may not be eaten, for though it chews the cud, it does not have split hooves.

Read: Leviticus 11:1-12:8

One of the things that have historically set the Jews apart from the rest of the world is the matter of their dietary restrictions. God gives the nation of Israel very clear and specific instructions as to what they can and cannot eat. Many Jews today adhere to these restrictions and will only eat 'kosher' food.

Some people have interpreted God's instructions to mean that there is something wrong with the animals that they were forbidden from eating. It is interesting that the Lord begins in His instructions by forbidding the eating of camels. If you have ever been around a camel, it is hard to imagine wanting to eat one. The instructions go on to forbid the eating of pigs and most of us would miss pork if it were forbidden to us.

It is not a matter of the animals being bad for us to eat. In fact, in the book of Acts the Lord tells Peter, a Jew, that all the forbidden animals of Leviticus are no longer forbidden. Peter resists what the Lord is saying to him because he was raised from birth knowing that certain foods were never to be eaten.

These instructions and prohibitions about food are not a judgment on the animals listed. God is creating a system of requirements that are designed to make the nation of Israel so unique that they stand out from all of the nations around them. And it worked; the Jews different diet is almost universally known.

What got lost over time was God's purpose in this different diet. God wasn't trying to ruin the pork industry. He was attempting to create a nation of people that had separated themselves from the world around them. The dietary laws were just one of the things that God was using to do that. His reason for doing that is so that others would become curious about their lives and come to learn about God. The LORD told Abraham that his descendants, the Jews, would be a blessing to all the nations. The blessing that they were to be was to be a conduit between a righteous and holy God and fallen man.

As Christians that role has now fallen to us. We don't have a list of dietary laws or other dos and don'ts that we are to adhere to. What we have is the Holy Spirit seeking to lead and guide our lives. God still wants us to be a separated people. He still wants His people to bless the nations by being a conduit of His grace, power, and blessings into this dark, fallen world. To do that we must be different than those around us that don't know God. If we are no different than the world around us, then the world won't be drawn to God through us. Jesus, help us to be spiritual magnets to draw others to You.

FEBRUARY 22 || LEVITICUS 13:41

And if he loses hair on his forehead, he simply has a bald forehead; he is still clean.

Read: Leviticus 13:1-59

God is giving the Israelites directions and instructions on how to keep them ceremonially clean. God is giving them the tools that they need to be a different kind of people; a people that are set apart from the nations around them. God is teaching them to tell the difference between things that are clean or wholesome and things that are not.

Many of these things were also designed by God to protect the nation of Israel, especially as they wander in the wilderness for forty years. Estimates place the population during the Exodus at between two and four million people. They were all living in very close proximity to one another and the conditions were very primitive. A contagious disease left uncontrolled would devastate the nation of Israel. God taught them how to recognize and deal with these diseases so that they would not be vulnerable in this area.

God is at all times practical as well as spiritual. Here in our text for today is a simple example of God being practical. He is telling the Israelites that just because a person loses their hair doesn't mean that they are unclean; they are just bald. It is almost a comical statement to make but it points to another reality in why God is giving them this instruction.

People have a way of twisting things to accomplish what they desire. People will even do this with God's word. It is as though God is predicting that the people will somehow interpret God's instructions to mean that a bald person is unclean because they have no hair on their head. So He inserts this caveat to prevent that interpretation.

As the leaders in God's ministries and churches we are called to hold people to the truth. We need to make sure that they are not interpreting God's word to mean what they want it to mean. Often they are doing it to justify their own sins.

To hold people to the truth, we must be students of the truth. We must know what the Bible says about different things. And we must be sensitive to the leading of the Holy Spirit. He will tell us when something that is said is not truth. Then we are to determine what the truth is and confront the false statement in love.

To be in a place where we are able to do this we must be living in the truth ourselves. Our witness must be such that others will receive what we have to say because they can see the truth being modeled for them. Your credibility is directly related to your integrity. If you are a person of integrity, then people are likely to hear what you say even when you are confronting them in their errors. Jesus, help us to walk in the truth so others will see the truth and follow us as we follow you.

Rick Lancaster / PLANTERS PERSPECTIVE

FEBRUARY 23 || LEVITICUS 14:34

When you arrive in Canaan, the land that I am giving you as an inheritance, I may contaminate some of your houses with an infectious mildew.

Read: Leviticus 14:1-57

The Lord is giving instructions to Moses and Aaron to give to the people so that they know how to deal with different things once they enter the land of Canaan. This one deals with what to do if they find a certain kind of mildew in their homes. God is teaching them how to protect themselves from diseases. These instructions helped the Jews throughout history to survive in times when other populations were being decimated by diseases and plagues.

What struck me about this verse was that it says 'I may contaminate'. Since it is the Lord speaking, He is saying that the Lord may contaminate some of their houses. Why in the world would He do something like that? Isn't that mean? Isn't that unfair? Be careful, asking those kinds of questions can quickly lead to blasphemy. It is against God's character to be mean or unjust.

The Hebrew word that is translated as 'mildew' is actually more accurately translated as 'leprosy'. In Scripture leprosy is often associated with judgment or punishment. You might remember the account of when Aaron and Miriam challenged Moses' leadership of the nation of Israel. God struck Miriam with leprosy as a punishment. Moses prayed for her and she was healed but not until after she had been driven from the camp for a period of time.

Contracting this disease would have been a terrible inconvenience for Miriam. A family living in a house with infectious mildew would also be greatly inconvenienced. The text of our verse doesn't say clearly whether God will do this as a form of punishment or for some other purpose. But for a period of time, their lives will be interrupted by this thing. Even in our modern times we need to be watching out for infectious mildew but I believe there is a different lesson in this verse than that.

Life is filled with interruptions, inconveniences, and disruptions. These are things that are not a part of our plan for life. Some of them might be small like a flat tire and some of them may be large like a serious illness. Usually we examine them in relation to how they affect our lives. What we usually forget to do is to use it to draw us to the Lord.

The Israelites were to go to the priests and report this problem and then a priest would come out and examine it to determine what they should do. And whatever the priest told them to do, they did. As Christians, we don't have priests that we can go to. You might be thinking that is what the pastor is for. He is no more a priest than you are. In fact, as Christians we are called into a holy priesthood. Jesus would have us to minister to one another. Surround yourself with people that are spiritually more mature than you are and then invite them into your life to examine the mildew that you find there. But if you do that, be prepared to do what they tell you. Jesus, help us to examine our lives.

FEBRUARY 24 || LEVITICUS 15:31

This is how you will guard the people of Israel from ceremonial uncleanness. Otherwise they would die, for their impurity would defile my Tabernacle that stands among them.

Read: Leviticus 15:1-16:28

God has just given to Moses to give to the people of Israel the laws of cleanliness. These laws deal with all sorts of things that will make the people unclean in the Lord's sight and also gives them the instructions of what they need to do to become clean in God's sight. The issue of 'clean' and 'unclean' served two purposes. The first was very practical. There were more than two million people living in close proximity to one another. Many of these laws are very practical for keeping contagious diseases from spreading through the camp. If these controls weren't in place, a contagious disease could easily have wiped out the population of the children of Israel.

The second and more important reason for these laws of cleanliness is given here in our text. These laws were to protect the Hebrews from the separation of uncleanness. God was living in their midst and He is perfectly clean. If they were to enter His tabernacle while they were unclean, His cleanness would have no choice but to separate Himself from it permanently.

The tabernacle was the place that God chose to live among them. It was a holy place. It was ceremonially clean. To enter into the presence of God, you also had to be ceremonially clean. To come into the tabernacle while being 'unclean' would defile the tabernacle making it 'unclean' and this was punishable by death. There is great symbolism in the laws of cleanliness and the tabernacle. Each of these laws spoke of a physical truth that also showed a spiritual truth. Jesus was speaking of that when He said that it is not what goes inside of us that defiles but what comes out. He said that the things that we say and do come from our heart and that are what defile us.

We are now the tabernacles of God. How much more important is it for us to be clean since God chooses to live in us rather than in our midst? While the dietary laws and cleanliness laws do not apply to us as New Testament Christians, we still need to separate ourselves from the things that make us unclean. Uncleanness will separate us from the blessings, provision, and protection of God.

And we need to teach others how to be 'clean' in the presence of the Lord. We do that through our testimony and the witness of our lives. Some of us are also have the responsibility of teaching these truths to others. It is a very high calling to be a priest in the Tabernacle of God. If you are in a ministry or starting a church then that is exactly what you have been called to. Even if you aren't involved in ministry, you are still called to keep your tabernacle clean. Jesus, help us to separate ourselves from anything that would defile us.

Rick Lancaster / PLANTERS PERSPECTIVE

FEBRUARY 25 || LEVITICUS 17:7

The people must no longer be unfaithful to the LORD by offering sacrifices to evil spirits out in the fields. This is a permanent law for them, to be kept generation after generation.

Read: Leviticus 16:29-18:30

The New King James translation has a little more impact than the NLT on this verse. It reads: *They shall no more offer their sacrifices to demons, after whom they have played the harlot. This shall be a statute forever for them throughout their generations.* The Israelites were God worshippers. They knew that there was one God; the God of their ancestors. However, for the last four hundred years they have been in Egypt where there were many gods that were worshipped. Each of these gods was worshipped in different ways; each having their own type of sacrifice. Over the years it is easy to imagine that the Israelites had picked up some of the habits of the Egyptians in their style of worship. One of the reasons for that is because up until this time they really hadn't received any instruction as to how they were supposed to worship God. As each new generation came, the things the previous generations were doing would slip into tradition. After a while, the people would have no idea where the tradition came from and would worship God in the way that they always had.

God now tells the Israelites that the way that they have been worshipping is no longer acceptable to Him. God is giving them very specific instructions on how they are to worship their God. To do anything else is to be worshipping evil spirits or demons. God closes this verse by saying that this is not going to change over time like some religious traditions do; it is forever. There is a strong warning in this text for us as Christians.

Why do we worship God the way that we do? Why do we practice the rituals that we do in our worship services? These are valid and important questions that we all ought to be asking. God expects us to worship Him in one way; His way. Any other way is wrong and in fact may be worshipping someone or something other than God; which He calls harlotry or prostitution. Sadly, there are many denominations and religious groups that are following the traditions of men in their worship rather than worshipping God the way that He wants us to.

This doesn't mean that we all need to worship God using the same methods and formulas. Only to the Israelites did God give specific instructions as to how He wanted to be worshipped and that was because He wanted to set them apart as distinctly different from the nations around them. God still wants us to be set apart from the nations around us but He wants that difference to be manifested in our love for one another. If you are in a religious organization that will not allow you to question the origins of the style and methods of worship, you MAY be in a group that is worshipping the traditions of men. Search your heart and God's Word; let Him reveal the truth to you. Jesus, help us to worship You in spirit and in truth and not according to the traditions of men.

PLANTERS PERSPECTIVE / *A Devotional*

FEBRUARY 26 || LEVITICUS 20:8

Keep all my laws and obey them, for I am the LORD, who makes you holy.

Read: Leviticus 19:1-20:21

God is continuing to instruct the Israelites about how to be holy. And here in our text for today God makes a powerful statement. God through Moses tells the Israelites and us that it is He that makes us holy. This is a critical thing for us to grasp about our relationship with Jesus. It is God that makes us holy.

It is important to understand and to communicate to those around us that it is not us that makes us holy; it is Jesus Christ. Without Christ, there can be no holiness. There are people that believe that they must get their lives together before they can come to God. The problem is that without God they cannot know what right is. The only way to get right is to come to Jesus and let Him guide you to holiness.

Scripture tells us to exercise ourselves toward godliness. It is our relationship with Jesus that teaches us the exercises that we use to become godly. Jesus paid for our eternal membership in God's Gym of holiness and then He sent to each of us the Holy Spirit to act as our personal trainer.

He also left us a training manual, the Bible, so that we would be able to learn the exercises that would lead us to holiness. The first half of our verse for today gives us the two parts of our exercise program. In the first part God instructs us to 'keep all my laws'. The Bible is filled with God's laws, statutes, and commands. Each one of these when exercised leads us toward godliness. God through Moses told the Israelites to keep them. This word "keep" means: to guard, or to protect, or to take care of. God's laws are something that we should treasure like we would something of great value. The place that God wants us to keep His laws is in our hearts and minds. You do that by reading, studying, and learning His laws as they are found in the Old and New Testament.

But it is not enough just to keep God's laws; we must also obey them. It does you no good to know what exercises you should be doing if you are not doing them. Keeping the laws and not obeying them is called religion. That is what the Pharisees of Jesus' time were doing. And sadly, much of the church today falls into this category as well.

Keeping and obeying God's laws is the relationship that Jesus wants to have with us and it is the method that He uses to lead us to holiness. Obedience to the laws can only come as a result of keeping the laws, and keeping the laws only matters if you are obeying the laws. God's plan for us is holiness and He has prepared the way that He can work out our salvation toward holiness through His laws in obedience. Jesus, teach us to hide your laws in our hearts and help us to obey them.

Rick Lancaster / PLANTERS PERSPECTIVE

FEBRUARY 27 || LEVITICUS 21:6

They must be set apart to God as holy and must never dishonor his name. After all, they are the ones who present the offerings to the LORD by fire, providing God with his food, and they must remain holy.

Read: Leviticus 20:22-22:16

Here in our reading for today, God is giving the instructions for the priests. All the Law and ordinances that God laid out for the Israelites were meant to cause the Israelites to be a separated people. This meant they were to be obviously different than the nations around them. Then God calls the Levites and priests to be a separated people from within the nation of Israel. The people were being called to be radically different than the rest of the world; specifically God was calling them to holiness or godliness. The priests were called to an even higher level, a greater level of holiness or godliness than the people.

Those that are called into service to lead God's people to worship have always been held to a higher standard than the rest of the people. There are some that might think that this is unfair or impossible to achieve. But there is great wisdom in this mandate from God. We were created to worship God and to bring honor to His name. Our actions and behaviors are the things that bring honor to God's name. If our actions do not glorify God, then we do not bring honor to His name and we may potentially bring dishonor to His name.

If you have been called to lead God's people in a family, ministry, or church you are in a position to lead people to worship and honor God. If your actions and behaviors are dishonoring to God then you are potentially leading others to dishonor God. You will bear a greater responsibility before God than someone that has not been placed in a place of leadership. You are the example that people will follow in how they will worship and honor God. Your holiness is the most important thing in your life. God cares more about how you are becoming like His Son Jesus Christ than He does about anything else that is going on in your life. And if you are a leader He cares about it even more because you are affecting the holiness of those around you. It is critical that we focus our attention on allowing our lives to reflect more of the holiness of God with every day that passes.

The priests had very strict rules that they were to live by. Failure to do so could have serious consequences. Those consequences were spelled out for them in advance so that they knew what would happen if they strayed from the way that God wanted them to live. God in His wisdom has given us the opportunity to interpret how He wants us to lead without the constraints of a religious system of rules and regulations. Instead He has given us Someone that if we will surrender to His influence will lead us better than any religious system ever could. The Holy Spirit in conjunction with God's Word is all we need to live lives that are examples to everyone around us of the holiness that God desires in everyone. Jesus, help us to do nothing that dishonors Your name.

FEBRUARY 28 || LEVITICUS 23:22

When you harvest the crops of your land, do not harvest the grain along the edges of your fields, and do not pick up what the harvesters drop. Leave it for the poor and the foreigners living among you. I, the LORD, am your God.

Read: Leviticus 22:17-23:44

As you are reading scripture and this devotional I pray that you are learning to catch some of the cool things that many people miss as they read the most incredible book ever written; the Bible. Today is another example of something cool that God would like us to glean from this reading. That was a play on words because what God is telling the Israelites is that they should not glean their grain or other crops. To glean is to come after the harvesters and gather what they missed.

God wants the Israelites to have giving attitudes about the things that God is going to give them in the Promised Land. Remember, right now they are living in the desert and living on manna. Before that they were living as slaves in Egypt. It is likely that the people would have a tendency to hoard everything they got from God because they had gone so long without anything. That was not how God wanted them to be.

God had promised them abundance and His desire was that they would share that abundance with others that had a need. By leaving the edges of the fields and what the harvesters dropped, the poor and foreigners would have something to eat. This precept is played out beautifully in the book of Ruth.

God has also promised us abundance and His desire is that we would share what we have with those that are in need. One of the truths that many people miss in their lives is that God gives us what He does so that we will share it with others. God wants us to take care of the poor and the foreigners. The problem is that most of us don't have fields that we are harvesting and even if we did we live in a culture that doesn't operate this way.

What God wants us to glean from this text is that our abundance serves a purpose. God will give to you all that you can safely enjoy without being drawn away from Him and all that you will give away. If you will not give away some of your abundance to those that need it, He will not give it to you. If you cannot have abundance without it drawing you away from God, He will not give it to you.

Here is the hard part for some people; God wants you to have a giving heart before He gives you abundance. If you are not willing to help those that have need with what you have right now; God may not give you any more. God will only give us what we can bear. That also means that He will only give us what we can carry. If you cannot carry abundance; He will not give it to you. God wants you to live today just as if you have abundance right now. Jesus, help us to give away what You have given us.

Rick Lancaster / PLANTERS PERSPECTIVE

FEBRUARY 29 || LEVITICUS 24:2

Command the people of Israel to provide you with pure olive oil for the lampstand, so it can be kept burning continually.

Read: Leviticus 24:1-25:46

There is tremendous symbolism in all of the furnishings of the tabernacle. In each item, its placement, and its use we are shown some aspect of Christ and God's plan of redemption for the world. The lampstand alone is rich in symbolism with its seven stems, the light, the flame, and the oil. Many of these things pointed to something that they would not see or understand in their lifetimes. The fulfillment of the symbols was not to take place for over a thousand years.

What caught my attention in today's verse was the word 'continually'. The Israelites were to provide oil for the lampstand so that it would burn without ceasing. The priests were also tasked to tend to the lampstand through the night so that it didn't go out.

The oil is a picture of the Holy Spirit. The light is a picture of Jesus Christ. The lampstand points to believers. The New Testament tells us that Jesus is the light of the world. Jesus instructed His followers to let their light shine for the whole world to see. The light is the declaration or witness of the gospel of Jesus Christ. And in the book of Acts, Jesus told His disciples that they would receive power from the Holy Spirit so that they could be witnesses.

What we sometimes forget is that God's instruction to keep the lamp burning continuously still applies to us today. The priests were instructed to tend the lampstand all through the night. All through the dark night they were to make sure that the light did not go out as they waited for the dawning of the day. We also wait for the dawning of the day, the day when Christ returns. While we wait we need to be tending the lamps of our life to keep the flame burning brightly.

This means keeping the oil of the Holy Spirit flowing in our lives. We must daily commit to being open to the moving of the Holy Spirit in all areas of our lives. This also means removing from our lives anything that might hinder the work of the Holy Spirit; which means eliminating sin, disobedience, and rebellion from our lives.

We also need to make sure that our lamps are placed where others can see the light. Sharing the gospel with others is the reason why we weren't taken to heaven the instant we accepted Jesus. There are as many ways to share Christ as there are believers in the world. Some will do it through sharing the gospel. Others will do it through good deeds. Some will do it by living the abundantly blessed life that Jesus promised.

We can't make the light or the oil. Our only part is to tend the lamp. If we will do that, the light will shine out from us in the way that Jesus wants it to. This is not something we can do once a week or even once a day. Tending to the lamp of our faith is a continual thing. Jesus, help us to not let the light dim for even a second.

MARCH

MARCH 1 || LEVITICUS 25:28

But if the original owner cannot afford to redeem it, then it will belong to the new owner until the next Year of Jubilee. In the jubilee year, the land will be returned to the original owner.

Read: Leviticus 24:1-25:46

In our society the concept of the Year of Jubilee is an alien one. The idea that every fifty years land would revert back to its original owners is hard to imagine. And the price to redeem it being based on the number of years until the Year of Jubilee and not on fair market value is definitely not a part of our culture. Today's verse paints a radical picture for all Christians and the way that we look at our things and life.

As Christians we are taught in the New Testament that this earth is not our home. In fact, we are citizens of heaven. We are foreigners in this land that we live in. Our home is in the very presence of God. Unfortunately, sin puts us into spiritual poverty and so we have lost our homeland. We also don't have the ability to redeem it for ourselves. There is no way that we can buy back our spiritual inheritance. As Christians we have the hope of salvation. Our hope is the knowledge that we have a relative that is able to redeem us; Jesus Christ.

However, even though we have been redeemed by the blood of Jesus, we still do not have our spiritual inheritance. We are waiting for the Year of Jubilee. That is not a specific calendar year that we can calculate but it is an event that is going to take place in the future. A day is coming, and could be very soon, in which God is going to give to Jesus everything He promised to Him. As co-heirs with Christ that is when we will receive all that God has promised us as well.

Knowing that, how should we live? Because this is not our home and the things of this world are only temporary we should live as though none of the things in this world matter that much. Our homes, cars, RVs, and all the rest of it are not a part of our inheritance. God has set aside for us some very cool stuff. No one can tell you what that stuff is but the Bible indicates that nothing in this world compares to it.

On top of that we are going to be in the presence of God. We will finally be free from the bondage that prevents us from being what we were created to be. In God's presence we will take all of the very cool things of heaven and lay them at His feet. Our selfish, self-centered hearts struggle with really grasping that concept but we will not care about anything else once we are in His presence. We will be free to worship Him the way that He created us to and we are going to love it. We will break out in spontaneous praise because of the wonder and majesty of his holiness. Stop looking at this world as your home. Spiritually speaking it is less than a weekend camping trip and what you have here is less than what you could fit in a backpack compared to eternity in heaven in the presence of God. Jesus, help us to look at heaven as our home.

MARCH 2 || LEVITICUS 26:3

"If you keep my laws and are careful to obey my commands..."

Read: Leviticus 25:47-27:13

Here in Leviticus chapter 26, God gives the people of Israel a very clear description of what will happen if they are obedient to His Law and commands. He also contrasts this description of His blessings with the curses that the people will experience if they are disobedient to His Law and commands. We see a similar accounting in Deuteronomy 28. And you will notice in both places that the curses take twice as long to describe as the blessings.

God expects the people to be obedient. And in these two chapters He describes all the good things that will happen to them if they will obey His Laws and commands. The curses are given to create a sense of fear. God doesn't give the curses to make the people afraid of Him but to give them a fear of the consequences of not obeying God. The curses listed in Leviticus 26 turn out to be prophetic. The people will turn away from God's Law and His commands and He does inflict the curses upon them. And ultimately the people are sent into exile and the land is given rest as is required in the Law. God never fails to do what he says He is going to do.

As you look at the curses listed there you will notice that they come in waves. And before describing each wave God says: 'If you fail to obey' and 'If you fail to listen'. Each curse is intended to get the attention of the people and cause them to start obeying God's Law and commands. It is God's desire that His people would stay in the place where He can bless them. But most of the blessings of God depend on our obedience.

If we choose to be disobedient, God will send a warning to us, maybe several warnings. And if we refuse to listen to the warnings and continue to be disobedient, God will begin to withdraw His hand of blessing from our lives. And if that still doesn't get our attention He will start allowing curses to come into our lives. And then if after experiencing the curse that he allows we still don't turn to Him and be obedient to Him, He will punish us Himself.

This applies not just to people but to ministries and churches as well. God has a plan for your life, your ministry, and your church. To fulfill that plan He has established laws, the Bible, that he expects you to follow. He will then through the Holy Spirit give you direction to cause you to fulfill the specific plan that he has for your ministry or church.

If you refuse to obey His Laws as they are described in the Bible and fail to listen to the Holy Spirit as He leads you, you should not expect to receive God's blessing on your life, your ministry, or your church. In fact, you should expect to experience the curses. God will bless your obedience and will curse your disobedience. As with most things with God, it is your choice. Jesus, help us to choose obedience and blessings.

Rick Lancaster / PLANTERS PERSPECTIVE

MARCH 3 || LEVITICUS 27:30

A tenth of the produce of the land, whether grain or fruit, belongs to the LORD and must be set apart to him as holy.

Read: Leviticus 27:14-Numbers 1:54

Here in the last chapter of Leviticus, God gives to Moses instructions about how the people are to devote things to the Lord. It was a practice of that time to dedicate things to the Lord for His use and purpose. This could be done with things, animals, and even people. God concludes this chapter describing those things that the people can't dedicate to the Lord. The reason they can't be dedicated to the Lord is because they already belong to Him. Certain things like the firstborn male of the people and the animals are holy and set apart for the Lord. They are His and they cannot be redeemed.

And in the verse above we are told that the first of the harvest is also the Lord's. That means that a portion of the things that the people produced also belonged to the Lord. This included not only the crops but the animals that were born to the people. God was to be given a portion, a tithe, of them as well.

The word tithe means a tenth. God told the people of Israel that of all that He gave them they were to give back to Him a tenth. The act of tithing is first seen being done by Abraham after rescuing Lot. Abraham gave a tenth of the spoils to the King of Salem.

About a thousand years after God spoke the above verse to Moses, God spoke to the prophet Malachi. God was upset because the people had neglected to give Him what was due to Him. Within the rebuke he made to the nation of Israel, He made a promise. God told the people that if they would bring the tithe in that He would bless them beyond their imagination. It was been about 2,400 years since the Lord spoke to Malachi and people need to be reminded all over again. There are some that say that we shouldn't talk about tithing. There are two reasons why we should. First, the first tenth of all we have belongs to God. It is holy; it has been set aside for His use. The only correct thing to do with God's portion is give it to God. Doing anything else would be treating holy things as common.

The second and much less important reason why we should encourage people to obey God and tithe is that they will receive a blessing as a result. God has never made a promise that He hasn't kept. If He says that He will 'open up the windows and pour out a blessing so great that you cannot contain it', then you can count on it coming true.

The New Testament teaches that God loves a cheerful giver. That doesn't mean that until you are happy about tithing that you shouldn't tithe. Tithe out of obedience and then let God work on your emotions. Teach your people that tithing is a natural and important part of their relationship with God. Jesus, teach us to give back to you a part of what you gave to us, not because we have to but because we love you.

MARCH 4 || NUMBERS 3:12

I have chosen the Levites from among the Israelites as substitutes for all the firstborn sons of the people of Israel. The Levites are mine...

Read: Numbers 2:1-3:51

This verse covers a lot of historical background. God chose the Levites from the people of Israel as His in Exodus 32 after the incident of the Gold Calf. Only the tribe of Levi chose to be on the Lord's side when challenged by Moses. The matter of firstborn sons goes back to Exodus 13 where God says that all firstborn sons belong to Him. This also relates to the last plague that God placed on Pharaoh and the land of Egypt when He killed all the firstborn sons in Egypt in Exodus 11. In our reading today we saw that God chose to take the Levites as substitutes for the all the firstborn sons of the nation of Israel. The Levites belonged to God; He owned them.

It is the issue of ownership that caught my attention in this verse. When you own something it means that you can do with it whatever you choose to do. What fascinates me about this verse is that God owns everything. Why would He single out the Levites to make a statement like this? Even though God owns everything and everyone in all creation He had a special purpose for the Levites. By saying that they were His, God was saying that He was going to treat them differently than He was everyone else.

Specifically it meant that He was going to be very active in directing their lives. This included determining what their roles in life were to be and even to their daily needs being met. Because the Levites chose God in Exodus 32 God chose them to be His special vessels to get His work done on the earth. To do that He provided for them everything they needed to accomplish the work that He assigned them.

Each of us has a choice to make in life too. At some point God is going to bring you to a place where He is going to ask you, just like Moses asked the Israelites, 'Whoever is on the Lord's side – come to me!' If you are one of the ones that respond as the Levites did, then you will be chosen just as they were to be special vessels and experience a different kind of relationship with God than others do. And if you are one of the ones that didn't respond when God called; He will call again. Be ready to respond the next time He calls.

This is not an issue of salvation; it is an issue of servant-hood. The Holy Spirit will never cease calling all to salvation. God's call to servant-hood as His chosen vessels is something that most people will ignore out of fear or ignorance. Doing so means they will miss the greatest blessing that is possible for a person on this side of heaven. The life of a person that chooses to be a servant of God may not be filled with the things of the world but it is filled with the things of God. It is difficult to put into words just what those things are; except to say that the things of the world pale in comparison. Jesus, help us to choose to be chosen.

MARCH 5 || NUMBERS 4:2

Take a census of the clans and families of the Kohathite division of the Levite tribe.

Read: Numbers 4:1-5:31

In Numbers chapter four God tells Moses to count all of the divisions of the tribe of Levi. The three divisions are based on the three sons of Levi. Each one of these divisions is counted and registered by name in this census. Then only the men that are aged thirty to fifty are chosen to do the work that God will assign to that division. It would be interesting to spend some time meditating on that for a while. Why would God pick people in that age range to do the work that He assigned to them? Most of the work was manual labor; it would seem to make more sense to let the younger men do that kind of work. But that study is for a different time.

What caught my attention in our text for today is that God chose the work that He wanted them to do. Yesterday we saw that God chose the tribe of Levi to be His own possession out of the Israelites, His chosen people. There is no explanation why God assigned the different divisions the work that he did. It seems almost to be arbitrary. It doesn't seem to be in order of their birth because in the previous chapter of Numbers Gershon is listed before Kohath.

The only explanation might be because that is the way that God wanted to assign the duties that he did. This is important for all of us to understand. Some of us might be chosen to carry the Ark of the Covenant and others might be called to carry the altar. Others might be called to carry the bases of the curtain that surround the tabernacle. It is not hard to imagine that some of those that were relegated to 'lesser' roles than their fellow Levites might have wondered why. It is also not hard to imagine people today that serve in what they see as 'lesser' roles might question why that is. The only explanation might be that is the way that God assigned the duties. There may be no more to it than that.

What is important for us to understand is that there are no 'lesser' roles in the kingdom of God. It took every piece of the tabernacle set into its place for it to be complete. That Levite that was carrying the base for the outer curtain of the courtyard was just as important in God's economy as the ones carrying the Ark of the Covenant. God doesn't look at any of His servants any differently when they are doing their assigned tasks. It doesn't matter what task has been assigned to you; do it as though it was the most important task that there is in your family, ministry, or church.

Whether it is preaching, making coffee, teaching Sunday school, or cleaning up trash in the parking lot; do it as though the tabernacle will not be complete until it is done. Do the task that was assigned to you and God will smile upon you as a faithful, obedient servant worthy of His blessing! Jesus, help us to look at our assigned task as the most important thing that we could be doing.

PLANTERS PERSPECTIVE / A Devotional

MARCH 6 || NUMBERS 6:4

As long as they are bound by their Nazirite vow, they are not allowed to eat or drink anything that comes from a grapevine, not even the grape seeds or skins.

Read: Numbers 6:1-7:89

The Nazirite vow is something that the Israelites were accustomed to but its origins have been lost over time. The idea of a Nazirite vow was that a man or a woman could choose to dedicate themselves, as in the case of Samson and John the Baptist a child, to the Lord. This could be for a period of time, typically thirty days, or for a lifetime. God gives them directions here as to how they were to conduct themselves during a vow like this. They are told to abstain from three things: anything that comes from grapes, cutting their hair, and contact with a dead body.

There is much that could be said about these three items but I was caught by the first one. God told them to stay away from anything that was made from the grape. The Israelites couldn't have known the significance of this yet because they were still in the wilderness and they did not know what the Promised Land was like. They didn't know yet that when their twelve spies came back that they would bring a cluster of grapes so large that it would take two men to carry it. Grapes would be one of the staples of their diet in the future.

God was telling them that if they take this vow to dedicate themselves to the Lord that they are to stay away from something that they would likely encounter almost every day of their lives. Grapes are used to make juice, wine, raisins, and cakes. It would be a tremendous sacrifice. There is nothing wrong with grapes or any of the things that come from the grape. The grape is not an evil or wicked thing. In fact, the grape is a good thing. It is often associated with the goodness of God and His bounty. The grape brings pleasure; it is desirable. What God is doing by telling the Nazirites to abstain from them is that they are to deny their flesh and its natural desires for pleasure while they are under this vow.

Dedicating your life to God is going to cost you something. To draw nearer to God means that you are going to have to stay away from some things that might bring pleasure into your life. Some of those things are so common that you can't go through a single day without coming into contact with them. God calls us to be a separated people. He calls us to be different than the rest of the world. One of the ways that we are different is by abstaining from some of the common pleasures of the world so that we can have the divine pleasure of fellowship with God. As Christians we have a choice. We can live our lives enjoying the common pleasures of the world or we can deny those common things from our flesh that we might experience the kind of relationship with God that He desires to have with us. A modern Nazirite vow might be to unplug your TV for a month. Take that time drawing nearer to God and watch what He might do in your life. Jesus, help us to live lives dedicated to You.

Rick Lancaster / PLANTERS PERSPECTIVE

MARCH 7 || NUMBERS 8:2

"Tell Aaron that when he sets up the seven lamps in the lampstand, he is to place them so their light shines forward."

Read: Numbers 8:1-9:23

One of the things that you will notice about these devotionals is that I am often drawn to the verses that create questions. Often those questions don't really have answers. Such is the case with our verse for the day. God instructed Moses to tell Aaron to arrange the lamps so that their light shines forward. The text doesn't explain why. It is left open to interpretation as to why God would want them arranged that way rather than to the sides or in all directions or backwards or upwards.

We can be sure that some theologian has come up with an explanation for this particular orientation of the lamps. In fact, I am sure that many have and they all probably have different opinions as to why it was done this way. You have probably heard me say before that if scripture does not give a clear answer on something, it probably means that it is not important for us to have an answer to that question.

Why did God want Aaron to do it the way that He did? Only God knows for sure. That is okay with me. It actually comforts me to know that there are things about God that I do not know and that I do not understand. It brings me comfort that God is so big and complex that I can't possibly understand Him. That brings me comfort because that helps me to see God as big enough to handle all of the stuff that is going to come into my life. If I could understand God; He wouldn't be big enough to help me with all of the things in life that I don't understand.

That also means that there are going to be times when He gives me instructions that I don't understand. He will tell me things that don't make sense and that create questions that I can't answer. He will allow circumstances and situations to happen in my life that I don't understand and that make me wonder what is going on. It is then that I can rest in His greatness and mystery. Even though I don't understand and can't find the answers that my heart cries out for; I know that He knows everything. And not just everything but more specifically, God knows everything about my life, my circumstances, what I am feeling, and the questions that I have.

Questions can sometimes create confusion when we don't get the answers that we are looking for. For me, these questions draw me nearer to God. They cause me to trust Him more with my life and with more areas of my life. They cause me to stand in awe and wonder as to His wonderful nature. They cause me to want to know Him better. Every question is a chance to know God better. Never stop asking God questions. Be that small child that wants to know 'why' everything is the way that it is. Just like a small child we will not always understand the answer but that's okay. Our loving Father loves it when we climb onto His lap and ask Him 'why'. Jesus, teach us to ask the right questions.

MARCH 8 || NUMBERS 11:11

And Moses said to the LORD, "Why are you treating me, your servant, so miserably? What did I do to deserve the burden of a people like this?"

Read: Numbers 10:1-11:23

There comes a time in every leader's life when they cry out to God as Moses does here and wonder why God is punishing them by giving them the people He has to lead. Moses is leading what most estimates say was between two and three million people through the desert. It would be a tremendous burden for anyone to carry. Moses is crying out to God because the people have come to him complaining that they have no meat to eat. It is not hard to imagine why Moses is responding this way. How do you provide meat for up three million people? You do it just the way that Moses did; you go to God. This is exactly the same way that you will provide for the needs of your family, ministry, or church; you go to God.

Too often as leaders we tend to take too much of the burden upon ourselves. For some bizarre reason we believe that we need to carry it all. This was definitely one of Moses' weaknesses and is the weakness of many leaders. We sometimes believe that there is no one else that can carry even a part of it. That is never the truth; there is always someone that God has in the wings to help carry the load.

After Moses cried out to God because the burden was so great, God chose seventy men to come alongside Moses to help carry the burden. God didn't wait for Moses to become over-burdened before He did something; He waited for Moses to realize that He was over-burdened. We need to not wait so long before we go to God and tell Him what we see as our needs. If they really are needs He has already seen them before you did and already has a solution that He is waiting to implement.

God chooses to operate in and through people. It must sadden God to have the solution to your circumstances all prepared and ready to go and you don't come to Him and ask for it. To see God work mightily in any circumstance we need to begin by asking God to work mightily within us. Ask God to do the work that he needs to do inside of your heart first and then ask Him to act in your circumstance. We usually do that the other way around.

Moses was trying to do it himself; he forgot that it was God that was going to care for the people, not Moses. God wanted Moses to realize that before He solved the problem. As you lead your family, ministry, or church are there things that you are trying to do by yourself that only God can do? If there are, then you are going to feel a tremendous burden that will bring you to cry out as Moses did in our verse today. The problem may not be the people. The problem might be that you are not learning the lesson that God wants to teach you. God has a solution and He is probably waiting for you to ask for it. Jesus, teach us to sense the burden quickly and cry out to You immediately.

MARCH 9 || NUMBERS 12:1

While they were at Hazeroth, Miriam and Aaron criticized Moses because he had married a Cushite woman.

Read: Numbers 11:24-13:33

Miriam and Aaron are Moses' older sister and brother. Both have played very influential roles in his life. Both have been used by God to provide for the deliverance of the children of Israel from the bondage of Egypt. Aaron recently has been appointed to be the High Priest and to minister before the Lord in the Tabernacle. And here we find them criticizing Moses.

This brought out God's anger toward Miriam and Aaron. He described His relationship with Moses to them and asked them why they weren't afraid to criticize him. It also came with a price; Miriam became leprous. Aaron pleaded with Moses for her to be healed. God did but had her sent out of the camp for seven days.

Moses was an incredibly humble man; in fact we see in today's reading that God considered Moses the most humble man on the face of the earth. And God comes to his defense and confronts Miriam and Aaron with their sin. We need to glean from this text that God considers it sin to criticize his anointed leaders.

There is no way to cover all the lessons that are taught in this single short account in a single devotional. Discover them for yourself. Most of the lessons are for the follower but there are also some for the leaders.

God selects people to lead His ministries and churches. He then brings people to come alongside those leaders to help that leader fulfill the tasks that He assigned to that leader. It is the responsibility of the follower to fulfill their role as follower until God calls them to lead elsewhere.

God told Miriam and Aaron that He had a special relationship with Moses and therefore they could not understand what it was that going on between them. Before you presume to criticize someone that is in a position of spiritual leadership you better know what you are talking about. If you had to stand before God, as Miriam and Aaron did, would He bless you or rebuke you for the words that you would use to criticize one of His leaders.

Miriam and Aaron were two of the people closest to Moses in his life and ministry. And yet because they criticized Moses God rebuked them. We have got to be very careful about criticizing anyone; especially someone in a spiritual leadership position. Notice that God did not say that they were right or wrong in their criticism of Moses. God was angry that they had criticized him at all. God considers it His responsibility to judge those that He has appointed to leadership; not yours! Jesus, help us to love, encourage, pray for, support, exhort, and submit to those you have placed in leadership over us.

MARCH 10 || NUMBERS 14:33

And your children will be like shepherds, wandering in the wilderness forty years. In this way, they will pay for your faithlessness, until the last of you lies dead in the wilderness.

Read: Numbers 14:1-15:16

God led the Israelites up to the Promised Land as He had told them that He would. Even though the report from the spies said that the land was exactly the way that God said it was going to be, they rebelled against God and wanted to return to Egypt where only suffering and bondage awaited them. Because of their rebellion God was going to strike them dead on the spot. Moses interceded on their behalf again and God relented from destroying them. While God did not strike them dead, He did not release them from the consequences of their sin.

Every time that we sin there are going to consequences. Sometimes those consequences will be small; sometimes they are huge and life-changing. God told the Israelites that they would not be allowed into the Promised Land because of their rebellion. Instead they were to wander around in the wilderness for forty years until every last one that was twenty years old at this point had died.

In today's verse we see that it was not just the adults that were going to experience those consequences. Their children were also going to have to pay a price for the sins of their parents. For forty years these children would wander around in the wilderness like shepherds. It was not their fault that they were going to suffer in this way. It was not their fault that they were not going to get to enter the Promised Land for another forty years. It was the fault of their parents.

Nothing has changed in the last 4,500 years. People are still rebelling against God and their children are suffering the consequences. When we sin against God we are usually only thinking of ourselves. If we do think of our children we will tend to minimize the damage that our sin will cause them. You have no idea what the consequences of your sin are going to be. Few things in life are as tragic as the pain and suffering that are inflicted upon children through the consequences of their parent's sins. Drugs, alcohol, pornography, divorce, sexual immorality, anger, gambling are just a few of the sins that parents commit that produce life-altering consequences for their children. Children are not the only victims; spouses often suffer as much as the children.

Our sin does not only affect us; it affects everyone that is close to us. Don't kid yourself into thinking that no one will ever find out. God knows and He will not allow you to hide your sin forever. He will expose it to the world and then you will experience the consequences and so will your spouse and your children. Confess and repent of it today before God makes you and the consequences will be less. Jesus, help us to obey you because that is what we should do and because it will protect our children from the consequences of our sins.

Rick Lancaster / PLANTERS PERSPECTIVE

MARCH 11 || NUMBERS 16:9

Does it seem a small thing to you that the God of Israel has chosen you from among all the people of Israel to be near him as you serve in the LORD's Tabernacle and to stand before the people to minister to them?

Read: Numbers 15:17-16:40

Korah and his 250 cohorts come to Moses and confront him about the manner in which he is conducting himself. In effect, they are accusing Moses of making himself someone important. They believe that Moses has exalted himself. They tell Moses that there is no difference between them and Moses. They say that God is with them all and so they all should share in the responsibilities.

It might be subtle but there are two things going on here. First, Korah and his cohorts are envious of the relationship that Moses has with God. For some reason they believe that Moses is manufacturing this and that he is keeping it from everyone else. They want Moses to share God with them; as though he is a favored toy.

Second, we see a power struggle going on. Korah wants control of the nation of Israel. And he can see that if he can gain control over the tabernacle he can control the whole nation of Israel. Moses is in charge and Korah wants to be in charge. Korah is questioning Moses' authority and ability to rule over the nation of Israel.

It is obvious from God's response that He did not approve of the attitude of Korah and his followers. He caused the earth to open up and swallow Korah and the other leaders and their families and possessions. He then sent fire to burn up Korah's followers.

Korah was one of the leaders of the tribe of Levi. God had set them apart to be used in a special way in the nation of Israel. They were the ones that would serve in and around the Tabernacle. They were serving in the presence of the Lord. God had also set them apart to be the ones in the nation of Israel that ministered to the people. They were to act on God's behalf for the people.

Moses asks them in our text for today, "Isn't that enough for you?" God chose them to the chosen people from among the chosen people. Unfortunately, it wasn't enough for them. And because of their hard hearts and rebellion, God had to take them out of the way.

We also have been chosen to serve in the presence of the Lord. We also have been chosen to minister to the people on behalf of God. God's relationship with the Levites was special and different than everyone else's. We also get to share in that special relationship. Korah wanted more and it cost him everything. Korah took his eyes off of his relationship with God and fixed his eyes on Moses' relationship with God and became jealous. God would also ask you, "Aren't I enough for you?" We risk our relationship with God when we start longing for someone else's relationship with God. Jesus, help us to see our relationship with you as the most valuable thing that we possess.

MARCH 12 || NUMBERS 18:7

But you and your sons, the priests, must personally handle all the sacred service associated with the altar and everything within the inner curtain. I am giving you the priesthood as your special gift of service. Any other person who comes too near the sanctuary will be put to death.

Read: Numbers 16:41-18:32

Aaron and his sons were selected by God to perform the most sacred duties in the whole nation of Israel. They were God's priests. They were to minister before the Lord on behalf of the people. To punctuate how important this was, God told them that if anyone other than a priest were to approach too close to the sanctuary that they would be struck dead. Even the people that were to carry the sacred objects from place to place were not allowed to approach them until Aaron or one of his sons had covered them up. What Aaron and his sons were to do was holy and God set them apart to make that work holy to the people.

God had given to Aaron and his descendants the priesthood. Our verse for the day says that it was 'a special gift of service'. Only Aaron and his sons received this gift and only they could do what was asked of them. No one else could come in and fill in for them. If they didn't do it, no one else could.

In Hebrews it teaches that as Christians we have been grafted into the royal priesthood by Christ. We also have been given a special gift of service. God calls us to perform the sacred work of ministering before the Lord on behalf of the people. The people are those that are in our families, ministries, and churches. It is also those all around us in this world that need to see Jesus.

This gift of service that God has given to us must be done by us. No one else can perform the work that has been assigned to us. Whatever your titles in this world might be, they are part of your sacred duty to those that give reason for those titles. Whether it be husband, wife, father, mother, son, daughter, employee, employer, pastor, ministry leader, or church member God has called you to perform the duties for all those titles as your special gift of service.

God took care of Aaron and his sons as they performed their special duties. They were provided for by God from the tithes and offerings of the people. As they performed their duties they were given from the people the best of their best. God is still providing for His faithful servants. He doesn't do it the same way now but He still gives His best to those that perform their sacred duties faithfully.

Aaron and his sons' whole lives revolved around the priesthood. Your whole life is also comprised of the priesthood. It is not just your time ministering to those that you are called to minister to. Your special gift of service applies to every aspect of your life. Jesus, teach us to live our lives exercising the special gift of service You have given us.

Rick Lancaster | PLANTERS PERSPECTIVE

MARCH 13 || NUMBERS 20:12

But the LORD said to Moses and Aaron, "Because you did not trust me enough to demonstrate my holiness to the people of Israel, you will not lead them into the land I am giving them!"

Read: Numbers 19:1-20:29

Our verse for today comes out of a text that many of us are familiar with. As leaders this is a text that we should study and become very familiar with. This is the account of when Moses responded to the people's request for water. Two million or so people and all of their animals are in the middle of the desert and they have no water. It seems like a reasonable request that they would want water. Scripture does record that they were grumbling and complaining and blaming God and Moses for this situation. Moses goes to God and is told to speak to the rock to bring forth water for the people. Instead Moses rebukes the people drawing attention to himself and then strikes the rock with his staff.

God does bring forth water from the rock but then tells Moses and Aaron that they will not be allowed to enter into the Promised Land. For nearly forty years Moses and Aaron will lead the nation of Israel around in the desert. It could not have been a pleasant life. The hope of the land filled with milk and honey had to be one of the things that drove them on. That hope was now gone. Moses would get to look upon the land but he was not allowed to enter into it.

Moses was accused by God of not trusting Him enough to demonstrate His holiness to the people. Because of his lack of trust in God, Moses lost the greatest physical blessing that he might have received. God did the miracle that He had planned to do through Moses and He continued to work through Moses after this event. It was a future blessing that Moses had sacrificed for this one moment of poor judgment. Moses allowed his flesh to get the best of him and it cost him dearly.

As God uses us to lead the families, ministries, or churches that He has entrusted to us He is going to give us opportunities to demonstrate His holiness to those around us. Moses should have simply gone out and told the people that their God had heard them and then spoken to the rock to produce the miracle. That would have focused the people on God and they would have honored and glorified His name. We will be given those same kinds of opportunities as we minister to the people that God has given us. Moses disobeyed God and paid a steep price for his disobedience. We need to take this for the warning that it is to us. God will use us as long as we let Him to lead and guide His people. He will bless us in ways that are beyond our ability to comprehend. But He demands our trust and obedience. If we fail to give them to Him as He deserves then we sacrifice our future blessings. How strongly do you think Moses wished he could take back those few seconds of time? Don't let a few seconds of the flesh ruin what God wants to give you. Jesus, help us to trust and obey.

MARCH 14 || NUMBERS 21:8

Then the LORD told him, "Make a replica of a poisonous snake and attach it to the top of a pole. Those who are bitten will live if they simply look at it!"

Read: Numbers 21:1-22:20

This is a section of scripture that has always fascinated me. The people are grumbling and complaining which seems to be their normal pattern. The problem is that the people do not trust God. Because they are faithless, God is punishing them. God has been traveling with them providing for them every step of the way and yet they still don't trust Him to do what he says He is going to do. God will only tolerate that from His people for so long before He starts to discipline them. God gets angry and sends poisonous snakes to punish them. They cry out to Moses and ask him to pray for them. God tells Moses to make this replica of a snake and put it on a pole.

There is a greater message in this text which we see explained in John chapter three as Jesus speaks with Nicodemus. Jesus refers to this incident in Numbers and says to Nicodemus that He must be raised up just as the bronze serpent was raised up so that anyone that looks upon Him will live.

One of the realities of our relationship with God is that He gives us the ability to choose. God does not make us love Him or trust Him. God will not make us believe in Jesus. God will not make us look upon Him upon the cross so that we can live. He gives us the ability to choose to look upon the bronze serpent.

While this is not in the text, it is not hard to imagine that there were some that chose not to look upon the bronze serpent. I can easily imagine people lying in their tents dying from the bite of the serpent and someone coming in to say that if they want to be healed they just need to come outside and look up at this serpent upon the pole. How many of those people refused to come outside because they didn't believe it was possible to be healed that way? It is not hard for me to imagine that because we see that on a regular basis as we share the truth of the gospel with others and they refuse to look up at Jesus on the cross so that they might have life.

We can't make them put their trust in Jesus; they have to choose. All we can do is be the ones that carry the pole around to as many people as we can and invite them to look up to the bronze serpent that brings healing from the poisonous snake of sin. We can't make them do it; they have to choose just like you did. Sadly, there will be many that will choose death rather than life. When that happens we need to be very clear that it was their choice not God's. God's desire was that they would choose life; eternal life with Him.

The Israelites chose not to trust God and it cost them dearly. God still expects His people to trust Him. Don't wait until the snakes are slithering around your ankles to believe and trust God. Jesus, teach us to trust You.

Rick Lancaster | PLANTERS PERSPECTIVE

MARCH 15 || NUMBERS 23:8

But how can I curse those whom God has not cursed? How can I condemn those whom the LORD has not condemned?

Read: Numbers 22:21-23:30

Here is an account that often gets relegated to a Sunday School story; the account of Balaam and his donkey. King Balak is freaked out about the nation of Israel camped out on his doorstep and so he sends for Balaam to curse them. His hopes are that if he can get Balaam to curse them that he can be successful at attacking them and driving them away from his land. Three times Balak requests Balaam to curse Israel and three times Balaam blesses them.

In Balaam's first blessing, which also has a prophetic element, we find our verse for the day. Balaam had warned Balak that he could only say what God wanted him to say. Because Balak didn't know or understand who the Lord is he thought he could manipulate the system to get what he wanted.

It is our misunderstanding of God that can lead to some of the weird ways that we look at life. There are people that believe that others can curse us or bring bad luck into our lives. What our verse for the day tells us is that if God hasn't cursed us, no one else can either. It also says that if God hasn't condemned us, that no one else can condemn us either. This can be a tremendously liberating truth when it is compared to Romans 8:1 where we are told that there is no condemnation to those that are in Christ Jesus. If you are in Christ, then God does not condemn you. Put that verse together with today's verse and you know that as a Christian that no one can condemn you.

God desires us to be free from the bondage of other people's judgment. Too many people are bound under what other people think of them. It only matters what one person thinks of us and He sees us through the eyes of His Son Jesus. What other people think of me is for them to work out with God, not with me. Balak thought that the people of Israel were a menace and needed to be destroyed. God thinks they were His chosen people. What God thinks always trumps what others think.

God looks at us and sees us as His children. While we may be flawed and in serious need of adjustment, He still views us as a loving Father. Others might try to curse us and condemn us but it matters not because that is not how God looks at us.

There is no indication that the people of Israel did anything while all of this was going on, the moving around and the altars being built and the sacrifices being made; they just went about their business. I believe God would tell us the same thing; don't waste time dealing with people that are trying to condemn you and curse you. You focus on what God is calling you to do now; you leave them to God who is much better equipped to deal with them. Jesus, help us to keep our eyes on You when others condemn us.

MARCH 16 || NUMBERS 25:3

Before long Israel was joining in the worship of Baal of Peor, causing the LORD's anger to blaze against his people.

Read: Numbers 24:1-25:18

God had led the nation of Israel through the wilderness for almost forty years. They will soon be entering into the Promised Land. God is traveling with them and providing for them every day and every step of the way. And yet, here they are in this text worshipping the false god of Baal. It started with the men seeing the women of Moab and being attracted to them. They then began to have sex with these women. Before long they are going to these women's festivals and religious ceremonies. And then ultimately they have turned away from the one true God to worship a god that allowed them to satisfy their sinful desires.

Baal was the supposed god of fertility and both male and female shrine prostitutes were available to assist in the worship of this pagan deity. As the men of Israel were prostituting themselves to this pagan false god, they were also acting as the prostitute to the one real God. God made it very clear to the descendants of Abraham that they were to have only one God. God is a jealous God and will not share our affections with anyone.

It is very unlikely that any of these men that were ultimately killed because of their sin believed that their first lustful look at the women of Moab would lead to Baal worship and then death. They simply saw something they wanted that would temporarily make them happy. God had warned them of this very thing. He had told them to separate themselves from the rest of the world because the world would draw them away from Him. As always, what God said would happen if they didn't listen to Him, is exactly what happened.

We live in a world today where there are so many more idols that can be worshipped than there were in the time of the Israelites. With television, movies, sports, and the internet there are literally thousands of idols that people can and do worship. And then there are the ones that have always been around; money, power, influence, and sex.

God gave the Israelites the Tabernacle and the sacrificial system and the Law to separate them and to protect them. We, as Christians, have something even more powerful than that, the Holy Spirit. The Holy Spirit was sent to us so that we could resist the temptation of the idols of this world. But we have to allow Him to work in our lives. We have to surrender control to Him so that he can teach us how to recognize and refuse the false gods of this world.

And we are called to reveal the futility and wickedness to others that are practicing these things. It is our role to let God use us to save them from the penalty of worshipping any god other than the Almighty God. Jesus, help us to see the unclean things as they are and help us to worship only You.

Rick Lancaster / PLANTERS PERSPECTIVE

MARCH 17 || NUMBERS 26:51

So the total number of Israelite men counted in the census numbered 601,730.

Read: Numbers 26:1-51

The Israelites have almost finished their forty year wilderness hike. They are camped out on the edge of the Promised Land and they will soon enter into it and begin to possess what God had promised their ancestors. Before they go in, God has them do a census to count all the men that are twenty years and older. Forty years earlier God did the same thing when He was preparing to take them in the first time. What caught my attention was that the totals were very close to the same. In the first chapter of Numbers the Israelites took a census and the total counted was 603,550; just a couple of thousand higher than the second count.

The interesting thing about the two counts was that none of the 603,500 that were counted in the first count was counted in the second count. That means that the 601,730 consisted of two groups of people. The first group was all the boys that were less than twenty years old when the first census was taken. The second group was all the boys that were born in the wilderness during the first twenty years of the wilderness journey.

This speaks to me of God's faithfulness. God had made a promise. That promise was that He was going to lead the people into the Promised Land. His plan was to take over 600,000 men and their families into the land. God's plan didn't change just because the people were unfaithful and rebelled against Him. Their unfaithfulness and rebellion just delayed God's plan for forty years. God was faithful and kept His promise and stuck to His plan to take more than 600,000 men and their families into the Promised Land.

This applies to us as well. God has a plan and He has made promises that apply to all of our lives, families, ministries, and churches. Our faithfulness and obedience will have an impact on how and when God fulfills those promises and plans. Nothing we do will stop them from happening but we do have a choice about our role and involvement in those things happening.

If the first 600,000 Israelites had trusted and believed God and acted upon their trust and belief, they would have entered into the land and seen God's promises fulfilled. Because of their disbelief and rebellion they didn't and another 600,000 were allowed to get what God had offered to them first. The first 600,000 had to live with the consequences of their bad decisions. We also have to live with the consequences of the way that we believe and act in relation to God. Many people are wandering around in the wilderness of their disbelief and rebellion against God, while someone else is reaping the fulfillment of God's promises. We owe it to our families, ministries, and churches to believe God and obey Him so that He can be glorified and they can experience the fulfillment of God's promises. Jesus, teach us to trust, believe, and obey.

MARCH 18 || NUMBERS 27:7

The daughters of Zelophehad are right. You must give them an inheritance of land along with their father's relatives. Assign them the property that would have been given to their father.

Read: Numbers 26:52-28:15

God was about to begin to fulfill His promise to Abraham and his descendants to give them a land that they could call their own. God told Moses to instruct the people about how to divide up the land which they will accomplish in the book of Joshua. As they are being instructed in how to do the division of the land the daughters of Zelophehad come to Moses to request land. They do this because the land was to be divided only to the male heads of the families of the tribes of Israel. Zelophehad had died leaving no male children just five daughters. That meant that these five women would have no land and that their father's name would disappear from the nation of Israel.

In our verse for the day, God said that what the Daughters had said was correct and then went on to give Moses directions on how to deal with this situation when it came up in the future. Because these women brought this situation to Moses, women for all the future generations would be taken care of. God acted on behalf of these women because they came and asked for God to act on their behalf.

For some reason we believe that life has to be fair. That is partly because we are usually raised with an emphasis on being fair. The fact of the matter is that life is not fair. Things are going to happen in your lives that just aren't fair. In our text for today it was not fair that the Daughters were not going to get an inheritance. They took it to God and God acted on their behalf.

That is cool because that means that when we come to some unfair thing in life that we can go to God and ask Him to do something about it. God might be waiting for someone with the faith to come to Him and ask for Him to act. And when that person does, it might have a tremendous impact on many others.

The thing we need to keep in mind is that God might not think that our situation is unfair. Just because we think it is unfair and ask God to do something about it doesn't mean that He is obligated to do something about it. He is God, not a magic genie. He will do what He thinks is correct; not what you think is correct or fair. We need to balance our sense of fairness with the fact that God is sovereign and He makes the final decision. Once He has made that decision we are to accept it and go on with our lives.

God loves it when His children come to Him and tell Him about some unfairness in their lives. It gives Him the opportunity to act on their behalf or to teach them about what He thinks is fair. Jesus, help us to understand what You think is fair and to accept it.

Rick Lancaster / PLANTERS PERSPECTIVE

MARCH 19 || NUMBERS 29:40

So Moses gave all these instructions to the people of Israel, just as the LORD had commanded him.

Read: Numbers 28:16-29:40

The Lord has just given Moses the instructions for the sacrifices required for several festivals including the Day of Atonement. Hundreds of animals will be sacrificed during these festivals. The people are expected to provide those animals. This chapter ends with the statement that Moses told the people what God expected from them.

We live in a culture that doesn't really care to hear what anyone expects of us. And for many that includes God. This can present a real problem for someone that listens to and hears from God. The problem is that God will sometimes give us messages that He would like us to share with others.

God's messages are all intended for people to come to know Him better and to move closer to Him in their relationship to Him and with Him. These messages are often asking people to change something about the way they are relating to God or to other people. As flawed and frail humans we will often wrestle with God over messages that are calling us or others to change.

We wrestle with God over these things because we forget that God is good. Everything that He does is born out of His goodness and love. We also forget that God has complete knowledge of everything and that we don't. It is highly unlikely that Moses truly understood why God wanted them to sacrifice all those animals, grain, and drink.

Moses did not question what God was saying or ask Him even to help Him to understand it. Moses simply told the people what God said. It was then up to the people to decide what they would do with what He had told them.

When God gives us a message to share with others, we need to share it. Moses didn't respond to God's instructions based on how he thought the people might receive it. He had already learned from his mistake at the burning bush about that. We also can't hold back what God wants to say to His people because we are not sure how they are going to respond to it. Their response is not our responsibility; it's God's.

Moses also learned that how we give God's messages is just as important as the act of doing it. Moses misrepresented God to the people in Numbers 20 at Meribah by suggesting that God was angry with them. That cost Moses his chance to enter into the Promised Land. If God gives you a message for someone, it is because he loves them in a way that you will never fully understand. We should do everything in our ability to help them to know that love. If God gives you a message for someone, give it to them humbly, gently, and with love. Jesus, help us to be loving conduits of your word.

MARCH 20 || NUMBERS 31:16

These are the very ones who followed Balaam's advice and caused the people of Israel to rebel against the LORD at Mount Peor. They are the ones who caused the plague to strike the LORD's people.

Read: Numbers 30:1-31:54

God instructed Moses to send out a military force to destroy the Midianites because they had been responsible for leading the people into the sin of idolatry. They send out twelve thousand men and kill every man. They come back with a great amount of spoils from their victory. Part of the spoils is all the women and children. Moses gets angry at the army commanders because they have allowed the women to live.

The Midianites were enemies of the people of Israel. But they weren't outwardly aggressive to them. Their plan was to cause the Israelites to rebel against God and then God would destroy them. That plan was working until Phineas stepped in and showed his passion and zeal for the Lord. The Midianite women were tempting the men physically and then leading them to worship their gods. By allowing them to live, the Israelites were placing themselves in great danger. The Midianite women would likely continue to lead the men of Israel away from God to worship their idols.

The enemy is very subtle in his schemes to lead us away from the Lord. If he was blatantly aggressive we would more easily detect him and prepare ourselves against him. He tends to attack us most often in the areas of our desires. The men of Israel were obviously attracted to the women of Midian and so the enemy used them to lure the men to idol worship. When we are faced with temptations to sin, God will call us to resist it. He will also lead us to destroy that sin from within our lives. By allowing the women to live, the Israelites were inviting the temptation to dwell among them. If we want to have victory over temptation and sin, we must absolutely destroy any possibility of temptation. While it is not usually possible to completely destroy temptation, you can at least not invite that temptation home with you.

It made good sense to the men of Israel to take these women captive; they would be used as servants to the people of Israel. The problem is that the men of Israel were attracted to them and so they would not remain as servants; the men of Israel would desire them. To defeat temptation and sin, we must deny ourselves the things that lead us toward sin. Some things that we need to deny ourselves are in themselves innocent but to us they may be just the tool that the enemy needs to defeat you. Jesus said that to follow Him that we need to deny ourselves and pick up our cross. To deny ourselves means that we will destroy anything in our lives that could lead us to sin or away from God. That means sacrifice! It would have been a great blessing to the people to have all those women serving them; doing all the menial tasks around the camp. The cost to their relationship with God was not worth it. Jesus, help us to destroy anything that does not lead us to You.

Rick Lancaster | PLANTERS PERSPECTIVE

MARCH 21 || NUMBERS 32:19

But we do not want any of the land on the other side of the Jordan. We would rather live here on the east side where we have received our inheritance.

Read: Numbers 32:1-33:39

The tribes of Rueben and Gad come to Moses and tell him that they want the land of Gilead rather than going into the Promised Land as the Lord had commanded them. They looked around at the land of Gilead and saw that it was good for all of their livestock. At first Moses is very upset and accuses them of rebelling against God and leading the rest of the nation into rebellion like their ancestors that died in the wilderness. Eventually Moses relents and gives them what they ask for after the leaders of Reuben and Gad make a deal with Moses.

The people of Reuben and Gad didn't want what God had promised them, they wanted what they saw. This is a sad testimony of how many of us relate to God. God has promised us tremendous blessings. He has promised us a life that is filled with His presence, power, and provision. But we tend to look around and say 'No thank you God, I like it right here'. The people had no idea what the Promised Land held for them except that God had told them that it was a land flowing with milk and honey. They couldn't have known what they were giving up to settle there. They would rather settle for what they could see, rather than obey God and experience His abundant blessings.

Sadly, God will allow us to settle for less than all that He has for us. He loves us so much that He will let us decide how much we want to be blessed by Him. We get to choose whether or not we live in His abundance or settle for what the world will give us.

The problem is that the world doesn't want to give us anything. In fact, it wants to take what we have from us. Because the people of Reuben and Gad settled on the wrong side of the Jordan they were the first tribes to fall into idolatry and they were the first tribes to be taken away into captivity.

There is a great danger in settling for the things of the world rather than the promises of God. When we settle for the world we are usually outside of God's protection and provision. That makes us vulnerable to attacks and temptations. Most of us are not strong enough to withstand those attacks and temptations for very long before we are over-run by our enemy.

To keep the enemy at bay we must always be moving toward the Promised Land; the life that God promised us. As we do, we draw closer and closer to God. The closer we get to God, the more that He protects and provides for us. Don't settle for what the world can give you. Only what God can give you will truly fill your life with all that you truly desire. Jesus, help us to see You as more precious than the things around us.

MARCH 22 || NUMBERS 34:2

Give these instructions to the Israelites: When you come into the land of Canaan, which I am giving you as your special possession, these will be the boundaries.

Read: Numbers 33:40-35:34

The Israelites are very close to entering the Promised Land. They are camped out on the East side of the Jordan River across from Jericho. Moses is going to give them some last minute instructions which we will read in the book of Deuteronomy and then he is going to die. Joshua will then lead them into the land that was promised to their ancestors.

In our text for today God tells Moses to instruct the people about dividing the land once they have entered it. He begins by describing the boundaries of the land that he is giving them. This is what caught my attention this morning; God set boundaries or limits to what he was giving them.

We often have the mindset that there is no limit to what God is going to give us. God could have given the Israelites the whole world and yet He only gave them the small area of Palestine. These were His chosen people and yet they had this tiny territory as their own. God in His sovereignty will decide what the boundaries of our lives are; we have no say in the matter. We can ask as Jabez did that our boundaries be expanded but it is still God's call whether or not it happens.

God set the boundaries of all things. In the book of Genesis we read of God setting the boundaries of the oceans and seas. God determined the limits and boundaries of all things that exist. That is important for us to know for all aspects of our lives. There is a point at which God will not allow us to pass.

The other side of that which we will see in the book of Joshua is that God wants us to occupy every bit of what He has given us. Too often we are asking for more territory and we are not occupying everything that God has already given us. God is not going to give you more if you are not using what He has already given you. In fact, the nation of Israel is a great picture of what happens if you do not use wisely what God has given you; He will take it away from you.

God has promised to us great and wonderful things. He wants us to possess those things and make them a part of our lives. God wants us to occupy every bit of the life that He has given us and to live right up to the boundary that He has set for our lives. Only then will He consider expanding your boundaries. Too many people are looking for a life that is outside of their boundaries and they are frustrated and discouraged. Keep your eyes on the Lord and get to work to develop all of the life that God has given you. Jesus, give us eyes to see all that You have already given us.

Rick Lancaster / PLANTERS PERSPECTIVE

MARCH 23 || DEUTERONOMY 1:2

Normally it takes only eleven days to travel from Mount Sinai to Kadesh-barnea, going by way of Mount Seir.

Read: Numbers 36:1-Deuteronomy 1:46

The first chapters of Deuteronomy are a recap of the Israelites wandering in the wilderness. It begins with this incredibly sad statement that we find in our verse for the day. It took them forty years to travel the distance that it should have only taken eleven days. Because the people were disobedient and didn't go into the land when God told them to they wasted forty years wandering around. All of the disobedient people died without having seen the land that was promised to them.

The sad thing about that is that is a picture of many people's lives today as well. They are wasting their lives wandering around in the wilderness of disobedience while they are only a few steps away from the life that God promised to them.

Jesus came to this world to give us eternal life and so that we could live a power-filled, abundant life. But to access this life we must do so through Jesus Christ and that means that we need to obey Him in everything. As we get to know more about Jesus and obey His commands we get to experience more of the life that He promised us

It is hard as a pastor to sit and watch people just outside of the abundant life wandering around in the wilderness. It breaks my heart to see them and know that they are just a few steps from enjoying the same kind of life that I am. I know what they need to do and have told them what they need to do but they must choose to do it. Only then can they enter into the promised life.

As leaders of families, ministries, and churches our responsibility is to draw people toward the promised life through Jesus Christ. We do that by first living that life ourselves. No one will be drawn to Jesus by you if you are not living an abundant life yourself. People must see Jesus working in you and through you and must see how Jesus has changed your life for the better.

You must also light the path for them to see the way to the promised life. You do that by sharing the truth of God's Word to them. As they see your life and hear the truth, they will begin to make the decision to follow you into the Promised life. Few things fill my heart with joy like seeing God's people entering into the life that Jesus came to give them. That might be the greatest reward that I can receive as a shepherd of God's flock; to see that flock enjoying the bounty of God. The greatest sadness is when we look and see those of God's flock that are in spiritual poverty as they wander in the wilderness of disobedience. God has this amazing life that He has given to anyone that will simply obey Him. Jesus, help us to enter into the fullness of the life that You came to give us and help us to lead others into it as well.

MARCH 24 || DEUTERONOMY 3:22

Do not be afraid of the nations there, for the LORD your God will fight for you.

Read: Deuteronomy 2:1-3:29

Moses is getting the people ready to enter into the Promised Land. God brought them out of Egypt and lead them to the edge of the land. God told them that He was going to drive out nations that were greater than they were so that they could possess the land. The spies that had gone into the land also reported that there were strong nations in the land. Moses tells them not to worry about those other nations because God is going to fight for them.

This is a beautiful picture of the Christian life, especially to someone that has fully surrendered their life to God and committed to serve Him. God has not promised us a land like He did the Israelites. What He promised us is a life that is rich, power-filled, and full of all the goodness of God. To get this life we need to go in and possess it just like the Israelites had to do with the Promised Land. And just like the Israelites had to dispossess enemies from the Promised Land, we need to dispossess enemies from the life that Jesus gave to us.

In our lives those enemies are sin. To experience all of the life that God wants us to, we must drive sin from our lives. We do that by surrendering our lives fully and completely to the work of the Holy Spirit and strive to obey every word of the Bible. Then we will find that God will drive those enemies from our lives.

As we surrender more of our lives and give ourselves to serve God and His people we will also find enemies in that area as well. The reason for that is that by committing to serve you are actually stepping further into the Promised Life. The enemies there are greater and fiercer. Now you are not just working on your life with God but you are also impacting the lives of others and their relationship with God.

Moses told the Israelites not to be afraid of the enemies they would face in the land because God was going to fight for them. God has not changed and He is still fighting the battles of those that are actively seeking to possess the life that He promised them and those that they serve. We have absolutely nothing to fear; God is bigger and badder than any enemy that could possibly come into our lives.

God wants us to fearlessly pursue the life that Jesus came to give us. He wants us to face those enemies just as David faced Goliath; with a bold confidence, not in his own ability but in the power of the living God. The people of God should be fearless as they face the things that the world throws at them. The people that have been called to serve Him (that is everyone) should be even more fearless. We are on God's side and no one or nothing can beat God. Jesus, help us to face our enemies with fearless confidence in You.

MARCH 25 || DEUTERONOMY 4:12

Do not add to or subtract from these commands I am giving you from the LORD your God. Just obey them.

Read: Deuteronomy 4:1-49

Moses is giving his last speech before he dies. In this speech he will remind the nation of Israel of all the great things that God has done for them and he will remind them of God's laws. Much of the book of Deuteronomy is a restatement of the laws of God. And here in our verse for the day we see Moses making a very important declaration. In a very simple statement Moses describes what our response to the laws of God should be.

First we are told not to add to or subtract from these laws. God's laws, commandments, and statutes are complete. They need nothing added to them. There is nothing that man can say that can add anything to what God has said. All man can do is to attempt to explain to others what God said. And even in that man has to be very careful that his explanation lines up with the Word of God.

There is no part of God's word that is not necessary. If you subtract anything from God's Word, you are making it incomplete. Every word is there for a reason. Only by examining all of God's Word do you get a complete picture of God. If you leave things out of what God said you have a lesser view of God's holiness. God is jealous of His holiness and anything that diminishes it will be met with His anger and judgment.

God's word is absolutely perfect and complete. It needs nothing and it has nothing extra. It contains everything that we need and nothing in it is unimportant. The only way the Bible can be viewed is completely. Anything less than that will cause you to view God in a way that cannot help you the way that you need to be helped.

Moses concludes this exhortation with a very simple instruction of what to do with the laws of God; 'just obey them'. How simple is that! We tend to spend too much time trying to understand the theology and prophetic aspects of scripture when the most important thing that God wants us to do is obey scripture. We need to understand scripture well enough that we can obey it.

Don't complicate scripture! Don't diminish scripture! Just do what it says! If we would spend more time obeying scripture and teaching others to obey scripture, there would be less conflict in the church and in ministry. Jesus, help us to see the Bible as a work of absolute perfection to be held in awe and reverence and to be obeyed absolutely.

MARCH 26 || DEUTERONOMY 6:6

And you must commit yourselves wholeheartedly to these commands I am giving you today.

Read: Deuteronomy 5:1-6:25

Moses is continuing his last speech to the people of Israel before he dies and Joshua takes them into the Promised Land. Moses is reminding them of everything that the Lord has told them. He is also reminding them of the mistakes that they and their fathers have made and exhorting them not to make the same mistakes again.

In our text for today Moses tells the Israelites to follow these commands wholeheartedly. The NKJV says that these commands 'shall be in your heart'. God is very concerned about the condition of the hearts of His people. God knows that it is in the heart that obedience begins. In the verse prior to this, Moses told the children of Israel to 'love the Lord your God with all your heart, with all your soul, and with all your strength'. Our obedience should be born out of our love for God.

The way that we show God that we love Him is by obeying Him. And the way that we obey God is by living a life that imitates the life of Christ. Christ lived a life that was sacrificed to others in service. The way that we show God that we love Him is by obeying Him in a life that is lived wholeheartedly for others.

That's where it sometimes can become difficult for some people. They love the Lord Jesus and they want to serve Him wholeheartedly but they are not in the ministry or church that they feel called to be in. Because of the needs of the ministry or church that they are in, they find themselves doing something that is not "their ministry" or "using their gifts". And unfortunately they are not serving wholeheartedly. They are doing it out of sense of duty or "because the pastor told me to".

Let us not forget that Jesus also served in a ministry that was not His primary calling. Jesus is God! But for a time the needs of His ministry to the world called Him to serve in a very humble way; as a man in Galilee. If Jesus could do that, is it too much to ask us to set up chairs, or to be an usher or greeter, or even to serve in the Children's Ministry. We should not think so highly of ourselves as to think that any service to God is below us.

God has you where you are in your ministry or church for a reason and a season. He is trying to teach you to be more like His Son and He is preparing you for the next step of the journey that he has you on. The length of the season may depend on whether or not you serve God wholeheartedly even in a ministry or place of service that you don't enjoy. Jesus, help us to love you so much that we will pour our heart completely into whatever act of service that YOU have placed before us.

Rick Lancaster | PLANTERS PERSPECTIVE

MARCH 27 || DEUTERONOMY 7:7

The LORD did not choose you and lavish his love on you because you were larger or greater than other nations, for you were the smallest of all nations!

Read: Deuteronomy 7:1-8:20

Moses continues to tell the Israelites what they need to know before they cross over into the Promised Land in just a few days. He has been telling them about all the promises that God has made that they are going to be able to benefit from. Then Moses makes this statement about the Israelites that probably didn't build up their self-esteem. Basically God was saying that He wasn't doing this because of them; they weren't really that special. They were the special possession of God but God is telling them here that they weren't all that special. God chose them because He loved them and because He had made a promise to their ancestors.

God was telling the Israelites that so that they didn't get big heads about their relationship with God. It is amazing how quickly pride can deceive you into thinking that something God did for you or through you was because of you. God does what He does for reasons that sometimes only He knows. His motivation is always love and not us. We are the object of His love but we are not the reason for it nor are we the source of it.

One of the most dangerous things for a Christian is success. Once we have success in something, we sometimes think that we had something to do with it. When we do that we are taking God's glory from Him which He is not too happy about. Or we might think that God made us successful because there is something special about us. God has no favorites; He loves those that love Him and those that don't.

All glory and honor belong to God. If God has placed you in a position where you lead other people there can be a great temptation to take some of God's glory. It happens when someone tells you how something you have done has blessed them or ministered to them. It can sometimes be very difficult to remember that you are not so special that you should take any credit for it. All glory belongs to God and should be given to Him immediately.

First this needs to take place in our hearts before it comes out of our mouths. If God does something through you and someone praises you for it, it can sound very fake if you are praising God just so that you sound humble. It is better just to say 'Thank you' and leave it at that. This can be especially true with someone that God is using in a tremendous way. There is nothing special about any of us, regardless what the world would try to convince you of. God does what He does in our lives because He loves us and because He wants to. Don't let your pride convince you of anything else. Jesus, help us to be truly humble and not convinced of our own importance.

MARCH 28 || DEUTERONOMY 10:12-13

And now, Israel, what does the LORD your God require of you? He requires you to fear him, to live according to his will, to love and worship him with all your heart and soul, and to obey the LORD's commands and laws that I am giving you today for your own good.

Read: Deuteronomy 9:1-10:22

Moses knows that his time on this earth is short. And so he wants to give to the Israelites everything he can before he dies. Moses is a loving shepherd that has a sincere desire to see the flock that God entrusted to him do well after he leaves. Here Moses gives the Israelites some very clear direction about what God expects from them.

There are five things that the Israelites are required by God to do. These five things are; to fear Him, to live according to His Word, to love Him, to worship Him, and to obey Him. Within these two verses we find the formula to living a life that pleases God. If we do these five things we will please God because this is what He expected of the Israelites and it is what He expects of us as Christians.

First, God expects us to fear Him. This is not fear as in being afraid. It means to hold Him in reverential awe. It means to treat Him with the greatest of dignity and respect. It means to hold Him in the highest regard, much like we would do with a king or a president.

Second, God expects us to live according to His Word. We are to live by His Word. The Bible is the source of all we need to know about God and what He expects from us. Within His Word we find His promises, we learn of His power and might, and we find examples, both good and bad of how to live this life.

Third, God expects us to love Him. God has done what He has for us because He loves us. Love is His very nature. God wants us to love Him back. Fourth, God expects us to worship Him. We were created to worship. God wants us to fill that need in our lives to worship with the worship of Him and no one or nothing else.

Fifth, God expects us to obey Him. It is interesting that this is the last one on the list. This seems to be the one that we struggle with the most. You would think that it ought to be the first one mentioned. I believe that is because we can put too much emphasis on obedience and neglect the other four things that God expects. If you practice the other four things that God expects of you, you are going to be much more likely to be obedient.

God doesn't want just our obedience. He wants all of us. Not only does He want it, He expects us to do all five of these things. It is required of us as Christians. Jesus, teach us how to do a spiritual inventory of these five areas every day so that we can be doing all that You require of us.

Rick Lancaster / PLANTERS PERSPECTIVE

MARCH 29 || DEUTERONOMY 11:2

Listen! I am not talking now to your children, who have never experienced the discipline of the LORD your God or seen his greatness and awesome power.

Read: Deuteronomy 11:1-12:32

Moses is laying out what the Israelites need to do when they cross over the Jordan River into the Promised Land. He is giving them instructions and letting them know what God is going to do on their behalf. Moses is telling them of all the great things that God is going to do. Then Moses makes this interesting statement in our verse for the day. His point is clear; they should know that everything that he is saying about God is true because they have seen the same things before. Besides Caleb, Joshua, and Moses the oldest people in the camp are sixty years old. Everyone that is from forty to sixty years old was alive when God brought the Israelites out of Egypt. Everyone less than forty years old was born during the wilderness wanderings.

These people that are between forty and sixty years of age are most likely the leaders of the community. Moses is reminding them that they have seen God do to the Egyptians what Moses is telling them that He is going to do the nations in the Promised Land. If God did something once and He says He is going to do it again we can absolutely trust Him that He will.

Anyone that has spiritual eyes to see what God is doing will see Him work powerfully in their lives or in the lives of those around them. Moses was telling the leaders of the community to remember these wonderful works of God and to tell their children so that they can believe as well. God is calling anyone that has seen God work in their life or someone else's to use that knowledge to encourage and exhort the others around them to believe God.

That belief is the source of the faith that is needed to see God work all around us. If we don't believe that God can work in our lives, we may not be able to see it when it happens. It is critical that we share what God is doing and has done in our lives so that others can have the same faith that we do that God is going to act and work in their lives. If we don't, then those people may not get to experience the amazing, power-filled life that God desires them to.

That can be a burden to think that someone else's life depends upon your actions but it is not a burden it is a privilege. God has chosen to use us to be His special vessel to share with others so that they can receive something very special from God. Instead of being a burden that we bear, this truth should give us tremendous boldness. We get to be a part of helping people experience God in a powerful and radical way. God has worked in your life; share that with others and watch how it affects their life. Jesus, give us good memories about the radical things that You have done in our lives and then give us the boldness to tell others.

MARCH 30 || DEUTERONOMY 14:2

You have been set apart as holy to the LORD your God, and he has chosen you to be his own special treasure from all the nations of the earth.

Read: Deuteronomy 13:1-15:23

Moses reminds the Israelites that God set them apart and chose them from among all the other nations of the world. This is not new; Moses has communicated this to the Israelites on numerous occasions. What struck me was that Moses used a different word to describe how God feels about the Israelites; treasure. God views the Israelites as a treasure. This is a powerful statement if you take a moment to reflect upon it.

God is the creator of the universe. Everything that exists, He created. Everything that exists belongs to God. Of all the things that God owns, the nation of Israel is a treasure. A treasure is something that you put more value on than anything else. It doesn't even need to have any intrinsic value to be a treasure. We determine what a treasure is and what isn't.

The wonderful thing for us as Christians is that we have been adopted into the family of God; this makes us a part of this treasure of God's. Because we accepted Jesus, we are now part of the treasure of God.

Think about how we treat the treasures of our life. We do everything that we can to protect them and preserve them. We will put them in places of prominence and display them for others to see. We take special care of the things that we treasure. That is how God treats us as well. He treats us as a treasure and protects us from harm. He preserves us so that He can put us in places of prominence so that the whole world can see this beautiful treasure that He has set apart as His own.

One of the things that we will often do with our treasures is clean them and polish them to be as beautiful as possible. We, as a treasure of God have been set apart from the rest of the world as God's. Because we have been set apart as God's we are expected to be holy. That doesn't mean that God expects you to be perfectly sinless; He knows you can't do that. What He expects is that you will allow the Holy Spirit to do the work inside of you to clean off the dirt (sin) from your life and to cause you to shine. That's where the big difference between our treasures and God's treasures come in. Our treasures have no say as to whether or not we polish them up and make them beautiful to see. As God's treasure, He has set us aside but we get to choose whether or not we allow the Holy Spirit to clean and polish us. Too often we resist this work of the Holy Spirit and the treasure of God is dirty and tarnished. It must sadden God greatly to look upon His treasure that He values over everything else in all of creation and see it dirty and rusted. We need to see ourselves as God sees us through the eyes of Jesus and allow the Holy Spirit free access to do all the work that He wants to. Jesus, help us to stop fighting what You want to do in us.

Rick Lancaster | PLANTERS PERSPECTIVE

MARCH 31 || DEUTERONOMY 17:19

He must always keep this copy of the law with him and read it daily as long as he lives. That way he will learn to fear the LORD his God by obeying all the terms of this law.

Read: Deuteronomy 16:1-17:20

Moses speaks out a prophecy that the Israelites are going to want a king to lead them in the future. This will happen in just a couple of generations from the time they enter the Promised Land. God gives them the key to making sure that king rules well. That key is God's Word. The king is to personally write a copy of the Law and keep it with him. And he is to read it every day.

If the king of Israel were to do this the king would learn to fear God. He would learn to fear God by obeying all the commandments written in the Law. By doing this it would also prevent the king from exalting himself above the people. God also promises that by doing that his days would be prolonged in his kingdom. God would extend the length of time that he would rule if he obeys the laws of God. And this promise is not just for the king but also for the king's children that would take his place when he dies.

God knew the hearts of the people. He knew that they were going to want a king, like the nations around them. And God also knew that this king could lead the people well only if he read and obeyed God's laws. God also knew that if the king did not read and obey His laws that it would result in the nation of Israel falling away from God. As the leader goes, so go the people.

In ministry and in churches, we have the awesome responsibility of leading people. The question is where we are leading them to. If we are leading them, where are we taking them? That is why God wanted the King to write a copy of the Law himself. And then to read it daily ensured that it never left his mind. The only way that we can know if we are leading in the direction that God wants us to is to read the directions that He left us; the Bible.

As leaders we have a greater obligation to be in the Word of God daily. This journey we are on is a difficult one. It has lots of twists and turns in the road that most of us are not equipped to deal with. God doesn't want us to get lost. God wants us to ask for directions. Because it is one thing when you are alone and you get lost. It is quite another when you get lost with a bunch of people following you.

God promises to 'prolong his days' to the king that reads and obeys His laws. As leaders in God's church we can know that God will lead, guide, and direct our path if we will learn to fear Him by reading and obeying His Word. Jesus, teach to read your Word like the roadmap of our lives and help us to follow those directions all the days of our lives.

APRIL

APRIL 1 || DEUTERONOMY 19:8-9

If the Lord your God enlarges your territory, as he solemnly promised your ancestors, and gives you all the land he promised them, you must designate three additional cities of refuge. (He will give you this land if you obey all the commands I have given you-if you always love the Lord your God and walk in his ways.)

Read: Deuteronomy 18:1-20:20

Moses is giving the Israelites some further instructions for when they enter into the Promised Land. In this section of chapter 19 Moses is giving directions about the cities of refuge. These are cities scattered all around the land to provide a place of refuge for someone that has accidentally killed another person. While that is a fascinating thing in itself, it is the verses above that caught my attention.

Moses tells the Israelites that should God expand their territory they should add more cities of refuge to make sure someone is able to reach them without having to travel too far. Moses compares the land that they are going in to possess to the land that God had promised to their ancestors.

God promised Abraham, Isaac, and Jacob a land that would be their own for all time. God defined that land and it is estimated to have been over 300,000 square miles. The land that God defines as the Promised Land to the people that Moses is speaking to is much smaller, about 10% of what God promised to their ancestors. Why the difference?

Elsewhere God told the Israelites that He wasn't going to drive all the Canaanites out of the land right away because then the land would be over-run with wild animals. As they grew as a nation, God would drive the Canaanites out before them. Moses then goes on to tell them how to get the other 90% of the land promised to their ancestors; love the Lord and walk in His ways.

As Christians, we have also been made amazing promises. God has promised us a life that is rich and full. The picture of the Israelites only getting 10% of the Promised Land is an example of how most people appropriate the things that God has promised them. They only ever get a small percentage of all that God wants for them.

The key to appropriating and experiencing the whole life that God wants for us is found in two things; loving God and obeying His commandments. Loving God is not a feeling but describes the manner in which we live our lives. Walking in His ways means to obey Him, whether it be the instructions found in His word or the leading of the Holy Spirit.

The Israelites were content to live a life that only encompassed 10% of what they could have enjoyed. How much of the Promised Life are you living? If it is less than 100%, ask God to reveal to you how you can move into new territory with Him. Jesus, help us to love You more and teach us to obey You better.

APRIL 2 || DEUTERONOMY 21:17

He must give the customary double portion to his oldest son, who represents the strength of his father's manhood and who owns the rights of the firstborn son, even though he is the son of the wife his father does not love.

Read: Deuteronomy 21:1-22:30

In today's reading Moses is laying out various instructions that have to do with everyday life and teaching the Israelites what it means to be set apart as the special possession of the Lord. Many of these things in our culture are alien and seemingly unimportant to us. Such is the case for our verse for the day. It has to do with a man that has two wives; one he loves and the other one he doesn't.

One of the regulations that God laid out for the Israelites was the rights of the firstborn son. The firstborn son was special in the sight of the Lord. There is an obvious correlation between this regulation and Jesus as the only son of God. The rights of the firstborn included a double portion of his father's estate. He would also assume leadership of the family after his father died.

In our verse for the day, God is telling the Israelites that if the firstborn son is born to the wife that is not loved that they must still get the rights of the firstborn son. The fact that the husband did not love the wife that gave him the firstborn son had no bearing on the regulation of the firstborn son. This is the part that applies to us in this day and in this culture.

It didn't matter how this man felt; the regulation of firstborn son was to be applied to the first son that was born to him. There are going to be things that God tells us in His Word or through His people that we are not going to like. That doesn't change the fact that we need to obey them and do them in spite of our feelings. That is not the way that world tells us to do things. The world would tell you that if you don't feel like it you don't have to do it. We even see that going on with the laws of the land. There is a great disrespect for authority and the laws of our country.

As Christians we don't have the luxury of using our feelings as the guiding force of our lives. If we do then we are no different than the rest of the world. Your feelings are irrelevant to God. It is not that He doesn't care about your feelings; it is that they don't change the way that you are to behave. What God says is the way that we are to behave without regard to our feelings. Your feelings are fickle and unreliable. God expects our obedience regardless of the way that we feel. I have heard it said, 'Fake it until you feel it'. In many respects I believe this applies to doing what God says. Do it even though you don't feel like it. God will change your feelings and bless your obedience. Jesus, help us to put our feelings aside and just do what You say.

APRIL 3 || DEUTERONOMY 24:5

A newly married man must not be drafted into the army or given any other special responsibilities. He must be free to be at home for one year, bring happiness to the wife he has married.

Read: Deuteronomy 23:1-25:19

The book of Deuteronomy is a review of the instructions that God gave to Moses to give to the nation of Israel. These instructions covered all areas of life, including their relationships. Many of those instructions were only relevant to a culture that existed 3,000 years ago, but some are just as relevant today as they were then. Such is the case for our verse today.

It is often amazing to discover how much of our language and culture has been impacted by the Bible without our realizing it. Here in a text written 3,400 years ago we see the concept of 'newlyweds'. A newlywed is a person that has been married for less than a year. Most people that use that term have no idea it came from the Bible.

Moses instructs the Israelites not to draft any newlywed men into the army and to refrain from giving them any special responsibilities. Instead the newlywed men are to focus their attention on 'bringing happiness' to their wife.

There is a saying that I adopted some years ago, 'Happy wife, happy life!' I have found in my own life, that when my wife is happy, I am happy. There is direct connection between her happiness and my own. I have also discovered that bringing happiness to my wife is not a natural thing. We have been married since 1981 and I am still learning what it means to bring happiness to her.

God's wisdom in this instruction is beyond question. In my own experience, if a man doesn't take the time to do this at the beginning of his marriage, it becomes increasingly difficult as the years pass. Life has a way of filling up our time and making it virtually impossible to invest this kind of time to learning how to bring happiness to a wife.

Whether you are leading a family, ministry, or church, take note of this concept. Give the newlyweds a great gift by not filling their lives with 'special responsibilities'. Give them time to better understand the meaning of 'one flesh'. Those other responsibilities will be taken care of by others or can wait. Trust God's wisdom in this and give the newlyweds the time they need to become happy in each other.

Our verse also says that they shouldn't be drafted into the army. It is not stated implicitly but I believe this speaks of God's promise to protect the nation or organization that follows this instruction. Sometimes we think we need every able-bodied man in the battle if we are going to win. Thinking like that assumes that you are the one that will determine the outcome of the battle. You aren't, God is. Leave the battle in His hands and follow His instructions. Jesus, help us to be bringers of happiness.

APRIL 4 | | DEUTERONOMY 26:19

And if you do, he will make you greater than any other nation. Then you will receive praise, honor, and renown. You will be a nation that is holy to the Lord your God, just as he promised."

Read: Deuteronomy 26:1-27:26

In these next few chapters of Deuteronomy Moses explains to the nation of Israel that God expects them to obey His commands. This is not a new concept that Moses is describing. But starting here Moses explains that there are benefits and consequences to the response of the Israelites. Within these chapters God explains to the people that there are great blessings to be experienced through obedience and that there are terrible curses resulting from disobedience. That is very graphically described in Deuteronomy chapter 28.

For some reason people have a hard time believing that God would curse them. Their view of God is that He will only bless and would never curse someone. There is no basis for that viewpoint in Scripture. God's blessings are a result of our obedience and God's curses are a result of our disobedience. This can become complicated because we can also experience the blessings or curses of someone else's obedience or disobedience. A great example of this is the people that Moses is talking to in this text. These are the children of the people that refused to obey God and enter the Promised Land at Kadesh-Barnea. As a result of that disobedience their children were forced to wander around in the wilderness for forty years until all of their parents had died.

But even though the children were experiencing the curse that was brought on by their parents, God used this time to teach them to obey His commands more readily. During this time God caused them to become a great nation that was feared and respected by every other nation around them.

Our role as leaders of families, ministries, or churches is to guide people through their wilderness times. Everyone, including those in leadership will experience those times; either self-inflicted as a result of sin and disobedience or as a result of someone else's disobedience. We need to show them the path that God has laid out for them through the wilderness time. We need to help them to see their sin and disobedience so that their wilderness time can be as short as possible. And we need to help them to see the lesson or lessons that God is trying to teach them through this time.

And if we will be faithful to do those things God will bring praise, honor, and renown to us. This is not the reason why we do these things; it is one of the fruits that you look for so that you know that you are doing it the way that God wants you to. God's promises are faithful; we can trust them no matter what. If our lives are marked by blessings, then we can feel confident that we are being obedient. If our lives are marked by curses; than we need to examine our lives for disobedience in our lives or the lives of those around us. Jesus, help us to obey your commands not just for the blessings but because we love You.

Rick Lancaster / PLANTERS PERSPECTIVE

APRIL 5 || DEUTERONOMY 28:2

You will experience all these blessings if you obey the LORD your God...

Read: Deuteronomy 28:1-68

The Israelites were the chosen people of God. The LORD has a very special relationship with them. This relationship was unlike His relationship with any other nation on the earth. Here in Deuteronomy 28 the LORD describes what the Israelites can expect from that relationship and it is fantastic. Twelve verses of every kind of blessing you might want; involving protection, provision, and presence. You can't help but read those verses and be envious of that relationship and those promises.

What we sometimes forget is that many, in fact most, of God's promises are conditional promises. For God to keep His side of the promise some condition must be met first. That is indicated by the word 'if' right in the middle of today's verse. God is faithful and because of His faithfulness the Israelites could be absolutely certain that His promises would be fulfilled but only IF they did their part.

In the case of our verse today the Israelites part was obedience to the LORD their God. They could absolutely depend on all the promises of God lists in verse three through fourteen to come to pass if they would simply obey the LORD their God. If they did their part they could be totally confident that God would do His.

Obedience is critical to our relationship with God. Some people believe that God doesn't really care all that much if we obey Him or not. They wrongly believe that they might not get all of His blessings but other than that it is no big deal. Those people need to read the rest of Deuteronomy 28. The LORD gives Moses 14 verses of blessings to give to the people and then gives him 54 verses of curses for disobedience.

These 54 verses describe everything that would happen if the Israelites chose not to obey God. Sadly, the Israelites ended up experiencing all of these curses throughout history and still to this day are still receiving them. God is just as faithful to fulfill His promises of curses as He is to fulfill His promises of blessings. What many people struggle with is the thought that God would curse them or us. In reality it makes perfect sense. God loves us so very much and longs for us to be in an intimate fellowship and communion with Him that He will do anything that He needs to bring us closer to Him. Only He knows how to do that. We can't possibly know how to be in that kind of relationship. It's not natural, we need to be instructed and directed.

That is why God demands and rewards obedience. Disobedience means we are wandering around aimlessly and not drawing nearer to Him. To discourage us from that the LORD will discipline and punish us to remind us to keep drawing nearer to Him. For some, the promise of God's blessings is enough to keep them drawing nearer. For others, it is the threat of discipline and punishment that holds them to the right path. God wants to bless us but He will punish us because we are His children and it is one of the ways that He proves His love for us. Jesus, help us to want to obey.

APRIL 6 || DEUTERONOMY 30:8

Then you will again obey the Lord and keep all the commands I am giving you today.

Read: Deuteronomy 29:1-30:20

In the reading for today, Moses prophesies that the people of Israel are going to be unfaithful to God and that He is going to drive them from the land of Canaan that He is just about to give them. Moses has just gotten through explaining to the people all the blessings that they will receive if they are obedient to God and the curses they will receive if they are disobedient. God told them very plainly what was going to happen in the future and then allowed them to choose the option that they wanted; His blessings or His curses.

God has not changed! He still allows us to choose whether or not we will receive His blessings or curses. People don't like to look at God that way; that He would send a curse to you. Their view of God is that He should always bless and never curse. What they fail to understand is that His love for us is so great that He must curse us when we are being disobedient. He does that because when we are disobedient or in sin (which is disobedience) it separates us from Him. We were created to be in intimate personal fellowship with Him. God will do anything to eliminate anything that separates us from Him; including sending curses.

In our verse for the day God tells the reason why He will allow all the bad to happen to Israel that he ultimately does. It is because they will turn away from Him and He wants them to turn back. By turning back to Him and obeying His voice and His commandments, they will again be in that place where God can be in fellowship with them and bless them.

God does not want to curse you or anyone else. To be cursed by God, you must make a decision to be cursed by God. The Bible teaches that God waits to bless us, not curse us. His desire is that we would be in a place where He can pour out blessings so great that we can't contain them. All we have to do is obey His voice and His commands. Our problem is that our sinful flesh would much rather do things our own way even if it means taking ourselves out of the blessings of God and placing us in the curses of God.

God cares so much for you that He will do anything to cause you to be in a place where you can receive all that He desires to give you. He will even allow great pain and suffering in your life if that is what it is going to take to get you to turn back to Him and obey His voice and His commands. The choice is yours! It is an absolutely incredible fact that God lets us choose whether or not He will bless us. I know for myself and for my family and for my church that I am going to choose to obey God as well as I am able. I am going to be looking for signs that I am out of God's blessing and then run back to Him as quickly as I can. What life will you choose? Jesus, help us to choose well.

Rick Lancaster / PLANTERS PERSPECTIVE

APRIL 7 || DEUTERONOMY 32:6

Is this the way you repay the LORD**, you foolish and senseless people? Isn't he your Father who created you? Has he not made you and established you?**

Read: Deuteronomy 31:1-32:27

God tells Moses to teach the people of Israel this song. The purpose is to warn them against turning away from God and also to teach them what will happen if they do turn away. There is also a warning to the nations that will ultimately persecute them after they have turned away. Everything that this song warns of happens to the nation of Israel. All God wanted them to do was to worship Him alone. If they had only obeyed God there is no telling what the world would look like today. God promised them blessings in abundance and that they would have no disease or sickness like other nations.

They chose to do things their own way and experienced the consequences of their poor choices. It would have been more excusable if they hadn't known what it was that God wanted them to do. They knew what God expected of them but they allowed the influences of the world to draw them away from God. In our verse for the day, God describes them as foolish and senseless people. God says in our verse for the day that we owe it to Him to obey Him.

We owe it to Him for two reasons; He created us and established us. The first one is pretty easy to understand, the reason why we exist is because God decided that He wanted us to exist. Your parents were the tool that God used to accomplish His plan for bringing you into the world. God created us because He wanted to. He didn't need to and He didn't have to; He wanted to. That is a good reason to do what He says.

Not only did He create us but He also established us. That means that God set everything up so that our lives would be what they are. Everything that you have or are is a result of God establishing you. Without God you would be lost, wandering aimlessly and pointlessly through life. God has provided all that you need to be right where you are and He is at the same time positioning everything that you need so that you can go where He wants you to. We, of course, get to choose whether or not we go where He wants us to. When we choose to go somewhere other than where He desires we are proving Moses' song to be true; that we are foolish and senseless people.

If we are truly honest with ourselves and God we would understand this more fully. If God created us and established us and He is a good God (which He is), than anywhere that He would want us to go would be good. Anywhere else that we might go would be bad. To choose to take the bad rather than the good is foolishness and senseless. It often amazes me that God puts up with us at all. Jesus, help us to have good sense.

PLANTERS PERSPECTIVE | *A Devotional*

APRIL 8 || DEUTERONOMY 32:47

These instructions are not mere words-they are your life! By obeying them you will enjoy a long life in the land you are crossing the Jordan River to occupy.

Read: Deuteronomy 32:28-52

Moses is best known for a couple of key events in history; leading the Israelites out of Egypt and the giving of the Law. It was through Moses that God gave the Law to the people of Israel. Moses is now nearing the end of his life at 120 years old. In the reading for today God told Moses that he is about to die but that he will get a chance to look at the Promised Land from a distance. Soon Joshua will take over leadership of the nation and lead the people across into the land that had been promised to Abraham, Isaac, and Jacob.

In what are some of Moses' last words he tells them that the instructions he has given them from God and not just mere words. People often look at the Bible as a mere book written by men that had an objective in mind. No honest student of the Bible can believe that. In Hebrews it says that the scriptures are living and powerful. The more I study the Bible, the more convinced I am about the truth of that. Every day it takes on greater beauty. As my knowledge grows of the Word of God, my appreciation for it and the God that inspired it grows as well.

Moses tells the Israelites, "they are your life!" This is echoed centuries later by Peter when he tells Jesus that He alone has the 'words of life'. The Bible is the best-selling book of all time. It is said that the Bible is in more homes than any other book ever written. Sadly, most people seldom, if ever, open the book that is filled with the words of life. Instead they are running to and fro looking for answers from the world. As they do they are slowly dying inside.

Moses told the Israelites that the words of God were the way to life and the source of life. Every other source of words leads not to life but to death. Probably not a physical death but certainly a spiritual death is the result of looking to the world's wisdom for life.

Moses' goal in saying this was to change the Israelites viewpoint regarding the instructions of God. Some people view God's instructions as boundaries or restrictive fences. They see God's commands as a list of things they can't do or must do to please God. Moses wanted them to see God's words as the pathway to a blessed life.

It is all about your perspective. If you approach God's Word as a list of things you can or cannot do, then it will be a lifeless experience. However, if you approach the Scriptures as the source of life and happiness, each time you read or hear it you will find life and blessing. Reading and studying the Bible has long ceased being a duty for me and is now one of the greatest joys of my life. Learn to fall in love with God's Word and it will change your life in radical ways. Jesus, help us to fall in love with Your Word.

Rick Lancaster / PLANTERS PERSPECTIVE

APRIL 9 || DEUTERONOMY 33:11

Bless the Levites, O LORD, and accept all their work. Crush the loins of their enemies; strike down their foes so they never rise again.

Read: Deuteronomy 33:1-29

Moses is praying a blessing over the people of Israel right before he dies. He gives a blessing to each of the tribes. It is fascinating to study the many times that the patriarchs blessed people. Often the blessings were prophetic; telling what was going to happen in the future of the person or tribe that was being blessed. In our verse for the day, Moses is blessing the Levites. It might be interesting to spend a little time thinking about Moses' request concerning the enemies of Levi but it was the reference to work that caught my attention.

The Levites were a special people among the Chosen people. They had the responsibility to assist Aaron and his sons in the work of the priesthood. They alone were to do the work in and around the tabernacle and ultimately in the temple that Solomon would build. No one else was allowed to do this work.

How does this relate to the modern church? The closest comparison we might have to Levites in the modern church is the volunteers that serve in our churches and ministries. The volunteers serve God by assisting the pastors and ministry leaders in the completion of their religious responsibilities.

There is a lesson in this verse for the ministry leaders and pastors; pray for God to bless your volunteers. We should also be praying for God to crush their enemies so that they cannot rise again to hinder the work of God that they are involved. I believe that if more pastors were praying for their volunteers, they would have more volunteers.

The main thing that caught my attention was that Moses asked God to accept their work. We might think that because we are working for God that He has to accept our work but that is not the case. When we think of giving to God we usually think of money but that is not the only thing that we have that we can and should give to Him. In addition to our treasures, we also have our time and our talents. When we are working for God we are often using both time and talents. These then become an offering to the LORD.

In many places in the Bible we are taught that there is more to giving to God than simply the giving part. God cares about the condition of the heart of the giver. Gifts and offerings that are given out of the wrong heart are not acceptable to God. Work done for the LORD, for the wrong reasons, is not acceptable to Him. If we are doing things for the LORD because we think we have to or because we believe that we are going to get something out of it is not acceptable to God. The Lord wants us to do work for Him because we love Him and because we know that it will please Him. He desires that we do the things that we do because it proves our love for our God. That kind of work, however small it might seem, is very pleasing to the LORD. Jesus, teach to be pleasing to You in all the works that we do for You.

APRIL 10 || JOSHUA 1:8

Study this Book of the Law continually. Meditate on it day and night so you may be sure to obey all that is written in it. Only then will you succeed.

Read: Deuteronomy 34:1-Joshua 2:24

Joshua has just replaced Moses as the leader of the nation of Israel. For the last forty years Moses has been leading the nation as it made one of the greatest journeys of history. Joshua has the enormous responsibility of leading the people on the last leg of this great journey; he will lead them into the Promised Land.

The book of Joshua opens with God speaking to Joshua about the mission that God has for Him to complete. In the paragraph that our text for today is drawn from, God tells Joshua three times to 'Be strong and courageous'. God encourages Joshua by telling him that he has nothing to be afraid of because God is going to be right there with him the whole time.

God also gives Joshua a command and then gives him a promise with it. God commands Joshua to study the book of the Law. The book of the Law are the first five books of the Bible; Genesis, Exodus, Leviticus, Numbers, and Deuteronomy. These books are also referred to as the Pentateuch. God told Joshua to study these five books. It is within these five books that God revealed Himself to the Nation of Israel and where His covenant with them is established.

God also commands Joshua to meditate on these books. God wants Joshua to fill his mind with God and His commands and His covenant with the people of Israel. God is telling Joshua that these things should be the thing that is on his mind the most. God then tells Joshua, that this is the only way that he will be successful.

Joshua is about to enter the Promised Land. This leg of the journey is going to be filled with one enemy after another and one battle after another. God wants Joshua to focus all of his attention on God and not on his circumstances or his enemies or his abilities to handle these situations.

God would say to those that lead His ministries and churches today to do the same thing. Study God's Word and meditate on His laws and commands. We need to fix our eyes on His promises and precepts. Only then can we be successful at leading God's people into the life that Jesus promised them in John 10:10. This world is determined to distract us from God. And if we allow our eyes and minds to be taken off of God, we will not be as successful as God would want us to be. Jesus, help us to devote more and more of our mind to you and your precepts so that we will be successful as we lead Your ministries and churches.

Rick Lancaster / PLANTERS PERSPECTIVE

APRIL 11 || JOSHUA 4:24

He did this so that all the nations of the earth might know the power of the Lord, and that you might fear the Lord your God forever.

Read: Joshua 3:1-4:24

God has just done this radical miracle of stopping the flooding Jordan River so that the nation of Israel could cross over into the Promised Land. He also reminds them that forty years ago He did a similar miracle at the Red Sea so that they could escape Egypt and the army of the Pharaoh. And then God explains why He did these two great miracles.

It is interesting to note that it wasn't because there was anything special about the people of Israel. It wasn't because He owed it to the Hebrews. It wasn't because of anything pertaining to the children of Israel. It was because of what God wanted to accomplish.

God did these great miracles because He wanted the rest of the world to witness His great power. God chose the nation of Israel, not because there was anything special about them, but because He wanted to use a group of people to reveal to the rest of the world what an awesome God that He is. God could have used any group of people to do the same thing.

He also did these great miracles so that this group of people, the Israelites, would fear Him. God wanted them to have a deep reverential respect for Him and so He gave them a powerful witness of who He was so that they would. Unfortunately, the Israelites thought these miracles had something to do with them and it became a source of pride. It had always been about God and it will always be about God, but at some point they forgot that.

God is still performing miracles. Every day God is causing some miraculous thing to take place in the world and in the lives of His children. But we have got to avoid the temptation to assume that it has something to do with us. God is still in the business of revealing Himself to all the nations and causing His people to fear Him.

We benefit from the miracles of God, especially when we are in the business of revealing God to others and when we do have that deep reverential respect for God, but He is still not doing those miraculous things for us. There is always a purpose much deeper and more complex than just to bless your life.

The Bible teaches that God is searching the whole earth looking for people that fear Him so that He can pour out His power and might in miraculous ways within their lives. It is part of His plan to bring the whole world into a saving relationship with His son Jesus Christ. The more we fear God, the more we will see His great power working in our lives. Jesus, help us to live powerful, miraculous lives.

APRIL 12 || JOSHUA 7:11

Israel has sinned and broken my covenant! They have stolen the things that I commanded to be set apart for me. And they have not only stolen them; they have also lied about it and hidden the things among their belongings.

Read: Joshua 5:1-7:15

God had told the nation of Israel in the sixth chapter of Joshua that everything in the city of Jericho belonged to God. Everything in the city had been set apart for God. Some things had been set apart for destruction and some things had been set apart for His use in the Lord's treasury. Unfortunately, one man, Achan, could not resist the temptation to take some of these things that He saw in Jericho.

God does not accuse just Achan; He accuses the whole nation of this sin. As a result God withdraws His hand of blessing and protection from the nation of Israel and they get soundly beaten at the city of Ai. God is calling the nation of Israel to a level of obedience that most of the world would say is unfair. The world would tell us that it is not fair for the whole nation to be punished because of one man's sin.

God's requirement of the Israelites was absolute obedience. He had told them that if anyone were to disobey, it would bring trouble into the camp. That is exactly what happened. God is not being unfair; He is being true to His word. God is being faithful while the people were being unfaithful.

This account teaches us very clearly that we cannot hide our sins of disobedience and rebellion from God. We may be successful at burying them in our tents, but we can't hide them from God. Achan's greed caused him to steal these things from God. The tragic aspect of this account is that in the very next town that they attacked and destroyed, God allowed them to keep the spoils.

For those of us that are in ministry and in churches, we are often handling things that have been set apart for God's use. We might also be in contact with money that has been given to the church for God's use. These things and this money are God's and we must resist the temptation to touch these holy things in an unholy manner. Any time we disobey God or rebel against His leading, we are stealing something that belongs to Him. Our lives and our obedience belong to God. We might be able to hide it from the rest of the world but we can't hide it from God.

By mishandling God's things or stealing from God, we are bringing trouble into the camp. And that trouble means that God will withdraw His hand of blessing and protection from your ministry, church, or life. As leaders in God's ministries and churches, it is our responsibility to jealously guard the things of God. We must ask God to help us to resist the temptation involving the things set apart for God and to help others to do the same. Jesus, help us to resist.

Rick Lancaster | PLANTERS PERSPECTIVE

APRIL 13 || JOSHUA 8:2

You will destroy them as you destroyed Jericho and its king. But this time you may keep the captured goods and the cattle for yourselves. Set an ambush behind the city.

Read: Joshua 7:16-9:2

The background for this verse is fascinating and important. Joshua and the nation of Israel have been in the Promised Land for about two weeks. They defeated the fortress city of Jericho in a spectacular way. The Lord had instructed them to utterly destroy the city and everyone and everything in it. Only the precious metals were to be spared and those were to be put into the Lord's treasury. For you Bible students this was a form of the first fruits of the Promised Land.

Israel's victory at Jericho went to their heads and they turned their gaze upon the much smaller city of Ai and attacked it. Israel was soundly defeated by a much weaker force. Upon seeking the Lord about the defeat they discovered that Achan had disobeyed God and had kept some of the spoils from Jericho for himself. Once that was dealt with, God told the Israelites to go back to Ai and destroy it.

God changed the rules when He sent them to Ai; He told them they could keep all the captured goods for themselves this time. This then became the pattern for most of the rest of the conquest of the Promised Land. The second time they attacked Ai, they were victorious and kept the captured goods for themselves. God had a plan to bless them abundantly, but they had to follow God's plan to receive God's blessings and abundance.

Many are like Achan, they see the riches of the world and don't want to wait for God's blessings. Because he wouldn't wait for God, Achan lost everything, including his life. For us to experience the fullness of God's blessings we must do what He tells us to do. Patient obedience always leads to blessing and disobedience always leads to destruction.

There are times when it doesn't make sense from a worldly perspective to give God what He is asking for. From a human perspective it would make more sense to take care of ourselves. Our problem is that we can't see clearly how God's plan is going to bless us. That's where faith comes in; we simply need to trust God and His Word to us.

Achan's lack of faith and impatience destroyed him and his family. Many Christians are also suffering from the same spiritual disease that Achan had. By grasping at a blessing today they are sacrificing even greater blessings in the future and potentially heading toward destruction.

Give God what He is asking for and wait for His blessings in your life. Trust God at His word even when it makes no sense to you. God is not a liar; He promised to bless us if we would just obey His Word without hesitation or question. Keep your eyes on the Lord and not on what you want or what you don't have. Jesus, teach us to trust You.

APRIL 14 | | JOSHUA 9:14

So the Israelite leaders examined their bread, but they did not consult the LORD.

Read: Joshua 9:3-10:43

As you study the life of Joshua you are not faced with many examples of poor choices or mistakes. This account is one of the few exceptions. The people of Gibeon hear about the Israelites and they understand that the Israelites are going to overthrow everyone in Canaan. In a step of self-preservation the Gibeonites devise a scheme to save themselves from destruction. They come to the leaders of Israel dressed as though they have traveled a very long distance from well outside of Canaan. Their plan is to trick Israel into a peace treaty.

The problem with that is the LORD told them not to make treaties with the people of Canaan but to drive them out of the land. The Gibeonites are wearing worn-out clothes and bring old, moldy bread. They present these as evidences of their truthfulness and convince the leaders of Israel that they are telling the truth.

One of the greatest tactics of the enemy is deception. Satan is a liar and the father of lies. If there is a lie involved we know that its source is Satan. One of Satan's objectives through lying is compromise. He wants us to compromise in our relationship with God. And so he brings worn-out clothes and moldy bread to us and tries to convince us to believe him and make peace with the world. If we fall for his scheme, we get no peace. Instead we are left with worn-out clothes and moldy bread.

Our verse for the day tells us that the leaders examined the bread, but they did not consult the LORD to get His opinion on the matter. The Israelites had the unique privilege of being able to come to the High Priest and get answers concerning God's will. If they had gone to the LORD and asked Him what He wanted them to do in this matter, He would have told them of the deception.

As Christians, we also have a great privilege; we have the Holy Spirit living within us. We are able to come to him any time we need to and ask for direction and instruction. Sadly, we too often do as the Israelites did here; we rely upon our own abilities and knowledge to make our decisions. And sadly, we often end up doing what the Israelites did here; we make mistakes that have far-reaching consequences.

The Holy Spirit was given to us to be a Companion, Comforter, and Counselor. The Lord desires that we would live in the center of His will. To do that we need to get out of our own will. That is only possible through the leading of the Holy Spirit directing your decisions and revealing truth to you. When we are outside of the LORD's will we will always end up with worn-out clothes and moldy bread. Turn to the LORD and do not lean on your own understanding and you will find yourself moving ever closer to the center of the LORD's will for your life. Jesus, help us to put You at the center.

APRIL 15 || JOSHUA 11:15

As the LORD commanded Moses his servant, so did Moses command Joshua, and so did Joshua; he left nothing undone of all that the LORD commanded Moses.

Read: Joshua 11:1-12:24

Joshua was one of the most successful leaders that Israel ever had. And in this verse we see the reason why. Joshua did what he was told! He had spent a large chunk of forty years under the tutoring of Moses. Joshua was there as many of the commands that he was to obey were given to Moses by God.

Joshua was a great leader. Few leaders have accomplished similar things in their lives. And his success can be directly linked to his obedience. Whatever he was commanded to do, he did. Even when he didn't understand the instructions, he did it anyway. Joshua's obedience was linked to his faith. Joshua believed God and so he obeyed God. So strong was his faith that he could ask God to make the sun stand still so he could destroy God's enemies and God did it. Joshua was a man of faithful obedience. And that faithful obedience allowed God to win great victories through Joshua.

God is always looking for someone that He can show Himself strong through. He is looking for men and women that have the faithful obedience of Joshua so that He can win great victories through them. He is looking for ministries and churches that will faithfully obey His calling and commands. And when He finds those faithful ones that will obey, there is no limit to the things that he will accomplish through them.

This world is in desperate need of people like Joshua. This world needs people that, in faith, will ask God for the impossible so that they can fulfill His will. No one had ever heard of God stopping the sun from setting. And yet Joshua asked for it because it was the only way he was going to be able to complete the task that God had given him. We need to have that same faith to ask God to do something that has never been done before so that we can accomplish His works.

This world needs leaders like Joshua that obey God and His commands without hesitation and without question. We need to be leaders that don't ask God for an explanation or even a confirmation. Just simply obey! If we will just believe and obey there is no limit to the things that God can accomplish through us. Joshua believed because he was there as God gave all the commands to Moses. God is no further away from us than He was from Joshua. Every time you read God's Word know, believe, and act as though every word is true; because it is true. And then, ask God for the impossible to complete the work He has given you.

God uses ordinary people, ministries, and churches to do extraordinary things. In fact, the more ordinary you are, the more God wants to use you because he will receive more glory when extraordinary things are done. Jesus, help us ordinary people be used by an extraordinary God by building in each us Joshua-sized faith and obedience.

APRIL 16 || JOSHUA 14:12

So I'm asking you to give me the hill country that the Lord promised me. You will remember that as scouts we found the Anakites living there in great, walled cities. But if the Lord is with me, I will drive them out of the land, just as the Lord said.

Read: Joshua 13:1-14:15

Caleb is one of the Bible characters that do not get a lot of recognition. But if you study his life you find a man of incredible integrity, consistent faith, and a quiet strength. He was originally one of the twelve men that Moses sent into the Promised Land at Kadesh-Barnea to spy out the land. Of the twelve, only two came back with a good report. The other ten aroused the people to the point that they were ready to stone Caleb and Joshua because they were telling the people that they should go and take the land as God had commanded.

Because of their faithfulness, Caleb and Joshua were the only two adults that lived long enough to enter into the Promised Land. All that generation died in the wilderness because of their disbelief of God's promises.

Caleb now comes to Joshua and asks him to keep the promise that Moses had made to him. Moses had promised to give Caleb the land that they had walked upon while in the land for forty days spying. Caleb asks for a very specific area and reminds Joshua about what they saw when the two of them were there. It is an area with giants and strong cities.

Caleb is convinced that God will help him to conquer that difficult area. He knows that if it is God's will that no giant or great city can possibly stand against him. As you read the account of his request you can almost sense that he is eager to go and see what God will do to help him defeat these enemies and conquer this land.

We need to have this same attitude about the land that God has promised to give us. Just like Caleb, God has set before us a good land. Within that land are giants and walled fortresses that we must defeat if we are to conquer this land. Caleb did not fear these obstacles to him getting what was promised to him. Neither should we as we go out to face our enemies.

The ministry or church you are in will also face giants and walled cities that must be destroyed. We can face them the same way that Caleb did, with the confidence of the Lord. If the Lord is with us, there is nothing that we can't overcome. Caleb was not content to wait for his inheritance to be given to him; he went after it, in spite of the obstacles. We must do the same. We must go after the victory and the promises of God with confidence and faith. Jesus, help us to see the giants and great fortresses as You do and help us to go after all that You have promised us just like Caleb did.

Rick Lancaster / PLANTERS PERSPECTIVE

APRIL 17 || JOSHUA 15:63

But the tribe of Judah could not drive out the Jebusites, who lived in the city of Jerusalem, so the Jebusites live there among the people of Judah to this day.

Read: Joshua 16:1-18:28

This is a recurrent theme with the nation of Israel. God promised the land of Canaan to Abram and his descendants. God then told Joshua that He would drive out all the inhabitants of the land from before them. Even with those promises we see the nation of Israel failing to drive out the inhabitants and failing to take the whole land.

There was nothing special about the Jebusites that prevented the tribe of Judah from driving them out of Jerusalem. They were not some great nation that was too powerful for the tribe of Judah to defeat. So why is it that the tribe of Judah could not drive out the Jebusites? Every other time that they had faced an enemy they had been greatly victorious. What has changed?

Each of the tribes is receiving its inheritance and going and taking possession of the land that was given to them. The greatest change that has taken place is leadership. Up until this point, Joshua has led the nation of Israel. Each tribe also has a leader that took Joshua's orders and carried them out through their tribe. Now each tribe is leading itself.

Any time there is a change in leadership there is usually some amount of chaos that comes with it. The preparation by the previous leader will determine how great that chaos might be. That doesn't really explain what is going on here; most of these leaders have been with Joshua for most of their adult lives. They have watched him very closely for the seven years of the conquest; they really have no good excuse.

The problem is not in the change of leadership but in who the leader is depending upon. Joshua has led the nation of Israel from one victory to the next. Joshua was a great example of a leader that depended upon the Lord to determine his steps. Every time the Israelites did what the Lord told them to do they were successful. Joshua had an intimate fellowship with God that allowed him to be victorious everywhere that he went.

The leaders of Judah have not developed this same level of intimacy with God. They were not able to hear from God the way that Joshua was and so they were not successful like Joshua was. Caleb is another leader that had this close fellowship with God and was successful at driving out the people that were living in the land that was allotted to him.

Success and victory can only come through a finely developed relationship with Jesus Christ. There are likely Jebusites that God has called you to drive out of the land of your life. You will not be able to do it completely until you have surrendered your whole life to God and allow Him to direct your path. Jesus, lead us to victory.

APRIL 18 || JOSHUA 18:3

Then Joshua asked them, "How long are you going to wait before taking possession of the remaining land the LORD, the God of your ancestors, has given to you?"

Read: Joshua 16:1-18:28

Seven of the tribes still have not taken possession of the land that had been promised to them. Joshua challenges them in our verse and asks them why they are still waiting around and not taking the gift that was given to them. God had promised them the entire land of Canaan and had promised to drive out all of the nations from before them. For the last seven years they have been marching through the land and defeating one enemy after another.

They have defeated all of the major enemies in the land and all that remains is that they go and take possession of the land that has been allotted to each individual tribe. It is difficult to say why they didn't do that. They had been fighting for seven years and so they might have been tired. It is hard to imagine a great leader like Joshua challenging them like that if that was the case.

It is more likely that they were just being lazy. They had conquered large chunks of the land of Canaan and they may have been satisfied living in the land of someone else's inheritance rather than going out and taking their own. The problem with that was that wasn't God's plan. God wanted them to spread out and fill the land and to drive out all the other nations so that He could make them a completely separated nation. God had a special blessing for each tribe that they could only receive from within their inheritance. And so Joshua tells them to stop sitting around and go out and take what God has given them.

We also can fall into this same problem in our lives, ministries, and churches. Sometimes it is much easier to just sit in the comfort of someone else's inheritance than it is to go and take possession of the one that was promised to you. The problem with that is that you will not experience all that God has for you nor will you be in the center of His will for your life if you do that.

God's promises are not just so that we can be blessed; they are also so that we can be positioned where God wants us so that He can fulfill the plan that He has for our lives. If we fail to take possession of the promises that He has made to us then we are not where He wants us to be. And because we are not where we are supposed to be we will miss out on the future blessings that God has for us there and we are not where He can use us most effectively.

Joshua told the seven tribes to stop free-loading off of the other tribes and to go and take what was theirs. Would God tell you the same thing? If you are not where you are supposed to be; stop sitting around and go there! Jesus, lead us to where we need to be.

Rick Lancaster | PLANTERS PERSPECTIVE

APRIL 19 || JOSHUA 20:3

Anyone who kills another person unintentionally can run to one of these cities and be protected from the relatives of the one who was killed, for the relative may seek to avenge the killing.

Read: Joshua 19:1-20:9

After the Promised Land has been divided God reminds Joshua of an instruction that He had given Moses regarding setting aside cities to serve as places of refuge. These cities had a very special purpose, to provide a place of sanctuary to anyone that unintentionally killed another person. The slayer could flee to one of these cities and would be safe there from anyone that might seek vengeance.

God considers the taking of any life a serious matter. In fact, He tells us that it is His responsibility; not man's. In God's economy there are serious consequences associated with the taking of a human life. Even if someone were to take a life unintentionally, the consequences were significant. They had to flee, ahead of the family avenger, and stay in a city of refuge until the ruling High Priest died. That could mean years of separation from their previous life.

On the other hand, someone that committed murder had no such hope. A murderer had no place to run to. If they run to a city of refuge, the leaders of the city were to determine his guilt and then turn him over to the family avenger who would execute him immediately.

In the Law that God gave to Moses to give to the people of Israel there were numerous capital offences. If someone were to break one of those laws, the punishment was death. God explained that this was so that the impurity could be cleansed from the land. God was trying to send a clear message that the only behavior that was acceptable to Him was one that conformed with His commands. He wanted people to think carefully before they decided to commit one of the capital offences listed in the Law.

God is absolutely just. This means that we can be absolutely certain that we will experience the consequences of our behaviors. If we violate one of the laws or commandments of God, we will experience some kind of consequence. We live in a society that gives hope to people that there will be no consequences for bad behavior. The legal system as it exists gives people hope that they can get away with breaking the law or at least not experience the full consequences that should come with breaking the law.

By giving people the hope of evading the consequences, they more freely challenge the laws and rules. We see this in all areas of our society, including in our homes. Society then begins to change our view of God; if we can get away with it in the world, maybe we can get away with things with God. God is gracious and merciful, but if you test Him you will find yourself on the wrong end of His rod of correction. Jesus, teach us to take Your commands seriously.

APRIL 20 || JOSHUA 21:44

And the LORD gave them rest on every side, just as he had solemnly promised their ancestors. None of their enemies could stand against them, for the LORD helped them conquer all their enemies.

Read: Joshua 21:1-22:20

The nation of Israel has successfully conquered all of the land that they have attempted to occupy. There was much of it that they still needed to occupy but God fought for them every time they went out to occupy the land that God had promised them.

For many years, the Israelites have been fighting to take the land that God had promised to their ancestors. God had promised that if they would go in and fight that He would drive their enemies out before them. And as always, God has been faithful to His promises. And now He is giving them rest. That doesn't mean that they don't have any more battles to fight. It just means that God is going to keep their enemies at bay for a while. Their enemies will not come after them for a while so that they can have a chance to rest.

We often forget this truth about God. He is in control of everything, including what our enemies can and cannot do. If God didn't want the enemies of Israel to attack them, then He would prevent them from being able to attack them. But the other side of that truth is that God can allow them to attack when it suits His purposes and plans.

As we go through this life, especially as we are involved in ministry, it seems like we are always in some battle or another. These battles and attacks come in all forms and effects. Some of them seem to wear us down and others seem to strengthen our resolve.

What we need to keep in mind is that we are in enemy territory. God may have promised us victory but there are still many enemies in the land that need to be defeated. And God intends to use our enemies to teach us and to discipline us. The battles and attacks that we face with our enemies teach us to depend upon God and His strength and not our own. And when we forget that, God will use our enemies to remind us to depend upon Him alone.

God will also provide for us times of rest. These times are for us to regain our strength and to focus our attention on Him and His grace and mercy in our lives. Unfortunately, we often take these times of rest and focus our attention on ourselves. And if we do that God will use an enemy to get our attention back where it belongs.

When the battles are raging, it seems like they will never end. But God has a plan and that plan includes us having victory over our enemies and having times of rest. This verse should bring great hope to those that are in the midst of great battles. The Lord has planned a time of rest for you. Keep at it until that time comes! Jesus, help us to keep marching forward until we reach Your place and time of rest.

Rick Lancaster / PLANTERS PERSPECTIVE

APRIL 21 || JOSHUA 23:14

Soon I will die, going the way of all the earth. Deep in your hearts you know that every promise of the Lord your God has come true. Not a single one has failed!

Read: Joshua 22:21-23:16

Joshua knows that his life is nearing its end. He brings all the leaders together and gives them his last instructions and warnings. Here in this text he warns them against turning away from the one true God to worship the idols of the nations that the Lord has driven out of the land. Joshua was concerned that after he was gone they would start to corrupt themselves by getting involved with the people of the land of Canaan which would ultimately corrupt their worship of God.

Joshua had good cause to be concerned because the people had already shown a tendency toward this behavior. Sadly, the people did not heed the warnings of Joshua and did get involved with the peoples of Canaan and did end up corrupting their worship of God. In his warning Joshua told them that God would not tolerate such behavior and that He would punish them if they did turn away from the Lord.

Joshua tells them to look deep within their hearts. He tells them what they will see there; that God has been faithful to keep every promise he has ever made. Their experience with God proves that God is faithful and that His word is absolute. His point was that if God has always kept His Word, He will do so again in regards to their association with the idols of the land of Canaan.

They did not listen and God did keep His word to punish them. Every time that they persisted in turning from Him to the false gods of the land, God sent a punisher into the land in the form of an enemy nation. Ultimately, He kicked them out of the land that He had promised to their ancestors because they would not remain faithful to Him.

God's word is just as absolute today as it was when Joshua uttered these words. If we persist in rejecting God's grace and chasing after things of this world rather than Him, we should expect to be punished. Some would tell you that a loving God would never punish His children. The fact is that if He is a loving God, He must punish us. It is one of the ways that He proves that He loves us.

We were created to be in intimate fellowship with God. Sin and rebellion breaks that fellowship and God will be faithful to do His part to restore that fellowship. God warned us not to rebel or sin and He promised us that He would punish us if we did. He could not be God if He did not follow through with those promises.

God's punishment of His children is for correction of behavior, not judgment. Thankfully, all of our sins and rebellion were judged on the cross of Christ. God's punishment is meant to bring us back to the cross and remind us what He did for us and so that He can continue to pour out His love, grace, and mercy. Jesus, don't spare the rod.

APRIL 22 || JOSHUA 24:15

But if you are unwilling to serve the Lord, then choose today whom you will serve. Would you prefer the gods your ancestors served beyond the Euphrates? Or will it be the gods of the Amorites in whose land you now live? But as for me and my family, we will serve the Lord."

Read: Joshua 24:1-33

Joshua is nearing the end of his life and he is giving the Israelites some last minute instructions before he leaves them. They have been in the Promised Land for about twenty-five years and have still not conquered the whole land. Joshua is concerned that after he dies that the Israelites are going to turn away from God and turn to either the gods of their ancestors or the gods of the people of Canaan.

Joshua challenges them by telling them to choose whom they will serve. He has just finished reminding them of all the great things that God has done for them and reminded them of the mistakes of their fathers that resulted in the anger of the Lord. Joshua finishes his challenge by telling the people what choice he is making.

The people respond by telling Joshua and then making a covenant with God to follow Joshua's example. They commit to follow the Lord and turn away from any of the worthless idols that they have been worshipping. Joshua reminds them of the punishment that awaits those that turn away from the Lord and they seem to respond in the right way.

The people do follow the Lord as long as Joshua lives. The text tells us that the people obeyed until all the elders that had witnessed the mighty works of God had died. We will see as we get into the book of Judges that it wasn't long after that the Israelites did what Joshua was warning them not to do.

We can learn from this text three things that every leader must do. First, we must teach people the truth. They need to understand what God expects of them and warn them of the danger of disobeying and rebelling against God.

Second, God's leaders must be examples of the things that they are teaching to the people. We should be living examples of the things that we are teaching to God's people. Our lives must model faith and obedience to God.

Third, as leaders in God's ministries and churches we must be raising up leaders to take our place that will continue in the first two steps. We must find and train leaders to teach and model God's truth. Any leader that is not recruiting and training leaders is not fulfilling his or her greatest responsibility. Who will lead the flock if something happens to you? A healthy ministry or church has shepherds ready to assume any responsibilities needed to protect and grow the flock no matter what happens to the leader. Jesus, help us to follow Your example of teaching the truth, living a life that models those truths, and teaching other leaders to do the same.

Rick Lancaster / PLANTERS PERSPECTIVE

APRIL 23 | | JUDGES 2:2

For your part, you were not to make any covenants with the people living in this land; instead, you were to destroy their altars. Why, then, have you disobeyed my command?

Read: Judges 1:1-2:9

God had told the nation of Israel not to make any covenants with the nations in the land of Canaan; the Promised Land. And He also promised them that He would drive out all of the people in the land. God had promised to give the land of Canaan to Abraham and his descendants forever. And the one thing that God wanted them to do was avoid making agreements with the nations that were in the land.

God had wanted them to do only one thing with those nations and that was to drive them out of the land. God had promised to drive those nations out before the nation of Israel. The nations that were living in the land were practicing all sorts of wickedness and evil and God knew that if those nations remained in the land that it was just a matter of time before His people turned away from Him and turned to the worthless idols of the people of Canaan. And that is exactly what happened.

The people of Israel did not drive out the nations that were living in the land and instead they started to get comfortable and began making agreements and covenants with the people of Canaan. And before very long they were intermarrying the people of Canaan and worshipping their gods.

The people of Canaan are a type or picture of the sin in our lives. They represent the evil and wickedness that lives within all of us. And God would also tell us not to make any agreements with those sins. Our only objective should be to conquer our lives for Jesus Christ and with the power of His Holy Spirit drive out all the sin in our lives. God has also promised that He will drive out those enemies to our life as we engage them in battle.

We must never get comfortable with the sin in our lives and we must never allow sin to exist peacefully within our lives. Because if we do, we will soon be bowing down to the altar that those sins will erect in our lives and we will hear God saying to us that we have not kept our part of the agreement with Him. The only way to live the life that God has promised us is to wage a never-ending war against the enemies to our soul; the sin that threatens to separate us from the God that gives us everything that we need and desire.

And when we engage in those battles, God is right there before us to defeat those enemies but it is up to us to march up to that enemy and attack. Jesus, help us to hate the sin in our lives as much as You do.

PLANTERS PERSPECTIVE | *A Devotional*

APRIL 24 || JUDGES 3:1-2

The LORD left certain nations in the land to test those Israelites who had not participated in the wars of Canaan. He did this to teach warfare to generations of Israelites who had no experience in battle.

Read: Judges 2:10-3:31

The nation of Israel has only been in the land of Canaan for a couple of generations and they are already turning away from God's ways. It seems that the more comfortable they became, the less they needed God. Sadly, this is the way most of us are also. God knows that and so allows certain things to remain in our lives to remind us that we really do need Him for every breath in our lungs.

In our verses for the day we see that the Lord left enemies in the land to test and teach the Israelites. This is a tremendous truth. If we will take hold of this truth it will help us to understand better why the world around us is the way that it is. God allows enemies to persist around us for our own good.

This goes contrary to human logic. We imagine that because we are God's children that He is going to eliminate every enemy within a thousand miles of us. That is not the case and there is a good reason for that. If He did, we would soon stop needing Him and we would turn to our own way. God loves us too much to allow that to happen. We were created to be in a fellowship relationship with Him and He is not going to allow us to forget that.

Another reason God allows some enemies to persist is so that we are always ready for a battle. If we are not taught how to defend ourselves through the practice of defending ourselves, then we will not be ready when a greater enemy approaches. God teaches us the art of spiritual warfare by allowing some enemies to come against us. If we will then turn to Him, He will teach us how to fight using the weapons that He has provided to us.

The battle belongs to the LORD, but He expects us to pick up the spiritual weapons He has equipped us with to do our part. Without testing and teaching, we will not know how to do that. It is an act of God's love and grace that He allows some enemies to persist in our lives. You may not have ever thought of it that way.

The next time one of your spiritual enemies attacks you, thank God for His love and acknowledge His grace. Then strap on your spiritual weapons and let the Holy Spirit teach you how to use them. I expect that will change the outcome of many of the battles that you will fight. You can't win fighting your way. Let the LORD teach you, and then fight beside Him and you cannot be defeated. Jesus, teach us to look forward to the lessons that you will send our way, knowing that they will make us stronger.

Rick Lancaster / PLANTERS PERSPECTIVE

APRIL 25 || JUDGES 4:9

"Very well," she replied, "I will go with you. But since you have made this choice, you will receive no honor. For the LORD's victory over Sisera will be at the hands of a woman." So Deborah went with Barak to Kedesh.

Read: Judges 4:1-5:31

The book of Judges reveals a very consistent pattern in the nation of Israel. While a prophet or judge is alive, they will follow the Lord. Shortly after the death of the prophet or judge, they turn away from the Lord and begin worshipping worthless idols. God then sends an enemy to remind them of their relationship with the Almighty God. Here in our account today we have the same scenario being played out. The Israelites have done what is evil in the Lord's sight and God has sent the Canaanite king Jabin to bring the Israelites back to God.

God selects Barak to be the one that He will use to defeat King Jabin and his commander Sisera. This is a great honor to be selected like this to do a great work for God. But Barak lacked the faith to go by himself and wanted Deborah to come with him. Because of his lack of faith some of the glory and honor that God had determined to give him was going to be given to a woman.

This would be a slap in the face to Barak. The person that defeated the enemy commander was the one that would be given great honor and respect. As the commander of the army of Israel, Barak would expect that to be him or at the very least, one of his soldiers. It was not uncommon for the soldiers to capture the enemy commander and bring him to their commander so that he would receive the honor of killing the enemy commander. Barak would be humiliated to have a woman do what he should have done.

As leaders of God's ministries and churches, God has given us the opportunity to do great things for Him. If we will have faith, He will win great victories and He will give us some measure of honor and glory. But if we lack the faith, He will still have the victory but He will use someone else and give them the honor and glory that He wanted to give you. And the person he picks will be someone that normally you would say is not capable of being used that way.

The Bible teaches that God is searching the whole world to find people with the faith to do great things for Him and then He shows His might and power through those people. Those people do not have great power or might, but they believe that God does. When we believe that God has great power and might, we then become conduits for the use of that power and might.

God used a donkey to speak to Balaam in Numbers 22. He could use anyone or anything to do the things that He has asked me to do. Jesus, help me to have the faith to respond to your will immediately and completely, so that I might receive the honor and glory that you have determined to give me, so that I in turn can give it back to you.

APRIL 26 | | JUDGES 6:14

Then the LORD turned to him and said, "Go with the strength you have and rescue Israel from the Midianites. I am sending you!"

Read: Judges 6:1-40

Gideon receives a visit from a very special person; the angel of the LORD. Some say that this person is a special messenger from heaven, possibly the archangel Gabriel. However, verses like the one above that in the Hebrew use the proper name of God, Yahweh, would lead us to see this as a Christophany, the physical appearance of the second person of the Trinity.

God had told the Israelites that if they rebelled against Him and turned to worship the false gods of the land they were occupying, that he would hand them over to enemies that would oppress them. That is exactly what has happened at the point in history that this account relates to. The Midianites regularly come in and steal their crops and cause havoc in Israel. Finally, they cry out to God for help and He responds by appearing to Gideon. The LORD addresses Gideon as 'Mighty hero'. The LORD saw him as He was going to be, not as he was.

Gideon didn't consider himself a hero. In our verse, the LORD tells Gideon to go and defeat the Midianites. He then assures Gideon by telling him that He was going with Gideon. At first Gideon is not sure that God is really going to do what He said and asks for proof, which to my surprise the Lord provides to Gideon.

The LORD tells Gideon to go with the strength that he had. That is one of the fascinating parts of this verse. What strength did Gideon have? If he had had any real strength he might already be doing something to resist the Midianites rather hiding in the bottom of a winepress threshing grain. To Gideon, this task was far beyond any puny strength he might have.

We all know the rest of the story. God uses Gideon and a small band of Israelites to route the Midianite army. All the work was done by God, Gideon and his little army were just allowed to be in the front row to watch what God was doing.

How much strength do you have? How much strength do you need to have to do the thing that God has told you to do? According to this verse you have enough strength to do what God is telling you do. The question then is, 'Will you obey?'

Gideon did and was allowed to participate in a great victory for the LORD. As small as your strength is, it is all you need when it is coupled with the LORD's strength and His command to 'Go.' Your little bit of strength and obedience combined with the LORD's infinite strength is a recipe for victory every time. Jesus, teach us to trust and obey.

Rick Lancaster / PLANTERS PERSPECTIVE

APRIL 27 || JUDGES 7:2

The LORD said to Gideon, "You have too many warriors with you. If I let all of you fight the Midianites, the Israelites will boast to me that they saved themselves by their own strength.

Read: Judges 7:1-8:17

Gideon has gathered an army with God's help to fight against the Midianite army that has been oppressing them. The Midianites are there because God was using them to bring the Israelites to a point where they turned away from their worthless idols and turned back to God. God will use this same method throughout the Old Testament every time the Israelites turn away from God.

This army that Gideon has collected is thirty-two thousand men. That is pretty impressive but not when compared to the army that they will face of about one hundred thirty five thousand. And then God does this amazing thing and tells Gideon that he has too many men. The army of Israel is outnumbered by more than four to one and God says that they have too many men.

Through a process of elimination God reduces Gideon's army down to three hundred men. Now the odds are a little fairer, right? Now the odds are more than 400 enemy soldiers to each Israelite soldier. God knew that even at the original odds, the Israelites would take credit for the victory. And the reason God didn't want them to do that was because they didn't deserve the credit and because they would quickly turn away from Him again. To have the effect that God was looking for; the victory had to be miraculous.

As leaders in God's ministries and churches, He has given us gifts, abilities, and experiences that have prepared us for the things that He wants us to accomplish. And for many of the things that we are going to face as we serve the Lord we are equipped to handle them. There is a great risk in our strength and abilities and our leaning on us rather than upon the Lord.

God is going to allow some battles with overwhelming odds into our lives so that we will remember who it is that supplies our every need; including the everyday ones. God will allow an enemy to come into our lives that there is no way for us to handle on our own so that we will come running back to Him.

Is there some overwhelming army in the valley below you? Praise God! That means that He wants to have a mighty victory and He wants to use you to do it. You can't defeat this enemy but God can! You don't have the strength to fight but God does! You don't have a plan that will work but God does! Surrender the battle, the enemy, and your life to God and let Him show you how He is going to defeat them. In our text today, Gideon and his little army didn't have to fight until after God had won the victory. Jesus, teach us to lean upon Your strength and to wait upon Your victory.

APRIL 28 || JUDGES 8:27

Gideon made a sacred ephod from the gold and put it in Ophrah, his hometown. But soon all the Israelites prostituted themselves by worshipping it, and it became a trap for Gideon and his family.

Read: Judges 8:18 – 9:21

God has just won a tremendous victory through Gideon and the nation of Israel by defeating the wicked Midianites. God had used the Midianites to punish Israel for turning away from Him to worship other gods. The Bible teaches that God is a jealous God; He will not share our affection with anything else.

Unfortunately, we humans have this bad habit of creating our own gods and objects of worship. If we would honestly evaluate our lives, all of us would probably find several objects of worship in our lives that God disapproves of. Many of them could have started out as good things. Gideon creates a golden ephod from the earrings of the fallen Midianites. The scriptures don't tell us why he does this. It is possible that it was done to serve as a memorial to God's victory.

Before long the Israelites are worshipping this object. God's description of that response is to call it prostitution. Prostitutes are not held in high regard in most cultures. In fact, they are shunned by most people because their lifestyle/profession is demeaning and offensive. By referring to their worship of the ephod as prostitution, the Lord is trying to help them to be repulsed by their own behavior.

The golden ephod became a trap for Gideon and his family. It is not hard to imagine that the attention that God's victory and the worship of this ephod had an intoxicating effect upon Gideon and his family. That was the bait that lured them into the trap. The trap was sprung when they didn't recognize what was going on and turn away from it.

Another feature of the human race is that we will often continue in behaviors long after they are productive or understood. We do what we do because that is the way we have always done it. We also refer to this trait as habits. We form habits that in some cases turn into tradition. If a tradition exists long enough, its source can be lost and therein lies the danger. For some reason we resist the urge to question tradition.

Gideon allowed his family to develop a tradition that drew them away from God and ultimately played a role in Israel's fall back into idolatry. There is nothing wrong with traditions, as long as they draw us to God and not away from Him. Traditions can be very useful and uplifting. It is up to us as leaders to challenge those traditions with God's Word and the guiding of the Holy Spirit to make sure that we are not allowing those we lead to spiritually prostitute themselves.

Traditions should draw us together and lead us to the Lord. If they don't, we are at risk of experiencing what the Israelites went through; the punishment of God. Because they allowed their tradition associated with Gideon's golden ephod to lead them away from the Lord, He used one of Gideon's own sons to bring trouble into his family. Jesus, help us to stay away from the traps.

Rick Lancaster / PLANTERS PERSPECTIVE

APRIL 29 || JUDGES 9:23

God stirred up trouble between Abimelech and the people of Shechem, and they revolted.

Read: Judges 9:22-10:18

God was going to punish the people of Shechem for murdering the seventy sons of Gideon. He did it through Abimelech. What is not obvious in the text above is how God stirred up the trouble in Shechem to get them to revolt. The NASB says "God sent an evil spirit". This is something that we wouldn't normally think about with God but does He have authority over the demons, which is what an evil spirit is? Of course He does! Nothing is outside of His power and authority. Even Satan must answer to God. It is nothing for God to appoint a demon to a task like this. We saw the same kind of thing with Saul when he turned away from God as the king of Israel; God sent a tormenting spirit to him.

The people of Shechem were godless and God had determined to judge them. Usually when we think of God judging we think of Sodom and Gomorrah with fire and brimstone falling from heaven. God is not limited in any way; He can judge or bless in ways that are well outside of our ability to imagine them. God can and does use angels and demons to work His will. We have to be very careful with this type of thought process though. The evil that is being done in this world is not being directed by God but by Satan. God has no plans for evil but to destroy it. But that doesn't prevent God from using the wicked people of this world to judge and punish the other wicked people of this world. And He will use whatever means that He chooses to; even some that we would think that He would not.

If trouble is being stirred up in the 'Shechem' near you it might be the Lord working out His plan to judge them. If you feel like you are living, or ministering, or your church might be a Shechem, then pray. Ask God to reveal to you what the source of the trouble is. If he reveals that He is judging your Shechem pray harder and ask Him to reveal to you what you should be doing. Get your heart right before God and you might find that is exactly what God is waiting for.

If it isn't then you are putting yourself where God can speak to you so that you know what you should be doing. If you don't do this you could find yourself sitting inside of a Shechem with the walls falling down all around you. God spared Nineveh because they repented; He will do the same with anyone or any group of people that does the same. Too often our pride prevents us from doing that.

Trouble isn't always from God; Satan is a master troublemaker. If there is trouble it is time to humble yourself seek God more diligently. More cities have been saved by a humble man on his knees than a strong man with a sword. Jesus, help us to kneel.

APRIL 30 || JUDGES 11:31

I will give to the LORD the first thing coming out of my house to greet me when I return in triumph. I will sacrifice it as a burnt offering.

Read: Judges 11:1-12:15

There are some accounts in Scripture that are difficult to understand and in some cases are a little disturbing. This is one such account. The armies of Ammon are preparing to attack Israel and the Israelites cry out to God to rescue them. The LORD accuses them of turning away from Him to worship false gods, again. They agree to change and so God raises Jephthah as leader of the Israelites.

The Spirit of the LORD comes upon Jephthah and he gathers together an army to fight against the Ammonites. Before going into the battle, Jephthah makes a vow to give the LORD the first thing that comes out of his house if the LORD gives him the victory. The disturbing part is that he promises to burn it as a sacrifice.

After the victory Jephthah returns home to be greeted by his daughter. The text says that his heart was broken because she was his only child. There is much controversy over what happened next in this account. Human sacrifice was forbidden by God for the Israelites but was practiced by the people of the surrounding nations. It is hard to imagine that God would allow Jephthah to sacrifice his daughter as a burnt offering.

The account ends in such a way to believe that rather than sacrificing her, she was never allowed to marry and ultimately died as a virgin, presumably of natural causes. So the outcome of this account is a little unclear. The outcome is not the main point of the account and it is easy to miss that. The main point of this account is that God had already determined to save the Israelites; Jephtath's vow was unnecessary and irrelevant.

God does not need our vows or promises, but He requires our obedience. Jephthah had already been given the victory; he only needed to obediently go out with his army and fight. He thought he was being spiritual by making a vow, and it is my guess this was not a private vow but very public. His vow was foolish and it cost him more than he ever imagined it would, regardless of the actual outcome.

If the LORD wants you to do something, you don't need to make a vow so that God will help you. If He wants you to do it He has already decided to help you. All you then need to do is just do it. Jesus, help us not to make foolish vows and simply obey.

Rick Lancaster / PLANTERS PERSPECTIVE

MAY

MAY 1 || JUDGES 13:8

Then Manoah prayed to the Lord. He said, "Lord, please let the man of God come back to us again and give us more instructions about this son who is to be born."

Read: Judges 13:1-14:20

An angel of the Lord has appeared the wife of Manoah and told her that she was going to have a son even though she was barren. Not only was she going to have a son, but this son was going to deliver the Israelites from the oppression of the Philistines. She tells her husband and he prays and asks that God would send back this messenger so that they can get additional instruction regarding this miracle.

What a great example of faith! Manoah did not question God about the miracle and he did not ask for proof. He asked God to provide them with more information so that he could complete the task that God was giving them. God answered Manoah's prayer and sent the messenger again. This is further proof of the heart of this man and his wife. God had selected them to do this great work because they had the faith to do it.

When the messenger returns he doesn't give them any more information than he did the first time. And his second visit serves no real purpose beyond blessing and encouraging Manoah and his wife. It was as though God was saying to them that He was pleased with their response to the first visit of the angel of the Lord.

When God speaks to us, He wants us to listen. He will send us messages in many different ways. He will speak to us through His Word, the Bible. He will speak to us in prayer. He will often give us a message while we are listening to someone teaching through the Word. He will also send people to deliver a message to you. When He does, He wants our response to be like that of Manoah and his wife.

They believed God and were ready to do whatever was asked of them. It wasn't a question of will God do this thing; it was a matter of what is our part in this thing that God is doing through us. And it is OK to ask God for more information but know that God might not give you any more information. That doesn't change the fact that He wants you to do what you can with the information you have. God will often only give us just enough information so that we can obey Him but not enough that we can do it without trusting Him to provide more in the future.

Men and women of faith receive messages from God. And when they do, they respond in faith to accomplish whatever it is that God is asking them to do. What has God asked you to do lately? What was your response? If you want God to do radical, supernatural, miraculous things in your life, you must believe that He can and will. And then when He tells you that He is going to do it, He will tell you what your part is. It is then up to you to do your part, trusting that God will do His. Jesus, help us to be men and women of faith that are used to do incredible things in Your name and for Your glory.

Rick Lancaster / PLANTERS PERSPECTIVE

MAY 2 || JUDGES 15:10

The men of Judah asked the Philistines, "Why have you attacked us?" The Philistines replied, "We've come to capture Sampson. We have come to pay him back for what he did to us."

Read: Judges 15:1-16:31

Sampson was a judge in the nation of Israel for twenty years. He was the most unusual of all of Israel's judges. As you study through the period of the judges you find that they were called upon for many duties, but mainly they would come forward to lead Israel when they were being oppressed by a foreign nation. Their primary role for the nation was to do as their title implies, to judge between the people settled disputes.

Sampson doesn't seem to fulfill any of the descriptions of what the other judges were doing. There is no sense that he assumed a role of leader at any point or that he acted as a judge for the people. In fact, Sampson could very well be the most selfish, self-centered person that God used in all of Scripture.

During the time of Sampson's life the Philistines were ruling over the nation of Israel. This was because they had once again turned away from the LORD and He punished them by letting them be tormented by a foreign nation. Once Israel figured out that they were out of God's will He would send someone to deliver them from their enemy. Sampson is the man that God has chosen to deliver Israel this time.

In today's reading the Philistines are once again harassing the Israelites but this time they are there because of what Sampson has done to them. He has just burned up all their fields of grain, their grapevines, and olive trees. They have come to get revenge upon Sampson. This is all leading up to the most famous thing that Sampson did; the killing of one thousand Philistines with the jawbone of a donkey.

What strikes me about our verse for the day is that the men of Judah asked the Philistines why they were attacking them. They were asking the right question, they were just asking the wrong person. They should have been asking the LORD. The tabernacle was still set up and the priests were still serving before the LORD. God was using Sampson to goad the Philistines into attacking and harassing the Israelites because they had turned away from Him. Instead of asking God what they should do, the men of Judah get three thousand men and go after Sampson themselves. Their goal was to get rid of the irritation and they hoped that would cause the Philistines to leave them alone.

God will allow enemies to come into our lives. We might be tempted, as the men of Judah were to find the source of the irritation and try to eliminate it. That might not be what God is trying to do. God might be trying to redirect you; He might be trying to draw you closer to Him. The men of Judah asked their enemy why they were being attacked. Your enemy can't and won't help you. Go to the LORD and ask Him why things are the way they are and ask Him how He would like you to respond. And then be prepared to see Him do something miraculous to drive that enemy from your life. Jesus, remind us to seek You out when we need answers.

MAY 3 | | JUDGES 17:6

In those days Israel had no king, so the people did whatever seemed right in their own eyes.

Read: Judges 17:1-18:31

The nation of Israel has dispersed to take control of and settle in their inheritance of land. Each tribe was given a section of Canaan as their portion of the Promised Land. They are in a period of time called the time of the Judges. It is the time in between when Moses and Joshua led the nation and the time of the kings that started with Saul.

It was God's desire to set up a theocracy. God would rule the people through His commands and through the revelation of His will through the Levites. But as we see throughout the Old Testament, the people can't quite seem to figure this out. The nation of Israel consistently and repeatedly turns away from God. They cease to seek God's will and do things that seem right to them.

We live in a society today that is no different than it was three thousand years ago. People are still doing things that seem right in their own eyes. God still wants to rule His people as a theocracy. He still wants His commands and instructions to be the guiding light of our lives. He still wants His people to seek His will and to follow Him.

This world has grown up, for the most part, not knowing the God that created them. A very small percentage of people attend church on a regular basis and many of the ones that do, don't really know the God that they are worshipping. And sadly, many of those churches are not doing a very good job of introducing people to the Savior of their souls. Here in our text for today we saw that a Levite accepted the role of priest to help this family and then the tribe of Dan to worship an idol. The very man that ought to be leading people back to God was helping them to do what seemed right in their own eyes.

As leaders in families, ministries, and churches we owe it to God to always be leading people to Christ. We can't just sit by and watch as people do what seems right in their eyes. They need to know the God that created them and loves them. They need to know Jesus. And as they get to know Him they will see the things that seem right to them are not right to God and then they will desire to change. We can't make people do the right things but we can lead them to Jesus and let Him show them the path of righteousness and eternal life.

We as leaders have a huge responsibility to always be checking ourselves to make sure that we are not doing things that seem right in our own eyes. We need to be on our face before God and asking Him to search us and reveal anything within us that displeases Him. Jesus, help us to love You like You love us and help us to love others so much that we will bring them to You.

Rick Lancaster / PLANTERS PERSPECTIVE

MAY 4 || JUDGES 19:1

Now in those days Israel had no king. There was a man from the tribe of Levi living in a remote area of the hill country of Ephraim. One day he brought home a woman from Bethlehem in Judah to be his concubine.

Read: Judges 19:1-20:48

Here we have the peculiar account of a Levite and his concubine from Bethlehem. This Levite is traveling home after finding this woman that he wants to bring to his home. She runs back to her home and then the Levite comes back to get her after four months. After several days of the father stalling, the Levite heads for home again.

They travel until dusk and stop in a town to rest. They bypass the city of Jerusalem because the Levite does not want to stay with foreigners. While in this town, they are invited into the home of an old man. While there, the men of the town, later identified as leaders of the town, come and tell the old man to send the visitors out so that they can have sex with them. Then the Levite does the unthinkable, he pushes his concubine out the door and locks it behind her.

The men of the town rape her all night and then she finally crawls back to the doorstep and dies. The Levite takes her body to his home and then dismembers it and sends the pieces to the twelve tribes of Israel. This creates great outrage within the nation and justice is demanded. The tribe of Benjamin is asked to hand over the wicked men that have done this evil thing. But instead they mobilize their army and a civil war breaks out that virtually wipes out the tribe of Benjamin.

Most of us cannot imagine many of these events taking place but to have them all take place in a single account is bizarre. We are reminded of the account of Sodom and Gomorrah being destroyed by God because of its great wickedness. And here the children of God are doing the same thing. The last verse in the book of Judges sums up what was going on. It reminds us that Israel did not have a king and so they did what they thought was right to do.

In the three thousand years since this event took place very little has changed. Most people still have no king and so they do what they think is right and best, usually for them. It is our responsibility as leaders in God's ministries and churches to bring them to the King of kings, Jesus Christ. Without a leader, people will do whatever feels right to them. We need to bring them back to the light of truth in the Bible and teach them to listen to the leading of the Holy Spirit.

Sadly, many of our churches also do what seems right in their own eyes and have forgotten their first love. Let us be the ones that relight that torch that provides light to lead God's people back to His throne so that they might find grace and mercy. Left to themselves people will do horrific things and think nothing of it. Jesus, teach us to chase after holiness and to lead others toward it as well.

MAY 5 || RUTH 1:16

But Ruth replied, "Don't ask me to leave you and turn back. I will go wherever you go and live wherever you live. Your people will be my people, and your God will be my God.

Read: Judges 21:1-Ruth 1:22

Naomi and her family travel to Moab to escape a famine that threatens their family. While there her husband dies and after her two sons marry Moabite women, they also die. Naomi learns that the famine is over in Israel and so she sets out to return to her homeland. On the way she tries to convince both of daughters-in-law to return to their homes because she doesn't think it is fair for them to have to come with her to Naomi's homeland.

One of the two Moabite women responds to Naomi's instructions but the other doesn't. This Moabite women Ruth tells her mother-in-law that she wants to go wherever she goes. This is an incredible act of loyalty on her part. It would have been perfectly acceptable and reasonable for Ruth to return to her parent's home and then re-marry from within her own people.

But instead this Moabite woman insists on following Naomi to her home. Ruth follows Naomi to a land that is strange to her and to a people that are strangers to her and that worship a God that is different than the gods of her people. All that awaits her in Naomi's homeland is strange to her. And yet she leaves all that is familiar to her to follow this woman. What beautiful, sacrificial loyalty!

Loyalty is a precious gift that is exchanged between leaders and followers. And it is absolutely critical that both give this gift. A leader must be loyal if he or she expects people to follow and a follower must be loyal if they desire that the ministry or church achieve its God-given objectives. And true loyalty often carries with it a price; it will often call for sacrifice on the part of the giver. Loyalty requires that we think of others more than ourselves and will cause us to do things that others don't understand.

God calls us to be loyal to Him first and then to those that He has called us to come alongside. This means that we can't just bail at the first hint of something we don't like. Ruth's loyalty to Naomi was stronger than her discomfort about leaving everything she knew behind her. Who has God called you to be loyal to? Does he or she know that you will be there no matter what happens? If not, let them know. It will be a great encouragement to them. Jesus, help us to be loyal to those that you have surrounded us with and teach to earn the loyalty of others.

Rick Lancaster / PLANTERS PERSPECTIVE

MAY 6 || RUTH 4:16

Naomi took care of the baby and cared for him as if he were her own.

Read: Ruth 2:1-4:22

While the main character in the book of Ruth is Ruth, the role of Naomi is fascinating and gives us much to learn from. Here as the book of Ruth comes to a close we see the happy ending. Ruth marries Boaz and they have a son that they name Obed. Naomi then cares for that son as though he was hers. By Jewish law this son would grow up to inherit all the land of Naomi's dead husband and sons. But he wasn't really related to her.

Ruth was a Moabite and Boaz was at best a distant relative of Naomi. And yet she cares for this child as if it were her own son. It almost makes you wonder if she had some sense of how precious this infant was. It is not likely that she was alive when this baby's grandson was born and even less likely that she was alive when he became the king of Israel. Obed's grandson was David, the son of Jesse.

As far as scripture tells us, she or no one else had been told of the incredible things that God was going to do through David. It wasn't until Samuel anointed David as the next king of Israel that we even know who he is. This has often caused me to wonder about the people around me. Are there children and people around me that are going to be used by God like He used David or Moses or Joshua?

As the leaders in God's ministries and churches, we need to be like Naomi. We need to care for God's children as though they were own. Not just because they may grow up to be used by God in some mighty way but because they are God's children. And this doesn't mean just the children. Some people used by God were called before their birth and others were called late in their life.

We need to take care of the people of God just as though they were our children. No matter how rebellious or stubborn they might be, we must care for them. No matter how wild and uncontrollable they are, we must take care of them as our own. We can never write them off and stop caring for them, because God never will.

There is no way for us to know what the future holds for ourselves, let alone anyone else in our ministry and so we must always try to look at the people in our ministries and churches with the eyes of Christ. Just like Naomi cared for the child Obed, we are to care for everyone that God places in our care. It is a huge responsibility and it carries with it eternal consequences and rewards. Jesus, help us to care for and love the people and children that you bring to us just like you would. Help us to see them through your eyes and to see that there are great things that you can do through them.

MAY 7 || 1 SAMUEL 2:17

So the sin of these young men was very serious in the Lord's sight, for they treated the Lord's offerings with contempt.

Read: 1 Samuel 1:1-2:21

Hophni and Phinehas have been doing some very wicked things. They are the two sons of Eli, the high priest. Because their father is the high priest they have a lot of authority with the people. They can get away with the things that they are doing because of their influence over the people. But they can't get away with it in God's eyes.

They would send their servants over as people were preparing their sacrifices and demand that choice pieces be given to them. They completely disregarded the sacrificial law given by Moses. They also seduced the women that were helping with the work around the Tabernacle. Both of these things would have a similar effect on the people that saw them. It would create a lack of respect for the things of God and for God. People would begin to question the whole system and wonder if any of it was real. They might even begin to believe that the whole sacrificial system was just a way to make the priests fat and allow them to satisfy their lusts. Does any of that sound familiar?

Three thousand years later, we are in the same place. There are people in ministry and in churches that are handling the holy things of God as though they were common and there for their use. And much of the world looks at them and sees a corrupt fleshly system that provides no more hope than anything else in the world. It creates a barrier that prevents people from coming to know the Lord.

Heaven forbid that any of us ever do that. The things of God are holy! They should be treated as though they belong to God, because they do. And if you are not sure if something is holy, treat it as holy; as if it belongs to God.

And as people in ministry and in churches, we must keep ourselves sexually pure. The world is watching and waiting for us to fall because of immorality so that it can have one more excuse why Jesus doesn't work. God will judge people like Hophni and Phinehas very harshly. But He also would have shown them mercy if they had repented of their sin.

It is our responsibility to show people and teach people about the holiness of God and His things. We need to model it in our behavior and we need to teach it to others. We need to exhort others in ministries and churches to do the same thing. The bride of Christ is too precious to allow people with soiled hands and hard hearts to fondle her. Jesus, give us a passion for Your bride that burns hot within us.

Rick Lancaster | PLANTERS PERSPECTIVE

MAY 8 || 1 SAMUEL 3:10

And the LORD came and called as before, "Samuel, Samuel!" And Samuel replied, "Yes, your servant is listening."

Read: 1 Samuel 2:22-4:22

The story of Samuel the Prophet is an interesting one. He was raised by Eli the priest. His mother Hannah had been praying for a son for a long time and she promised to give her first son to the LORD. God answered her prayers by giving her Samuel. Hannah kept her word to the LORD and He then gave her three more sons and two daughters.

The role of a prophet is to receive messages from the Lord and then to pass them on to the people that they are directed to. It seems that one of the main messages that the prophets were entrusted with were warnings against turning away from God. Many of the books of the Old Testament are filled with these warnings.

Samuel was raised in the area of the Tabernacle and in service to the LORD. In our text for today he is sleeping in the Tabernacle when he hears a voice calling out to him. He responds by going to Eli to see if he needs anything. Eli tells him to go back to sleep. This happens three times and then Eli understands that it is the LORD. He tells Samuel how to respond if it happens again.

Samuel lies down again and a fourth time he hears the LORD call out to him. That begins a long life of direct communication between the LORD and Samuel. Few people will ever hear the voice of the LORD is this way in this life. It is not a matter of worthiness or ability; it is a matter of God's sovereign choice. For most people He chooses to communicate to them in a different way.

It is pretty common as a pastor to be asked how you know if the LORD is speaking to you about something. That can be a difficult question to answer because the fact of the matter is you can't always know for sure it is His voice. You can run some tests to attempt to verify His voice such as compare what He is telling you to Scripture, to His character, to His previous instructions and the like. But the fact is that you will probably have to exercise some amount of faith to respond to the LORD's voice.

There are a couple of things that we can do to prepare ourselves to hear from the LORD. Samuel was sleeping in the Tabernacle near the Ark of the Covenant. To me this is a picture of living a life of worship. It is more than showing up to church once in a while; it is viewing your whole life as an act of worship to God.

Then prepare yourself to respond. The first thing Samuel said was 'Yes'. For someone that truly wants to hear from the LORD, they must already know that they are going to say 'Yes' to whatever the LORD tells them to do. Second, Samuel described himself as a servant. To hear from the LORD, acknowledge that He is the Master and you are a servant. Third, he was listening. The only way to hear from the LORD is to be listening for Him. It took four attempts before the Lord reached Samuel. How many times will He need to call out to you? Jesus, help us to be ready to listen.

MAY 9 || 1 SAMUEL 6:6

Don't be stubborn and rebellious as Pharaoh and the Egyptians were. They wouldn't let Israel go until God had ravaged them with dreadful plagues.

Read: 1 Samuel 5:1-7:17

The Ark of the Covenant has been captured by the Philistines. They first put it into the temple with their god Dagon but his statue keeps falling over and pieces are breaking off. The people also start breaking out in tumors. These must have been large ugly things growing on their bodies because they will eventually make five gold tumors as part of the offering to appease God.

The leaders decide to send the Ark back to Israel because they are suffering from the plague of tumors. In addition to the five gold tumors they make five gold rats. It appears that they were having a problem with rats that they associated with the presence of the Ark. The leaders determine that the only solution is to send the Ark back to Israel.

They do it in an interesting way; they hook a cart up to two cows that had just had calves. Then they shut up the calves away from the cows. Once released the natural thing for those cows to do would have been to return to their calves. Instead, they walk right down the road toward Israel. The Philistines did it this way to prove whether or not it was God that had inflicted them.

What fascinates me about this account is the fact that the people of Philistia knew about God. They knew about the history of the people of Israel. They knew that God had miraculously delivered them from the mighty power of Pharaoh and the Egyptians. They knew that the God of the Israelites was more powerful than the gods of Egypt. They had also just witnessed that God was more powerful than their god Dagon. They understood that these judgments were coming from God.

Their response is not to worship Him but to appease Him so that He will stop punishing them. Today, people still come to God the same way. They are looking for something from God or they want their suffering to stop. They only want to know God enough to figure out what the formula is for success or peace. Once they have that they go right back to their old life and their old gods.

God will send tumors and rats if that is what it is going to take to get you to humble your heart before Him. Once you are humbled before Him it is His love, grace, and mercy that will alter your life. As Christians it is our responsibility to be ready to give that love, to show that grace, to offer mercy to those that come to God for the wrong reasons.

They might know God and they might know that they need God but they probably don't know how to love God. They will learn to love him by watching His people loving one another. It is a tremendous responsibility to understand that you are a vessel of God's unconditional, sacrificial love. That love has the power to save lives. We need to let God use us to pour that love into the lives of others. Jesus, help us to let You love them through us.

Rick Lancaster / PLANTERS PERSPECTIVE

MAY 10 || 1 SAMUEL 8:20

We want to be like the nations around us. Our king will govern us and lead us into battle.

Read: 1 Samuel 8:1-9:27

The people came to Samuel and asked him to give them a king. They didn't like the fact that Samuel's sons weren't very good judges and so they decided that a better option would be that they have a king. Samuel was not happy about this but he took it to God to ask Him what he should do. God told Samuel to try to talk the people out of it. He tried but the people insisted that they wanted a king just like the other nations.

Sadly, this is how most people live their lives. Rather than have God govern their lives they want their lives to be like to lives of everyone around them. God will try to talk them out of this decision but ultimately we get to choose whom we will follow; God or the world. God let the Israelites choose and told Samuel to give them a king. And He gave them a king that matched what they thought a king should be, Saul. Unfortunately, Saul turned out to be just the kind of king that God had warned them about.

Too often we allow the world to influence our decisions. Every time that we do we are taking ourselves out of the gracious blessings of God and settling for something much less than what God has for us. Only God can lead us to victory over the enemies of our lives. Only God can give us all that we need and desire.

As leaders of families, ministries, or churches we will also face this same temptation to ignore the leading of God to follow the ways of men and the world. We must resist that temptation because if we don't those that are following us will also follow us into a lesser life than what they could have. You owe it to those that are following you to live the rich, abundant life that God gave to you through His Son Jesus.

Even though you do that there are going to be those that look at the ways of the world and are tempted to follow that path. Your responsibility is to warn them of the dangers and pitfalls that they will experience on that path. Sadly, you can't make them do the right thing. If after you have warned them they still choose that path you must let them go. Your prayer should be that God will help them to realize their mistake quickly so that they can get back to the pathway that leads to life.

Your responsibility also includes being ready to receive them back and help them to deal with whatever damage was done while they wandered. We are not to condemn but to forgive. We are not to reject but to receive. We are not bind in guilt but to free through repentance and love. Jesus, help us to bring them to You so that You can set them free from the ways of the world.

MAY 11 || 1 SAMUEL 10:1

Then Samuel took a flask of olive oil and poured it over Saul's head. He kissed Saul on the cheek and said, "I am doing this because the LORD has appointed you to be the leader of his people Israel."

Read: 1 Samuel 10:1-11:15

Saul was the first king of Israel. He was the man that God selected for the people because they wanted a king like all the other nations around them. God tried to talk them out of it but they persisted and God let them have what they wanted even though He warned them that they wouldn't be happy with how it was going to turn out.

Unfortunately, that is how God operates with us also. God will sometimes give us the things that we ask for even though He knows that they will be bad for us. I often wish this weren't so because it would be much better for me if God would only give me those things that are good for me. But He loves me enough to let me choose what I want for my life; even the bad things.

Saul didn't start out as a bad king. He had some success at the beginning but his true colors started to show after he had a little success. That is always the case when we ask God for something that He doesn't want us to have. In the beginning it looks great like Saul did and it is even successful in the beginning. But before too long we can see that it was a mistake and that it was not the best thing for us.

God told the people that they didn't really want a king to rule over them. It meant that they were rejected God's leadership over them. God told them it was a bad idea. God will always tell His children when they ask for things that they shouldn't have. He will even help them to understand why they shouldn't have it.

But ultimately He will let us have those things. Even in that God has a plan. God knows that this thing that you want is not good for you and He knows that at some point you are going to figure that out. His plan is to let you make the mistake in the hopes that you will realize it and come back to Him more fully than before.

God works more in our mistakes than He does in our successes and obedience to draw us nearer to Him. That is because we are more open to be taught by God after we have made a mistake. Our successes and obedience can sometimes cause us to take our eyes off of God while our failures tend to draw our eyes to God.

Once we realize that we have made a mistake we need to repent to God immediately and ask Him to forgive us. There are probably still going to be consequences and repercussions to deal with but God will carry you through those challenges as He teaches you to listen better to His voice and to trust Him. When God says no He wants you to accept that and go on with your life. Jesus, teach us to take 'no' as God's final answer.

Rick Lancaster / PLANTERS PERSPECTIVE

MAY 12 || 1 SAMUEL 12:23

As for me, I will certainly not sin against the LORD by ending my prayers for you. And I will continue to teach you what is good and right.

Read: 1 Samuel 12:1-13:23

Saul has been named the first king of Israel. The prophet Samuel tried to talk them out of it but they were insistent; they wanted to be like the other kingdoms around them. Samuel knew it was a bad idea. In fact, it was a form of rebellion against God. What might not be obvious in this account is the fact that Samuel is turning over leadership of the nation to Saul. Israel was a theocracy; a nation ruled by the LORD. By asking for a king, they wanted to be ruled by a man and not God. As one of the LORD's prophets, Samuel was given instructions from the LORD to give to the people.

Samuel prepares the people to see that what they have done is sinful and rebellious by telling them it is going to rain in the summer when it normally does not. Once they have seen it rain, the people realize that they have sinned against God and ask Samuel to pray for them. Samuel tells them to do what is right from this moment on. He tells them to leave the past in the past and do what is right in the today and in the future.

In today's verse Samuel goes on to tell them that it would be sin for him to stop praying for them. As Saul moves into his role as the king of Israel, Samuel's role of leader will subside. As the outgoing leader Samuel might be tempted to retire and go fishing. Samuel recognizes that his role in leadership is changing but not ending. Samuel assures them that he will not stop praying for them. He will continue to intercede on their behalf even though he is not going to be leading them.

He also goes on to tell them that he will continue to teach them what things are good and right. The LORD had given Samuel certain knowledge and experience that was helpful for the people. He grew up in the temple around the priests and so he had an insight into spiritual things that most people don't have. It can be inferred from the verse that he believed it would be sinful on his part not to continue to share that with others.

As leaders, there may be times when decisions are made that affect our leadership and might even remove us from leadership. Our natural instinct is to turn away from those that we were leading and never look back. But it appears from this verse that there is a higher road that can be taken.

First, continue to pray for those that you used to lead. This will accomplish a couple of things. First, it will help them to experience the blessings and presence of God more fully. The second thing it will do is guard your heart from bitterness and hardness. It is more difficult to be angry and bitter towards someone that you are regularly bringing before the throne of God.

Then, continue to teach them what God has taught you as much as you are able to. God has given you a gift and He expects you to use it for His purposes and for His glory. Pray for them and teach them; that is the higher road. Jesus, help us to take the road less traveled.

MAY 13 || 1 SAMUEL 14:6

"Let's go across to see those pagans," Jonathan said to his armor bearer. "Perhaps the LORD will help us, for nothing can hinder the LORD. He can win a battle whether he has many warriors or only a few!"

Read: 1 Samuel 14:1-52

Jonathan takes his armor bearer and goes over toward the camp of the Philistines. It is just the two of them and they approach this army that is enormous. With chariots alone the Philistines had a larger army than Israel. In the previous chapter we are told that the people of Israel when faced with this terrible army ran and hid in caves and holes. This left Saul with only six hundred men.

So Jonathan takes his armor bearer to check out this army. And then Jonathan proposes this wild idea to his armor bearer. He suggests that they go and show themselves to the army of the Philistines and see what they do. And he makes this radical statement: 'Perhaps the Lord will help us'. Jonathan was going to face this incredible foe and he wasn't even certain that God was going to go with him.

But Jonathan was certain of something; he was certain that if God wanted him to fight the Philistines, that there was nothing that the Philistines could do to stop him. Jonathan had the faith to believe that if God revealed to him that he was to fight the Philistines that God would win the victory. Jonathan knew that it would not be him that was doing the fighting but it would be God and nothing could hinder God in His victory.

That is the kind of faith that allows God to do the incredible things that He wants to do around us. All of us are faced with an army of Philistines; an enemy too great for us to defeat. While it usually isn't a physical army, it is some kind of hindrance to the life that God intended for you to have.

In our ministries and churches, the thing that prevents us from achieving great things for God is our lack of faith when faced with an overwhelming opponent. And often that opponent doesn't even exist; it is something in our minds. We have been asked to do something that is far beyond our abilities or God has revealed to us or our leaders a vision that is impossible. Impossible for whom; you or God?

It was impossible for Jonathan to defeat thirty thousand chariots, six thousand horsemen, and countless foot soldiers. But it wasn't impossible for God. All Jonathan needed was one little confirmation from God to convince him to attempt the impossible. Jonathan was risking his life. Usually when God leads us to attempt the impossible, He is not asking us to risk that much. And if God is telling you to do something, where is the risk? Remember, 'nothing can hinder the Lord'. Jesus, help us to go boldly where You lead.

Rick Lancaster / PLANTERS PERSPECTIVE

MAY 14 || 1 SAMUEL 15:22

But Samuel replied, "What is more pleasing to the LORD: your burnt offerings and sacrifices or your obedience to his voice? Obedience is far better than sacrifice. Listening to him is much better than offering the fat of rams.

Read: 1 Samuel 15:1-16:23

Samuel came to King Saul with instructions from God. Saul was to utterly destroy the nation of Amalek because of the things that they had done to Israel. God, through Samuel, told King Saul that everyone and everything was to be destroyed. The army of Israel was victorious in their battle against Amalek and destroyed all the people and most of the things.

However, they spared the king and brought him to King Saul. And they kept all the finest of the animals. The text says that they were unwilling to destroy them. Samuel confronts Saul and asks why he didn't do what God told him to do. Saul then starts making excuses and blame-shifting. He tells Samuel he did what God said and also that he was afraid of the people so he didn't make them do what they were supposed to do.

Saul was selected as the leader of the nation of Israel and God's expectation of the leader he appointed was that he would be obedient to him regardless of the consequences. Saul's failure here reveals his true nature and could be used to teach us much about leadership. But the main point of this text is that obedience is more important than any sacrifice that we could make to God.

Saul said that the people intended to sacrifice the animals that they kept to the Lord. Whether or not that was true doesn't change the fact that they were likely doing it for selfish reasons because seldom was the entire animal burned up. Usually the person making the sacrifice would keep a portion of the sacrifice for themselves and some would be given to the priests as their food. Saul allowed the desires of the people to sway his judgment and this cost him everything.

God expects His leaders to obey His voice implicitly, without hesitation and without compromise. God took the kingdom away from Saul because he chose to disobey God and then justified his actions by making a sacrifice to God. Our sacrifices are meaningless if we aren't being obedient. As God's leaders we are called to sacrifice much, and if we want those sacrifices to be of any worth we must be obedient. Obedience becomes difficult when it means it is going to cost us something or like with Saul, it means that we will experience conflict with those that want to do it a different way. Jesus, help us to respond to your voice without looking to the left, right, or behind.

MAY 15 || 1 SAMUEL 17:37

"The LORD who saved me from the claws of the lion and the bear will save me from this Philistine!" Saul finally consented. "All right, go ahead," he said. "And may the LORD be with you!"

Read: 1 Samuel 17:1-18:4

Today's verse comes out of one of the more famous of the stories in Scripture; David and Goliath. There are many lessons to be learned from the account. David is young, probably around seventeen or eighteen and is visiting his brothers who are a part of King Saul's army. Samuel has already anointed David to be the next king of Israel but Saul doesn't know that. David sees Goliath taunting the army of Israel and is outraged that no one has stood up to fight him. Word gets to King Saul that this young man is willing to fight Goliath.

As David speaks with King Saul he explains why he is not afraid to fight Goliath. He has already fought with a lion and a bear and was victorious. David recognized that his victory did not come from his own strengths or abilities but from the power of God. To David, Goliath was no different than a lion or a bear. He was a foe that the LORD wanted to defeat and he was willing to be the weapon that God would use to do it.

King Saul then tried to give David his armor but it didn't fit him and so he refused it. David instead used what God had already given him to fight the foe that the LORD had placed before him. David is a great example of how God wants us to face the enemies that rise up in our lives. David used his experience with the LORD to direct his actions.

For forty days the nation of Israel stood cowering before Goliath. David shows up and responds immediately to the threat by using the weapons he had coupled with the experience he had previously gained to win a great victory through the LORD. That was David's faith in action. Our response to the giants that show up in our lives should be no different.

Whatever comes into your life has been allowed to be there by the LORD. He permits giants for a number of reasons. One of the greatest of those reasons is that He wants His glory to be seen by others. To do that He uses simple people with simple faith to do supernatural things like David did with Goliath. You and I can be like David; we simply need to believe.

When you face your giant today, remember that the LORD placed him or it there so that others would be able to see His mighty power at work within your life. Also remember that He has been there for you in the past. That is all the proof that you need that He will do the same for you today. And then don't wait, step up and face your giant in the name of the living God. You will see giants falling at your feet and the name of God will be glorified. Jesus, strengthen us as we run toward our giants.

Rick Lancaster / PLANTERS PERSPECTIVE

MAY 16 | | 1 SAMUEL 18:9

So from that time on Saul kept a jealous eye on David.

Read: 1 Samuel 18:5-19:24

David has just recently killed the giant Goliath and the people are celebrating the great victory that Israel has won against their enemy, the Philistines. It is hard to imagine that Saul believed that David would be able to defeat Goliath. And so when he did, it was probably quite a shock and I would imagine a blow to his ego. To have this kid do something neither he nor anyone else in his army was willing to do would have been humiliating. And then to top it off, the women celebrate this great victory by singing a song that attributes ten times the success to David as to King Saul.

David's success was being celebrated and Saul's response was jealousy. This should have been a time of rejoicing in the Lord for what He had done for the nation of Israel. But Saul is jealous for his kingdom which God has already told him through Samuel that he is going to lose because of his disobedience. Saul keeps a jealous eye on David from this day on.

We see this same scenario played out in ministries and churches all around us. God is working and in some people's lives He is working very powerfully. And there is a great temptation in all of us to respond like Saul did with a jealous eye turned toward that person. Everyone wants to kill giants for God but not everyone gets to. Our response to the giant-killers around us will determine our usefulness to God in the future. What Saul should have done is celebrate this victory with David rather than be jealous of it. When God puts a giant-killer in our midst, we need to celebrate the victories that God will have through them and rejoice in the fact that we get to witness the power of God at work.

Saul was concerned that the people were going to give the kingdom to David instead of him. God had already done that. He just hadn't made the transition of leadership yet. What if that's what God wants to do with the giant-killer that He has put in your midst? What if God wants this person to take your 'position' in the ministry or church that you are in? Are you going to be like Saul and jealously fight to retain what God may have already taken away from you? If this is what God is doing, it doesn't necessarily mean that you were disobedient like Saul was. But it is very likely part of a plan for your life, their life, and the life of the ministry that you do not understand.

As leaders in ministries and churches, God would call us to look for those unlikely people that He might want to use to be giant-killers and then to encourage them to fight the giants around us. He would then call us to celebrate the victories that God wins through them. Jesus, help us to rejoice in the things that you are doing in other people even when it threatens our 'position'.

MAY 17 || 1 SAMUEL 21:13

So he pretended to be insane, scratching on the doors and drooling down his beard.

Read: 1 Samuel 20:1-21:15

David will some day be one of the greatest kings that the nation of Israel ever had. During his rule, he will conquer almost all the enemies of Israel. When his son Solomon takes over the kingdom, he will experience a lifetime of peace and prosperity because of David's efforts before him. But here we see David acting insane, scratching at the door like a dog and drooling down his beard. How did that happen?

Partly we can understand; he is running away from King Saul who is trying to kill him. King Saul wants to kill him because the people like David more than him, or at least that is what his paranoia is telling him. Because of King Saul's disobedience the LORD has taken the kingdom away from Saul and given it to David. It will still be many years before David sits as king.

In the meantime he is in Gath acting insane. The main problem with this picture is where David is. Gath is enemy territory. King Achish is a pagan king whose kingdom is in conflict with the nation of Israel. David's reputation has preceded him and King Achish's officers are not happy about David being there. David is famous for killing Philistines and where is he but in Philistine territory. It was a foolish decision for David to go to Gath and so now he must act foolish to try to get back out of Gath.

As Christians we can do the same thing. We might find ourselves in a place where we have to leave a circumstance because it is uncomfortable or possibly even dangerous but don't consult the LORD about what it is that He thinks we ought to do. Then we find ourselves in a place that might be just as bad as or worse than where we were.

To escape this new situation we must do something that under normal circumstances we would never even consider. David didn't consider that where he was headed to might be worse than from where he came. God had a different plan for David and as soon as David was following that plan God started blessing him.

The LORD didn't want David in Gath and so wouldn't bless him there. God will not bless us while we are wandering around in enemy territory acting insane. If you want to experience the blessing and promises of God fully, you must determine where He wants you and go there. For some people that means simply a change of perspective. For David, he had to go somewhere but went the wrong direction. For some God might want them to stay where they are and stop looking for something different.

Spiritually, Gath is any place that you go or desire to go that is outside of God's will for you. If you insist on going, you will find yourself doing something foolish to try to save yourself. It is so much better to go where the LORD wants you to or to stay where you are until He moves you. Jesus, help us to stay out of Gath.

Rick Lancaster | PLANTERS PERSPECTIVE

MAY 18 || 1 SAMUEL 22:2

Then others began coming—men who were in trouble or in debt or who were just discontented—until David was the leader of about four hundred men.

Read: 1 Samuel 22:1-23:29

David is still running from Saul. He has just returned from his mistaken journey to the enemy city of Gath and the prophet Gad tells him to go to Judah. He ends up in the cave of Adullam in the Judean wilderness. It is obvious by the psalms that he wrote during this time that he was desperate for and clinging to the Lord. There were enemies on all sides and David was suspicious of many.

During this time, people started coming out to find him and join him. He had been a popular leader in the nation of Israel and people still wanted to follow him even though he was on the run from the king. It would have been a difficult life living as outlaws and fugitives.

It is interesting the types of men that came to David. There were mighty warriors as we see in the First Chronicles reading. But here in our verse for today we have three different kinds of people: ones that were in trouble, ones that were in debt, and ones that were discontent. Out of this diverse group of men David built a force of men that would be called "David's Mighty Men". Many of these men did incredibly heroic things in the service of David and the Lord. But most of them didn't start out as heroes.

In ministry and the church you will see this same dynamic taking place. When you begin a work especially one that is new, God will start sending people to you. And you might wonder what God is doing. He will send you some mighty warriors; those are the ones that we really like. But then He will also send you people that are in trouble or that make trouble. He will send you those that are in debt financially, physically, emotionally, or spiritually. And He will also send you the ones that are discontent, they didn't like the way it was at the last place they were at.

God expects us to take these people, all of them, and minister to their needs first. And then God will build them up to make them into a mighty force for the work of His kingdom. And your role as the leader of that ministry or church is to guide them along their path of growth. Remember, if God can take the dust of the earth and make a man; He can take a man or woman and use you to make them into a mighty man or woman of God.

However, before you start looking at your people and trying to figure out what category they fall into; take a look in the mirror. Are you a mighty warrior ready to do the will of God by the power of the Holy Spirit? Or are you a troublemaker, or a debtor, or discontented? Jesus, help us to be the people that You want Your whole church to be.

MAY 19 || 1 SAMUEL 24:5

But then David's conscience began bothering him because he had cut Saul's robe.

Read: 1 Samuel 24:1-25:44

King Saul is pursuing David in hopes of killing him and eliminating him as a threat to 'his' kingdom. He pauses to relieve himself in a cave which just happens to be occupied by David and his men. David is encouraged by his men to kill Saul. Instead, he sneaks up and cuts off a part of his robe. As soon as he does, his conscience starts to bother him. He knows that he shouldn't have done it and recognizes that it was not pleasing to the LORD.

We might look at a story like this and wonder what the big deal is. Why would God be upset with David for simply cutting his robe? A study of David can teach us a lot about how God wants us to relate to our leaders. David looked at King Saul as his leader; placed in the position of leadership by God Himself. David trusted God to deal with Saul when He was ready to and in the way that He wanted to.

David did not feel free to do or say anything he wanted to as far as King Saul was concerned. Even though Saul was seeking his life and slandering him, David refused to speak against or attempt to harm Saul. The leaders in our life should be respected even when they are not worthy of respect. The Bible teaches that those leaders were placed there by God Himself. To speak against them is to question God's wisdom. To attempt to harm them is to fight against God.

We live in a country that promotes the exercise of 'free speech'. This means that no one can prevent us from speaking as our heart leads us to speak. For Christians, that should mean that we are free to speak about our faith without fear of repercussion. It should also mean that we speak with a fear of God that causes us to respect the leaders that He has allowed to lead us.

Because of Saul's sin, David had to flee and hide. There might come a time in your life where God calls you to depart from where you are because a leader's actions are harmful to you or to others. Until then, you are called by God to support your leaders to the best of your ability. This is true in your family, ministry, church, work, and country.

Attacking the leaders that God has placed in their positions above you is against God and will result in God's hand of judgment in your own life. God doesn't need our help dealing with His leaders. God wants followers that will do everything in their ability to bring a godly influence into even the most wicked of environments.

There are no perfect leaders and once we get into the habit of attacking our leaders because of their weaknesses, it is very difficult to stop. We start looking for weakness, instead of looking for their strengths and looking for ways to cover over their weaknesses. To the best of your ability pray for your leaders, encourage them, and look for ways to help them. Then trust them to God for everything else. Jesus, teach us to look up to our leaders, rather than down upon them.

Rick Lancaster | PLANTERS PERSPECTIVE

MAY 20 || 1 SAMUEL 26:9

"No!" David said. "Don't kill him. For who can remain innocent after attacking the LORD's anointed one?

Read: 1 Samuel 26:1-28:25

King Saul is still pursuing David and has chased him to the Wilderness of Ziph. Saul has three thousand of his best troops to attack David. And no matter what he does, God protects David from Saul. Saul should have had his focus on dealing with the Philistines rather than David and his few hundred men. Saul couldn't see past his selfish ambition that David wasn't his enemy.

This is the second occasion that David has been in a position to easily kill Saul. The first time Saul came into the cave that David and his were hiding in to relieve himself. David spared his life because he felt it wasn't his place to judge Saul. In today's reading David takes Abishai and walks right into the camp of King Saul and right past all those men that are there to protect him while they sleep.

Abishai is convinced that David should kill Saul because God had handed him over to David. David refuses and in so doing reveals a great truth that we need to understand about how God deals with his leaders. David refused to kill Saul because God had anointed him. He knew it was not his place to punish him; it was God's place to punish Saul. When a leader that God has placed in the body needs to be punished, it is God that will punish them.

To be deserving of punishment, you need to be in willful disobedience of God and you will have refused His attempts to correct you on numerous occasions. God is patient and full of grace and mercy but He will punish anyone that refuses to obey. David describes in the reading for today the three ways that God will punish His disobedient leaders. He will punish them Himself by withdrawing His hand of blessing and allowing the curse to fall upon them. Or He will allow them to experience the natural consequences of their sin. Or finally, He will use an enemy to punish them. In the case of Saul, God used the Philistines to punish Saul, ultimately ending his life in battle with them.

Nowhere in scripture will you find a place where God says that it is OK for us to attack those that are placed in authority over us. God is very clear on this, if they are in a position of authority over you, they are not your responsibility; they are God's. If they are in sin or are being disobedient to God, He will deal with them. Your role is to submit, encourage, exhort, support, and love that leader. If doing that compromises your relationship with God then you must take yourself out from under the authority of that leader quietly and respectfully. But before you do that, make sure it is not you that is in sin or being disobedient to God. Jesus, help us to stand with the leaders you have anointed.

MAY 21 || 1 SAMUEL 30:6

David was now in serious trouble because his men were very bitter about losing their wives and children, and they began to talk of stoning him. But David found strength in the LORD his God.

Read: 1 Samuel 29:1-31:13

David is in trouble again. King Saul is still hoping to catch him and kill him so he has fled to the Philistines. The Philistine commanders do not trust him, so they send David away from the upcoming battle. And when David and his six hundred men get back to their town, they find it burned to the ground by the Amalekites. All their wives and children and possessions are gone. This is too much for David's men and they turn on him and are talking about stoning him.

Among those taken away were David's two wives. Everything that they had was gone. They were in a foreign land and everything had been taken away from them. The text tells us that they grieved until they had no more strength to grieve.

As we lead God's ministries and churches, there are going to be times when we feel like David did here. Even as we attempt to lead our families we can feel as David did. On every side are enemies and everything that is important to us or has value has been taken away from you. And then even those that are closest to you, that you have fought and battled with, have turned on you. You feel incredibly, painfully, desperately alone. It is at those moments that we need to turn our eyes, as David did, to God.

David found strength in the Lord 'his' God. At that moment of his most desperate need David reminded himself that the awesome Creator of the universe was his God and that knowledge brought him the strength that he needed. David realized that his strength wasn't enough, because he didn't have any left.

Too many men and women of God forget this principle at just this time. God is our strength! Because David turned to God for strength and then for guidance, God helped David and his men get back everything that had been taken from them. It also appears from the text that they actually ended up with more than had been taken from them.

There will come a time in every leader's life, in every person's life when he or she will feel as David did. You will feel surrounded by enemies and everything that you treasure is gone. Will you do as David did? Will you get your strength from the Lord 'your' God? I pray that you will! Jesus, help us to look up every time things around us are looking down.

Rick Lancaster / PLANTERS PERSPECTIVE

MAY 22 || 2 SAMUEL 1:16

"You die self-condemned," David said, "for you yourself confessed that you killed the LORD's anointed one."

Read: 2 Samuel 1:1-2:11

King Saul and his sons died in battle with the Philistines at the end of 1 Samuel. 2 Samuel opens with the news of this defeat reaching David. The news is brought to David by a young Amalekite man. King Saul had asked his armor bearer to run him through but when he refused Saul fell on his own sword. It appears that Saul failed to kill himself and this young Amalekite came along and finished him off.

One of the great lessons of David's life is how a leader follows another leader. Even though David had been anointed to be the leader of Israel decades earlier, he refused to harm the man that God had anointed before him. He trusted God to deal with that man and so David did all he could to assist Saul even while Saul was trying to kill him.

One of the interesting side-notes on this account is the fact that the young man is an Amalekite. In 1 Samuel 15 Saul had been instructed to utterly destroy the nation of Amalek so that nothing remained of it. It was God's judgment upon a wicked nation. Saul obeyed but not completely. He and his men didn't destroy the things that pleased them. Among those spoils were likely young women. This young man is likely a descendant of one of those women that was spared on that day.

David doesn't give the young man a chance to explain or change his story but has him killed immediately. His hopes of reward are crushed as a sword ends his life suddenly. This young man was following the behaviors that were natural for people of the nations around Israel. He didn't know that God had called His people to be different.

God doesn't want us to conform to the world so that we can be successful. He wants us to be different. This young man got exactly what he deserved. The fact that he was alive was because the previous leader had failed to fully follow God. David was a man that didn't make that mistake. He was not perfect but his heart was fully devoted to the LORD.

Leaders of God's people, whether in families, ministries, or churches need to follow David's example of dealing with sin immediately and decisively. We can't look the other way or minimize it; we need to proactively and aggressively put it to spiritual death. That will mean doing some things that people in the world will not understand. That's all right; it is the LORD you will answer to, not them. Give your heart fully to the LORD and let Him direct your path and He will make you successful in whatever you do. Jesus, help us to give You all of our heart.

MAY 23 || 2 SAMUEL 3:36

This pleased the people very much. In fact, everything the king did pleased them!

Read: 2 Samuel 2:12-3:39

David is finally king over Judah. Eventually he will be king over all of Israel. Saul was the people's choice for a king and David was God's choice for a king. In our verse for the day we see why that makes a difference in the response of the people. Everything that David did pleased the people. More than that, it is said of David that he was a man after God's own heart. David was God's man and because he was, the things that He did pleased the people.

The lesson in that for us is that when we are in alignment with God's will and plan, things will go pretty well. It is an amazing thing that when we do what God wants us to that He can also make it so that everyone that we are in contact with are pleased by the things that we are doing. God is able to do that but it begins with us being exactly where God wants us to be.

Of course there are no guarantees on things like this. Because God's ways are so much higher than our ways, God's plan might include a little friction and opposition. King David is a perfect example of that. Even though David was God's man he had to deal with people that did things their way rather than God's way. We see that all through David's life.

If you have been chosen by God to lead His people, then you need to lead. One of the greatest blessings of life is the realization of being where God has called you to be and fulfilling the plan that He has for your life. The ways that God blesses you are as varied as the people that He blesses. The way that He will bless you is going to be different than the way that He blesses me. For some it will be peace, others will experience prosperity, and still others will experience a spiritual blessing that cannot be measured.

Leading or following we need to recognize who God wants to lead and then respond accordingly. In our verse, the people recognized that David was God's choice to lead the nation of Israel and they were pleased with all that he did as he followed the leading of the Lord.

Too often people challenge the authority that God has given to people that He has called to lead his people and church. And because they are challenging this authority, nothing pleases them. Sometimes this is because they feel that they should be in authority or that some other person should be in authority. A study of David's life will show just how sinful that type of attitude is. Even though David was anointed to be the next king of Israel, it was twenty years before he ascended to the throne. David waited patiently for God's plan to come to pass. Jesus, help us to wait.

Rick Lancaster / PLANTERS PERSPECTIVE

MAY 24 || 2 SAMUEL 5:2

For a long time, even while Saul was our king, you were the one who really led Israel. And the LORD has told you, 'You will be the shepherd of my people Israel. You will be their leader.'

Read: 2 Samuel 4:1-6:23

All the tribes of Israel gather together to proclaim that David is the king of Israel. Saul, Israel's first king has recently been killed in battle. After a short period of upheaval, everyone gets together and names David as the second king of the nation of Israel. The interesting thing about that to me is that this is about twenty years after the prophet told Saul that the kingdom was no longer his and that it was to be given to someone else. Twenty years earlier God told Samuel to go to Jesse the Bethlemite and anoint one of his sons as the next king of Israel.

Samuel did as he was told and anointed David, Jesse's youngest son, to be the next king of Israel. Estimates place David's age somewhere in his mid teens; he was a very young man. For the next twenty years Saul continued to rule over the nation that was no longer his to rule. And even though David was given a couple of opportunities to kill Saul and take his rightful place, he waited until God removed Saul from the throne of Israel.

Being in a place like David's must have been very difficult. He knew that he was the rightful anointed king of Israel and yet it took twenty or more years for him to be recognized by the people. It must have been especially difficult for him as he became increasingly successful at everything that he did.

You may be in a place like David's; you know in your heart that God has called you to something big and yet those around you cannot see it. You know that it is the call of God on your life but the doors seem to stay locked no matter what you do. If that is you then take a lesson from the life of David and from our verse for the day. God called David to be the leader, the shepherd, of the nation of Israel. Even though he was not given the title of 'king' he did what he could to fulfill the calling that God had on his life.

Are you fulfilling the calling of God on your life even though others have not recognized it yet? David was continually faced with danger and attacks as he attempted to fulfill God's call. You need to do what you can no matter what the opposition is or what others say; be faithful to God. God used the twenty years that David waited to assume the role that he was waiting for to train him to be the king that God would describe as 'a man after My own heart'. In this time of waiting, God is training you to be the man or woman that He desires you to be. In His perfect timing you will assume the role that He anointed you for. Jesus, help us to wait for You to open the doors.

MAY 25 || 2 SAMUEL 8:15

David reigned over all Israel and was fair to everyone.

Read: 2 Samuel 7:1-8:18

David is widely regarded as the best king that Israel ever had. During his reign the nation of Israel was unified and defeated many of their long-time enemies in the land of Canaan. Few men had the effect on the nation of Israel that King David did. It is interesting to me that the Holy Spirit chose to describe him as 'fair' in this text.

We don't often think of fairness as an indicator of the quality of a leader. But if the Holy Spirit thought it was important enough to be used to describe the best king that Israel had then we should consider it important enough to take a look at in our own leadership.

Fairness is one of the principles that we learn about early in life. Though it is usually based on our interpretation of what is not fair. All of us have seen children complain that something is not fair and it usually revolves around the fact that they didn't get what they thought they should have. It is usually during our childhood that we learn that fairness is not about getting what we think we deserve. Fairness is getting what is right for the person and the situation. And sometimes that means that someone else gets more than you do or something better than you do.

As leaders in our families, ministries and churches fairness is a matter of great importance. Strife and division often takes place when someone feels that the leader has not been fair. But the challenge is that as the leader you have to make decisions that can result in feelings of unfairness. King David would have been faced with those decisions every day. How is it that he was described as being fair to everyone?

Fairness has very little to do with how people feel. It has everything to do with the heart of the leader. A leader that loves God and others more than himself is more likely to be fair. A leader that considers others more highly than themselves is more likely to be fair. A leader that is not looking at every situation as a way to promote themselves is more likely to be fair. After all, it's not about you.

Leaders of God's families, ministries, and churches should be fair. Fair leaders care more about those that they are serving than they do about themselves. Fair leaders are looking for ways to make sure that those that have been entrusted to their care have everything that they need; even if it means giving up what the leader wants and needs. Fair leaders think of God first, others second, and self last. Jesus, teach us to play fair.

Rick Lancaster / PLANTERS PERSPECTIVE

MAY 26 || 2 SAMUEL 9:1

One day David began wondering if anyone in Saul's family was still alive, for he promised Jonathan that he would show kindness to them.

Read: 2 Samuel 9:1-11:27

David is firmly established as the king of Israel. Things begin to settle into a routine and David's mind wanders from the affairs of the kingdom to reflect upon the past. In doing that he remembers a promise that he made to Jonathan, King Saul's son. Jonathan was David's friend and David had promised that he would take care of Jonathan's family. This chapter describes King David fulfilling that promise in a very generous manner.

As I read a chapter of the Bible like this I find myself asking why this particular account is in there. Jonathan's son, Mephibosheth, is crippled in both feet. We will hear about him again briefly during the account of Absalom's revolt. He seems to be an insignificant character in Scripture. Why did the LORD inspire this particular account to be recorded? The answer is simple; the account is not really about Mephibosheth, it is about David's character.

David was a man of great character. He takes Mephibosheth into the palace and treats him as one of his own sons. He blesses him with all of Saul's land and provides servants to take care of it. To keep his promise to Jonathan, he didn't need to do that much. David is described in Scripture by God as a man after God's own heart. That is important for us to keep in mind as we go into some of the next chapters of David's life. There we will see his sin with Bathsheba and ultimately the murder of her husband.

David was not perfect. He made mistakes. And yet God used him powerfully to accomplish great things for the LORD. David was used by God because his heart belonged to the LORD. His character reflected his love for the LORD even though his sinful nature occasionally peeked out.

David kept his promise to Jonathan through Mephibosheth even though he could have gotten away with not keeping it. Or he certainly didn't have to keep it as graciously as he did. Mephibosheth grew to love and respect David greatly. How many of us can say that we have even considered keeping a promise in such a way?

David's position and power did not exclude him from keeping promises and maintaining a high character. In fact, his position and power required that he do so. That is how it should be for each of us as well. If you are in a position of authority and you have made a promise, keep it! Regardless of the cost or inconvenience. Jesus, help us to be faithful to you by being faithful to our promises.

MAY 27 || 2 SAMUEL 12:28

Now bring the rest of the army and finish the job, so you will get credit for the victory instead of me.

Read: 2 Samuel 12:1-31

Joab is the commander of Israel's army. King David sent him and the army to Rabbah to besiege it and to conquer it. As usual Joab has been successful at the task that was assigned to him. He has captured the water supply to the city. This means that they are just about to conquer the city. Joab in great humility calls for King David and asks him to come out and claim the victory rather than Joab defeating the enemy and getting credit for it. David responds by coming out and finishing off the enemy and taking the crown from the king of Rabbah.

At first glance this looks like a very noble thing that Joab did and in many respects that is exactly what it is. There is something else that warrants our attention in this matter. 2 Samuel 11 begins with a statement that David stayed at home at a time when kings would go out to war. Because David stayed behind he fell into sin with Bathsheba. This sin was compounded when David had her husband, Uriah, killed. Joab knew at least partly about the sins that David had committed. Joab called King David to be where he was supposed to be.

There is a lesson in that for those of us that are called to follow someone. No matter how good a man or woman might be they are still human and they still carry the sin nature within them. We might like to believe that our leaders will never stumble or fall but the fact is that they all probably will. Those closest to them will see it more clearly than others might. It is then that Joab's behavior becomes so important to us.

Joab called King David to come out to do those things that he knew that he was supposed to be doing. Joab knew that David had committed the sin of murder and yet rather than abandoning him and rebuking him he humbly encouraged him to do what he should have been doing in the first place. Joab knew that God would deal with David's sin; he didn't have to.

We need to love our leaders enough to help them to get to where they are supposed to be; even if it means overlooking some sin in their lives. If they are a leader that has a heart for God, then God is going to deal with their sins. Of course there are times when God would call us to confront our leaders in love and help them to see their sin as Joab does later with David. Then there are times to call to your leaders and encourage them as best you can to walk the higher walk that God called them to.

God would ultimately call King David 'a man after My own heart' because of the way that David would respond to God. Let us be men and women that will help our leaders rather than hindering them. Jesus, teach us to trust You to discipline our leaders.

Rick Lancaster / PLANTERS PERSPECTIVE

MAY 28 || 2 SAMUEL 13:15

Then suddenly Amnon's love turned to hate, and he hated her even more than he had loved her. "Get out of here!" he snarled at her.

Read: 2 Samuel 13:1-39

King David had many sons. Solomon is probably best known and would ultimately succeed David as king of Israel. Absalom and Amnon are not as well known but through them we see God's prediction of unrest within David's family fulfilled. One of the consequences of David's sin with Bathsheba was that there would be conflict within his home for the rest of his life. Much of it will be centered on Absalom.

Absalom had a beautiful sister, Tamar, and she caught the attention of Amnon. Amnon was her half-brother. King David was their father, but they had different mothers. Amnon saw her and fell in love with her; in fact, he became obsessed with her. Amnon conspires to have Tamar come and tend to him and then rapes her. Our verse tells us that once he had his way with her, his love turned to hatred and he rejected her.

The account doesn't tell us their ages but it is not hard for me to imagine them both in their late teens. If you have ever raised teenagers, then you know how this could have happened. This is a time of life when passions run wild and make radical swings from hot to cold in a moment. It certainly doesn't justify Amnon's actions but it is easy enough to see how it might have occurred.

What I think is the greater lesson in this is the effect that a father can have in a child's life. Fathers have been endowed with a supernatural ability to influence their children. If used properly, meaning as God directs, they can help their children grow to healthy, productive maturity. If neglected or abused, the children will follow the influence of their peers or their own selfish desires.

Of course, just because we use our influence as well as we can doesn't guarantee that our children won't make foolish decisions, but it certainly improves the odds in your favor. It should our goal as parents to give our children the best chances we can in life to make the best possible choices. To do otherwise is to condemn them to a life of pain and suffering.

As a result of Amnon's selfish, undisciplined actions Tamar lived as a 'desolate woman' in her brother Absalom's house. This meant that she did not marry, because no man would have her after having been raped. Two years later Absalom schemed against Amnon and murdered him. This resulted in Absalom running away from Israel to escape the consequences of his actions.

In one event we see the lives of many people of one family altered forever. As fathers we need to do everything we can to prevent these kinds of things from happening. We do that by leading our family as the LORD directs and by using the supernatural influence that He has given us to help them grow to maturity in the LORD. Jesus, teach us to lead them to You.

MAY 29 || 2 SAMUEL 14:1

Joab realized how much the king longed to see Absalom.

Read: 2 Samuel 14:1-15:22

Absalom has been banished from David's presence because he killed David's son Amnon, Absalom's half-brother. Amnon had raped and then rejected Absalom's sister Tamar. Two years after the rape, Absalom took revenge upon Amnon. David was reconciled to the death of Amnon and was now missing his son Absalom.

Joab recognized this state of mind in his king and decided to do something about it. He brought a woman in to make a request of the king that caused him to look at the matter of Absalom's banishment from a different perspective. David did and allowed Absalom to return to Jerusalem and ultimately their relationship was restored, at least for a little while.

Joab knew his king well enough to see that there was something that David needed that he couldn't provide for himself. David had banished Absalom and this decision was causing him much pain. Joab knew that David was a man of integrity and would not readily reverse his decision. Joab, through this woman, brought the matter before David so they he could see it from a different perspective.

In this Joab showed two characteristics that every person that follows a leader must exhibit. The first is awareness. You must be aware of the needs and emotions of your leader. He or she may not be able to express what is going on inside of them and they may not be able to even see the source of their pain or discomfort. For our leaders to be effective, we must love them enough to care about what is going on in their lives.

The second characteristic of a follower that will help his leader is courage. Joab showed great courage when he brought this matter before the king. Joab couldn't have known how the king might respond to his approach but he cared enough about David to risk it. We must have the courage to go to our leaders in love and humility to help them to see the matter from a different perspective.

Leaders are not perfect and they are not invincible. All leaders will go through times when they are not sure about themselves or their decisions. All leaders will have circumstances that challenge them. A good leader has good people that are there to lovingly help them through their times of need. In fact, without good people fulfilling that role, it is difficult for a leader to achieve success. For a leader to be a leader, they must have people following them. Those people have the responsibility to love that leader and to help him or her through whatever they might be going through. Jesus, teach us to be good followers.

Rick Lancaster / PLANTERS PERSPECTIVE

MAY 30 || 2 SAMUEL 16:10

"No!" the king said. "What am I going to do with you sons of Zeruiah! If the LORD has told him to curse me, who am I to stop him?"

Read: 2 Samuel 15:23-16:23

King David is fleeing for his life. His son Absalom has crowned himself king and is coming to Jerusalem where he hopes to find his father, whom he intends to kill. Rather than exposing the city and its people to the destruction of war, David leaves with his family and those that are loyal to him. Along the way this guy, Shimei comes out to curse David. Shimei is upset because David took the kingdom from Saul. Of course David didn't take the kingdom at all; God gave it to him. But as far as Shimei is concerned David stole it from Saul and he feels that David was now getting what he deserved.

Abishai doesn't like that this guy is cursing the king and so he begs David to let him go and cut off Shimei's head. David tells him 'no'. David is exhibiting a Christian trait a thousand years before Jesus taught it; to bless those that curse you. You can be sure that David wasn't too happy about this guy cursing him but then that was the least of his concerns; his own son was out to take by force the kingdom from him.

As you read this text, do you wonder how you might have responded to Shimei's curses? Would you have responded like Abishai or like David? If we were honest with ourselves, most of us would admit that we would be most likely to respond like Abishai.

David didn't know what was in the heart of Shimei and David didn't know whether or not God had told Shimei to curse him. David preferred to let God be his defender than to try to defend himself. This can be hard to do when someone is hurling curses and stones at you. There is a part of you that rages to get into a fight and defend your own honor; that is called 'pride'. Pride is a deadly sin that we can allow in our lives.

God allowed Shimei to curse David for reasons that we may never understand. God may allow someone into your life that will also do the same to you. They curse you and hurl spiritual and emotional stones at you for reasons that may be based completely on their wrong understanding of what God is doing in your life. How we respond will be a testimony of our faith and trust in God. David believed that God would defend him and he had faith that God would turn Shimei's curses to blessings.

In 2 Samuel 19 we see that David's trust and faith are validated as God brings David back to Jerusalem after Absalom is killed and his rebellion ended. The first person to meet King David at the Jordan River is Shimei to confess his sin to the king. Again Abishai wants to kill him but King David graciously forgives Shimei. Sadly, David doesn't forget the sin of Shimei and he tells his son Solomon to kill Shimei after his own death. Jesus, help us to be forgetful forgivers of those who maliciously curse us.

PLANTERS PERSPECTIVE / *A Devotional*

MAY 31 || 2 SAMUEL 17:14

Then Absalom and all the leaders of Israel said, "Hushai's advice is better than Ahithophel's." For the LORD had arranged to defeat the counsel of Ahithophel, which was really the better plan, so that he could bring disaster upon Absalom!

Read: 2 Samuel 17:1-29

Absalom, King David's son has rebelled against his father and is attempting to take David's throne from him. So far he has been pretty successful. David has evacuated the City of David so that Absalom will not come and besiege it. To cement his hold upon the throne, Absalom must destroy his father. So he calls in his advisors.

Ahithophel is loyal to Absalom and suggests that Absalom attack David immediately before David has a chance to gather troops or get into a fortified city. Hushai is loyal to King David and suggests that Absalom wait and gather the whole army of Israel together before attacking David. Absalom rejects Ahithophel's plan and accepts the plan that Hushai proposed.

All of that seems like pretty normal stuff until you get to the verse for the day. According to today's verse Absalom picked the wrong plan, and not because he wasn't wise enough but because God had arranged it so he would choose the wrong plan. God had determined to 'bring disaster upon Absalom.' Part of God's plan to accomplish that was to defeat Ahithophel's advice.

We sometimes forget that God is God and that there is nothing that He can't do. There are some things that He chooses not to do but there is nothing that He can't do. We often think that God is not going to make my choices for me; He leaves me the freewill to choose for myself. That is true but that doesn't mean that God can't cause us to choose what He wants rather than what we want.

Today's text is a great example of that. Absalom was outside of the will of God. Absalom wanted to destroy his father and the best plan presented to him was Ahithophel's. God's plan was to bring disaster upon Absalom and He caused Absalom to pick Hushai's plan which was the inferior plan. The LORD influenced Absalom's decision to accomplish His plan.

We might wonder why God doesn't do that all the time so that we are always doing what He desires rather than making some of the foolish decisions that we do. If He did do that our will would not come into the picture and we would not have the kind of relationship with Him that He desires. It is often because of the poor choices and bad decisions that we grow to recognize our great need for a close relationship with Him. If the LORD always influenced us to make only the right choices, then there would be no choice at all. God chooses to let us choose, but there are times when God influences the choice according to His will and plan. Understanding when that is happening is one of the great mysteries of life. Jesus, teach us look for You in all of our choices.

Rick Lancaster | PLANTERS PERSPECTIVE

JUNE

JUNE 1 || 2 SAMUEL 19:2

As the troops heard of the king's deep grief for his son, the joy of that day's victory was turned into deep sadness.

Read: 2 Samuel 18:1-19:10

Absalom has just been killed by Joab after he had rebelled against his father King David. Absalom was leading the entire army of Israel against the forces that had remained loyal to his father with the intent of killing David and thus cementing his hold upon the throne.

David had instructed his generals and commanders to deal kindly with Absalom. Even though Absalom was trying to kill him, David didn't want Absalom to be harmed. Joab knew that as long as Absalom was allowed to live that he would not cease trying to get the throne from his father. King David is crushed by the news that his son Absalom is dead. As a man with two sons of my own, I can't say that my response would be any different than David's.

The troops are returning from this tremendous victory. They have just defeated a much stronger force and defended their king. This was a time for celebration and rejoicing. But as they enter the city they are faced with the knowledge that their king is in deep mourning over the loss of his son. Instead of marching in as a victorious army, they sneak into the city as though they are ashamed of what they have done.

Joab confronts his king and lets him know the effect that his grief is having on the people. His words are not words of comfort, but strong and harsh. David was king and his people needed him now. Joab knew that if David didn't do something immediately that David might not regain the kingdom and the kingdom would collapse into chaos.

David was mourning his son. And the problem with grief is that it is a very selfish emotion. Grief only cares about what I have lost. Grief seldom cares what impact it has on those that are around us. Grief can turn a victorious time of celebration into a time of shame and defeat. There is a time and place for grief. Grief in moderation is healthy and cleansing. But as leaders in our families, ministries, and churches we do not have the luxury of allowing our emotions to control us. We must exercise self-control and deliberately think of what the people around us need, not just who we are missing.

David got up and went down to the gate of the city. Word soon spread that he was there and it encouraged the people and they came to him at the gate. As Christians, even in our deepest grief, we must consider others over ourselves. And as leaders we may need to lay our time of grieving aside so that we can minister to the needs of those that God has called us to shepherd. Jesus, help us to think of others more than ourselves even when our hearts are crushed.

JUNE 2 || 2 SAMUEL 19:41

But the men of Israel complained to the king that the men of Judah had gotten to do most of the work in helping him cross the Jordan.

Read: 2 Samuel 19:11-20:13

David is in the process of coming home after the death of Absalom and being reconfirmed as king of Israel. They have just crossed over the Jordan River and the text suggests that the tribe of Judah did all the work getting David and his family and the others that were traveling with him across the river. This apparently offends the other ten tribes of Israel and so they start complaining about it.

It is absolutely amazing the things that people will complain about. A revolution has just been thrown down and it is a time of celebration. The rightful king is returning to his throne. And these people are complaining because they didn't get to carry David's luggage across the river.

Then one man, Sheba, a troublemaker, is so upset that he incites another revolt. He obviously wasn't paying attention during the last one. He leads the men of Israel away from David and goes off to build support for his position. It doesn't take long before he loses his head over this.

People will complain over the littlest things and they will allow their complaints to escalate to the point that it becomes incredibly damaging. Sheba and the other complainers were upset because they didn't get to carry David's bags. And they took this so seriously that they were willing to go to war over it. It is amazing the foolish things that we will complain about. And it is even more amazing the things that we will allow these complaints to develop into.

Complainers are never satisfied and have the potential to split families, ministries, and churches. As Christians we must resist the temptation to complain. It accomplishes nothing except to create dissension and discord. The Bible teaches that we should not allow anything to leave our lips that is not edifying. That means that we should be building up, not tearing down.

As leaders in families, ministries, and churches we must do everything that we can to curb our own complaining and then do everything we can to curb complaining around us. Complainers are contagious and they can infect entire churches. In love, we must teach people to appreciate what they have and not to complain about what they don't. It seems silly to start a war over who carried the king's dirty laundry over the Jordan River but churches have been split over equally silly things. Jesus, teach us to be forgiving and content so that no word of complaint ever leaves our lips.

JUNE 3 || 2 SAMUEL 21:17

But Abishai son of Zeruiah came to his rescue and killed the Philistine. After that, David's men declared, "You are not going out to battle again! Why should we risk snuffing out the light of Israel?"

Read: 2 Samuel 20:14-21:22

David is out in a battle with the Philistines again. During this battle David becomes weary and is cornered by one of the descendants of the giants who is about to kill him. One of David's men, Abishai, comes and kills the giant to save David. The men then all agree that David should not come out to battle any longer. They are concerned that he will be killed.

David was a warrior-king. He had fought in many battles and been victorious. Some of those accounts, like the one with Goliath, are the best known stories in the Bible. But things have changed. The biggest thing that has changed is David; he is a lot older than he was when he fought Goliath. David's men see that age has caught up to their king and so they discourage him from joining them in any future battles.

It is not difficult to imagine that David resisted this suggestion at first but ultimately saw the wisdom in it. There is a lesson in this for us as well. As we go through life there will be a few things that will be the trademarks of our life. They are the things that people know about us when they look at our lives. In David's life it was his skill in battle. In Sampson's life it was strength. In Solomon's life it was wisdom. We can often find some one thing that defines our lives.

The problem arises when the circumstances of our life change. Sometimes the very thing that we are best known for becomes a liability. In David's life his prowess in battle could not be carried by his physical body; he was no longer able to fight like his reputation. He could have tried to continue but it ultimately would have cost him his life. His men were not willing to sacrifice David on the battlefield.

His men were not being cruel or prideful; they cared about their king. They believed he was of more value in the palace than on the battlefield. David could have let his pride get in the way in this but it appears that he did not and this was the last battle that David fought.

As the circumstances of our lives change we must be prepared to change along with them. It was as a warrior that David ascended to the throne but once there God wanted him to be a king. The warrior would never be totally gone from David but his role needed to change to match his circumstances. The pathways of life are not straight, well-lit, and filled with signs directing us. That is why it is so important for us to have an intimate relationship with our God. The closer we are to Him, the fewer times we will find ourselves backed into a corner with a giant trying to kill us. Jesus, teach us to stay close.

JUNE 4 || 2 SAMUEL 23:8

These are the names of David's mightiest men. The first was Jashobeam the Hacmonite, who was commander of the Three—the three greatest warriors among David's men. He once used his spear to kill eight hundred enemy warriors in a single battle.

Read: 2 Samuel 22:1-23:23

In today's reading we learn of David's Mighty Men. These guys did some amazing things. They were indeed mighty in the deeds that they did. The fascinating thing to me about them is that there is very little said about them in the Scriptures. These guys were a vital part of David's army and played a significant role in many his conquests and yet they are given only a minor reference, a footnote in the Bible.

These men were faithful and loyal to David and did not hesitate to risk their lives for their king. It can be said that they poured out their lives for him. What made these men 'Mighty' was their dedication and loyalty. These men cared about what their king wanted more than what they were going to get out of it.

We also have a king that deserves our dedication and loyalty; Jesus Christ. How we relate to our King will determine if we someday will earn the label of Mighty men and women of our King. Men and women of God must be dedicated to the King. To be dedicated means that your whole life is committed to and revolves around the needs and wants of the king. To be dedicated is to be set aside for a special use and purpose. The truly mighty men and women of God are not concerned what the world thinks or does, except as the King directs them to care.

Mighty men and women of God are loyal to the King. That means that they put their interests behind those of the King. The King will sometimes ask us to do things that we don't want to do or that we are afraid to do. He might ask us to do things that we might think are beneath us. The loyal man or woman of God will do whatever is asked of them regardless how they feel or think about it.

The main characteristic of a mighty man or woman of God is that they do not expect to get the credit for their efforts; they expect the King to get the credit for what they did. If you are looking for recognition or respect or awards for the things that you are doing for God then it is very unlikely that you will ever become a Mighty man or woman of God. The mighty ones do not even expect to be a footnote in God's plan; that is called humility. David's men were humble men that were mighty because of their humility, dedication, and loyalty. We have got to stop being so consumed with being mighty men and women of God and start being consumed with being humble, dedicated, and loyal. Jesus, help us to stop looking for the recognition of men and start looking for the King.

JUNE 5 || 2 SAMUEL 24:15

So the LORD sent a plague upon Israel that morning, and it lasted for three days. Seventy thousand people died throughout the nation.

Read: 2 Samuel 23:24-24:25

King David decides to count the people of the nation of Israel. That does not seem like that big of a deal but God had forbidden it because it would be a source of pride for the king. Joab even tried to dissuade David from taking the census but he insisted. Joab obeyed his king and counted the people as he was told. David then felt the conviction of the Lord in his heart and he went to God and confessed his sin before Him. God sends the prophet Gad to David to give him a choice of three punishments. David selects the third option which is a three day plague. In the three days that follow seventy thousand people die. David's punishment was that seventy thousand of his people died.

When a leader makes a mistake, it is often the people that are following him that pay the greatest price. In my own heart this truth is constantly before me. If I make a mistake or if I sin, I have no problem experiencing the consequences of that. That is easy for me to accept. But the thought that my sin or my mistake might cause others suffering and consequences is very painful to me. It keeps me from sinning and it keeps me dependent upon God.

Our sins and poor decisions seldom affect only us. And often the consequences of our sins and mistakes will be felt by those people that are closest to us. The very ones that we are called to protect and to keep safe are the ones that will suffer because of our failures. Few things should hurt our hearts like the thought of this happening in our lives.

No matter where you find yourself leading, your home, your workplace, your ministry, or your church you have the potential to bring a plague upon those around you. A leader like David would be greatly grieved by the thought of people suffering because of his failure. It will not absolutely guarantee that we won't sin, but it should deter us most of the time from being willfully disobedient to God.

David deliberately sinned against God and God punished him by sending a plague that killed seventy thousand people. We don't need to be concerned that every little sin or mistake is going to cost someone their life. God is gracious and merciful and His punishment fits the sin. But if we get to the place where we are doing what we want rather than what God wants, He will deal with us and we will probably not like the way He does it. Jesus, help us to care so much about the people around us that we don't expose them to risk of punishment because of our sin.

Rick Lancaster / PLANTERS PERSPECTIVE

JUNE 6 || 1 KINGS 1:5

About that time David's son Adonijah, whose mother was Haggith, decided to make himself king in place of his aged father. So he provided himself with chariots and horses and recruited fifty men to run in front of him.

Read: 1 Kings 1-53

This is one of those odd accounts in scripture that you might wonder what the point is. Adonijah decides that he wants to be king in the place of his father King David. The problem with that idea is God has already selected Solomon to be the next king and David has already announced that to the whole world.

There is a sense in the text that Adonijah was spoiled as a child; David never disciplined him in any way. That might explain his actions; he might have just decided one day that he should be king rather than Solomon and so he acted upon his desires. There is a message in that alone about men fulfilling their role as fathers to their children; especially to their sons.

The thing that struck me about this text is that Adonijah managed to get Joab and Abiathar to agree to his plan. Joab was David's army commander and Abiathar was one of the chief priests. Joab had been with David from very early in his time as king. It is difficult to understand fully why these two men would do something like this. King David was close to death and a new king was going to be selected; it is possible that they thought Adonijah would be a better king than Solomon.

In life, ministry, and church there will come times when there is a need for a change in leadership. Life happens and things change! This is one of the must vulnerable times for ministries and churches and any other organization because it is then that the people looking to advance themselves are most likely to act. As is the case with Adonijah, they can act very foolishly. He had no chance of success and yet he acted anyway

This can create great strife and division. From our text, we know that Nathan handled it very well and there was very little fallout from it. As we approach the inevitable changes that must take place within our ministries, we should do so upon our knees. We should be praying that God's chosen people will be raised up to the places that he wants them and those that would try to take advantage would be held back from acting. This is not likely to prevent it from happening but it will prepare your heart for it when it does.

Ministry and life is about people and people have a tendency to do the wrong things. As leaders, we should be ready for that through an active prayer life and because of a sincere desire to shepherd the flock of God that has been entrusted to us. Sheep have a tendency to wander wherever they want to and sometimes it is the sheep that are closest to you that wander the farthest. We don't need to fear it; we need to expect it and prepare for it. Jesus, help us to stay close to the Good Shepherd as we shepherd Your flock.

JUNE 7 || 1 KINGS 2:3

Observe the requirements of the Lord your God and follow all his ways. Keep each of the laws, commands, regulations, and stipulations written in the law of Moses so that you will be successful in all you do and wherever you go.

Read: 1 Kings 2:1-3:2

King David is now very old and will die soon. Before he dies he calls his son Solomon to himself and gives him some last minute instructions. He tells Solomon to take care of some people for him. Some he tells him to be kind to and others he instructs Solomon to arrange for a bloody death for. In this short section of scripture there is an interesting study in the contrasts of David's life. But that is for another time.

His first instruction to Solomon has to do with the Law of Moses. David is very specific about what he thinks Solomon should do with these laws. David told Solomon to observe, follow, and keep them. And seemingly to make sure there were no loopholes in his statement David told Solomon to do these things with the laws, commands, regulations, and stipulations.

To observe carries with it the idea of studying. The kings of Israel were told to write out a copy of the Law of Moses when they took the throne and they were to keep the Law with them. This personally hand-written copy was to be a continual reminder of who they were to answer to; God. Only as we study God's Word can we truly get to know the God that we serve. Our studies of His Word form the basis of all our understanding of life and this world that we are in.

David told Solomon to follow all of 'his ways'. This means that Solomon was to obey what was written within the Law of Moses. It is not enough to know God's Word, we need to obey it. If we are not following the Lord's directions as found in His Word we can be sure that we are going the wrong way. Sadly, this is what happened to Solomon.

Solomon is also instructed to keep these laws as well. The word 'keep' carries the idea of guarding and protecting. God's Word is a precious thing and should be guarded, first in our hearts and then in our lives and in the lives of those around us. Frequently in Scripture we are counseled to guard our hearts. This is because where our heart dwells is where our love is. God wants us to love Him and that is more easily done as we guard God's Word within our hearts.

David ended this verse with a promise. If Solomon would observe, follow, and keep the laws, commands, regulations, and stipulations he would be successful in everything he did and everywhere he went. That is a promise that I can really embrace; I want to be successful in everything and everywhere. For that to happen I simply need to observe, follow, and keep. Jesus, help me hide Your Word in my heart.

JUNE 8 || 1 KINGS 3:28

Word of the king's decision spread quickly throughout all Israel, and the people were awed as they realized the great wisdom God had given him to render decisions with justice.

Read: 1 Kings 3:3-4:34

God blessed King Solomon with great wisdom; greater wisdom than anyone else that lived. Because of this great wisdom the toughest cases of justice were brought to him so that he could judge fairly, when the local judges could not. We will see as the story of Solomon's life unfolds over the next few weeks that this wisdom did not remain as it is here. Because of disobedience Solomon's wisdom was polluted by the ways of the world and ended up no better than anyone else's.

Solomon's life is a sobering example that having everything does not give us a happy or successful life. Solomon started very well but finished very poorly. Solomon is known for many things; wisdom being one of the greatest things. This wisdom was a gift given from God to Solomon so that he could rule over the people of God wisely. God was pleased by Solomon's request for wisdom and also blessed Solomon with wealth, fame, and protection from his enemies.

While none of us are likely to be blessed in the way that Solomon was, each of us was blessed with some special gift that God has given us for the purpose of blessing His people. Solomon knew exactly what that thing was that he was given by God for His people. It is our responsibility to determine what gift or gifts that God has given us for His people. Once we have determined what those gifts are we are then expected by God to use them; not for ourselves but for the benefit of God's people.

When Solomon exercised his God-given gift, the people were awed and gave glory to God. That is exactly the response that God is looking for. When people see us exercising the gifts that God has given us they will be amazed. They will recognize that what we are doing is beyond us and so they will understand that it is God at work. And as people see God working in our lives their hearts will be turned to Him.

But there is a terrible temptation that comes with exercising the gifts that God has given us, to take credit for any part of the work that God did. Our flesh seems to think that just because God chose to use us for some small part of His work here on the earth that we should get some of the glory. The problem with that is that all of the glory belongs to God and to take any of it for yourself is stealing from God; which He frowns upon. If we are faithful to exercise our gifts to serve God by serving His people He will glorify us. It is then up to us to give that glory back to God. By doing that we open up the door for God to give us greater gifts, which will result in greater glory for God, which will result in greater blessings in our own lives. Jesus, give us the greater gifts so that we can bring greater glory to You.

JUNE 9 || 1 KINGS 6:12-13

Concerning the temple you are building, if you keep all my laws and regulations and obey all my commandments, I will fulfill through you the promise I made to your father, David. I will live among the people of Israel and never forsake my people.

Read: 1 Kings 5:1-6:38

Solomon is in the process of building the temple to the LORD that his father David wanted to build. God told David that he was not allowed to build it because of all the wars that he had fought. It was to be done by his son Solomon. God then promised David that if he would keep God's laws and regulations and obey His commandments that the nation of Israel would enjoy a special relationship with God. He would live among them. The Lord is now repeating this promise to Solomon.

That is an astounding promise. The LORD said that He would live among them. God had made no such promise to any other nation or group of people. He wanted to have a very personal relationship with them. It doesn't take a lot of imagination to figure out that there would be some real advantages to having the Almighty Creator of the universe living among you.

There was one condition on that promise and that was that they do what God says. And one of the primary commands that God wanted obeyed was that they worship no other gods. God is a jealous God. That means that He will not share our affections with anyone or anything. To please God He must be our only God.

All of God's laws, regulations, and commandments were meant to make the nation of Israel a separated nation. The Lord wanted to separate them out from the rest of the world. He wanted them to be peculiar. His intention was to bless them so abundantly that other nations would see and desire to know why. It was also God's intention that the nation of Israel bless the whole world by showing them God.

Sadly, Solomon didn't do his part and the nation of Israel started into a spiritual decline that ended up with them being kicked out of the Promised Land and sent away into exile. God is not finished with the Jews. In the end-times He will restore them back to the place that He has always desired for them.

In the meantime, the church is to step up and do its part to draw the whole world to the Lord God. Thankfully, none of us is responsible for reaching the world for Jesus Christ. Our responsibility is just the same as it was stated to Solomon; obey God. If we will simply do what He tells us we can rest assured of the fact that He will live with us and never forsake us. Obedience will lead us into a full and abundant life. The Almighty Creator of the Universe wants to live with you. All you have to do to see that happen is say, 'Yes, LORD', whenever He speaks to you. Jesus, help us to always say 'Yes' to You.

Rick Lancaster / PLANTERS PERSPECTIVE

JUNE 10 || 1 KINGS 7:51

So King Solomon finished all his work on the Temple of the LORD. Then Solomon brought all the gifts his father, David, had dedicated—the silver, the gold, and the other utensils—and he stored them in the treasuries of the LORD's Temple.

Read: 1 Kings 7:1-51

Solomon faithfully completed the work that God had given him through his father King David. The temple has been built and is a stunning example of the things that men can do for God. It took seven years and a tremendous amount of wealth to construct this temple and Solomon followed the plans precisely to build this tremendous structure. It is here that I believe we see what happened to Solomon that ultimately led to his poor finish after such a spectacular beginning. Solomon finished the work that God gave him to do.

Actually I don't believe that is true at all; Solomon only finished the first big project that God gave him. There is no indication as you read about Solomon's life that he went back to God after completing the temple and asking Him what God wanted him to do next. Instead you see Solomon focusing on his palaces and wives and building his kingdom. It seems that Solomon believed he had done everything he needed to do for God and so he was doing what he wanted for his own life.

Obviously we can't know what was in Solomon's heart but we can look at the evidence of his life. The more time that passed after completing the temple, the further away from God Solomon seemed to get. It proves that there is a direct connection between our service to God and our relationship with Him. Our relationship with God is linked closely with our service to Him. It is impossible to have a close relationship with Jesus if you are not doing something for Him in service.

We can't sit back and look behind us to see what great things we did for God. The question is: 'What are you doing for God right now?' Success in the past is not a guarantee of success in the future or does it guarantee a close relationship with God. Every day must be a fresh opportunity to come to know God through serving Him using the special gifts and abilities that He gave you for that purpose.

Solomon started his rule in a very spectacular way. He was a great example of faithfulness and obedience. Something happened to him and he didn't finish the way he started. In fact, he finished so poorly that after his death his kingdom was split and the nation of Israel never again achieved the place of honor and influence that it had before his death. It is not enough to start well; it is how you finish that will matter eternally. To achieve a good finish we must be continually going to God and asking Him to give us new marching orders. We are fond of telling people to leave their failures in the past and starting fresh with God. I believe that God would tell us to do the same thing with our successes. Jesus, teach us to come to you often so that we will daily draw closer to You.

JUNE 11 || 1 KINGS 8:11

The priests could not continue their work because the glorious presence of the LORD filled the Temple.

Read: 1 Kings 8:1-66

This image has always been very cool to me; even before I was involved in the ministry. The priests are going about their duties preparing the temple for daily worship and then suddenly the presence of the Lord fills the temple and they can no longer do their work. What an amazing thing that must have been! It is sad that we don't sense the presence of the Lord in such powerful ways as the priests did here in our account.

God only did this a couple of times in the Bible but I believe that we should be sensing His presence in powerful ways more often than we do. There should be times when His presence overwhelms us to the point that we are not able to do anything else but just stand in awe of His presence. God had promised to the nation of Israel that He would live with them within this temple. Solomon faithfully built the temple and God fulfilled His promise to dwell there among them.

The nation of Israel, through Solomon's leadership, did what God had told them to do and He rewarded by them with this very special appearance of His glorious presence. It is probably not too likely that God is going to do this in this way in your home, ministry, or church but I do believe that there are special awards awaiting those faithful to the calling of the Lord. There should be a sense of the overwhelming presence of the Lord that is powerful and amazing.

For every person it will be different. That is because God has called each of us to a different work. God's blessings and presence are felt in different ways by every person. What one person might perceive as the presence of God might have no effect on someone else. Only the priests inside the temple experienced this awesome display of God's presence. Everyone else only heard about it.

This display also came very suddenly; the priests weren't expecting it. They were just going about the work that was assigned to them and they got to experience God's presence. We need to simply go about our work; not expecting the Lord to do anything like this but always aware that he can.

We should also note that this display was not as a result of the priest's work; it was because God was fulfilling a promise that he had made to the nation of Israel and this was how He wanted to display His glorious presence. We should never assume that just because we are doing what we are supposed to that God is going to appear in a great cloud in our midst. God is God and he will do what He wants to do when he wants to do it. We need to faithfully go about the work that has been assigned to each of us and wait on the glorious appearance of the Lord. Jesus, help us to see you when you visit us.

Rick Lancaster | PLANTERS PERSPECTIVE

JUNE 12 || 1 KINGS 9:4-5

As for you, if you will follow me with integrity and godliness, as David your father did, always obeying my commands and keeping my laws and regulations, then I will establish the throne of your dynasty over Israel forever. For I made this promise to your father, David: 'You will never fail to have a successor on the throne of Israel.'

Read: 1 Kings 9:1-10:29

This is the second time that the Lord has appeared to Solomon. In this appearance the Lord makes a tremendous promise to Solomon. In this promise the Lord tells Solomon that there will always be one of his descendants on the throne of the nation of Israel. This promise was a continuation of the promise that the Lord had made to Solomon's father King David.

The thing that we should note is that this was a conditional promise. Most of God's promises include conditions that we must fulfill in order to see the promise fulfilled by the Lord. Many people often forget that part of how God's promises work is that they must fulfill their part first.

In the case of Solomon, God called him to follow the Lord with integrity and godliness. He also directed him to obey His commands and keep His laws and regulations. For Solomon to see this promise fulfilled, that he would have a successor on the throne, he would have to do all of these things. Sadly we will see that Solomon was not faithful to do these things and God did not keep the promise that He made first to David and then to Solomon. After Solomon's death, the kingdom was divided and someone else sat on the throne of the ten tribes in the North.

The rules haven't changed since the days of Solomon; God still expects his leaders to do the same things that He told David to do and then Solomon to do; follow Him in integrity and godliness, and obey His commands and keeps His laws and regulations. If we will do that as the leaders of our families, ministries, and churches then we can rest assured that God will keep His promises to us and will bless us and those that we are leading.

God is faithful; God is always faithful! He never fails to keep His promises. What we need to keep in mind is that those promises come with conditions that must be met by us. Those conditions are part of the promise and God will not give to us what He promised until we give to Him what He asked for. This doesn't mean that we have to be perfect, but it does mean that our lives are marked by a desire to follow God the way that he wants us to. This means that we are living our lives fulfilling the conditions that He gave us. Jesus, help us to be worthy of receiving the promises that You desire to give us.

JUNE 13 || 1 KINGS 12:15

So the king paid no attention to the people's demands. This turn of events was the will of the LORD, for it fulfilled the LORD's message to Jeroboam son of Nebat through the prophet Ahijah from Shiloh.

Read: 1 Kings 11:1-12:19

Rehoboam has just become king over all of the twelve tribes of Israel after the death of his father Solomon. The people come to Rehoboam and ask him to lighten the load that was placed on them by his father and in exchange they promise to be loyal subjects to him. Solomon had been very strong with the people. For forty years he has put a difficult burden upon them so that he could experience the comfort and success that he desired. The kingdom was prosperous and successful beyond most people's imagination. Rehoboam inherited the greatest kingdom on the planet. He inherited from Solomon wealth beyond measure. The kingdom was safe and secure from his enemies. It would have made perfect sense for Rehoboam to give the people what they wanted and he could have lived in great comfort and security for his entire life. There was just one little obstacle to that life; God had made a promise to Solomon and Jeroboam.

God is always faithful to His promises; nothing in life is as sure as the promises of God. Because Solomon was unfaithful to God, he was told that most of the kingdom would be taken away from his son. At the same time Jeroboam was told that ten of the tribes would be given to him to rule. God then orchestrated things so that His promises would be fulfilled. I think this is something that we sometimes forget about God; that He can cause to happen whatever He wants. God caused Rehoboam to reject the council of King Solomon's advisors which would have been the correct way to go. Instead Rehoboam used the foolish council of his friends. By following that advice, Rehoboam succeeded in accomplishing God's promise of splitting the nation of Israel into two parts.

This is an important truth for us to understand as we go through this life. As we follow leaders we must remember what God did through Rehoboam in this text; He caused him to make a foolish decision so that His plans could be completed. There are going to come times when God will direct our leaders to make decisions that are perplexing to us so that He can accomplish a greater goal. When that happens we need to determine what our responsibility is in that. In the case of the people of Judah they were to continue to follow Rehoboam. In the case of the ten tribes, they were to split and follow Jeroboam.

By following Rehoboam, the tribe of Judah was being obedient to God even though Rehoboam had made a foolish decision. Don't let a single bad decision by your leader cause you to desert him; seek to determine what the Lord is trying to do and then do it. Jesus, help us to follow where You are leading our leaders.

Rick Lancaster | PLANTERS PERSPECTIVE

JUNE 14 || 1 KINGS 13:7

Then the king said to the man of God, "Come to the palace with me and have something to eat, and I will give you a gift."

Read: 1 Kings 12:20-13:34

Here in 1 Kings 13 we have this fascinating but somewhat disturbing account of a man of God that in the beginning is used by God but then is killed by God. This man of God who is not named in this account is used by God to confront Jeroboam who has sinned greatly against God by making gold calves which he himself is making sacrifices to and leading the people to do likewise. God is very upset with Jeroboam and so sends this man of God to speak out a prophecy to him.

God tells this man of God to speak out the prophecy and then to return home. God protects the man of God from the anger of Jeroboam. Jeroboam recognizes the Spirit of God upon this man of God and so invites him back to his palace for food and gifts. The man of God was told by God not eat any food or drink while he was on this mission and so he refuses the offer and returns home by a different route as he was instructed.

Then an old prophet of Bethel comes to the man of God and lies to him and convinces him to come to his home for food and drink. The man of God is told while at the table that he has disobeyed God and that his body would not be buried with his relatives. As he gets back on the road he is killed by a lion. We see the supernatural aspect of this as we read that the lion and the donkey stood by the body until the old prophet came to get it. This doesn't seem fair. After all the old prophet lied to the man of God.

The reason why this offends our sense of fairness is because we are likely to have done the same thing. God's instructions to this man of God were clear. Do not eat, do not drink, and do not stay. He was told to do his job and get back to his home. He was probably tired, hungry, and thirsty. He chose to disobey God.

Often God's instructions to us are as clear as these were to the man of God. But often we will allow our flesh to offer us a different interpretation of God's instructions. God can only use us effectively if we are following his instructions exactly. When we start allowing our flesh to determine what we do with God's instructions we are removing ourselves from God's provision and protection.

As men and women of God we must see God's instructions as absolute. We must determine to do things exactly the way that God said for us to do it. Anything else is disobedience and brings the risk of punishment. Jesus, help us to 'don't' when you say 'don't' and to 'go' when you say 'go'.

JUNE 15 || 1 KINGS 14:7

Give your husband, Jeroboam, this message from the Lord, the God of Israel: 'I promoted you from the ranks of the common people and made you ruler over my people Israel.'

Read: 1 Kings 14:1-15:24

God chose Jeroboam and made him king over the ten tribes of Israel. There is no real indication why God chose him over any other person except that he was a good worker. Jeroboam was an ordinary guy that God selected to be king over ten of the twelve tribes of the Chosen People. King Solomon recognized that he was a worthy worker and placed him over the laborers of his many projects. Something seems to have happened to Jeroboam that caused him to start thinking of himself as someone that was more important than he was.

In this word from the Lord Jeroboam is rebuked by God because he has failed to follow and obey God like he was told to. God pulled him out of the common people and used him to fulfill God's plan in the nation of Israel. God made Jeroboam one of the most important people in the nation of Israel. All that God required of Jeroboam was obedience.

Many of us might also be in this same place with God. God has elevated us up from the common people and given us places of responsibility and authority within our families, ministries, and churches. And He only requires one thing from us; obedience. Because God chose us doesn't make us better or more important than anyone else; it just means that God in His sovereignty chose us rather than someone else.

Jeroboam allowed the fact that God chose him to make him think that he was somebody important. That is pride and it is one of the most dangerous sins that we can inflict upon ourselves and those that we are called to lead. We must always remember that we are where we are because God chose us to be there. He could just as easily have chosen someone else to do what you do. We must never presume that God's choice had anything to do with us; it had everything to do with God's supreme sovereignty.

As leaders, nothing is more important to us than the traits of humility and obedience. If we will just humble ourselves before our Almighty God and be obedient to His will and Word than we can rest assured that He will fight for us in the battles that will come into our lives. God had promised Jeroboam that his kingdom would last forever IF he would humble himself and obey God. Because Jeroboam didn't humble himself and obey God, God ripped the kingdom from him and killed all of his family. Jesus, teach us humility and help us to obey.

JUNE 16 || 1 KINGS 17:16

For no matter how much they used, there was always enough left in the containers, just as the LORD had promised through Elijah.

Read: 1 Kings 15:25-17:24

This is one of the accounts of scripture that I have enjoyed since I first read it. God supernaturally takes care of Elijah by taking care of this widow and her son. They have just enough food for one last meal when Elijah shows up and asks the widow to make him some bread. She tells him that she is about to cook up her last meal and then she and her son are going to die. Elijah tells her not to worry because God is going to provide for her. Then no matter how much food she prepares she has enough for her 'last meal'.

In faith this widow prepared the bread for Elijah, trusting God to do what Elijah had said that He would do. She couldn't have known for sure that there was going to be enough food for them to eat more than one more meal. There was a famine in the land and she had no one else that she could depend upon. The widow's circumstances were desperate. But, in faith she put her own needs aside to meet the needs of Elijah and God blessed her because of it.

All of us will encounter circumstances that cause us to think we are having our 'last meal'. For each of us the circumstances will be different. For some it might be financial desperation. Others could be struggling in their jobs or relationships and feel that there is just enough left in them to go one more day. Or it could be that the consequences of sins that have been allowed into their lives are weighing so heavily upon them that they feel that they will be crushed. Our verse for the day should give all of us hope that regardless of our circumstances we can make it one more day if we will just have faith in Jesus Christ and go about our life as best we can.

After each meal that the widow prepared she had left just enough for one 'last meal'. God did not give her an abundance that she could depend upon. After each meal her situation was just as desperate as it was before the meal. Too often we want God to deliver us completely from the desperate situations that we are in. He would remind us that He has provided for us this far; He will continue to provide for us.

Don't expect more than what you need for this moment; that's all that you need. Be content that you have enough for this moment and trust God for what you need next. Don't worry about your 'next meal'; let God worry about that. Have faith, believe that God loves you and will never leave you nor forsake you. Believe that He will continue to provide for you just as He has up to this point and then go about this day as best as you can. The text of our reading tells us that God provided for the widow and her son for several months in this way. Be patient; trust God. Jesus, thank You that You never fail to provide for those that trust You.

JUNE 17 || 1 KINGS 18:21

Then Elijah stood in front of them and said, "How long are you going to waver between two opinions? If the LORD is God, follow him! But if Baal is God, then follow him!" But the people were completely silent.

Read: 1 Kings 18:1-46

Elijah is confronting the people of Israel. They have been following the example of King Ahab as he leads them to worship Baal and other false gods. They are also still worshipping the True God. Elijah confronts them and tells them to decide for themselves who the one and true God is and worship him only. God is telling them through Elijah that there room in their hearts for only one God. It is up to them which one they will pick.

God then gives them a very powerful proof that He is the one and only God by burning up the sacrifice that Elijah has prepared after the prophets of Baal failed to cause their sacrifice to be burned. The people seem to turn to God but it is unfortunately short-lived.

To most of us, God would say the same thing: "How long will you waver between two opinions?" We have allowed something else to come in and divide our heart in two. In one breath we say that we are Christians and in the next we are worshipping the gods of this world; money, possessions, success, beauty, positions, and the like. There is only room in your heart for one god. Which one will you pick; the one that satisfies your flesh or the one and true God? The choice is yours and your actions and life will reveal your choice to God and to the world.

King Ahab had the choice of leading the people of Israel to God or away from God. He chose poorly! As a leader in your family, ministry, or church you have the opportunity to make the same choice that King Ahab did. Your choice affects not only you but all of those around you. One of the rules of leadership is that where the leader goes, the people follow. Where are you going? Are you going to God?

Later in our text we see God supernaturally delivering King Ahab and the people of Israel from the hand of the king of Aram. He will do this so that Ahab will realize that there is only one God and turn back to Him. God will do amazing and incredible things to remind His children that He alone is God. And incredibly, we miss those tremendous events and look at them as coincidence or as ordinary.

It is our role as leaders to draw people to God. It is our responsibility to first empty our hearts of all the gods of this world that do not belong there. And then we are to teach the people who are following us to do the same. We must first chose and help them to make the right choice as well. As a leader you have a tremendous influence on those around you. Use that God-given influence to direct people to the Lover of their souls. Jesus, help us to choose well and to lead others to the right choice also.

Rick Lancaster / PLANTERS PERSPECTIVE

JUNE 18 || 1 KINGS 19:10

Elijah replied, "I have zealously served the LORD God Almighty. But the people of Israel have broken their covenant with you, torn down your altars, and killed every one of your prophets. I alone am left, and now they are trying to kill me, too."

Read: 1 Kings 19:1-21

In the previous chapter Elijah has just won a tremendous victory over the prophets of Baal. The LORD sends down fire from heaven to consume his sacrifice in a spectacular display of God's power. While King Ahab stands by Elijah has the 500 prophets taken away and killed. Ahab goes back and tells his wife Jezebel about the incident and she becomes very angry and threatens Elijah's life.

He ends up on Mount Sinai, where Moses received the Ten Commandments from the LORD. He finds a cave and spends the night. The Lord speaks to him and asks Elijah what he is doing there? He responds in the verse above.

In ministry there come times in our life when we have a Mount Carmel experience; we have experienced the mighty power of God at work in us or around us. Elijah has just had a Mount Carmel experience. It is fairly common to experience a spiritual low after the high of a mountaintop experience. Elijah becomes fearful and depressed. Rather than responding to Elijah where he was, God sent him on a long journey. God took him away from his normal environment.

Once on Mount Sinai, the Lord asked Elijah to explain why he was there. The Lord's response is interesting. The Lord tells Elijah to go out of the cave. As Elijah stands there a windstorm comes up and then an earthquake and then a fire. Finally there was a gentle whisper. The Lord was reminding Elijah who He was. At no time does He address Elijah's concerns.

The Lord asks Elijah a second time why he is there and Elijah gives the same response. The Lord then does something peculiar; he assigns Elijah some tasks to accomplish. In responding to Elijah's complaints the Lord simply puts Elijah back to work.

The lesson for us all in this is when we are in the dark valley and feel like the world is closing in around us we need to get to Mount Sinai. I don't mean literally, but spiritually. You need to get to that place where you can come face-to-face with God. You need to be reminded about God's power and love. And then you need to get back to work for the LORD. If you need to take a break from some spiritual work to re-evaluate, do it. But understand that God is not through with you yet. Once you have taken a break to refresh your Spirit, get back to work doing whatever the LORD directs, even if it is the same thing as before. Never forget that we are His servants. Jesus, refresh us when the valley gets especially dark.

JUNE 19 || 1 KINGS 20:28

Then the man of God went to the king of Israel and said, "This is what the LORD says: The Arameans have said that the LORD is a god of the hills and not of the plains. So I will help you defeat this vast army. Then you will know that I am the LORD."

Read: 1 Kings 20:1-21:29

King Ben-hadad is determined to defeat King Ahab and conquer Israel. God previously had defeated Ben-hadad's forces and sent them packing. The king's advisers explain why a smaller Israelite army had been able to defeat a stronger military force. They told the king that it was because the battle had been fought in the hills and the Israelite gods were stronger there. Their suggestion was to move the battle down onto the plains where the Israelite gods would be weaker.

It is fascinating to see the unbelieving mind at work in a text like this. As believers we might even scoff at the ignorance of comments like these. For some, myself included, I can still remember thinking thoughts that were similar to the suggestions of Ben-hadad's advisers. To them the Lord was similar to the gods that they worshipped, which means they weren't gods at all. Because these gods were not all-powerful, there were places where they were weak or unconcerned. They believed that by changing the circumstances they could change the outcome.

People still think and act the same way. If some plan or desire is not fulfilled in the way that they think it should be, they will change the circumstances thinking that something new will change the outcome. The problem with that type of thinking is that it takes God out of the equation. The most important part of the verse that we are looking at today is the last part. God's reason for giving King Ahab the victory in this battle that was coming was so that he would 'know that I am the Lord' says God. God does the things that he does in our lives so that we will come to know Him better and better.

It is through an intimate knowledge of God and His will that we know how to live this life. There may be times that God wants us to change the circumstances so that we can experience a different outcome in our lives. More often I think God wants us to change the outcome we desire so that He can change the circumstances. Many people have the wrong understanding of God and His will and this misunderstanding is reflected in the way that they are living their lives. They will change spouses, jobs, churches, or friendships every time something doesn't go the way they want it to.

God is at work in your circumstance attempting to show you more of who He is. Until you recognize this and submit to His plan in your life, you will continue striving after one thing or another and never find what you are seeking. Get to know Him better through your particular circumstances and then ask Him what, if any, changes you should make in your circumstances. Jesus, help us to let You be God in our life.

Rick Lancaster / PLANTERS PERSPECTIVE

JUNE 20 || 1 KINGS 22:14

But Micaiah replied, "As surely as the LORD lives, I will say only what the LORD tells me to say."

Read: 1 Kings 22:1-53

King Ahab and King Jehoshaphat are trying to decide if they are going to go to war against the Arameans. King Ahab's 'prophets' are encouraging him telling him he will have a glorious victory. King Jehoshaphat has suggested to Ahab that they enquire of a prophet of the Lord. Ahab tells him that there is only one, but he hates him because he always gives him bad news. That speaks a lot about the character of Ahab and the condition of the nation of Israel.

A messenger is sent to Micaiah to have him come and prophecy for the kings. He is instructed to agree with the other prophets and say to the king what he wanted to hear. Micaiah, being a true prophet of God, told the messenger that he would not do that; he was going to tell the king only what God told him to say.

Upon getting to the king he begins by telling the king what he wanted to hear. There must have been something in the way that he said it because the king recognized that he was not telling the truth immediately and challenged him. Micaiah then tells him what God has revealed is going to happen; King Ahab is going to be killed and Israel scattered on the hills.

King Ahab responds to Micaiah by having him arrested and thrown into prison. He was to be fed bread and water until King Ahab returned from the battle. King Ahab never returned from the battle and the Bible does not tell us what became of Micaiah. He may have spent the rest of his life in prison eating nothing but bread and water.

Micaiah knew that telling the truth could cost him everything. He knew what the likely response of King Ahab was going to be. And yet he spoke only as the Lord directed him to. How many of us would have the faith to do that? How many of us would believe God and obey God even if it meant that we would be thrown into prison? Sadly, most Christians believe God for far less than this.

God wants us to say only what He tells us to, no matter what the potential consequences might be. God is responsible for the consequences when we are being obedient to Him. Too often we don't trust God enough to trust him with the consequences of our obedience. In my heart I believe that God acted on Micaiah's behalf and rescued him from that prison but I have no proof of it. It doesn't matter anyways because even if he didn't he was right where God allowed him to be. Micaiah's reward in heaven will be great. Jesus, help us to have the faith of Miciah to obey even when it might cost us greatly.

JUNE 21 || 2 KINGS 1:6

They replied, "A man came up to us and said, 'Go back to the king and give him this message from the LORD: Why are you sending men to Baal-zebub, the god of Ekron, to ask whether you will get well? Is there no God in Israel? Now, since you have done this, you will never leave the bed on which you are lying, but you will surely die.' "

Read: 2 Kings 1:1-2:25

King Ahaziah has fallen and seriously injured himself. He can tell that he may be dying and he wants to know if he is going to live. The king of Israel sends some messengers to enquire of Baal-zebub, the god of Ekron. Baal-zebub was said to have the power of prophecy. Ekron was one of the cities of the Philistines. God sends an angel to tell Elijah to intercept the king's messengers and to give them a message for the king. The message is that because the king did not enquire of Him that Ahaziah would not survive his injuries.

In the message the Lord asks the question: 'Is there no God in Israel?' By going to the god of their enemy, Ahaziah was totally rejecting the only True God. By going to ask of Baal-zebub he was rejecting the God that could actually help him in his time of need. God had proved Himself time and again to the ancestors of Ahaziah and yet he turned to some other god. One of the sad things about this is that Ahaziah didn't even believe that Baal-zebub could heal him; he only wanted to know whether he was going to live or not.

Because of Ahaziah's lack of faith God sent him a message that he wasn't going to live much longer. Before we are too quick to judge Ahaziah we should examine our own lives to see if we have done the same thing. It is amazing how often we will turn to the gods of this world when we should be turning to the True God. The Bible teaches that God has supplied everything we need for life and godliness and yet we will often turn to the world for its wisdom and help.

God allowed Ahaziah to fall and become critically injured. He probably wanted Ahaziah to turn to Him and ask for His help. God may have even planned to use this to turn Ahaziah back to Him by healing him from this injury. We often miss the radical things that God wants to do because we fail to go to Him in our times of need. Instead we will turn to gods that neither see nor hear and cannot help us.

Go to the Lord for everything that is going on in your life. Seek the counsel of the godly but trust God only for true wisdom. There is no way to imagine the blessings that God would bestow upon the person that will live their life like that. Trust God and give no place in your life for the gods of this world. Jesus, teach us to see You as the only true source of wisdom and power in this life.

Rick Lancaster | PLANTERS PERSPECTIVE

JUNE 22 || 2 KINGS 4:8

One day Elisha went to the town of Shunem. A wealthy woman lived there, and she invited him to eat some food. From then on, whenever he passed that way, he would stop there to eat.

Read: 2 Kings 3:1-4:17

As Elisha traveled about fulfilling his role as a Prophet of the Lord he happened upon the home of this woman from Shunem. Our verse tells us that she was wealthy. We read later that she was also married which fascinated me because the focus is on the woman and not her husband in this account. It is obvious from this that if it were not for this woman her husband would not have helped Elisha.

We do not learn of the name of this woman. In fact we know very little about her and yet she has found a place in history and in the living Word of God for a reason. It was not her wealth because many wealthy woman in history have died and been forgotten. It wasn't even her generosity for putting Elisha up whenever he came into town. We will read later that it was her faith that earned her this amazing place in scripture; she believed God.

Her faith led her to open her home to this odd man of God that would drop by occasionally. She even went so far as to prepare a room for him to stay in if he desired. I believe it was her faith that caused Elisha to continue to stop and to allow her to minister to him the way that she did.

We live in a time where some Christians have either an unhealthy desire for or fear of wealth. Some people want to be near to wealthy people because of the advantages and blessings that they might be able to partake of. Others might be afraid to be around the wealthy because of what others might think or for fear of temptation. Having these wrong views of wealth has caused some people to miss what God might want to do.

Elisha, the man of God, had no problem allowing this woman of Shunem to minister to him with the gifts that God had given to her. Wealth is a gift that God gives to some for ministering to the rest of the body. We should neither desire nor fear this gift in an unhealthy way. God led this woman to share her gifts with Elisha and obviously He led Elisha to accept them. We can interpret from this that her motives were pure; she just wanted to be used by God.

If God has blessed those around you with some type of abundance and He then leads them to bless you in some way, let them; accept their gifts. You don't need to be concerned about their motives, but you do need to be concerned about your own. If their motives are not pure God will reveal that to you and you can respond accordingly. Do not despise the gifts that God might want to give to you through the gifts that He has given to others. Jesus, help us to be cheerful givers and receivers of Your good gifts.

JUNE 23 || 2 KINGS 5:13

But his officers tried to reason with him and said, "Sir, if the prophet had told you to do some great thing, wouldn't you have done it? So you should certainly obey him when he says simply to go and wash and be cured!"

Read: 2 Kings 4:18-5:27

Naaman is the commander Aram's army. He is well admired by his king. He has been very successful for the king of Aram but he has contracted leprosy. A slave girl from Israel informs Naaman's wife that there is a prophet in Israel that can heal him. So Naaman comes to Elisha in Samaria to be healed of leprosy, a very contagious skin disease.

When Naaman shows up at Elisha's door, he sends a messenger out to tell Naaman to go to the Jordan River and wash himself and be healed. Naaman gets very upset; this was not how he expected to be treated. He expected to be shown a great deal more respect and he expected some kind of ritual that led to his healing.

In our verse for the day, his officers attempt to reason with him. They point to the error in his logic. Naaman believed he was a great man and so believed he should be treated in some great way including in the manner in which he was to be healed. To go and wash in the Jordan River was simply too simple.

There is a great picture of salvation here, in that salvation is simply accepting what Jesus did for us at Calvary. It is not involved in some great ritual or process; simply believe in Jesus. That bothers some people, and some people try to add to it to make it seem more important. Salvation is simple enough for a child to understand it and accept and I thank God that it is.

Some people approach serving God in the same way that Naaman approached being healed by God. They expect that their importance will determine where and how they serve God. Their problem is that they are comparing themselves to the people they are serving instead of the God they are serving. People that are important in the world sometimes expect to have important positions in serving God.

When we come to God and tell Him that we are ready to serve Him we must be ready to serve wherever He might direct us. As a pastor people regularly come to me and tell me that they believe that God is telling them that they should be serving Him in some way but they are not sure how. I can always tell if they have a heart like Naaman's when I suggest they do something small or simple. If they are upset because they were not given a task as great as they are, it is proof that the pride of Naaman lives in their heart.

The only way that they can be healed of that is through obedience and the washing of the blood of Christ. Naaman did as Elisha instructed and was healed and he came back to Elisha a changed man. We must never think ourselves so great that there is any task that is below us, especially when it comes from a God that is so much greater than us. Jesus, teach to gladly do the simple tasks for our great God.

Rick Lancaster | PLANTERS PERSPECTIVE

JUNE 24 || 2 KINGS 6:16

"Don't be afraid!" Elisha told him. "For there are more on our side than on theirs!"

Read: 2 Kings 6:1-7:20

This is one of those accounts in scripture that I always enjoy coming to and it has much to teach us about this world that we live in. The king of Syria has been making war against Israel. Elisha, the prophet of God, has been feeding information to the king of Israel warning him of the plans of the Syrian army. Elisha was getting this information from God and passing it on to the king of Israel. The Syrian king decides that the only thing to do is to capture Elisha and do away with him. Have you ever thought what a foolish decision that was by the Syrian king; Elisha had been getting all the king's plans from God, why did he think this plan would be any different?

The Syrian king sends a great army to capture Elisha and surrounds the city which he is staying in. His servant goes out in the morning and sees this vast army and is terrified. Elisha takes one look at the situation and then tells Gehazi, his servant, not to be concerned. As Elisha's servant Gehazi should have known that his master would have known this was coming and would have been prepared for it.

Elisha then prays that his servant's spiritual eyes would be opened. Gehazi couldn't see the spiritual side of the circumstances that he was involved in. All he could see was that he was in deep trouble. Most people look at life the same way that Gehazi looked at his circumstances that morning; there was an overwhelming obstacle that was going to destroy them. This is a lack of faith; it is a failure to believe and trust God.

Every last one of us is going to wake up some morning and find an enemy army surrounding our city. This army is going to be vast and overwhelming and your initial response might be to panic. Don't panic; remember that the army that is there to defend you is greater than the one that is coming against you. Gehazi forgot that God had been very faithful to protect his master Elisha. From that viewpoint Gehazi should have realized that this was no big deal for God. God has also been very faithful to you. He has provided and protected you up to this point and unless you have turned away from God, He will continue to do so. God did a radical thing with Gehazi; He showed him the spiritual world so that his faith would increase.

God probably won't do that with us because He has given us the Holy Spirit to testify of the presence of God in our lives. We are called to walk by faith. That means that we walk through this life choosing to believe the things that we cannot see. That means that when we look out upon the overwhelming circumstances of our lives; we believe that God is bigger and more powerful than those circumstances. Having those kinds of spiritual eyes will allow us to see the mighty hand of God at work in our circumstances. Jesus, please give us 20/20 spiritual vision.

JUNE 25 || 2 KINGS 8:5

And Gehazi was telling the king about the time Elisha had brought a boy back to life. At that very moment, the mother of the boy walked in to make her appeal to the king about her house and land. "Look, my lord the king!" Gehazi exclaimed. "Here is the woman now, and this is her son—the very one Elisha brought back to life!"

Read: 2 Kings 8:1-9:13

Gehazi is Elisha's servant. He has just been telling the king of Israel some stories about Elisha. He chooses as one of the stories of Elisha's displays of God's power the account of raising a boy from the dead. As he is reaching the climax of that account, in walks the woman. At first read this might seem like an amazing coincidence. I have grown to recognize that there is no such thing as a coincidence in the things of God.

Seven years earlier, this woman, who is not named in Scripture, is told by Elisha that there is going to be a seven-year famine and that she should leave. She packs up her family and leaves to live in the land of the Philistines for seven years. What is not obvious from the text is that someone has moved into her house and been using her land while she was gone. That is the only reason she would have to the king to ask for his help.

God has blessed this woman before by raising her son from the dead. This son was a gift from God to her, as her husband was old and not able to produce children. The reason that He has done this is because she has been helping Elisha for years. Every time Elisha would pass through, they would give him a place to sleep and feed him. She eventually had a room prepared just for him.

God's sovereign power is at work in this account. He put it into the mind of the king to ask to her some of the stories of the power of God being used through Elisha. The LORD put it in the mind of Gehazi to share the account of raising this woman's son from the dead. And He coordinated all of these things to happen just as she is approaching the king to make a request of him to get her land back.

The king responds by doing exactly what she wants. We might think, "Well, of course he did! That was the right thing to do!" If you read about the kings of Israel, they were not famous for doing the right things. It is very likely that this king would have sided with the current possessors of the land and not with this woman. God supernaturally intervened so that He could bless her because she had blessed His servant, Elisha.

This woman is a great example of the maxim that no good deed goes unrewarded. This is especially true of the good things that we do for God's people. We have to be careful not to presume upon God some reward for our efforts because God will be a debtor to no man. But it fills my heart with joy to know that God can not only move heaven and earth to bless me, but He can also influence the hearts of men in my favor. Jesus, give us eyes to see Your hand of providence in all things.

Rick Lancaster | PLANTERS PERSPECTIVE

JUNE 26 || 2 KINGS 10:27

They broke down the sacred pillar of Baal and wrecked the temple of Baal, converting it into a public toilet. That is what it is used for to this day.

Read: 2 Kings 9:14-10:31

The books of the kings of Judah contain some odd and some fascinating characters. Some of the kings are pleasing to God and some are evil and do not please God. Bad kings follow good kings and good kings follow bad kings. Some of them start well but then don't finish well in following the commands of the LORD. In many respects it is a fascinating study in the effects of sin in the lives of those in leadership and the impact that has on the people they lead.

Jehu is one of those characters that was used by the LORD in a powerful way. It was prophesied that all of King Ahab's descendants would be destroyed. Jehu was the man selected to accomplish this work for the LORD. He was ruthless in fulfilling this terrible task. After accomplishing that task, he sets out to destroy those that worship the false god Baal. He lures them into their temple and then kills them all.

To ensure that this idolatry does not happen again, Jehu destroys the objects of Baal worship. In our verse for the day, Jehu wrecks the temple of Baal worship and turns it into a public toilet. Jehu is making a powerful statement regarding the worship of false gods. A toilet is where we go to rid ourselves of the waste that our bodies produce. We flush away the impurities of our lives so that they don't contaminate us.

Putting something up as an idol in your life is the same as setting up a toilet in your life. The only difference is that instead of flushing your waste away, you flushing away something that is actually valuable. In the case of the Baal worshippers, they flushed away their very lives. Anything that you apply toward the worship of anything other than the Lord is wasted; it is flushed away as waste.

An idol is anything or anyone that we put higher in our lives than Jesus. It can be our spouse or our kids. It can be a career or a hobby. It can be someone famous or popular. It can be an object like a car, motorcycle, or a house. It can be a sin or a temptation that you refuse to deal with. Whatever it is, you are regularly sacrificing your time, talents, treasure, and thoughts to it. It is not a sacrifice of worship; it is a flushing away of something that God gave to you for His purposes.

Jehu was pretty zealous in his seeking to destroy false worship but he didn't destroy the gold calves that Jeroboam set up. It doesn't say why he didn't; he just didn't. He may not have recognized them as idols. This is one of the reasons that we need to daily draw nearer to the Lord. He will show us those things that we are flushing our lives down. We need to prepare ourselves by holding everything in our lives with open hands. This means that we would be content if the Lord chose to take something away. Jesus, help us not to waste this precious gift of life that You have given us.

JUNE 27 || 2 KINGS 12:2

All his life Joash did what was pleasing in the LORD's sight because Jehoiada the priest instructed him.

Read: 2 Kings 10:32-12:21

Joash was made the king of Judah at the young age of seven years old. Of course he could not rule at that young age so Jehoiada ruled in his place until the king was old enough to assume the leadership of the nation. Under Jehoiada's leadership the nation of Judah turned back to the Lord. We see in the text that King Joash did at some point assume the leadership of the nation and that he continued to lead the people to the Lord.

But then the priest Jehoiada dies. And very soon after that Joash is convinced by others to abandon the temple of the Lord and begin worshipping idols. The verse above is better translated in 2 Chronicles as 'for as long as Jehoiada lived, Joash did what was pleasing to the Lord.'

Joash was raised in the temple. The very first thing that Jehoiada did when Joash was crowned king was place a copy of the Law in his hands. Joash was brought up in the church and knew the truth. But soon after his mentor is gone, he turns away from what he knows is the truth. This is so difficult to understand and to prepare for.

As we do what we can to build a family, or a ministry, or a church we cannot guarantee what is going to happen to it once our influence is removed or replaced. Our children, no matter how well we do at raising them will decide for themselves if or how they will follow the Lord. Our ministries and churches no matter how well they are equipped and prepared will be led by someone other than you that may lead it in a direction that is not pleasing to the Lord.

It is certain that Jehoiada would have been angry, frustrated, and saddened by what happened to Joash and the nation of Judah. We can't determine what is going to happen after we are gone or move on. This is a part of trusting God with everything. All you are responsible for is what God told you to do. Once your leadership is removed from a situation, such as when a child leaves home or you move on to a new ministry or church, then it is God's responsibility. You are only responsible for your part.

Jehoiada did everything he could to prepare Joash to be a king that was pleasing to the Lord all his life. We need to do everything we can with our children, ministries, and churches to make sure that they are able to follow the Lord all the days of their lives. Then it becomes their choice. Jesus, help us to prepare them and ourselves for whatever future you have prepared for us.

Rick Lancaster | PLANTERS PERSPECTIVE

JUNE 28 || 2 KINGS 13:23

But the LORD was gracious to the people of Israel, and they were not totally destroyed. He pitied them because of his covenant with Abraham, Isaac, and Jacob. And to this day he still has not completely destroyed them or banished them from his presence.

Read: 2 Kings 13:1-14:29

God is such an amazing God! He is full of compassion and love. His mercies are new and fresh every day. Israel has turned away from Him and has been following after all the pagan gods that He had warned them not to follow after. Because of their disobedience He has abandoned them to their enemies. This is all happening just the way that He had said that it would while He was leading them through the forty years in the wilderness. He had told them that they would be tempted to worship the gods of the pagan nations they were replacing in the land and He told them that if they did that they would be destroyed. God is faithful to His word. Because the nation of Israel was unfaithful to Him God has turned them over to the pagan nations that He had helped them to defeat to possess the land.

Even though He has turned them over to their enemies He will not allow those enemies to completely destroy them. God in His infinite grace will save some of them as a remnant because of His promises to Abraham, Isaac, and Jacob. In this can be found a great seed of hope for those that have wandered away from the Lord or for those that know someone that has wandered away.

God, in His supreme sovereignty, has the right to completely destroy anyone that rejects Him or disobeys Him. Because of His infinite grace He will often stop short of complete destruction. He does this because His desire is to see everyone come to repentance and be restored into a right relationship with Him. The nation of Israel during the time of the kings is a great example of this. Every time they followed Him and obeyed the Lord He blessed them. Every time they turned away to follow pagan idols and disobey the Lord He withdrew His hand of blessing and allowed their enemies to attack and oppress them.

But He never did let any nation totally destroy His people. As we pray for those that have wandered from the path of God's provision and protection we should be praying that God would do whatever He needs to so that they can come to a complete restoration to Him; even if that means that they are nearly destroyed. There is nothing in this world that is worth sacrificing your soul for. And if it is necessary for someone to lose everything so that they can finally see the Lord and turn back to Him, it is well worth it. We pray poorly when we ask God to remove the consequences of rebellion if there is no repentance in the person we are praying for. It is better that we pray that God strip them of everything that hinders them from complete repentance and brokenness before the Lord. Jesus, teach us to pray that You would destroy all obstacles to repentance in those that we care for.

JUNE 29 || 2 KINGS 16:10

King Ahaz then went to Damascus to meet with King Tiglath-pileser of Assyria. While he was there, he noticed an unusual altar. So he sent a model of it to Uriah the priest, along with its design in full detail.

Read: 2 Kings 15:1-16:20

King Ahaz is the king of Judah. While he is king, the kings of Israel and Aram declare war on him. Judah and Israel are relatives and Aram should be a common enemy. King Ahaz hired the king of Assyria to come and save him. After saving him, King Ahaz goes to visit the king of Assyria. While there he sees an altar that catches his attention. He then sends the plans for that altar back to Uriah the priest, who promptly duplicates it for the king.

Ahaz is not a good king in the eyes of God. He did not do things that were pleasing to God. He even sacrificed his own children in the fire. His religious practices were very much like the people of Canaan before God drove them out. God had warned the people not to look at or study the way that these people worshipped. He warned them because He knew that there would be things about the way that they worship that they would find attractive. He knew that this would begin a process of them turning away from the LORD.

As soon as Ahaz got his new altar built, he started changing the way the people worshipped in the temple. God had given very clear and specific instructions as to how He wanted His people to worship Him. Ahaz substituted his own form of worship.

As God's people, we need to be so careful not to fall into this trap. It can be so subtle but it is so dangerous. There are some fascinating things being done today that are being called worship. That is not to say that everything that is different is evil. God has led some to worship Him in ways that are different.

It is impossible to say what the motives of King Ahaz were as he had this altar built and then worshipped at it. We cannot presume to know where his heart was because the Scriptures do not tell us. All the Scriptures say is that he did evil in the sight of the LORD. He had access to the same five books that make up the first books of our Bibles. He could have and should have known how God wanted to be worshipped. It appears that He had no desire to please God in his worship.

Being New Testament Christians, we are not bound by the Law. But we also have clear instruction regarding what will please our Lord in worship. And where the Scriptures are not clear or silent, we have the Holy Spirit to guide us. True worship begins not in the way that we worship but in the desire of our heart to please our Savior and Creator. Be careful not to let the world's ways of worship to distract you from a pure and undefiled worship. Jesus, you are worthy of our worship.

Rick Lancaster / PLANTERS PERSPECTIVE

JUNE 30 || 2 KINGS 17:7

This disaster came upon the nation of Israel because the people worshiped other gods, sinning against the LORD **their God, who had brought them safely out of their slavery in Egypt.**

Read: 2 Kings 17:1-18:12

For almost three hundred years God has been speaking to the people of Israel trying to get them to return to Him and turn away from the worthless idols that they have been worshipping. God has sent numerous prophets and judges to lead them and guide them but they resolutely refused to acknowledge them and turn from their wicked ways. God promised them that if they would follow Him and Him alone that they would be secure in the land forever. He also promised them that if they turned away from Him and worshipped the pagan gods of the nations around them that He would expel them from the good land that He had given them and hand them over to their enemies.

God's promises are sure; both the ones that promise blessing and the ones that promise disaster. God's promise of disaster was fulfilled when Assyria came and overthrew Samaria and took away the people of Israel. The Assyrian king also took people from other lands and moved them into Israel to live there. God used the Assyrian king to accomplish His plans in the nation of Israel.

God does the same things in our lives. God has promised to bless us with an abundant life, ministry, and church. All we have to do to experience that life is to simply worship and obey God and Him alone. The moment that we turn away from God, even if it is only to share our affection with something else, He then begins a process of warning and exhorting us to return to Him. God is patient and He will not punish us the moment that we turn away from Him. But there will come a time when God will send someone or something into our lives to remind us that He is God and that He deserves every bit of our worship.

The nation of Israel looked around at the nations around them and took their eyes off of the Lord. The longer they did this the harder it became for them to see Him and to follow Him. It is so critical that we don't take our eyes off of Jesus, even for a moment, because it can result in the loss of the blessings that God desired to give to us and we might see others getting the blessing instead.

If we will just let God be God in our lives He has promised to protect us and provide for us. He has promised to lead us and guide us to the abundant, victorious life. He has promised us a sweet communion and fellowship that this world can not understand nor can it duplicate. And all we need to do to have this is to keep our eyes on Jesus and do what He tells us to. Jesus, teach us to humble ourselves and obey You so that we can experience all of the life that You promised to give us.

JULY

JULY 1 || 2 KINGS 18:22

"But perhaps you will say, 'We are trusting in the LORD our God!' But isn't he the one who was insulted by King Hezekiah? Didn't Hezekiah tear down his shrines and altars and make everyone in Judah worship only at the altar here in Jerusalem?

Read: 2 Kings 18:13-19:37

Sennacherib, the king of Assyria has come to attack some of the cities in Israel. King Hezekiah sends him money to leave them alone. This doesn't work and Sennacherib sends a representative with a huge army to confront Hezekiah in Jerusalem. This representative makes a speech calling for the surrender of Jerusalem. This speech is filled with boasting in the power of the Assyrian army and arrogantly claims that not even God could stand against them. He even claims that it was 'the Lord' that told them to come up to Jerusalem to destroy it.

The representative also makes this interesting statement that we find in our verse for the day. He says that God is mad at Hezekiah because Hezekiah tore down all of the altars that the people were sacrificing on and made them come to Jerusalem to sacrifice to the Lord. Why would he say something like that? It could be possible that they became aware that Hezekiah had done this and out of ignorance of God's commands assumed that this would have angered God. In fact, Hezekiah was doing it in obedience to God.

What I believe is the more likely scenario is that as the army of Assyria is making its way into the land of Israel they are coming across people that are upset about the fact that Hezekiah has torn down these altars that people were sacrificing on. And it is very likely that these people are so upset with Hezekiah that they are even helping the enemy to destroy him. Hezekiah obeyed God by tearing down those altars. But there were people using those altars that didn't want to do things God's way; they wanted to worship God (or whatever else they were worshipping) their way. And because they couldn't do it their way they were upset enough to let the enemy into their land and help the Assyrians defeat their king.

Brothers and sisters in ministry, you need to know that if you obey God that there may be some people that don't agree with you and don't like it. And if they get upset enough about it they might even allow the enemy to come into your ministry and church in an attempt to eliminate you. Trust God just like King Hezekiah did and He will rescue you just He did for King Hezekiah. In the next chapter of 2 Kings we see that God in fact turns the king of Assyria away from Israel and spares them. We must be obedient and faithful to God even when it means that some people will be upset with us. Only God can protect us! Only God can save us from the attacks of our enemies. Jesus, help us to trust you so much that we will be obedient even if it means that others are upset with us.

JULY 2 | | 2 KINGS 20:3

"Remember, O LORD, how I have always tried to be faithful to you and do what is pleasing in your sight." Then he broke down and wept bitterly.

Read: 2 Kings 20:1-22:2

There is something fascinating about this account of when Hezekiah became deathly ill. Hezekiah was one of the best kings that Israel ever had. He instituted a great many reforms and did a great job of drawing the people back to the worship of God. At this point in his life he becomes very ill. God sends the prophet Isaiah to him to let him know that he will not recover from this illness. We see Hezekiah's response in our verse for the day. He is very upset and weeps bitterly.

First, I would like you to recognize Hezekiah's faith; he believed the report of Isaiah. This is one of the things that made Hezekiah such a good king; he believed the things that God told him. We would do well to follow Hezekiah's example in this area of our lives. We may not have a prophet like Isaiah around but we do have the Bible, the Holy Spirit, and those that have been appointed to teach and disciple us. Start believing what they say and do what the Bible and Holy Spirit are telling you to.

Hezekiah also reminds God of all the things that he had done for God. There was one word in this reminder that really caught my attention and I believe bears reflection upon; 'tried'. Hezekiah did not say that he had always been faithful or that he had always done what was pleasing; he said that he had tried to do those things. As we continue to read this account we see that God answers Hezekiah's prayer almost immediately and sends Isaiah back to the king with the news that God has decided to extend his life by fifteen years.

God will never ask us to be perfect; because He knows that we can't be perfect. He asks us to try to be perfect. Our goal in life is to try to be faithful to God and to try to always do what is pleasing to Him. Our problem is that our ability to achieve that is limited by our sinful flesh. God knows that we are going to blow it occasionally; but He wants us to keep trying.

God gave King Hezekiah an extra fifteen years to live. This was partly because Hezekiah had the faith to ask God to intervene on his behalf but we need to be careful not to create a theology that claims enough faith can extend your life. God extended Hezekiah's life because He wanted to and because Hezekiah asked in faith. Your faith is irrelevant if it is outside of God's will. What would you do if you knew that God had extended your life by fifteen years? What would you do with those fifteen years? Remember that every day that you are alive is a day that God extended to you. Live it as though it were your last. Jesus, help us to thank you for every day that we are here and to live each day faithfully and in a way that is pleasing to You.

JULY 3 || 2 KINGS 23:3

The king took his place of authority beside the pillar and renewed the covenant in the LORD's presence. He pledged to obey the Lord by keeping all his commands, regulations, and laws with all his heart and soul. In this way, he confirmed all the terms of the covenant that were written in the scroll, and all the people pledged themselves to the covenant.

Read: 2 Kings 22:3-23:30

King Josiah had been made king at the age of eight. The kingdom was well established and everyone was living their lives as they thought was the best way to live. As Josiah grew up he began leading the people back to God by first having the priests repair the temple. During this process they discovered the scroll of the Law of Moses. Upon reading it, Josiah knew that they were in trouble. He knew that God was upset with the nation of Israel and that He was going to judge them for their sins of idolatry.

Josiah's response was repentance. This is amazing! Josiah inherited the kingdom the way that it was. It was his ancestors, starting as far back as King Solomon that had allowed the sins of idolatry to defile the people. But Josiah is repentant and goes to God to seek His will. Josiah found out that the prophecies of impending doom for the nation of Israel were true but because of his repentance it would not happen in his lifetime.

Josiah then did what every leader should do in a time of crisis; he 'took his place of authority'. Josiah knew that it was his place to lead the people, especially in their relationship with God. Josiah was not responsible for the past but he knew he would be responsible for the future. He went to great lengths to bring the people back to God.

Some of us will have the opportunity to start ministries and churches but more of us will inherit ministries and churches that are already established. We may go into those situations and see as Josiah did a temple that is run down and neglected and determine that there are serious problems including sin and idolatry throughout the ministry and church. Your role is to take your place of authority and bring people back to God. That may involve tearing down idols and shrines to other gods and removing the priests of those gods. You can probably imagine that many of the people of Josiah's time were wondering what he was doing because that was the way that they had always worshipped. Josiah used his authority to drive the sin from the land and to draw the people back to God.

The very first thing that Josiah did after he 'took his place of authority' was to renew his covenant with the Lord. He started the process of cleansing the land by cleansing himself. Nothing that you do 'for God' will matter as much as what you do 'with God'. Begin by cleansing yourself and letting Jesus do the work in you before you try to do it in others. Jesus, help us to see your church the way that you see it and give us the courage to take our place of authority.

JULY 4 || 2 KINGS 25:5

But the Babylonians chased after them and caught the king on the plains of Jericho, for by then his men had all abandoned him.

Read: 2 Kings 23:31-25:30

King Zedekiah was placed on the throne by Nebuchadnezzar of Babylon after the Babylonians conquered Judah. He was to maintain order in Judah and send tribute to Babylon. Zedekiah did that for nine years and then rebelled against Nebuchadnezzar. The Babylonians laid siege to the city of Jerusalem for two years. Zedekiah and the soldiers attempted to escape in the dark of night through a section of the wall that had broken down. Zedekiah was caught and taken to Nebuchadnezzar where he was made to watch as all his sons were killed and then his eyes were gouged out. Zedekiah was then led away as a captive to Babylon where he remained until his death.

When Zedekiah rebelled against Nebuchadnezzar he was actually rebelling against God. The LORD had sent the Babylonians to punish Judah for rebelling against God. They had turned from the LORD and were following their own way. Through the prophets, the LORD had warned them about doing that. The LORD said very plainly that if they rebelled that He would send in foreign nations to remove them from the land. The LORD was being faithful to His word.

Something that struck me about our verse for the day is that the Babylonians caught Zedekiah after all his men had abandoned him. The Bible doesn't explain why Zedekiah rebelled, just that he did. It could be that he felt that he was strong enough to withstand the Babylonian army. But by resisting the Babylonians, Zedekiah was resisting the chastisement of God. God brings chastisement to correct us; to turn us from our evil ways and back to Him again. If we resist this chastisement, we only bring more severe disciplines into our lives.

God will strip away everything that prevents His children from humbling their hearts and turning to them. For some people, a simple rebuke from the Lord is enough to correct their behaviors. For others, they must be stripped of everything, blinded, and led away in chains before they submit to the mighty hand of God. In all of this, God's purpose is to restore His people in personal, intimate fellowship with Him.

The problem for many people is that they want God, but they want Him on their own terms and in their own ways. God will send discipline and chastisement to remind that He is God and it is His way that matters, not ours. When the people of Israel followed the LORD with their whole heart, God blessed them abundantly. After they had sinned, God withdrew His hand of blessing. If they had repented once they felt His chastisement, He would have once again blessed them abundantly. They same is true for us. If you feel the heavy hand of God upon you, humble your heart and turn back to Him in everything. Jesus, help us to not kick against the goads of Your love.

Rick Lancaster / PLANTERS PERSPECTIVE

JULY 5 || 1 CHRONICLES 1:10

Cush was also the ancestor of Nimrod, who was known across the earth as a heroic warrior.

Read: 1 Chronicles 1:1-2:17

Reading through the genealogies can sometimes be a laborious and difficult thing. The names are sometimes hard to pronounce and there is a drone to the rhythm of the text that can lull you to sleep. Over the years as I have become more familiar with the Scriptures, the genealogies have become more interesting. Now as I read each name, the story of this person's life as it is revealed in Scripture also pops up.

Nimrod in our verse is described as a great warrior. His fame was so great that everyone in the whole world knew about him. That is a pretty amazing statement considering there was no news coverage on television. Elsewhere Nimrod is described as a mighty hunter. He is also given credit for building a number of cities.

The most famous of the cities that Nimrod built was Babel. We are familiar with Babel; that is where the people decided to build a tower to reach up to God. They were attempting to elevate themselves to be equal with God. It is not certain that Nimrod was responsible for starting that project but It would not be a surprise if he was. God came and saw what they were doing and confused their language and dispersed the peoples to the ends of the earth.

Babel was later renamed Babylon and was a center of pagan worship practices. Babylon would later become a great world power that would be used by God to discipline His Chosen People, Israel, when they were disobedient. Babylon will also play a role in the end times as the Antichrist rebuilds it and uses it as his capital during the seven-year Tribulation period.

All of this started with a man by the name of Nimrod. As I grow in knowledge of the Scriptures my love of them grows. They are beautiful, not just in the content, but also in the way that they are put together. As time goes by and I grow in my understanding of this amazing book, I find myself more awe-struck by how wonderful it truly is. Only God could create something this beautiful and detailed.

The Bible teaches that man is God's highest creation. We were made in the image of God so that we could fellowship and commune with Him. His Word is given to us so that we might know how to do that. As my love of God grows, so does my love of His Word. As my love of the Bible grows, so does my love of God. I am convinced that someone that does not love God's Word cannot truly love God.

Choose to Love God more fully by choosing to love His Word. Not just the interesting stories, but every single word. Even the genealogies are given for a reason. Don't skip over them. Ask God to speak to you through the genealogies and through all the more difficult texts. You'll be amazed by what might come out. Jesus, help us to love You more by loving Your Word more.

JULY 6 || 1 CHRONICLES 3:4

These six sons were born to David in Hebron, where he reigned seven and a half years. Then David moved the capital to Jerusalem, where he reigned another thirty-three years.

Read: 1 Chronicles 2:18-4:4

Often as you read through the genealogies you will come across brief commentaries inserted by the writers. We have one of those commentaries in today's reading. Every time I come across one I pause to reflect upon it. I wonder why the writer chose to insert this bit of information at this point. Reading through the genealogies can sometimes be like walking through an arid desert; it is dry and seems to be dead. Then you come across an oasis that seems to be bursting with life.

All Scripture is inspired by God. Even the dry, seemingly dead genealogies have a place and a lesson to teach. Just as in the most arid of deserts, there is life; you just need to know where to look for it. Sometimes it is so well hidden that someone has to point it out to you. Don't be discouraged when you read something in the Bible and don't understand it. It could be that God hasn't chosen to reveal it to you yet. Be patient and diligent, He will. He loves to reveal Himself to those that love Him and are seeking to know Him.

In our verse for the day we are told that David ruled for over forty years. He had seven wives and an unspecified number of concubines. He had numerous children and I would imagine a large number of grandchildren. It is hard for me to imagine what that must have been like. Having been married to the same woman for over 26 years (by the grace of God as of this writing in 2008) and having two sons and a daughter, it is difficult to imagine what it would be like having ten times as many women and children in my life.

Life is a balancing act; we must balance our family life with our work life, and our leisure time, and our church life. If one of them gets out of balance, it throws everything else out of balance as well. Something had to have suffered in David's life. It is interesting to me that God had told the Israelites that their leaders should not take multiple wives. There was no explanation given; they were simply told not to do it. Culturally, it was very common to have multiple wives. It was a sign of wealth and position. Marriage was also a common way to seal agreements with neighboring kings to ensure peace.

A study of David's family shows that it was not the healthiest group of people. Among the six sons born to David in Hebron, three died violent deaths. One raped his half-sister. Absalom killed Amnon for that and also tried to take his father's kingdom by force, losing his life in the process.

David was a great king and was called by God 'a man after My own heart'. But he made some mistakes that cost him dearly. His family life was not in balance and it caused pain and frustration throughout his life. God's instructions are often simple and if we follow them we prosper. If we ignore them we suffer. Jesus, teach us to simply follow Your simple directions.

Rick Lancaster / PLANTERS PERSPECTIVE

JULY 7 || 1 CHRONICLES 4:10

He was the one who prayed to the God of Israel, "Oh, that you would bless me and extend my lands! Please be with me in all that I do, and keep me from all trouble and pain!" And God granted him his request.

Read: 1 Chronicles 4:5 – 5:17

This little prayer that is recorded in the middle of the genealogies has become pretty famous. Books have been written about it and countless sermons have been preached on it. It is commonly referred to by people that proclaim certain types of theologies that suggest that God will give you anything you ask for. It is often associated with the belief that if you have enough faith you can ask God for the moon and He will give it to you.

It is placed here in the Scriptures for a reason; it is there to teach us something. The challenge as always is to try to figure out just what that is. One of the clues that we need to look at is context. In this case this account gives us very little to go on. Jabez was more distinguished than his brothers and his birth was difficult. Neither of those facts give us that much to go on. Other men in Scripture were very distinguished and did not have their prayers answered like this. Other people were born through difficult births. Neither of those facts warrant the kind of response that Jabez received here.

The danger we run into with a verse like this one is that we attempt to discover a method hidden in the request. If we can figure out what Jabez did than we can pray like this and get the same results. There is one little problem with that, God doesn't work that way. God works outside of our understanding and comprehension. We cannot put methods on our relationship with God.

God is absolutely faithful; He will never deviate from His character. In those areas where He has spoken on a subject, we can be absolutely certain how things are going to happen. The Bible tells us that if we confess our sins that God will forgive us. That is an absolute guarantee. If the Bible has not spoken clearly on a subject God is free to operate any way that He chooses, within the confines of His character.

People are looking for a formula to getting everything they want from God. He is not a genie in a bottle. That is approaching God with the wrong attitude. There is no clear explanation as to why God answered this prayer of Jabez so completely. We only have two verses to tell us about the man, the prayer, and about God's response.

God granted Jabez all of His requests. We don't know any more than that. The prayer of Jabez can then be used to teach us about what God can do. It cannot be used to teach us about what we should do to get our prayers answered. God chose to grant all of the requests that Jabez laid before Him. It is not important why God did that; he simply did! God may grant all your requests and He may not. That is His choice. He is God after all! Approach Him as though He can answer any and every request that you have. But understand that He is God and it is His will that determines what He will do, not your method or process, or even how much 'faith' you have. Jesus, teach to believe that you answer every prayer.

PLANTERS PERSPECTIVE | A Devotional

JULY 8 || 1 CHRONICLES 5:25

But they were unfaithful and violated their covenant with the God of their ancestors. They worshiped the gods of the nations that God had destroyed.

Read: 1 Chronicles 5:18-6:81

As I read this I can't get over how foolish it sounds. This is speaking about the leaders of the half tribe of Manasseh. They are described as great warriors but then this statement above is made about them. Even though they were great warriors they worshipped the gods that God had destroyed while He was giving them the land that they were living in. Maybe it is just me but that sounds very foolish.

There are a couple of lessons in that for all of us. We need to examine our hearts on a regular basis and determine what we have allowed into our lives that would be described by God as foolish acts of worship. It is difficult to know for sure but I would guess that the leaders of Manasseh did not turn to idol worship overnight. It would be more likely that some subtle bit of it was allowed in and accepted as innocent and normal. Over time, more and more of it was allowed until they found themselves in full-blown idolatry. It can happen the same way in our lives. Everything should be questioned in our lives and compared to God's word for correctness. Anything that doesn't belong there should be eliminated immediately. There are no innocent sins!

As leaders of families, ministries, and churches this is especially important. The things that we 'allow' as innocent and normal will be practiced by the people we lead as acceptable before God. And even though every person will stand before God and give an accounting for their own action, we leaders will give an account for the things that we allowed them to do without warning and correction. We owe it to God first and then to those that are following us to warn them of all those innocent and normal sins that will lead them into idolatry.

One of the things that I desire for my life, family, and ministry is that it would never be described as foolish. It is my great desire that my life would matter and be of great value to God and to others. The only way that I can be sure of that is to have a regular practice of examining myself. That is done in a number of ways. God's word is one of the best tools for examining my life. The Holy Spirit also does a great job of helping me to see any foolish things in my life. God also uses other people to reveal the foolish things that I have allowed in my life. It is up to me to humble my heart and use these things to guide me toward the kind of life that God desires for me. If, in my pride, I decide I don't need one or more of these things in my life, I will soon find myself being compared to the leaders of Manasseh. Humble your heart before God and let Him reveal the foolishness that you will find there and then be obedient to do what is necessary to rid yourself of it. Jesus, teach us to open our hearts fully to You.

Rick Lancaster | PLANTERS PERSPECTIVE

JULY 9 || 1 CHRONICLES 7:33

The sons of Japhlet were Pasach, Bimhal, and Ashvath.

Read: 1 Chronicles 7:1-8:40

In today's reading we continue through the genealogies. This section of the Bible is very difficult for people. It is filled with long lists of names that are difficult to pronounce. Very little information is given about many of these people except that they lived and they had children. Today's verse is an example of that. This is the only place in Scripture where this man and his three sons appear.

The genealogies were (and still are) important to the Jews. Originally the land of Canaan was divided among the tribes of Israel. Everyone within the tribe was allotted land within their ancestral boundaries. Land could also be bought and sold. Every fifty years there was a Year of Jubilee. All land had to be returned to the original owner or to his descendants.

There were also specific roles within the community that had to be accomplished by people from certain groups. To be a High Priest you had to be descended from Aaron. To do the work of a priest you had to be able to prove that you were from the tribe of Levi. God created a culture within Israel that made the genealogies important because some of the prophecies concerning the arrival of the Messiah involved his ancestry. He was to be descended from King David. The genealogies given for both Joseph and Mary indicate that they were descended from King David, thus fulfilling the prophecy from whatever direction you might view it.

Japhlet and his sons were descended from the tribe of Asher. Asher was one of those tribes that didn't get much mention in Scripture. We might wonder what kind of men they were or imagine them one way or another. Is the fact that they did not get a lot of mention because they were disobedient or rebellious? What stopped them from becoming great men that performed great feats for the Lord?

The Scriptures are often silent on such things as that to remind us that God is sovereign; He is in absolute control of everything. These men did not become more than they were because God did not require them to. It was God's sovereign will that they were born in the tribe they were at the time they were. They lived the life that they were destined to live.

We also were born into the family that God chose for us to be born into. We didn't have a choice in that. We should strive for greatness, especially in works for the Lord, but He might not need us to be great in the way that the world defines great. He might have created you to simply be one that continues the line of descendants. It may be that your destiny is to have a single line of mention in the history of the world.

It brings me comfort that I don't need to be great to be pleasing to God. He doesn't ask me to be great. He asks me to love Him and to love others. If I do that with my whole heart, soul, mind, and strength the Lord will be pleased. Nothing else really matters. If He wants me to be great, that's His responsibility. Jesus, help me to concentrate on loving You and others.

JULY 10 || 1 CHRONICLES 10:13-14

So Saul died because he was unfaithful to the LORD. He failed to obey the Lord's command, and he even consulted a medium instead of asking the LORD for guidance. So the LORD killed him and turned his kingdom over to David son of Jesse.

Read: 1 Chronicles 9:1-10:14

Saul's rule of Israel was hardly something to brag about. He was disobedient to the LORD right from the beginning. The prophet Samuel tried to warn him and teach him the right way to go but Saul insisted on doing things his own way. The Lord sent a number of things into Saul's life in an attempt to turn him back to the LORD. Saul was determined to be his own man.

Saul's life was ended at the hands of the Philistines over twenty years after David had been anointed to be the next king of Israel. It is not clear why the LORD waited so long before making the transition to David as king of Israel. It could have been to give David time to become more mature and gain experience. It could also have been to give Saul time to repent and turn back to the LORD.

Saul failed to respond and so the LORD killed him in battle with the Philistines. This verse reminds us that God is in control of everything. As those arrows were flying in the battle, the LORD directed one to fly to the target He had placed on King Saul. He had no chance of escape. His fate had been sealed.

What is tragic about this is the two things that Saul depended upon became trophies of his enemies; his armor and his head. Saul's armor was placed in the temple of their gods and his head was placed on the wall of the temple of Dagon. Saul depended upon his own strength which is pictured in his armor and his own wisdom. The enemy took both and mounted them on their walls like they might the head of an animal they had hunted. It was a way of saying that our gods are stronger than yours.

All of this happened because Saul was unfaithful to the LORD. As leaders of families, ministries, churches, or in industry we need to take careful note of what happened to Saul. Because he was unfaithful, the LORD took him out. In this case, He did it literally by taking his life. There are other ways that the LORD can take you out. He can take away your position or authority or ability. Humble your heart before you find yourself hanging on some enemy's wall as a trophy.

God will be patient, desiring that you would humble your heart before Him and repent. But don't think even for a second that a rebellious leader is going to get away with his sins forever. In His time, the LORD will act. If you find yourself under the leadership of a leader that is rebelling against God, remember to let Him deal with that leader. It is your responsibility before the LORD to follow as if He were the LORD until the LORD acts or causes you to move on. Jesus, help us to be faithful to you whether we are leading or following.

Rick Lancaster / PLANTERS PERSPECTIVE

JULY 11 || 1 CHRONICLES 11:2

For a long time, even while Saul was our king, you were the one who really led Israel. And the LORD your God has told you, 'You will be the shepherd of my people Israel. You will be their leader.'

Read: 1 Chronicles 11:1-12:18

King Saul was recently killed in a battle with the Philistines. Once word gets out that he is dead the leaders come to David to crown him as king of Israel. It has been more than twenty years since Samuel came to David's father's house and anointed him as the next king of Israel. In that time David has experienced a lifetime of things to prepare him for the next part of his life. He went on to be a great king for the nation of Israel, even with some tremendous mistakes.

What speaks to me loudest about the leadership of David is a statement made in the beginning of today's verse, 'you were the one who really led Israel'. Part of what made David a great king was his attitude when he wasn't king. His attitude was not to try to push Saul out of the way so that he could take his rightful place. David trusted God to deal with Saul when He was ready to. David's attitude was to do everything he could to help Saul lead, even though Saul was trying to kill him most of the time.

How many of us could have that kind of trust and patience in God. If our employer was determined to destroy us and God had not opened the door for us to leave, could we stay there and work toward their success. That is exactly what David was doing. As hard as it was, it was exactly the training that David needed to be a great king.

Too often we have interpreted the saying, 'When the going gets tough, the tough get going' to mean, 'If it gets hard to work somewhere, leave!' That may not be what God's plan is. He may be trying to teach you something that you need to learn before He can move you up to the next level of responsibility. If you don't learn the lesson in the position you are in, you will probably have to learn it in the next one.

David learned to lead effectively even when he wasn't the leader. It was his attitude that determined that. He knew that it was more important that the nation of Israel prosper than for he himself to prosper. He was more concerned about larger things than himself. He also maintained a close walk with the LORD. I believe that is ultimately how David was able to do such a difficult thing.

Thankfully, most of us will not have leaders in our lives that will throw spears at us and seek to kill us. But we are all likely to have leaders that are not following the LORD. It can be very difficult to keep a good attitude in some environments. Stay close to the LORD and seek the greater good than your own. God has you in that organization for a reason that He may never declare to you. Trust Him and be faithful to Him. Do your work as though the Lord Jesus Christ was your boss. Do your work as though it was the most important thing in all of heaven and earth. And then patiently wait for the Lord to work in your life. Jesus, help us with our attitudes.

JULY 12 || 1 CHRONICLES 12:40

And people from as far away as Issachar, Zebulun, and Naphtali brought food on donkeys, camels, mules, and oxen. Vast supplies of flour, fig cakes, raisins, wine, olive oil, cattle, and sheep were brought to the celebration. There was great joy throughout the land of Israel.

Read: 1 Chronicles 12:19-14:17

David is finally king of Israel. People come from all over Israel to celebrate the rise of this new king. Somehow the people knew something about David that they did not know about Saul. They were celebrating the fact that there was a new king with great enthusiasm. Somehow they knew that God was going to bless Israel because David was now king. Somehow they knew this was God's perfect plan at work and it filled them with joy.

This is not the way people usually feel when there is a significant change taking place. More often than not, there is fear or concern whenever a change is coming. There is uncertainty about what the future holds and questions about how the change will affect them personally.

It would be great if we could all face change the way that Israel faced this change of leadership. The people may not have known exactly why they had joy; it just welled up within them. The same can be said of us in our own walk with the Lord. There are times when joy seems to flow like a rushing river and there are other times when it is glaringly absent.

Joy is not easy to manufacture. It can be done but it is difficult to maintain. Joy is a fruit; one of the fruits of the Holy Spirit. As a fruit it grows spontaneously from the source that produces it. Joy springs forth from faith and trust. When faith and trust are nurtured in your life, joy is the natural byproduct. Obviously our faith and trust must be in something that can generate joy for it to produce any. I can believe and trust an apple tree will produce oranges but it never will; it can't.

When we put our faith in God's Word and trust Him implicitly, we are in the fertile ground that produces healthy fruit, including joy. As we nurture and tend to our faith and trust we will see fruit to grow naturally. We will experience joy in our lives without effort. Even in normally stressful or difficult times, there will be an underlying sense of joy in the faith and trust you have in the Lord.

If there is no joy in our lives it is often an indication that we need to tend to our faith and trust. The Holy Spirit might be trying to show you an area of your life that you have not fully surrendered to the Lord. Humble your heart and ask the Spirit to show you clearly what you are holding on to. Then lay it down at the feet of Jesus. Open up your Bible and find something that speaks to that subject and then choose to believe it.

Joy is a choice; it is a choice to believe God's Word and trust in Him. After you have made the right choice, celebrate. Jesus, strengthen our faith and trust.

Rick Lancaster / PLANTERS PERSPECTIVE

JULY 13 || 1 CHRONICLES 15:14

So the priests and the Levites purified themselves in order to bring the Ark of the Lord, the God of Israel, to Jerusalem.

Read: 1 Chronicles 15:1-16:36

David is recovering from a mistake that he made earlier in regards to the moving of the Ark of the Lord. He had tried to move it but failed to ask God how to do it. As a result Uzzah made the mistake of touching the Ark and was killed instantly. David then determined that it was the role of the Levites to transport the Ark and so he summoned them to Jerusalem. The Levites successfully transported the Ark to Jerusalem by carrying it the way that Moses had instructed them to.

We are told in this verse that the Levites purified themselves before attempting to perform this task. For the Levites this was a very specific set of activities and rituals that they performed. Once completed, they were considered purified and ready to work for the Lord.

As Christians, we don't have rituals for purification. One of the benefits of being Christians is that God looks upon us as having the purity of Christ. But this doesn't make us pure. In fact, the Bible teaches us Christians that we need to actively pursue purity and holiness. And that is especially true of those that have responded to the Lord's call to serve Him. (Everyone has been called but not everyone responds.)

All of the ceremonies and rituals that the priests and Levites performed to become purified are symbolic of things that we need to be doing in our lives to be purified ourselves. There were sacrifices that are a picture of the sacrifice of Christ to provide us a pathway to God. As servants of God we will also be called upon to sacrifice to help others find their way to Christ. That sacrifice might come in our time, or our talents, or in our treasures. Serving God will cost you something. If it doesn't; you might need to examine whether or not you are truly serving God.

The priests also performed rituals of cleansing to purify themselves. These rituals are a picture of the cleansing that we receive from Christ through the forgiveness of sins. It is also a picture that we have a role in becoming cleansed. We need to wash ourselves from the uncleanness of this world. We do this through a process that we call sanctification. This is the process of allowing the Word of God, the Bible, to fill our minds and hearts and change us. As we learn about God through His Word and open our heart to the purifying work of the Holy Spirit we are slowly changed into the image of His Son Jesus.

The priests performed these rituals every time they were about to go on duty for God. One big difference between the priests and Christians is that we are always on duty. Our purification needs to be a regular and constant process. Only then can we be ready to serve God when He desires. Jesus, help us to be pure.

JULY 14 || 1 CHRONICLES 17:6

Yet no matter where I have gone with the Israelites, I have never once complained to Israel's leaders, the shepherds of my people. I have never asked them, "Why haven't you built me a beautiful cedar house?"

Read: 1 Chronicles 16:37-18:17

King David is secure is his control of the nation of Israel. He has built for himself a great palace in the City of David on the outskirts of Jerusalem. It then occurs to him that God is 'dwelling' in a tent. David consults with the prophet Nathan who encourages David to go ahead with his plans to build a temple for God. The Lord then speaks to Nathan and reverses Nathan's opinion. There is an important lesson in that for all of us. Nathan's first opinion about David's plan to build a temple was that it was a good idea. It was a good idea and God was going to have a great temple built in His name. But God's timing was different than both Nathan and David's timing. God would have David's son Solomon build Him a temple. It is a wise leader that will allow God to change his plan, even after he has sought counsel.

God told Nathan to go back to David and give him a message. The main point of the message was that God didn't want him to build him a temple. And the Lord makes this interesting statement above. He wants Nathan to tell David that He has never complained to men about where He lived. God's dwelling place was the tabernacle, which was basically a large tent. God's dwelling place was a portable, temporary structure. It was built while the Israelites were wandering in the wilderness after they had been delivered from slavery in Egypt.

As a pastor that ministers in a 'mobile' church this verse strikes a note deep within my heart. We meet (2008) in an elementary school multi-purpose room. Every Sunday we set up church from two trailers. And just about every Sunday we are asking God to provide a permanent home for our church. There are numerous practical reasons why we should want a permanent church home, not the least of which is that we will be able to do more ministry.

The primary question that a verse like this tells me is that God doesn't need a beautiful building to minister to His people. We often think that we need to build God some large beautiful structure so that He can be glorified. We need to keep in mind that God told them to build the Tabernacle and He allowed them to build the Temple. God wants to tabernacle in our hearts. He doesn't need some ornate edifice to be glorified.

Our buildings should be more practical than ornate. They should be designed to help people discover the fullness of their relationship with the Living God. Our church buildings should not be monuments to our glory but factories that are busy 'making disciples' that will be living displays of God's glory. Jesus, thank you for the tabernacle that you provided to us.

Rick Lancaster / PLANTERS PERSPECTIVE

JULY 15 || 1 CHRONICLES 21:1

Satan rose up against Israel and caused David to take a census of the Israelites.

Read: 1 Chronicles 19:1-21:30

In our culture a census is not that big of a deal; every ten years a census is taken. It seems odd to us that a census would be something that God would call a sin. The thing was that God had promised David and the nation of Israel to multiply them until their numbers were like the sands of the seashore; meaning too great to count. For David to do a census was to test God to see if His promise had come true or not. God also had a concern that this census would provide a source of pride and independence in the heart of the king and the people.

God had caused David to be very successful. David had taken control over the nation of Israel and it was prospering under his leadership and control. David had done a pretty good job of depending upon and following the will of God in his life. But David slipped into that dangerous phase of a leader's life; comfort. David had become comfortable and nothing is more dangerous to a leader's ability to lead than to become very successful and becoming comfortable in that success.

Satan used David's success against him and the nation of Israel by planting the idea of a census in David's mind. This is the place that David could have had the victory; if he had only rejected the idea while it was still in his mind. David was given another opportunity to do the right thing when Joab tried to talk him out of it. David allowed his pride to get in the way of the right decision.

Too many leaders within God's churches, ministries, and families fall into the same kind of traps. God blesses them and they become successful. They then fall into the trap of being comfortable in that success and forget who made them successful. Then Satan very gently plants the seed of an idea in their minds. That seed is then fed and nurtured by our pride and selfishness and before long they find themselves involved in some kind of sin. The sad thing about that is that it is not just the leader that suffers from sin. When David sinned, the whole nation suffered as a result of that. The same is true in the churches, ministries, and families of God; when the leader sins it is not just the leader that pays for that sin.

God wants us all to be successful; though we need to understand and accept His description of success. God doesn't want us to allow our success to open a door into our lives for sin. The best way to defend ourselves from this is to keep our focus on God and to continually point to God as the source of any good thing in our lives. This must be done in the heart before it is done with the mouth but both must take place if you desire to see God's continued blessings and protection. Jesus, help us to only look at our successes as a way of glorifying and praising You.

JULY 16 || 1 CHRONICLES 23:1

When David was an old man, he appointed his son Solomon to be king over Israel.

Read: 1 Chronicles 22:1-23:32

David is getting old and he is nearing the end of his life. God has already told him that Solomon is to replace him as king of Israel. David has been preparing for this transition in leadership for some time. He had been preparing the materials to build the temple and teaching Solomon everything he needed to know so that he could build the temple. He had also been preparing the people that would assist Solomon.

We see also in our text for today that David is preparing and assigning the people that will minister in the temple once it is complete. David is doing everything he can to get everyone ready for the change in leaders.

It was common in these times for the king to rule until he died and then their heir would assume the throne. While it was common, it also led to many challenges in the transition. Often there were conflicts over who should be king and sometimes wars would break out over the issue. David showed great humility and wisdom by preparing for and appointing Solomon to be king before he died. We will see in a few chapters that David will step down from the throne and make Solomon king in his place. This puts David in the unique position of being able to help Solomon as he assumes the responsibility of king.

David loved God and God's people so much that he worked to make sure that the transition would be smooth and that Solomon would have the greatest chance of success. In life and ministry we will have opportunities to act as David has acted here. We will regularly be faced with transitions that will test our humility and wisdom. Changes in jobs, homes, schools, family, ministry, and churches all provide opportunities for us to show the same humility and wisdom that David did.

We should prepare for the transition so that the person that is replacing us has the greatest chance of success. This is easier to do when we are being promoted or moving to something better but the real test comes when we are losing our job or ministry or it is a 'negative' move. This is the time that God will test your humility. Will you show your love for God by preparing for your replacement so that they will succeed? And even more than that, will you help them to be more successful than you were? God would call you to do this in all areas of your life. The humility and wisdom that David showed here is available to everyone that trusts in Jesus. He is the source and the reason for both. Jesus, help us to show our love for you by trying to make this a better place after we move on.

Rick Lancaster | PLANTERS PERSPECTIVE

JULY 17 || 1 CHRONICLES 24:5

All tasks were assigned to the various groups by means of sacred lots so that no preference would be shown, for there were many qualified officials serving God in the sanctuary from among the descendants of both Eleazar and Ithamar.

Read: 1 Chronicles 24:1-26:11

As part of the preparations for building the temple, King David arranged so that the priests were assigned to do the various tasks that would needed to be done. David proved in his actions that his heart was right before God. He would not live to see the temple built and he knew that but he exhausted all of his resources to make sure that when it was built that it would be magnificent. What a beautiful picture of a man after God's own heart.

David used sacred lots to determine which groups of priests would be assigned to which tasks. This was done in a way that showed no preference to any one group. That is a beautiful picture of how we should conduct our lives and ministries. David had many qualified people to pick from and it would have been easy for him to decide to pick people based on the abilities and skills that he saw in them.

The reason why that is important is because God gets very little glory when highly qualified people do things for God. God gets great glory and His name is lifted up when everyday, ordinary people accomplish the great things that God wants to do. When we go about the process of selecting people to serve God in various areas of His house we should be more interested in their heart than we are in their talent. Talented people without a heart for God will not bring glory to God. Ordinary people with a heart for God tend to depend upon God more and get to experience His power and mighty works more often.

All of us regardless of our ability ought to try to remember that all of our abilities and skills were gifts from God to us and that his desire is that we would be dependent upon Him for everything that we do. Our talents and abilities are nothing to God if our hearts are not right toward God. If you are one of those people that is blessed with natural talent and abilities, you need to be careful and more diligent about the things that you do for God. It can be very natural for you to do something and forget to give the credit to God. That is a sure way to make yourself unusable to God.

What are you building for God? Are you building it for God's glory or your own? Are you selecting people to help you based on their heart for God and not based only on their ability? The temple that Solomon built was called Solomon's temple; though a lot of the work to build it was done by his father David. Would you work just as hard if you knew that you wouldn't be able to finish it and someone else will? Jesus, help us to go about the work that you have assigned us without playing favorites or looking for personal glory.

JULY 18 || 1 CHRONICLES 27:24

Joab son of Zeruiah began the census but never finished it because the anger of God fell on Israel. The total number was never recorded in King David's official records.

Read: 1 Chronicles 26:12-27:34

This is one of those confusing sections of Scripture. At first glance it is difficult to understand what God was angry about. There several accounts of God commanding the leaders of Israel to conduct a census. Why then would God get angry at David for doing one here? The answer is simple; God didn't tell David to do it here. Prior to this, every census had a purpose for God. This census of David's did not have a purpose for the Lord. This census was all about David.

Joab realized this when David ordered it and tried to talk David out of it. He knew that it would displease God and tried to convince David to change his mind. But David wouldn't listen and insisted that Joab conduct the census. This was a matter of pride for David. God knew David's heart was not to glorify God in this census but to bring glory to Himself.

The consequences of David's pride were severe. The text simply says that the 'anger of God fell on Israel', but elsewhere this meant that He sent a plague to punish His rebellious people. Because of King David's sin of pride, the people of Israel suffered. As leaders, we need to grow to be intimately familiar with accounts like this one. David's sin carried immense consequences to the people that he was leading. Your sins will impact more than just yourself.

Joab tried to talk David out of the census. Having failed to do so, he was faithful to his king and did what was asked. Joab sensed what he was doing was wrong and yet he was faithful to his king. There may be times in life and ministry when you are called to do something that you are not sure about. It is then that you must choose; you choose to follow your wisdom or the wisdom of your leader.

What David did was wrong, but Joab did the right thing. If your leader calls you to do something that you do not agree with, it doesn't necessarily mean that he is wrong or in sin. Unless his request is in direct violation of Scripture, is illegal, immoral, or unethical, then your obligation before God is to be faithful to your leader. Trust God by trusting your leader. Every good leader is going to make mistakes. That you can be absolutely sure of. God knows that and it is why he surrounds good leaders with people to help him. If you can't follow an imperfect leader then you can't follow anyone, because there are no perfect leaders.

The only perfect leader is Jesus Christ. Follow Him with your whole heart, soul, mind, and strength. One of the ways that you do that is to submit yourself to the authority of the leader that God placed above you. If you cannot do that, you should tell him so privately and then leave quietly. But always make sure your heart is right with God first. Jesus, teach us to be better leaders by teaching us to follow.

Rick Lancaster / PLANTERS PERSPECTIVE

JULY 19 || 1 CHRONICLES 28:5

And from among my sons—for the LORD has given me many children—he chose Solomon to succeed me on the throne of his kingdom of Israel.

Read: 1 Chronicles 28:1-29:30

David, in our text for today is still in the process of handing the kingdom of Israel to his son Solomon. David gathers together all of the leaders of the nation and tells them Solomon has been chosen by God to be the next leader of the Israelites. Many would question Solomon being selected as the next king.

It was common during this period and still is in some areas that the oldest son would be first in line to ascend the throne. That was tradition and it was expected. Solomon was not David's oldest son. In fact there were several other sons that were older than Solomon. We will be reading in the next few days that one of David's sons wasn't paying attention when David made this announcement and decided he should be the king anyway. His plan did not work well.

God had spoken to David and told him that it would be Solomon that would take his place as king and it would be Solomon that would build the temple where God's name would be honored. Solomon was described by his father as "inexperienced". God did not select the logical choice to be the next king; He selected one according to His wisdom.

God will never change. He still selects the people to lead the same way today as He did with David and Solomon. He still picks people that the world and we might look at and wonder what God was thinking when made them the leader. But it is often these 'unlikely' leaders that do some of the most incredible things.

We need to have the same faith in God's selection process. It is not our place to question why God picks certain leaders over others. This is especially hard when we are a likely candidate for that leadership position. We must never forget that God has a plan that is much greater than we can perceive and that our role has been set from before the beginning of time.

We often let our pride interfere with our relationship with God by trying to help God make these kinds of decisions or by trying to correct one that we think was a mistake. The last time I checked God had never made a mistake. We should be praising God every time we see a 'Solomon' take a leadership position. We should be praying for this leader and doing everything we can to help them be successful. In this way, it will bless them and God will bless you and your ministry or church will be blessed. We will see that fighting against God's choices will get you into trouble. Jesus, help us to choose to accept the person you have chosen to lead.

JULY 20 || 2 CHRONICLES 1:1

Solomon, the son of King David, now took firm control of the kingdom, for the LORD his God was with him and made him very powerful.

Read: 2 Chronicles 1:1-3:17

A study of the life of Solomon can teach a leader of God's people a great deal. Solomon had it all; He was chosen by and blessed with great abilities. His father David had left him a strong kingdom and equipped him to be very successful; which he was. But then as you dig into his life you find evidence that he made some tremendous mistakes that can be directly related to his success and power.

This should serve as a warning to all of God's leaders; it is not enough to have everything you need to be successful, you must also have God with you. Solomon started his reign as king of Israel with God right there making him successful and powerful. At some point in Solomon's life he determined that he didn't need God's help anymore. I am certain that this was not a conscious decision and I would guess that when he finally realized what had happened that he wondered how it happened. The plain fact remains that it did happen because Solomon allowed it to happen.

Because of Solomon's failure in this area, the nation of Israel was divided after his death and would never regain its power and influence in the world. God had promised David that He would be there for Solomon as long as Solomon would treat Him as God. Solomon failed to keep God in His rightful place in his heart and soon found his heart filled with idols and false worship.

No person has ever had the potential to succeed as King Solomon and from the world's viewpoint: most people would say that his life was very successful. The problem is that his success did not survive after he died. Jesus tells us that godly fruit, or success, will remain; it will last after we are gone. Solomon had the success but he had lost the one thing that would have made it last; God's presence.

There is nothing wrong with desiring to be successful, especially in doing things for the Lord. But for that success to be lasting and worthwhile we need to be cultivating a strong sense of the presence of God in our lives. If we will focus on keeping our lives close to the Lord, then we can be sure that we will be doing tings that will have significance long past our lives. Solomon probably didn't notice the Lord's presence leaving him; it was probably gradual and over an extended period of time. It takes deliberate effort to refocus on our relationship with God and maintaining a close relationship with Jesus. If we focus on being successful, we will not focus on the person that makes us successful; God. Focus instead on being exactly where God wants you to be and then leave your success in His hands where it belongs. Jesus, don't let our success be a source of distraction from You.

Rick Lancaster / PLANTERS PERSPECTIVE

JULY 21 || 2 CHRONICLES 5:11

Then the priests left the Holy Place. All the priests who were present had purified themselves, whether or not they were on duty that day.

Read: 2 Chronicles 4:1-6:11

Solomon has completed the construction of the temple. They have moved the Ark of the Covenant into the Most Holy Place and also brought all of the furnishings and the tent that the Ark was housed in into the temple. It seems from the text that there were a lot of priests present for this event. The priests had the responsibility and duties within the temple. Back in 1 Chronicles 24, David had divided the descendants of Aaron into 24 divisions. Each division had an assigned time to serve in the temple. Many priests were present that were not on duty.

What caught my attention here in this text is not that they were there, but that they had purified themselves. For the Hebrew priest this was a ritual act of cleansing that would make them presentable and acceptable to God. There were also certain things that they had to stay away from so that they would not become defiled which would prevent them from serving for a period of time.

Even though these priests were not going to be serving in the temple they had prepared themselves as though they were. What a great lesson for us to keep in mind. We also need to be prepared for what God might want to do through us. Too often people think about their relationship to God and their service to Him in relation to when they are going to church. Our time of service is not limited to once or twice a week when the church meets to hold services. Our time of service to God is 24 hours a day and seven days a week. We need to be ready whenever He might call.

The priests got ready by going through a cleansing ritual and by staying away from things that would defile them. We stay ready the same way but using different methods. We are cleansed by the blood of Jesus as we go to the Lord and seek forgiveness of our sins. We also need to stay away from things that defile us. Things like sexual immorality, drugs, alcohol, and pornography just to name a few. By staying away from these things we keep ourselves ready to serve the Lord when He wants to use us.

It doesn't matter who you are or where you are, as a Christian you have a responsibility to serve God when He says that he wants you to. That could be in a ministry, or a church, or a home Bible study, or in your family. Wherever it is, you must be prepared to serve; you must keep yourself ready. Your opportunity to serve might happen at the gas station, grocery store, at work, at home, and of course at church. We are not on a rotating schedule of service; we are on call all the time. Jesus, help us to prepare ourselves so that we can serve you when you want us to.

JULY 22 || 2 CHRONICLES 7:14

Then if my people who are called by my name will humble themselves and pray and seek my face and turn from their wicked ways, I will hear from heaven and will forgive their sins and heal their land.

Read: 2 Chronicles 6:12-8:10

Solomon has completed the construction of the temple and prayed and asked God's blessing on it and the people of Israel. That evening God appears to Solomon and tells him that He has heard Solomon's prayers. That is such an amazing thing; God told Solomon that He had received his prayer. Don't we sometimes wonder if God actually hears our prayers? And then here in our verse for the day God gives us some conditions that we need to consider when we are praying.

First, this verse is directed to those that are called by His name. Christian that means you! Because we are called by the name of God's Son, we have the privilege of being able to pray to Him and expect Him to hear our prayers. Second, for God to respond the way that we desire we must be humble. God resists the proud. If you come to God with arrogance and pride then you should not expect a positive response from God.

Third, we must pray! If you don't pray, then you won't get a response. Jesus taught extensively about prayer; both how to pray and how not to pray. Persistence and diligence in prayer is a powerful thing. Fourth, to receive a positive response from God we must be seeking Him with our whole being. Our desire should be that we get so close to God that we can see His face. And to see the face of God, you need only look to Jesus. Get close to Jesus!

Fifth, we must turn away from the things that separate us from God. If we don't then we are being double-minded; saying that we want to hear from God but living the life that we want to. To experience all that it means to have God hearing your prayers we must repent of our sins and turn away from anything that displeases Him.

And if we will do that, than no matter where we are God will hear us in heaven and respond. God was speaking specifically about the trials that He would allow to happen in the Israelite's land if they turned away from worshipping the True God. But the same truth applies to the trials and tribulations that God allows into our lives when we allow sin to control us. To have our trials and tribulations that are caused by our sin removed we must humble ourselves, pray, seek Him, and turn from our sin. If we will do that, this verse says that God will take away the trial or tribulation. Keep in mind that all trials and tribulations are not because of sin. But if you will follow these steps, you can absolutely rest in the knowledge that God hears your prayers and is preparing a response for you. Jesus, teach us to pray!

Rick Lancaster / PLANTERS PERSPECTIVE

JULY 23 || 2 CHRONICLES 10:15

So the king paid no attention to the people. This turn of events was the will of God, for it fulfilled the LORD's message to Jeroboam son of Nebat through the prophet Ahijah from Shiloh.

Read: 2 Chronicles 8:11-10:19

King Rehoboam has taken his father Solomon's place as the king of Israel. Jeroboam has returned from exile in Egypt where he had fled from King Solomon. Before leaving for Egypt the prophet Ahijah prophesied that he would be given ten of the twelve tribes to rule over. It was also prophesied that he would do terrible things after he became king.

All the leaders of Israel come to King Rehoboam with Jeroboam and make a request of him; to lighten the heavy workload that Solomon had placed on all of them. Solomon was famous for his many building projects. To complete all the many projects that he wanted done, Solomon made the leaders of Israel pay for them and provide laborers to do the work. The leaders of Israel wanted Rehoboam to slow down on the building projects. In return they were assured that they would be totally loyal to him.

Instead Rehoboam suggests that he will increase their workload and make life even more difficult. The leaders respond by telling them that they will not follow him at all. After the conversation is over, ten of the tribe choose Jeroboam as their king. Only Judah and Benjamin remain under the control of Rehoboam. The nation of Israel is divided from this moment until after the exile is over.

This is hardly the outcome that Rehoboam desired. Our verse for the day tells us that this was the 'will of God'. This was God's plan! It was His will that Rehoboam listen to the wrong counselors and take bad advice and make the wrong decision. It was God's will that the people rebel against Rehoboam and split the nation of Israel. This was the result of King Solomon's sins. It is another testimony to the fact that our sins will ripple through eternity and sometimes it is our children that pay the greatest price.

Rehoboam was a foolish king and God used his foolishness to punish him. By allowing him to make this foolish choice, he would be reduced to a fraction of the king that he was just moments before. God's will is His sovereign ability to cause events to take place that fulfill His plans in the world. What God has determined will come to pass; will without fail come to pass and nothing in this universe can change that.

What makes this confusing is that God also gives us the ability to choose to obey Him or to reject Him. But He doesn't allow us to choose in every situation. Sometimes circumstances are forced upon us and we have no choices at all. What can get your mind twisted up is that God gives us choices and already knows what we are going to choose and His plan includes our choice even before we make it. It brings me comfort to know that God knows what I am going to choose and that His plan is working for the good of those that love and obey Him. So my most important choice is whether or not I will love and obey God; everything else is under His control. Jesus, help me to make good choices.

JULY 24 || 2 CHRONICLES 12:8

But they will become his subjects, so they will know the difference between serving me and serving earthly rulers.

Read: 2 Chronicles 11:1-13:22

King Rehoboam of Judah was the son of Solomon and grandson of David. King David was described as a man after God's own heart. This means that he followed God in all his ways. It doesn't mean that he was perfect, but he lived a life that was centered imperfectly around the LORD. His grandson Rehoboam was not that way; he went his own way and turned away from the law of the LORD.

The Lord then sent King Shishak from Egypt to punish Rehoboam for his unfaithfulness. Upon seeing Shishak come and his huge army destroying everything in their path Rehoboam and the leaders of Israel humbled themselves and confessed their sins before the Lord. That was what the Lord was hoping would happen.

God gives us the choice; humble your heart before Him or He will send a destroyer that will force you to humble your heart. If we would just logically examine this choice we would quickly recognize the foolishness of many of our actions. God is a loving, generous Father who cares for us and protects and provides for us. The destroyer seeks only to destroy some part or all of our life. Which does it make more sense to humble your heart before? And yet all too often we resist God and refuse to humble our hearts before Him.

When I was in boot camp as a young man I quickly realized one of the objectives of the instructors was to break our will to teach us how to follow commands. This is necessary in a military unit; it can mean life and death, not just for the one following the commands but for their entire unit. I learned quickly that by humbling myself before these instructors that I would be more successful. I saw that some men resisted the leadership and instruction and paid a price in various forms of discipline or punishment.

God's purposes are the same in my life. He wants me to learn to follow His commands quickly and without question. I have come to recognize the direct connection between a humble heart and God's blessings. The more quickly I respond, the more successful I am in this Christian life.

This is so important to God that if we do not do it, He will send someone or something into our lives to teach it to us. The problem with that is that other 'instructor' doesn't love us or desire to see us prosper as God does. But if that is what it will take to teach us how to serve God with a humble heart, God is will to let us endure it.

The choice is ours; serve God with a humble heart or endure the forced humbling of our heart by an unloving destroyer. If you are in the hands of the destroyer now, simply humble your heart before God and ask Him to help you to learn to serve Him. God may not deliver you until you have done that, because that may be exactly why you are in the hands of the destroyer. Jesus, teach us to serve with a humble heart.

Rick Lancaster / PLANTERS PERSPECTIVE

JULY 25 || 2 CHRONICLES 16:7

At that time Hanani the seer came to King Asa and told him, "Because you have put your trust in the king of Aram instead of in the LORD your God, you missed your chance to destroy the army of the king of Aram."

Read: 2 Chronicles 14:1-16:14

King Asa was one of the better kings of Judah. He spent most of his life doing what was pleasing to the Lord. Here we have an account of King Asa missing the mark in God's opinion. Because of King Solomon's sin, the nation of Israel is split in half and they are in constant conflict for hundreds of years. Wars rage on and off between Israel and Judah even though they are both the children of God and part of the nation of Israel. That is an interesting study all unto itself.

King Baasha of Israel has attacked again and taken Ramah. Asa's response is to bribe Ben-Hadad the king of Aram (Syria) to break his treaty with Baasha. Asa's plan works; at least in his eyes. Ben-Hadad attacks the territory of Baasha and so Baasha withdraws from Ramah. Then the seer Hanani comes and tells Asa that he has made a mistake.

The problem is that Aram is an enemy nation and God had told the nation of Israel not to make any treatys with them. It was God's desire to give the land of King Ben Hadad to the nation of Israel. And to do that they would have to destroy the king and his army. God wanted Asa to come to Him with this problem and allow Him to solve it for Asa. This was an ongoing weakness of Asa. As this chapter ends we are told that Asa had a disease in his feet that he would not go to the Lord about and so he died.

Asa missed an opportunity to do a great work for God. He missed it because he trusted in something that he could see and understand rather than going in faith to God. Because of his lack of faith he missed an opportunity to win a great victory for God. How many of us have done the same thing? As we look at a situation, we determine how to deal with it without ever even consulting the Lord. We might even do something like Asa did and work out a deal with the enemy to help us.

Twice in this chapter it is mentioned that Asa did not trust fully in the Lord and it cost him something. Trusting in the Lord means that we go to Him with absolutely everything and ask for His wisdom and direction. And while you wait for a response from God you keep working on plans and strategies, but you must trust the Lord to direct your path because that is exactly what He wants to and will do.

As leaders in families, ministries, and churches we must trust God with all of our decisions. If we don't, then we risk missing an opportunity to something tremendous for God. God wants to use us, no matter how insignificant we might think we are, to do mighty miraculous things. Jesus, help us so that we don't miss an opportunity that You set before us to change someone's life or to change the world.

JULY 26 || 2 CHRONICLES 17:10

Then the fear of the LORD fell over all the surrounding kingdoms so that none of them declared war on Jehoshaphat.

Read: 2 Chronicles 17:1-18:34

Jehoshaphat was one of the good kings of Judah. He did what was pleasing to the Lord. He made a point of destroying the pagan altars and shrines that had been erected in Judah during and since the time of King Solomon. He didn't get them all but he at least tried to do something about the idolatry. Then he sent priests and Levites out with the Book of the Law to teach people about God.

God was pleased with Jehoshaphat's actions and so He protected the king and the nation of Judah from the surrounding nations. Our verse tells us that 'the fear of the Lord fell over' them. One might assume from this that the surrounding nations were afraid to declare war on the nation of Judah and King Jehoshaphat because of the Lord. And this is partly true but it is not the whole picture.

The fear of the Lord is not just about being afraid. In fact it usually has nothing at all to do with being afraid in the sense that we usually use the word. The fear that is being described here is a reverential awe of God. The surrounding nations looked at what God was doing in Judah and they were blown away by it. They recognized that what was going on in Judah was because of God; not because of King Jehoshaphat.

There is a valuable lesson for all of us as we lead our families, ministries, and churches. God can cause all of those around us to be so blown away by what He is doing in our lives, marriages, families, ministries, and churches that they will not do anything to 'wage war' with us. How this came about is something that we also need to take note of. Jehoshaphat did what he could to eliminate the sin in Judah. Then he did what he could to teach the people about God and His Laws so that they would walk with God.

As leaders, we must also try to follow Jehoshaphat's example; we need to work to eliminate sin from every area of our lives and from everything that we are called to be leaders of. We then should be serious about learning God's Word and teaching it to others as best as we can. Each of us has been given at least a few people that we can influence toward a closer walk with God. We need to be faithful to do whatever we can regardless if it is only one person or a whole church full of people. Jehoshaphat was in a position that allowed him to influence millions toward God. God may have only called you to influence one person; be faithful to that one and God will bless you by keeping your 'enemies' at bay. Jesus, teach us how to be faithful shepherds of the flock that you have entrusted to us regardless of how big it is.

Rick Lancaster | PLANTERS PERSPECTIVE

JULY 27 || 2 CHRONICLES 20:33

During his reign, however, he failed to remove all the pagan shrines, and the people never fully committed themselves to following the God of their ancestors.

Read: 2 Chronicles 19:1-20:37

King Jehoshaphat was a pretty good king in Judah. For the most part he did what was pleasing to the Lord. He did make some mistakes that the Bible declares. That is one of the amazing things about Scripture; it doesn't hide the mistakes of the children of God. And for one, I am very happy about that. Because if all we ever saw in the Bible is people that were very pleasing to the Lord it would cause all the rest of us normal people to feel like we could never possibly measure up.

But the Bible reveals that many of God's people made mistakes and sometimes did things that displeased Him and resulted in punishment or loss of reward. That should give the rest of us hope in the knowledge that God uses imperfect people to get His work done on the earth. After all, that's all that He has to work with.

In our text for today we see this comment during the summary of Jehoshaphat's reign in Judah. He failed to do something that God wanted him to do and there was a consequence to Jehoshaphat's failure. God wanted His land cleansed of all the pagan places of worship. This is not a new request of God. When God led them into the Promised Land He told them to drive out all the nations that were living there and to utterly destroy their idols and places of worship.

God knew that if the people of Canaan, their places of worship, or their idols remained in the land that the children of Israel would be drawn to them. God knew that as long as those pagan shrines remained that it was just a matter of time before the Israelites turned away from God and to the idols.

Johoshaphat was the leader of the nation and he was in a place where he could have had a tremendous effect on the people towards God. It was his responsibility to lead the people toward God. Too often leaders define their role based on some task that they are trying to accomplish. As leaders, our first and most important priority is to lead people to Christ. And that is not completed once they come to Christ, but when they become like Christ.

Everything else that we do as leaders must be secondary to that. As leaders of families, ministries, or churches we must see our most important task as helping people to follow their God, Jesus Christ. The other things that we do are just tools and techniques for doing that. Helping them to follow Jesus means helping them tear down the pagan shrines that are in their lives. Jesus, help us to follow you so that we can lead others.

JULY 28 || 2 CHRONICLES 22:4

He did what was evil in the LORD's sight, just as Ahab had done. After the death of his father, members of Ahab's family became his advisers, and they led him to ruin.

Read: 2 Chronicles 22:1-23:21

Ahaziah becomes king after his father has been struck by God and killed in a most terrible way. His father had married one of King Ahab's daughters. King Ahab was one of the most wicked and evil kings that the nation of Israel ever endured. Ahaziah adopted the ways of his father-in-law King Ahab and was also a wicked king. The thing is that he wasn't a king of Israel but of Judah. In our verse for the day it says that the king of Judah took as his advisers men from the nation of Israel.

The ten tribes of Israel had a long almost uninterrupted series of wicked kings that did what was evil in the Lord's sight. Many of the God-fearing people in the land of the ten tribes escaped to Judah so as not to defile themselves with the sins that the kings were leading the people into. Now some of the very men that had helped King Ahab to be the wickedest king of Israel are the men that are advising Ahaziah. The result is that these people led him to his ruin.

The people that we allow to be our counselors and advisers will have an impact on us. In some respects you might understand why Ahaziah went to them for advice; after all, they were part of his family. Bloodlines are not enough to determine if someone should be your adviser or not. There must be something more than just relation that determines who will be appropriate to counsel you and advise you.

Only one person should be your adviser and that is God. The only way that we can live this life is to listen only to God and then do what He says. Ahaziah's advisers didn't follow God and weren't listening to God. Ahaziah only reigned in Judah for one year because He despised the counsel of the Lord.

Who are the people that are advising you and where are they leading you to? The Bible does teach us to seek counsel and advice from others. It tells us to seek that advice from people with wisdom. We also know from Scripture that wisdom is found in God and God alone. This should teach us to seek counsel from godly people. We determine whether someone is giving godly counsel based on comparing what they tell us to what the Bible teaches and what the Holy Spirit confirms in our heart.

Just because someone is part of your family doesn't qualify them as your adviser. The people that you should go to for advice are the ones that are going to God for advice. Anything else and you are being led to ruin and destruction. God's counsel is always good and leads to you to Jesus and the life that He came to give you. Jesus, reveal to us who we should be allowing to counsel and advise us.

Rick Lancaster / PLANTERS PERSPECTIVE

JULY 29 || 2 CHRONICLES 24:20

Then the Spirit of God came upon Zechariah son of Jehoiada the priest. He stood before the people and said, "This is what God says: Why do you disobey the LORD's commands so that you cannot prosper? You have abandoned the LORD, and now he has abandoned you!"

Read: 2 Chronicles 24:1-25:28

Joash, the king of Judah, has turned his back on the God that his mentor Jehoiada the priest has raised him to follow. Jehoiada's son Zechariah tries to tell Joash of his mistake and tries to warn him to come back to the Lord by abandoning all of the idols that he is worshipping and leading others to worship. Zechariah makes two powerful statements in our verse for today.

First, Zechariah asks the question: 'Why do you disobey the Lord's commands so that you cannot prosper?' There is a link described here between obedience and our prosperity. In Deuteronomy 28 this is also described in great detail as Moses tells of God's blessings for obedience and curses for disobedience. We need to understand very clearly that God is under no obligation to bless us when we are being disobedient. In fact, when we are disobedient we are very likely to experience God's curses.

A lot of people struggle with the idea that a gracious and loving God would curse anyone; especially one of His children. We must never forget that God loves us so much that He will do anything it takes to draw us into a right relationship with Him; including curse us. This is no different than when a two or three year needs a spanking because they are being defiant and rebellious. We discipline our children because we love them. God loves us more than we can imagine and He will 'spank' us if we will not obey Him.

The second word from Zechariah to the people of Israel is even more frightening; God told them that because they had abandoned Him that He was abandoning them. The first statement concerned God's provision to His people; this second one relates to His protection. God is not required to protect those that have abandoned Him. He might, but He doesn't have to. God promised to never leave us nor forsake us but there is an implied obedience on our part. To experience and partake of the blessings of God, we must be in obedience to His commands.

In our verse for the day it is obvious from the text that the people of Judah chose to disobey God. It wasn't that they sinned ignorantly; they made a conscious decision to do what they wanted as opposed to what God wanted. It is our choices that determine our relationship with God. Disobedience is a choice that carries serious consequences. Many of the trials and tribulations of our lives would be avoided if we would simply obey. Jesus, teach us to do what you want so that we might experience the life that You want to give us.

JULY 30 || 2 CHRONICLES 26:16

But when he had become powerful, he also became proud, which led to his downfall. He sinned against the LORD his God by entering the sanctuary of the LORD's Temple and personally burning incense on the altar.

Read: 2 Chronicles 26:1-28:27

King Uzziah was another of Judah's kings that did what was pleasing in the Lord's sight. But then a very dangerous thing happened; he became successful. Few things are as dangerous to a Christian as success. Nothing will tempt a Christian leader like the smell of great success. Uzziah had been very successful. And like many successful people, Uzziah allowed his success to go to his head.

Uzziah began to think that he had something to do with his success. He began to think that it was him that had won the victories and built up the nation of Judah. He thought he was somebody important. He came to believe it so strongly that he convinced himself that it was okay to do things that God has said not to do.

In his pride, Uzziah decided to worship God the way that he wanted to rather than the way that God had instructed him to. God had been very clear that only the descendants of Aaron and the Levites were allowed to enter into the temple and burn incense before God. By worshipping the way that he wanted to he was placing his ways above God's ways. God's response was immediate; Uzziah was stricken with leprosy.

As leaders of the family of God, His ministries, and His churches we must be so careful to watch out for the sin of Uzziah. When we are obedient and submitted to God, it is very likely that he is going to bless the work that we are doing. When He does, we must focus our eyes more firmly upon Him. It is at those times of success, especially public success that the sin of pride begins to grow.

Everyone around Uzziah was probably telling him what an awesome guy he was and what a great leader he was. He began to believe what they were saying about him. Uzziah was successful because God made him successful. If you are successful, it is because God has made you successful. Don't ever lose sight of that. If you do, God will remind you. Uzziah was stricken with leprosy and spent the rest of his life isolated from the people that were telling him how great he was. Don't make God put you on a time-out.

If God blesses you with success focus your eyes, mind, and heart on the Lord. The more successful you are, the more you need to keep your eyes off of yourself. Pride will take down one of God's leaders faster than virtually any other sin. Jesus, help us to look at our success and see only You.

Rick Lancaster | PLANTERS PERSPECTIVE

JULY 31 || 2 CHRONICLES 29:3

In the very first month of the first year of his reign, Hezekiah reopened the doors of the Temple of the LORD and repaired them.

Read: 2 Chronicles 29:1-36

Hezekiah takes over the kingdom after his father Ahaz dies. The very first thing that he does is open the doors of the temple which had been closed for some time. This is just the first of many things that Hezekiah did as he was king to bring the people of Israel back into a right relationship with God.

The temple was the focal point of all Jewish worship. When the nation of Israel wanted to worship God it was supposed to be at the temple in Jerusalem. Because it had been closed, the people were not able to worship God as they had been instructed and raised to. Instead they started turning to the pagan idols of the nations that surrounded them.

This verse spoke to me about the importance of the role of leader in the worship of God. God places leaders over us to lead and guide us so that we don't wander from the path that he has set before us. God sets them up and then tells us to follow them. Their role is to lead us to God and His plans for our lives. What we have that the Israelites lacked was the Holy Spirit living within us. He now leads us as we become attuned to His voice. There are still leaders in our lives and we are still to follow them but now we don't need to depend upon them as we follow God.

Some people have not attuned their ears to the voice of the Holy Spirit and there are those that sometimes 'tune out'. At those times the leader is the one that should be leading us back to the 'temple' to worship God. The leader has the responsibility of opening the doors to the temple. Once the doors are open it is up to each person whether or not they go into the temple and worship God.

As leaders, everything that we do should be drawing people closer to God. We must be very careful not to close the doors to God through our bad or sinful behaviors. God will hold us to account for the times that we have allowed that to happen. Everything that we do should open the doors and clear the way for people to enter into an intimate relationship with Jesus.

As followers, we should be doing everything we can to learn to hear from the Holy Spirit as He leads us to that relationship. To help us learn to do that God has given us godly leaders to follow. We need to faithfully pray for them as they work to open the doors to worship, not just for you but for everyone they are called to shepherd. And if God has called you to follow Jesus by following their example; then do it. That means when they open the door for you that you go through it into the place that has been prepared for you. Jesus, teach us to listen and obey.

AUGUST

AUGUST 1 || 2 CHRONICLES 30:9

For if you return to the LORD, your relatives and your children will be treated mercifully by their captors, and they will be able to return to this land. For the LORD your God is gracious and merciful. If you return to him, he will not continue to turn his face from you.

Read: 2 Chronicles 30:1-31:21

The very first thing that King Hezekiah does after becoming king is to open the temple and reinstate proper worship of God. Hezekiah has the priests cleanse and purify the temple of all the idols and other unclean things that had been placed there by previous kings. He then invites all the people to come and celebrate the Passover which had not been celebrated on a large scale for a long time.

Hezekiah's invitation is not just to celebrate the Passover but to return to the Lord. And then within that invitation to return to the Lord, Hezekiah gives the people a promise that is very powerful. Not only would the people benefit from coming back to the Lord but so would their relatives that were still in captivity.

God had turned His face away from the people of Israel because they had turned from Him and were worshipping worthless Idols. Ultimately, God allowed the Assyrians to come in and capture many of the Israelites and take them away into captivity. God's promise to those remaining in the land was that if they would turn back to God that He would turn His face back to them and not just them but also to their families that were in captivity. Hezekiah reminds us that God does this because He is gracious and merciful.

What hope that this should give us! This means that for us, if we will worship the Lord Jesus, that because of God's graciousness and mercy, that not only will we be blessed but that God will also bless us by blessing our family and friends that are in captivity. The Assyrians are long gone but the powerful enemy that they represent to us is not; the enemy of sin. Many of our family and friends are in bondage and captivity to sin.

Your faithfulness will play a role in bringing them to a place where they can encounter God in a powerful way. Because of your worship and service to God, He may protect and provide for them while they are in rebellion. He may do this to bless you. Never underestimate the power of your worship of God. Your worship unleashes the power of God in your life and in the lives of others. You may never know the impact of your worship of God. You may never realize the effect that your worship has on those around you and even on those that you don't even know.

As we bow our hearts in worship to God, He draws nearer to us and as a result He is nearer to those around us. I desire that I will grow to be as near to Jesus as is humanly possible so that those around me can't help but see God more clearly. Jesus, help us to clear our hearts of anything that separates us from that intimate closeness with You.

AUGUST 2 || 2 CHRONICLES 33:10

The LORD spoke to Manasseh and his people, but they ignored all his warnings.

Read: 2 Chronicles 32:1-33:13

God is always faithful to warn us about the dangers of our sin and rebellion. Our problem is that we don't listen. Manasseh was the king of Judah after his father Hezekiah died. Hezekiah was a good king and for some reason his son was not. It is hard for me to completely understand how these guys could deviate so far from what is right in a single generation but we see this tendency repeated throughout the history of the nation of Israel. Manasseh did what was evil in the sight of the Lord and so the Lord sent to Manasseh prophets to warn him of the danger that he was in and that he was leading the people into.

Our verse for the day says that the Lord spoke to Manasseh and his people. The Lord does not just speak to a single person usually. While He typically will select a single person to be His primary tool for a particular group or time, He will usually confirm what He is saying to all those around this person as well.

Manasseh and his people ignored God. Because they ignored Him, God brought the nation of Assyria against them to punish them. That was not God's desire in the life of Manasseh and the people of Judah. It was God's desire to bless them abundantly and to protect them from their enemies. But you can't ignore God and expect Him to bless and protect you; it just doesn't work that way.

It is so important for us to not ignore God; especially when we He is trying to warn us. We need to get into the habit of listening to God and knowing His voice when we hear it. Listening is not a natural thing; especially when it comes to God. Our natural self does not want to hear from God because that means that we cannot be on the throne of our lives. We need to learn how to listen to God's voice. That begins by knowing how He talks to people. We begin to learn that as we read and study God's word. The longer that we spend time in the Bible the more likely we are to hear His voice.

In addition to being in His word, we also need to be taking time alone with God in prayer. We need to keep in mind that in order for us to hear God that we need to be quiet occasionally. In your prayer time set aside some time to just be still and wait for the Lord to speak to you.

The single most important thing that you need to do when the Lord speaks to you is do what He tells you to do. How do we know that Manasseh and his people ignored the Lord? They didn't obey Him! If you are involved in any kind of sin or rebellion, you can know that God is speaking to you through the work of the Holy Spirit in your life. If you keep ignoring Him you need to understand that He is preparing an Assyrian army to get your attention. Jesus, teach us to shut up and listen to You.

Rick Lancaster | PLANTERS PERSPECTIVE

AUGUST 3 || 2 CHRONICLES 34:33

So Josiah removed all detestable idols from the entire land of Israel and required everyone to worship the LORD their God. And throughout the rest of his lifetime, they did not turn away from the LORD, the God of their ancestors.

Read: 2 Chronicles 33:14-34:33

Josiah was one of the good kings of Israel. From early in his reign he sought to follow the LORD. In the eighteenth year of his reign, one of the priests found the Book of the Law in the Temple. This in itself is a sad testimony to how far Israel had drifted from the LORD. It took over a decade to uncover God's instructions to the people of Israel. Once Josiah heard the words that the scroll contained he realized that God was going to judge Israel for her sins of rebellion and idolatry. His response was to humble his heart before God and repent for the whole nation.

Josiah had been trying to seek the LORD for the last decade, but he had been doing it without God's written word. Once he heard God's word Josiah realized that his best efforts still left the whole nation under the impending judgment of God. Man' best efforts or best intentions will never substitute for obeying His word. Doing what we think God wants will never replace what God's says that He wants.

Even though Josiah was seeking the LORD, there were still things in his kingdom that were offensive to God. Without God's word Josiah did not know that the idols that were everywhere in the land was one of the key things that God was about to judge the nation for. He didn't see anything wrong with them until God's word was presented to him.

This is why it is so important for leaders of God's people to be in the Word of God often. They should have an intimate knowledge of what God says and wants from His people. When they counsel others it should be from God's Word and not from man's opinions. It is only as the Word of God comes to life within them that they will see the idols that litter their lives and set them up as targets of God's judgment.

It is also important for God's leaders to be in God's Word so that they can see the idols in their own lives. Josiah didn't see the idols in his kingdom as idols until God's Word revealed them as idols. Up to that point, they were just places where people worshipped whatever god they believed in. He didn't see that as sin until God's Word helped him to see it as sin. Just because we are seeking the LORD, doesn't mean that we can see every area of sin in our lives. As leaders seeking to serve God and please Him, we need to invite the Holy Spirit to use the Word of God to illuminate all the dark areas of our lives, especially all the areas that are hidden even to us.

Only God's Word has the power to change our lives to the level of perfection that God desires for us. Our best efforts are not good enough. Our best intentions will always fall short. Only the Holy Spirit quickened Word of God is able to bring about that kind of change. Jesus, help us to make Your Word a greater part of our lives.

AUGUST 4 || 2 CHRONICLES 36:14

All the leaders of the priests and the people became more and more unfaithful. They followed the pagan practices of the surrounding nations, desecrating the Temple of the LORD in Jerusalem.

Read: 2 Chronicles 35:1-36:23

Nebuchadnezzar, king of Babylon, has conquered Jerusalem and taken much of the treasures and people back with him to Babylonia. He appointed Zedekiah to be king over Israel. Zedekiah was part of the royal family and a descendant of King David. Nebuchadnezzar left Zedekiah to rule over Israel so that he could get tribute from Israel. There was a benefit in this for the Israelites. They did not have an oppressing government ruling over them. One of their own people was placed to lead them. God did this so that the national identity of Israel would not fade away.

Zedekiah had the opportunity to be a good or an evil king. He chose to do what was evil in the Lord's sight as did many of his ancestors. The really tragic part of all this is that it didn't have to happen. God had warned them through the prophets for a couple hundred years that this was going to happen. Both of the prophets Jeremiah and Ezekiel spoke very clearly to the people that this was going to happen soon and why it was happening. God told them that He was going to kick them out of the land because they were worshipping idols instead of Him.

Even with all the warnings and then the prophecies being fulfilled in their very presence the people did not respond. Many of these prophecies and warnings were spoken directly to the king and the leaders of the people and priests. But even with this mountain of evidence our verse for the day says that they became more and more unfaithful.

It is no wonder that the people were doing the wrong things. They were doing what they saw and heard. While this is no excuse, they should have also known to do the right thing but where the leaders go, so go the people. A leader's role is to go somewhere or do something and have other people follow. A leader can have tremendous influence upon those that are following him.

God doesn't call us to be perfect; He calls us to follow Him as well as we are able to. Then He calls us to lead others to follow us as well as they can. It is an enormous responsibility to assume the role of leader. Often we don't choose the role of leader; God does. Zedekiah was appointed by Nebuchadnezzar to be king. It was Zedekiah's choice of what kind of king he was. We also may not get to vote on whether we are to be leaders or not, but we do get to choose what kind of leader that we will be. Choose to follow Christ with your whole heart, soul, mind, and strength. That's all God needs to make you into a leader. Jesus, help us to choose you.

AUGUST 5 || EZRA 1:2

This is what King Cyrus of Persia says: "The LORD, the God of heaven, has given me all the kingdoms of the earth. He has appointed me to build him a Temple at Jerusalem, which is in Judah."

Read: Ezra 1:1-2:70

As I reflected upon this verse there were so many different things that I could have touched on. This proclamation by King Cyrus of Persia was the fulfillment of a prophecy given by Jeremiah. The prophecy was so specific that it mentioned Cyrus by name before he was born. The previous verse mentions that God stirred Cyrus' heart. We sometimes overlook the fact that God can touch the hearts of those that are not believers. What struck me about this verse is what God stirred Cyrus' heart to do; to build God a temple.

The first temple was built by Solomon. Cyrus is here ordering the construction of the second temple. This temple was later renovated and the temple mount was built around it by Herod the Great. This second temple is the one that Jesus visited some 500 later. The second temple was destroyed by the Romans in 70 AD. A third temple is predicted in Scripture to be built in the end days in a terrible period of time known as the Tribulation.

As a pastor of a small church that currently meets in an elementary school, this verse encourages me. From a human standpoint it is impossible for us to buy a piece of land and build a church. There simply is not enough money. The Jews coming out of the exile were in exactly the same position. There were not very many of them and they did not have a lot of resources to work with. They had to rebuild their whole country. Without God's intervention, the temple might never have been built.

It is going to take God's direct intervention in the hearts of people with resources for our church to find itself in a building that it can call its own. As most people would do I would pray and ask God to send someone, a Christian, to the church that would catch the vision of what we are doing and want to help see it come to life. I was praying too small. God has the sovereign ability to control anything and anyone. My prayer is now that God would send whoever He is preparing to do this work.

God can operate through unbelievers just as easily as He can through believers. We need to trust Him to accomplish His work using His methods and not our own. What great thing has God called you to do? Maybe God is preparing a Cyrus to help it to happen. We need to keep our eyes open and be prepared to work even when the work seems impossible. It is impossible to you but it is not impossible to God. Jesus, help us to learn that Your power is greater than our ability to dream.

AUGUST 6 || EZRA 3:3

Even though the people were afraid of the local residents, they rebuilt the altar at its old site. Then they immediately began to sacrifice burnt offerings on the altar to the LORD. They did this each morning and evening.

Read: Ezra 3:1-4:23

About fifty thousand Israelites return to Judah from their exile in Babylon. Once back they begin to rebuild the towns and cities where they had lived. They also begin to rebuild the temple. Part of rebuilding the temple was rebuilding the altar so that they could reinstate the sacrificial system that God had instructed Moses to teach the people. It has been a long time since they had been able to perform these sacrifices.

After the Israelites had been exiled, the Babylonians had moved other people into the land to farm it and to live in it. These foreigners had settled into the land and made homes and livings there. In many respects they would now look upon the Israelites as foreigners.

Our verse for the day gives us an idea that there was a tension that existed between the two groups. The Israelites were afraid of the people that were living in the land. This could be for many different reasons but it was real enough to get into scripture. One of the likely things that would have created a tension between the two groups was their religions. What people worship and the way that they worship can be a very divisive force.

The returning Israelites wanted to return to the manner of worship that Moses had taught them; they had to build a large altar and started the sacrifices again. The Israelites were obeying God by doing this. This verse is a testimony of their faith; even though they were afraid, they rebuilt the altar and began making sacrifices upon it. What an important lesson for all of us to learn. God expects us to be obedient regardless of the external circumstances. God had exiled the Israelites because they had turned away from Him. They were determined to start over again, the right way.

We are also surrounded by people that desire to worship their gods in ways that are contrary to what God would have us to do. That will create a tension between you and them. It may also create a fear in you because of what they might be able to do to you. This is not referring just to other religious groups but also to people that worship themselves or some other idol like money or position. They are in our neighborhoods, at work, where we play, even at church. We need to have the faith to believe that if God wants us to do something that He is also strong enough to help us to accomplish it. Too often we let fear stop us from worshipping God the way that He desires. When we do that we are robbing God of His glory and ourselves of His blessings. Fear should never stop us from acting, it should teach us to depend upon God as we act. Jesus, help us to do what You want even when we are afraid.

AUGUST 7 || EZRA 5:5

But because their God was watching over them, the leaders of the Jews were not prevented from building until a report was sent to Darius and he returned his decision.

Read: Ezra 4:24-6:22

The Jews had stopped rebuilding the temple for a time but based on the words of some prophets they get back to work. As soon as they start working the governor of the area comes and challenges them about what they are doing. He sends a letter to King Darius to let him know what the Jews are doing. But the governor did not stop the Jews from continuing their work on the temple.

The reason why they were not stopped was because God was watching over them. The task of rebuilding the temple had been given to them by God through His prophets. There was nothing or no one that was going to be able to stop that from happening; at least as long as those assigned the task were obedient. Even though he had control over the territory the governor had no power over the situation because God was in control over everything.

This truth should give us great courage to go about the work that God has assigned to us. Whatever tasks or roles that God has assigned to you (each of us has many of these), trust that as long as you are obedient that God is watching over you and will not allow the work to be hindered. The only thing that hinders the work that God wants us to do is our own sin. If we will just make it our goal to go through this life with clean hands and a pure heart we can rest in the knowledge that God's mighty power will bring to pass everything that He desires to see happen.

In our reading for the day we know that King Darius told the governor to stay away from the Jews and to pay for the construction of the temple. He also told him that anyone that violated this decree would be severely punished. God not only protected the Jews as they faithfully went about their work, He also provided for the work through their enemies. Never underestimate the power of God to function on your behalf. God can rearrange heaven and earth to cause things to happen in your life, marriage, family, ministry, or church to accomplish the work that He desires to accomplish. God only needs faithful workers to go about the work.

The Bible teaches that God is searching for people like that. In some ways that makes me sad because it sounds as though there are not many that God finds with hearts that are loyal to Him. The unlimited, supernatural power of God is available to anyone and everyone that is faithful to God. All we have to do is open up our hearts and ask God to use us to accomplish His good will in the world. We need to cry out as the prophet did; 'Here am I Lord, send me!' Jesus, help us to be those people that seek Your face and desire Your power to flow through us to accomplish mighty things in this world.

AUGUST 8 || EZRA 7:10

This was because Ezra had determined to study and obey the law of the LORD and to teach those laws and regulations to the people of Israel.

Read: Ezra 7:1-8:20

Several times during our reading for today the idea that the hand of the Lord was on Ezra is expressed. This means that God was blessing the things of Ezra; He was causing good things to happen in Ezra's life. The things that Ezra was trying to accomplish were happening because God was helping him. In our verse for the day we are given the reason why God was doing so much for Ezra. Ezra was doing three things that allowed him to be in a place where he could receive such an ample outpouring of God's grace; he was studying, obeying, and teaching the Law of God. It is within these three things that we also can experience the same blessing that Ezra did. It revolves around the Word of God.

Ezra started by studying the Law of the Lord. This is so different than just reading. We must study the Bible which means that we are striving to understand what it says. Lots of people can tell you what the Bible says about something but they have not studied to tell you what that means. Not only did Ezra study what the Law said but he was obedient to what he learned. Knowing and understanding what the Bible says is useless unless you are doing what you understand. Obedience is one of the keys to receiving God's blessing in your life.

The last step in Ezra's path to abundant blessing is teaching the Law of the Lord to others. This is the step that many people leave out in their relationship with God; teaching others. The Great Commission tells us to teach others to obey. This is not the role of just the pastors or elders or leaders; it is everyone's responsibility. Everyone that wants to experience the kind of relationship with God that Ezra was experiencing, needs to be being all three of these things; studying, obeying, and teaching.

The phrase that really struck me in this verse was 'Ezra had determined'. Ezra had made a decision and was determined to do these things that we have seen above. It is in our choices that all of our relationship with God is found. Ezra chose to do the things that he believed would please God. He was right; they did please God and He blessed Ezra because of this choice.

Too many people in this world have made choices that do not allow them to do the things that Ezra did. If you are too busy to study God's Word so that you understand it; you are too busy. If you are struggling obeying God's word it is because you have made decisions that draw you away from God. If there is too much going on in your life to take the time to teach others about God, than the things you are doing may not be pleasing to God. Determine to do what you know will please God and He will be pleased to bless you. Jesus, help us to choose to study, obey, and teach others about You.

Rick Lancaster | PLANTERS PERSPECTIVE

AUGUST 9 || EZRA 9:2

For the men of Israel have married women from these people and have taken them as wives for their sons. So the holy race has become polluted by these mixed marriages. To make matters worse, the officials and leaders are some of the worst offenders.

Read: Ezra 8:21-9:15

Ezra is confronted with the fact that many of the people of the children of Israel have married women from the pagan people that are living around them. Ezra is very upset about this and confronts the leaders about this and they go about dealing with it. The idea of inter-racial marriages is one that we as a culture are not that concerned about. Most of us are probably a mixture of nationalities; with some being so mixed that it is virtually impossible to describe. When marrying someone, the matter of race is seldom addressed beyond simple curiosity. However, for the Jews it was a completely different matter. God had very specifically told them not to inter-marry with the pagan nations around them. God had called them to be a separated people; separated from the nations around them. By marrying these women they were in direct disobedience and rebellion to God.

Ezra knew this and he was upset because he understood what the consequences would be if this were allowed to continue and grow. Ezra knew that God would not bless the nation of Israel while they were in disobedience. Ezra knew that the pagan women were likely to cause their Jewish husbands to worship false gods. This is the very thing that caused God to kick them out of the land in the first place. They have just returned to the land and here they are setting themselves up to do the very thing that brought God's judgment on them before.

And to make matters worse, the officials and leaders were some of the worst offenders. Those people that should have been setting the right example were the ones that were saying it was OK to do. Leaders are not above the rules. The leaders should be the one setting the greatest example; an example of obedience and purity.

As non-Jews, we are not held to this strict requirement about marrying into other nationalities. However we are restricted about the family that we are to marry from. As Christians, God calls us to marry from within the family of God. For the very same reason that God didn't want the Jews marrying outside of their family, He doesn't want us marrying outside of ours. The New Testament calls it being unequally yoked and we are told not to do it. If we do then we need to understand that we are being disobedient to God and that we are setting ourselves up to fall away from God and possibly to experience His judgment in our lives. As leaders of the family of God, we need to set the example by marrying within the family of God and encouraging all those around us to do the same. This applies to all of our close relationships and not just that of husband and wife. Do not be unequally yoked to unbelievers. Jesus, help us to separate ourselves from a world that will pollute us.

AUGUST 10 || EZRA 10:4

Take courage, for it is your duty to tell us how to proceed in setting things straight, and we will cooperate fully.

Read: Ezra 10:1-44

Ezra was a prophet that had come with a remnant of the Jewish people back from the exile. God had sent conquering nations to drive the people from their land because they had been unfaithful to Him. As was the custom of many of these conquering nations, they brought people from other nations they had conquered to maintain the land so that it wouldn't go wild.

When the remnant of Jews returned from captivity, the land was once again occupied by people from pagan nations. It wasn't long after they returned that the Jewish men, including many of the leaders of the nation and priests were marrying pagan women. God had chosen the Jewish people to be a separated people. He commanded them not to marry pagan women. The reason was simple; they would lead the nation of Israel into the sin of idolatry. Israel's own history proved God to be right in this.

When Ezra found out that this was going on he was greatly upset. He tore his clothes and went before God in an attitude of confession and mourning. He knew that the people were sinning and that God would end up judging them again for their sin. Ezra's heart was broken and everyone around him could see that. Shecaniah seems to speak for all the people to confess that they had indeed acted shamefully in marrying pagan women.

In today's verse, Shecaniah tells Ezra three things. First, he tells Ezra to 'take courage'. Ezra was discouraged. They had just been delivered from captivity and had a chance at a fresh start with God. Now here the people were committing a sin against the simple word of God. The people knew they weren't supposed to marry these women but they did it anyway. Shecaniah tells Ezra to 'get up', he has work to do.

The second thing that Shecaniah tells Ezra is that it is Ezra's duty to tell them how to do things that correct the mistakes of the people. One of the reasons that Ezra is in such deep mourning over this is not just because the people are now subject to God's punishment but because they are not in the place that God can bless them. God had been blessing them since they had returned and Ezra wept because he knew that would not continue while they were in rebellion and sin. One of the roles of the leader of families, churches, or any organization is to tell people how to move from rebellion against God, disobedience to His Word, and His curses to a place of surrender, obedience, and blessing. That is our duty; if we don't tell them then we are in disobedience.

The third thing that Shecaniah told Ezra was that the people would all listen and do what he told them to do. It would be great if that was the way it always worked, but the reality of things is that it doesn't. Sometimes people don't want to know what God wants and have no intention of turning away from their sin and rebellion. That is not your problem. Tell them the truth and tell them what they need to do to get right with God. The rest is up to the Holy Spirit. Trust Him to deal with them. Jesus, help us to tell them what they need to hear.

Rick Lancaster | PLANTERS PERSPECTIVE

AUGUST 11 | | NEHEMIAH 3:1

Then Eliashib the high priest and the other priests started to rebuild at the Sheep Gate. They dedicated it and set up its doors, building the wall as far as the Tower of the Hundred, which they dedicated, and the Tower of Hananel.

Read: Nehemiah 1:1-3:14

The wall around Jerusalem was destroyed when Nebuchadnezzar conquered Judah and exiled its people. The fact that the wall is down is a reproach to the Jewish people and Nehemiah sets about to do something about it. In our verse for the day we see that the high priest is one of the first ones mentioned as taking part in the reconstruction. Whether or not he was physically involved is impossible to tell but the text suggests that he was. The high priest was one of the highest positions in the nation of Israel.

The fact that the high priest and the other priests were the first ones mentioned speaks of a spiritual principle that we all should be sensitive to. As spiritual leaders we ought to be the first ones on the wall to do the work that needs to get done. We need to set the example of what is expected. We should never fall into the trap of believing that we are someone important and therefore above certain activities. The moment that we do, we have disqualified ourselves from our 'greater' positions.

God can only use us while we realize that we are where we are because God placed us there. He placed us there to do a certain type of task but that does not elevate us above other necessary tasks. To accomplish the task of rebuilding the wall it was going to take everyone's efforts. It encourages me that the high priest was right there in the midst of the work.

Often as I go about working around during the time that we set up the church on Sunday morning someone will see me doing something and will come over to take it from me and do it. I am one of those types that can't sit still while others are working. When they do that I go and find something else to do. My goal is to set the example that the work that needs to get done can be done by anyone and that no one is above any kind of work.

This applies to all aspects of our lives, not just at church. At home, in our neighborhoods, at work, and at play we can set the example of a people that don't think too highly of ourselves and do what we can to help other people wherever we can. Even little things like picking up trash in the parking lot at the grocery store can make a tremendous difference. There are so many little things that we could do to make life a little easier for someone else that cost us virtually nothing; except our pride.

We need to humble ourselves and actually want to find things to do that show the world that Christians care about someone or something other than themselves. We can say it and we can preach it but until we practice it, it means nothing. Jesus, help us to help.

AUGUST 12 || NEHEMIAH 5:9

Then I pressed further, "What you are doing is not right! Should you not walk in the fear of our God in order to avoid being mocked by enemy nations?"

Read: Nehemiah 3:15-5:13

Nehemiah has done a great job of getting the returned exiles organized and the wall around the city of Jerusalem is being rebuilt. Then Nehemiah finds out that the wealthy Jews are taking advantage of their poorer relatives. They are charging interest on loans and even taking their children as slaves to pay for food. Both of these things are against the law of God and Nehemiah is very upset about it. Nehemiah rebukes the nobles and officials and then tells them to return everything that they took.

In our verse he tells them why they should do this. Nehemiah asks them a rhetorical question. This means that the answer is obvious in the manner that the question was asked. He asks them, 'Should you not walk in fear of our God...?' The obvious answer is, 'Yes!' To walk in fear of God, means that we humbly obey all of God's commands. We do this because we recognize His ultimate authority and power in the universe and our lives.

Nehemiah goes on to explain why they should walk in fear of God; to avoid being mocked by enemy nations. The Jews are surrounded by the nations that the Babylonians moved into Israel after they exiled the Jews. These conquering nations would often bring other conquered nations in to maintain the land to provide food and other resources to the capitals of the conquering nations. These nations were watching what was going with the rebuilding of the wall and seeing what the nobles and officials were doing to their own people. Their poor behavior was causing these enemy nations to mock Israel and God and this upset Nehemiah.

We should take a lesson from this account as well. The way that we treat other Christians is being watched by the enemies of God. We must be so careful not to give them reason to mock God. The New Testament has over fifty 'one another' verses. These are Scriptures that specifically deal with how Christians relate to one another. If we disregard these instructions and do things the way we think we should or the way the world would, we are giving the enemies of God the opportunity to make fun of God.

Obeying God will cost us something that we think is fair or right for us to have. The nobles and officials felt that is was fair to collect interest on the money that they loaned to their relatives. God said it wasn't. Trusting God means that we believe that God will give us what He thinks is fair. God promised to bless the Jews if they obeyed Him completely. That promise applies to us as well. Jesus, help us to walk in the 'fear of God.'

Rick Lancaster | PLANTERS PERSPECTIVE

AUGUST 13 || NEHEMIAH 6:9

They were just trying to intimidate us, imagining that they could break our resolve and stop the work. So I prayed for strength to continue the work.

Read: Nehemiah 5:14-7:73a

Nehemiah and the Jews that returned from the exile have rebuilt the wall around Jerusalem. Soon they will hang the gates which will complete the project and will remove the reproach that is upon the city and the nation of Israel. It is then that the enemies of the Jews really step up their attempts to interfere. They send Nehemiah a message to try to get him to meet them. Their intent is to harm him, probably kill him but Nehemiah realizes that and refuses to go.

Five times these enemies attempt to get Nehemiah where they can do him harm. The fifth time they send a letter that accuses Nehemiah of conspiring to rebel. The letter goes on to say that they are going to send word to the king informing him of their plan to set Nehemiah up as their king. Nehemiah's response is simple; he told them that it was a lie.

In our verse for the day, Nehemiah acknowledges that their purpose was to delay or stop the work that they were doing. Nehemiah was doing a work that God had appointed for him to do. Some people might point to the rebuilding of the wall as some great work that God wanted to do. I think that is a mistake. How do we measure the greatness of the works that God gives us? To do that we would need to understand fully the significance of this work in God's overall plan. And that is something that we can't do, because only God sees it all.

Each and every work that God gives to us to do should be seen as a great work. Just like any one of the hundreds of people working on the wall might not have thought that their part was significant, it was a part of the whole and so therefore it is significant. We can't know the significance of our work and so we should treat every thing that God gives us to do as a great work. That child in the Sunday School class might be the next Billy Graham. Those signs you put out for church might direct that person that is close to suicide to find hope. That hug of greeting might be the only human affection that someone has received all week.

There are no small works with God, only small people that will not ses God as a big God. He is able to take my small offering and 'feed' thousands. Never see your offering, however small, as unimportant to God and His church. That is exactly what the enemy will try to do. If he can't intimidate you, he will try to discourage you. He will try to delay you or stop you. When that happens, you do as Nehemiah did, become even more determined to continue.

Our verse says that Nehemiah prayed for the strength to continue. When the enemy comes knocking on your door, don't answer, knock on God's door and ask for strength. You don't have time to be arguing and fighting with your enemies, you have work that God has appointed for you to do. Jesus, give us the strength we need to do the work.

AUGUST 14 || NEHEMIAH 8:17

So everyone who had returned from captivity lived in these shelters for the seven days of the festival, and everyone was filled with great joy! The Israelites had not celebrated this way since the days of Joshua son of Nun.

Read: Nehemiah 7:73b-9:21

The priests had been going through the book of the Law and learning about God and what He expected of them when they discovered that there was a festival that they were supposed to be celebrating during that month. It was the festival of shelters and was meant to remind the Israelites of how they had lived in shelters while brought the Lord them out of Egypt. The people respond to this information by celebrating this festival and they do it with great joy.

What really struck me about this verse was the time since they had last practiced this festival; it had been since the days of Joshua son of Nun. That was at least eight hundred years earlier. It had been at least eight hundred years since they had celebrated what God had done to give them the life that they were living in the land of the Promise. That seems very sad to me and I believe is a warning to all of us.

The Israelites had forgotten what it was that God had expected of them; they had forgotten how to worship God. And because they had forgotten, they had just returned from exile after God had kicked them out of the land that He had promised their ancestors. The promise was made to be an everlasting promise. The Jewish people were given the Promised Land and it was to be theirs for all time. There was a condition to that promise; they were to remain faithful to God and worship Him only. The Israelites forgot that and God kept His promise to kick them out if they did.

It was only after the priests started studying the book of the Law that they realized what they had done wrong. The lesson for us is that we should not stop studying the Bible. It is our lifeline to being in fellowship with God. Human nature will naturally draw us away from God. It is His word in conjunction with His Holy Spirit that keeps us close to where He wants us to be.

God has also made promises to us and given us things that we can celebrate in recognition of the amazing things that he has done. When we begin to forget those things it is just a matter of time before He must remove us from the land so that we remember that we need to remember what He told us. It is so much better just to stay close to Him by staying deep within His word. In yesterday's reading it said that Ezra helped them to understand what it all meant. Find somebody that can help you to understand and then stay connected. God desires to bless us beyond our abilities to think or ask but we must be in obedience and submission to Him to receive those blessings. To be obedient and submitted we need to know what he expects. Jesus, give us a hunger for Your word.

Rick Lancaster | PLANTERS PERSPECTIVE

AUGUST 15 || NEHEMIAH 10:32

In addition, we promise to obey the command to pay the annual Temple tax of one-eighth of an ounce of silver for the care of the Temple of our God.

Read: Nehemiah 9:22-10:39

The wall around Jerusalem has been rebuilt, though not to its original height. This is a time of great rejoicing within the nation of Israel. No longer is the city a reproach to its people. No longer can its enemies mock and ridicule them. All the people gathered together and Ezra the scribe read from the book of the law and reminded them of their past and called them to a right walk with God. A great revival swept through the land of Israel at this time and the people committed to follow the Lord with their whole hearts.

This revival resulted in a renewed interest in the Temple of God and other religious observances like the Sabbath. This is one of the evidences that revival is taking place; the things of God are given more attention and more respect. This is true when there is revival in a country, church, or a person's life.

God had commanded the Israelites pay an annual tax for the purpose of maintaining the Temple of God. While the text doesn't say this, this tax probably had not been collected for over 100 years. To maintain the temple and see that all the ceremonies and religious observances were held according to the Law of Moses, the people were going to have to do their part.

It wasn't just this tax that they promised to bring. They also promised to bring the wood that was needed for the altar. They would need grain for the special bread that was put out and they would also have to bring animals for the daily sacrifices that were required by the Law.

As New Testament Christians, we don't have the same requirements. We are not required to pay an annual tax or bring certain kinds of gifts to the Church. Instead we are simply told to give as we are able. Instead of following the direction of the Law of Moses we are to follow the leading of the Holy Spirit.

One of the signs of revival within a person's life today is still a desire to see God's house built and maintained. The enemy has done a masterful job of making it almost taboo for pastors to speak about money or tithing. The courageous ones do it anyway because God does expect His people to give to the work that needs to get done and to maintain His house. We should not be ashamed to tell people that God gave them money so that they could give a part of it back to Him. It is one of the ways that they prove that they trust God. Jesus, teach us to trust, obey, and give.

AUGUST 16 || NEHEMIAH 11:2

And the people commended everyone who volunteered to resettle in Jerusalem.

Read: Nehemiah 11:1-12:26

The people of Israel are re-establishing themselves in the land. They have been returning from exile in waves. In Jerusalem, the temple has been rebuilt and the walls of the city have recently been rebuilt. The city itself does not have a lot of people living in it. Most of the people that have returned have returned to the land that was their ancestral inheritance.

Jerusalem was the center of Hebrew worship. It was there that the temple of God was located. It was there that the only altar for making sacrifices to God was found. Jerusalem was the city that God said that he would live in among the children of Israel. Jerusalem was and still is a very important city to the nation of Israel.

The leaders determined that there were not enough people living in the city to maintain it and the temple of God and so they determined that some people would need to leave their ancestral homes to come and live in Jerusalem. They determined that one out of every ten would come and live in Jerusalem. To determine who would make the move they cast sacred lots to determine God's will in the matter.

There were some that willingly volunteered to make this move. They could see the need and decided to meet the need. This was a sacrifice. It meant giving up their ancestral home to go and live in the city of Jerusalem. It is not possible to know the level of significance of this sacrifice but it was enough that the other people recognized it and commended those that would do such a thing.

Life is filled with opportunities to sacrifice something that is important or valuable to you for the needs of others or the greater good. As leaders of families, ministries, or churches sacrifice should be second nature to us. It should be something that we do almost without thinking. But there will come times when there is a need to give up something very valuable to us. And the question will be; 'Will God have to tell you to give it up or will you volunteer to give it up?'

Some of the people were told to leave their homes and move to Jerusalem. Others went voluntarily. Those that chose to move to Jerusalem received the commendation of their peers. We don't do our deeds to be seen by men but you should note that the only people that were recognized by God by being recorded in scripture were the ones that volunteered to move to Jerusalem. Men noticed their choice but that is recorded so that we know that God noticed their choice. Life is all about our choices. Jesus, help us to move toward You with all of our choices.

Rick Lancaster / PLANTERS PERSPECTIVE

AUGUST 17 || NEHEMIAH 12:30

The priests and Levites first dedicated themselves, then the people, the gates, and the wall.

Read: Nehemiah 12:27-13:31

The wall that surrounded the city of Jerusalem has just been rebuilt. Nehemiah then prepares everyone to dedicate the wall. This was an ancient practice that was done at the completion of any project. Even the pagan cultures would dedicate their structures to their gods. In this case the Israelites are dedicating the wall to the One and Only God.

Our verse for today says that the priests and Levites dedicated themselves first. It was only after they had been dedicated did they do the work of dedicating the wall, the gates, and the people. There is a great lesson in that for the Christian today. We must also be dedicated before we can go and do the work of the ministry. Too often we do the work without a consideration of our own preparation for that work.

For the Levites and the priests preparation involved a ritual of cleansing. It was a ritual of changing their clothes and bathing. Ceremonially they would be cleansed of all the sin that defiles them. By doing this they would be ceremonially prepared to minister to the people.

We also need to go through a ritual of cleansing as we prepare ourselves to be used by God to do His work. The difference is that ours is an internal cleansing not external as the Levites and priests did. Their rituals of cleansing were meant to be a picture of what we are to do. By changing their clothes they were removing the effects of the physical world. We as Christian servants do the same thing as we repent of the sins that infect us. By repenting and turning from the sin that soils us we are in effect removing them from ourselves and changing into clean clothes.

The Levites ritual of washing is a picture of Christ's forgiveness. When we repent or turn away from the sins in our life and ask for God to forgive us He does every single time and then the blood of Christ washes over us and makes us clean. This cleansing makes us white as snow in the sight of the Lord. It is only then that we can truly serve with the power, grace, mercy, and love that God provides.

Before you are ready to do anything for the Lord, He wants you to be dedicated to Him. This involves a ritual of cleansing. Open your heart to the searchlight of the Holy Spirit. Allow Him to reveal to you those areas that you need to repent of and be forgiven for. And then receive from Jesus the power of His forgiveness. Allow God to cleanse you and purify you. Then you are ready to do something for God. Jesus, help us to dedicate ourselves before we try to dedicate others.

AUGUST 18 || ESTHER 1:22

He sent letters to all parts of the empire, to each province in its own script and language, proclaiming that every man should be the ruler of his home.

Read: Esther 1:1-3:15

King Xerxes was the most powerful man in the world at this time. The Persian Empire stretched across much of the known world. King Xerxes had little to concern himself with and so threw a huge party that lasted six months. After that party was over, the king threw a feast for all the servants and officials of the palace. While half drunk he decided to parade his beautiful wife before everyone to show off. She refused to come and Xerxes flew into a rage. Xerxes' counselors told him that if he didn't do something, all the wives in the kingdom would soon rebel because of her actions. The beautiful Queen Vashti was forever banished from the king's presence and Xerxes sent a decree throughout his kingdom.

This decree, as our verse for the day tells us, was that every man should be ruler in his home. This meant that husbands were given the power to treat their wives the same way that Xerxes had just treated Vashti. Husbands now had ultimate, unquestionable authority over their wives. It is not hard to imagine the abuse that was spawned by this sinful decree. This may also be the source of the idea that 'a man is the king of his castle'.

Xerxes' mistake is the same mistake that men have been making for thousands of years; believing that they are superior to women. There is no question that God made men different than women. Generally speaking men are stronger physically than women. They also respond differently in certain situations causing men to attribute superiority over women. What these men fail to recognize is that women excel in areas that men are weak. These same men don't recognize this because they perceive those areas to be unimportant.

God's view of men and women are as equals. Neither is superior over the other. Both are uniquely designed to complement one another to accomplish something miraculous; living together in marriage and raising children. Unhealthy views about our roles in marriage and family is the source of many of our society's woes and struggles. If more men stood up to be who God created them to be, our world would be radically different than it is today.

God didn't create men to the rulers of their homes; He created them to lead their homes. The distinction might appear to be small but is, in fact, enormous. A ruler has absolute authority. No one has permission to question or challenge his authority or rule. A leader uses influence to guide people toward a desired objective. A man that is fulfilling his God-given roles as a husband and father is not so much a ruler as he is a servant, steward, and shepherd. That kind of a man will enjoy blessings beyond his imaginings as God rearranges heaven and earth to pour out his grace upon him. Jesus, help men to be real men, not as the world says but as You say.

Rick Lancaster | PLANTERS PERSPECTIVE

AUGUST 19 || ESTHER 6:1

That night the king had trouble sleeping, so he ordered an attendant to bring the historical records of his kingdom so they could be read to him.

Read: Esther 4:1-7:10

The book of Esther describes an event that took place while the Hebrews were in exile. It is obvious as we read this text that the Jews were not being oppressed like they were in Egypt. They are living among the people of the land. One of the primary themes of the book of Esther is the sovereignty of God. Repeatedly throughout this fascinating book we see the mighty hand of God at work on behalf of the Jews.

Haman is plotting against the Jews because of his hatred for Mordecai. He has convinced the king to issue an order for them all to be exterminated. Earlier Esther, a Jew, was picked as Queen. Her nationality was not known to the king or to Haman. Haman is so consumed with hatred for the Jew Mordecai that he erects a gallows and is coming to the king to ask permission to hang Mordecai.

That night the king has trouble sleeping and has the historical records read to him. During this reading he is reminded that Mordecai had earlier uncovered a plot to assassinate him and Mordecai had not been rewarded. Just as the king is reading this Haman comes in to ask the king to hand Mordecai over to him to hang him. Instead the king tells Haman to honor Mordecai. Can you imagine the humiliation that Haman would have felt to be honoring the man that he was determined to kill? Ultimately Haman is hanged on the gallows that he planned to hang Mordecai on.

God is sovereign! That means that He is in complete and total control. God arranged for Mordecai to uncover the plot to kill the king. He arranged that Mordecai would get no immediate reward for this good act of service. God arranged that Esther, Mordecai's uncle's daughter, would become Queen rather than one of the other several hundred women that were being 'interviewed'. God arranges for the king to have trouble sleeping and then arranges that the thing that is read to him be the very thing needed to prevent Haman's plot from succeeding.

Every detail of this account is laid out by God so that we can see that God sometimes works in very unusual ways to get to the place where He can do a great thing for His people. No detail of our lives is accidental. Everything that goes on in our lives is part of this great plan that God is unfolding in front of us. No detail is unimportant. Some seemingly unimportant event in your life, like a bad night's sleep, might be the very thing that God is going to use to do something miraculous. We need to see every event in our lives as the sovereign hand of God at work and be watching for what He is going to do next. Jesus, help me to look for You in the smallest details of my life.

AUGUST 20 || ESTHER 8:8

Now go ahead and send a message to the Jews in the king's name, telling them whatever you want, and seal it with the king's signet ring. But remember that whatever is written in the king's name and sealed with his ring can never be revoked.

Read: Esther 8:1-10:3

There are many parts of the book of Esther that are difficult for modern readers to relate to. The whole process that led to Esther becoming queen is certainly pretty strange. When we think of the ancient kings we usually picture in our minds men that did pretty much whatever they wanted to. King Xerxes was the ruler of the Medes and the Persians, one of the largest empires ever formed. From our text we see that Xerxes wasn't free to do whatever he wanted. There were rules that he had to abide by, even though he was the most powerful man in the world at that time.

The main message of the book of Esther is God's providential care for His people. Haman had planned to destroy the Jews but God frustrated his plan by placing Esther, a Jew, in the palace as queen. As a little side-note, Haman is an Agagite, his ancestor was King Agag the Amalekite. King Saul had been commanded by God to utterly destroy the Amalekites from the face of the earth. King Saul rebelled against God and spared some of the Amalekites. Haman and his treachery are the result of King Saul's rebellion.

King Xerxes gives Esther permission to do whatever she wants to but she cannot reverse what has already been ordered. King Xerxes is a symbol of the world and the flesh. Queen Esther is a symbol of God's people. God's people are in close proximity to the world. In the New Testament we are told that we are in the world but not of the world. There is a fascinating lesson in this verse for all of us.

The king of this world, Satan, has instituted things that are designed and determined to destroy God's people. Many of those things we have no power to alter or change. While we have no power to change the way things are, we do have power to act to try to produce a different outcome. Esther and Mordecai sent a decree in the king's name and sealed with his signet ring telling the Jews to defend themselves and attack their enemies.

We also have received a decree that has the same purpose. The Bible's primary purpose is to teach us how to know, love, and worship God. It points us always to His Son Jesus. This decree is written in King Jesus' name and is sealed with the Holy Spirit. Nothing within this decree can ever be revoked. Jesus referred to God's Word as eternal. But it is also a powerful tool to teach us how to defend ourselves from our enemies and how to attack his spiritual strongholds. To do that we must know, believe, and obey God's Word. Jesus, teach us to go to Your Word for our defense.

Rick Lancaster / PLANTERS PERSPECTIVE

AUGUST 21 || JOB 1:10

You have always protected him and his home and his property from harm. You have made him prosperous in everything he does. Look how rich he is!

Read: Job 1:1-3:26

As we begin the book of Job we have this fascinating exchange between God and Satan. God is telling Satan how proud He is of Job. How many times have we read that and missed how cool that really is. God is proud of Job for his righteous behavior and so He is telling Satan about it. God does this twice in the beginning of the book. It is like a proud father boasting about his son's football game. God loves us and wants to see us do well and when we do He is proud of us. Satan responds to God with a challenge. He tells God that the only reason that Job is righteous is because of God's gracious hand of blessing in his life. God has protected Job and prospered him in everything. Satan tells God that is why Job is righteous. He goes on to tell God that if Job lost God's protection and blessing that Job would not be so righteous.

This shows you the foolishness of Satan and the power of God. God knows the end from the beginning; He knew exactly how Job was going to respond to the testing that he was put through. Satan believed that Job would melt into a pathetic puddle as soon as the heat got turned up on his life. God used His complete and perfect knowledge to permit Satan to provide us with an excellent example of how we can stand up under the heat of this life.

Job was rich; probably the richest man alive at the time. Satan accused him of loving his riches more than God. Satan accused Job of loving God only because of his great wealth. God knew differently. God knew that Job understood that the wealth that he possessed had been given to him by God. Job knew that God could take it away if he chose to.

Most of us will never find ourselves in a place where we are the richest people around. Many of us will live our whole lives with just enough to live. That should not change our view of this great book. What Satan said in our verse for today was true; both for Job and for you. You may not be rich monetarily but the Bible says that you are rich spiritually if you are in Christ. God still protects and provides for all of His people. Just because He chose not to make you rich is hardly a judgment regarding His love for you.

One of the messages that God tried to teach us through the book of Job is that He does provide or allow absolutely everything that comes into our lives. The problem begins when we start to expect God to provide and protect us in certain ways as a result of our relationship with Jesus. God will challenge some of the things that Job will say in this book to give us a picture that it is OK not to understand God. If God was small enough to understand, He wouldn't be big enough to be God. Jesus, thank you for everything that we have, but mostly for what You did.

AUGUST 22 || JOB 5:8

My advice to you is this: Go to God and present your case to him.

Read: Job 4:1-7:21

Eliphaz the Temanite is the first of Job's friends to speak out concerning what is going on in Job's life. For seven days and nights these men sat with him and none of them said a word. However you might judge the things that they end up telling Job about his circumstances you have to at least note that they cared enough about him to come to him in his time of need and take the time to mourn with him.

In his first speech to Job, Eliphaz makes a number of statements about God and then in our verse for today he tells Job that he should take his case to God. As we continue to read through the book of Job we are going to see that one of the great mistakes that Job's friends make is that they have already judged him guilty of sin. They make the wrong assumption that all of these things happened to Job because of some sin in his life. They assume that because these disasters have struck him it is because God is punishing him. Even though they can point to no obvious sin; they assume that there must be some. What Eliphaz was saying to Job was that if he were to take his case before God that he would be able to see the sin in his life. Eliphaz makes some great statements about God. The problem is that he has a wrong view of the circumstances that He is speaking about.

The main problem that Job and his friends seem to have in this book is that they do not understand that they have an enemy that they cannot see. They associate everything both good and evil with God. This wrong view of God affects the way that they relate to God. The same thing is true of us; if we have the wrong view of God it affects the way that we relate to Him. And part of our problem will always be that we have a wrong view about God because we see an infinite, perfect, and eternal God through the finite, sinful, and temporal eyes.

Eliphaz's advice was right, Job needed to take his case to God. God is the perfect judge. When we go to Him with the circumstances of our life we need to go with the attitude that we might have the wrong view of God and of what He is doing in our lives. Our desire should be to have Him show us where we do not see Him clearly and to better understand why things are going the way that they are. Too often we want to explain to God why things should be different, instead of humbly going to God and telling Him that we have no idea why things are the way that they are.

In Job's case it was not a matter of guilt or sin. God was doing a special work and using these circumstances in Job's life to do it. Just because things are not going the way that you desire them to doesn't mean that you are in sin (but it could) and it doesn't mean that God is judging you (but He could be); it might be because He is working to accomplish something that you can't see. Jesus, teach to come to You humbly so that we might see You more clearly.

Rick Lancaster / PLANTERS PERSPECTIVE

AUGUST 23 | | JOB 9:4

For God is so wise and so mighty. Who has ever challenged him successfully?

Read: Job 8:1-11:20

As Job responds to Bildad he makes some interesting statements about God. One of the truths of the book of Job is that within this book we can find most of the things that many people over time have thought about God. Within this single book you will find most of the ways that people view God of the Bible. Most people will interpret the book of Job to be a lesson in patience through adversity; I believe there are many much deeper lessons to be learned from this book. If you will study this book from the viewpoint of getting your viewpoint about God right, you will gain a lot more from it than just a better understanding of perseverance.

One such lesson is here in this chapter of Job. Job asks the question: 'Who has ever challenged Him successfully?' This question is raised out of Job's desire to challenge God about the things that have happened in his life. But Job is torn between his desire to challenge God and his understanding of the wisdom and power of God. Job knows that there is no possible way that anyone will ever be as wise or as powerful as God. He knows that to challenge Him is to invite defeat and humiliation.

This doesn't change the fact that his heart wants to challenge God. This is one of the cool things about this book; Job's heart is revealed throughout it. If we could put into words the things that were going on in our heart, we would be saying things much like Job does here. In Job's statement above, there is a sense of futility; He wants to challenge God but knows that he can't.

Job's problem is much like ours is; he doesn't see God correctly. All of us have a viewpoint of God that is based on our knowledge, experience, and maturity. The problem is that in all three areas we are not complete. The first verse of the book of Job describes him as blameless and as a man of complete integrity. Then as you read through the book you see that he was not perfect. That should give us all hope. None of us are perfect and our viewpoint of God is not exactly what it ought to be. You are going to find yourself being right where Job is with a desire to challenge God but with an understanding that to do so would be futile. That conflict in your heart is the Holy Spirit talking to you about your viewpoint of God.

When you come to that point of conflict it is time to stop and ask God to reveal Himself to you more fully. As you draw nearer to God through a deeper understanding of who He is and how He is going to work in your life you will find that these conflicts will diminish over time. They will not go away completely in this lifetime but as your viewpoint of God lines up with the reality of who He is they will diminish. Jesus, use the conflicts in our heart to draw us nearer to You that we might see You more clearly.

AUGUST 24 || JOB 13:3

Oh, how I long to speak directly to the Almighty. I want to argue my case with God himself.

Read: Job 12:1-15:35

Job wants to talk to God. As he argues with his 'friends' he becomes more frustrated at their attempts to get him to confess the sin that has brought this tragedy into Job's life. And because they won't listen to him and believe him Job turns his words to God.

Haven't we all been here at some point in our lives? A situation will get so out of control that we think to ourselves; if I could just speak with God directly, I could figure this out. Well, in a little over a week in our reading Job is going to get a chance to do just that. And it doesn't turn out the way that he wants it to. And trust me when I say this that you wouldn't like the results either.

As righteous and just as Job was, he was lacking in faith. Earlier in the book Job made a statement that showed great faith. But here we have evidence that his faith was not complete. The reason why he wanted to speak to God was so that he could argue his case with God. This word 'argue' is like the word used to describe what an attorney does in the courtroom. Job wanted to present his case before God and influence His decision.

What is it that Job could have said to God that He didn't already know? What evidence could Job have presented before God that He hadn't already seen? God is omniscient! He knows everything about everything and everyone. There is nothing that God does not know. There is no evidence or argument that you could bring that would change His decision.

Job is asking the question: Why is this happening to me? He wants to know why God is doing this to Him. We know from our earlier reading that these kinds of things are not done by God, but that they are allowed by God. And as Job's friends probe him for his guilt, Job's faith is tested.

In ministry we are going to have 'friends' like Job's friends. And those friends are going to test our faith and patience. We live in a world where bad things happen. Eventually those bad things happen to almost everyone. And if something bad happens in your church or ministry, your 'friends' are going to come try to 'comfort' you. And they are going to try to 'help' you by encouraging you to get right with God.

If you have sin in your life, confess it to God and get right. If you don't, then you have only one option left, trust God. God allows the bad things in our lives for more reasons than we can possibly know. You don't have to understand. All you have to do is believe God and trust Him with your life, your ministry, and your church. Jesus, teach us to trust You and to stop arguing.

Rick Lancaster | PLANTERS PERSPECTIVE

AUGUST 25 || JOB 16:9

God hates me and tears angrily at my flesh. He gnashes his teeth at me and pierces me with his eyes.

Read: Job 16:1-19:29

Job is expressing a great sense of frustration because of his circumstances. God has allowed Satan to take everything from him except his life and Job places the blame on why his life is the way that it is on God. His friends resolutely try to cause him to see that it is his sin that has brought about the judgment of God but Job just as resolutely stands in his blamelessness.

It is almost as if the more Job's friends try to convince him that it is his sin that has brought this upon him that Job gets angrier with God. He will eventually lash out at his friends but most of his frustration is being targeted at God. Job is blaming God and speaks as though he believes that God hates him and is trying to destroy him.

Job was operating from a place of blindness and ignorance. As far as we can tell, he had no knowledge that there was a creature named Satan. This lack of information is the basis for his attitude toward God. This is also the source of his friends questioning Job's righteousness. They only knew about God and assumed that only He was active in the world.

Before we can dismiss this book because of our more complete knowledge we need to understand something. The book of Job is a picture of what happens in the way that we behave when we have the wrong understanding of God. Because we know about Satan and have more knowledge, we think these kinds of attitudes cannot happen with us. That is very far from the truth. Just because we have more complete knowledge about God and Satan and spiritual things doesn't mean that we know everything. In fact, the Bible teaches that our knowledge is far from complete.

This means that we are just as likely to have a wrong attitude about God as Job and his friends did. Even though we have greater knowledge of spiritual things we don't know why God does or allows all the things that He does. We can easily find ourselves in a place just like Job's, wondering why God is picking on us.

God loves us with an infinite, eternal, immeasurable love. That doesn't mean that our lives are going to be totally free from any forms of trials and troubles. You can be just as blameless as Job, or even more, and still experience great pain and suffering. The part that we struggle with is that God does not owe us an explanation for why He does or allows the things that He does. He is God and part of being God is never having to explain yourself. That doesn't change His love for us. God will never, ever hate us. Even when it feels as though He is tearing angrily at your flesh, He loves you and has a plan for your troubles and suffering. Jesus, help us to never forget the depth of your love.

AUGUST 26 || JOB 21:34

How can you comfort me? All your explanations are wrong!

Read: Job 20:1-22:30

Job's 'friends' have come in the pretense that they are there to comfort him. And they resolutely stick to the belief that Job has committed some sin against God that he is being judged for. And Job just as resolutely sticks to his claims that he has not committed any sins worthy of the punishment that he has received.

Job needs comfort. He needs someone to give him some answers for the things that are going on in his life. His children are all gone and his wife is no comfort to him and so his friends are his only source of comfort. And yet they are not very comforting to him.

Can you imagine how alone Job must feel at this moment? Unfortunately, I know that some of you can! There are going to be times in our life, in our ministry, in our church, when it feels like we are all alone. No one knows what you are feeling, and they can't see things the way that you can. It is very lonely!

And everyone that comes to comfort you will do so with the wrong information or ideas. They are probably only seeing things from their perspective or from a perspective that is based on incorrect information. Their comfort will leave you questioning yourself, your ministry, your church, and maybe even God.

Only God can comfort us. Of course God can and will use others to do that comforting but we must understand that the source of all comfort is God. Going to any other source will always lead to disappointment and frustration. It is the Holy Spirit who comforts us when we need it the most.

Part of Job's problem is that he spends too much time with his eyes focused on the wrong thing. Job has experienced a tremendous tragedy in his life. But that is just a circumstance! While we see Job look up to God through his many speeches, he spends too much time with his eyes focused on his problem.

As the trials and tribulations of life and ministry come and go from your view, you must maintain the proper viewpoint. And that is of a servant of the living God. And even though we are His servants, we are also His children and He loves us with an infinite, eternal love. As a servant, our eyes should always be on the master looking for His leading and guiding, especially when things are tough. As His children, we can plead with Him for mercy and expect to receive it. Our ability to weather the storms of life and ministry will depend largely upon our ability to keep our eyes off of our circumstances and keep our eyes on the Lord Jesus. Jesus, help us to keep looking up.

Rick Lancaster / PLANTERS PERSPECTIVE

AUGUST 27 || JOB 23:13

Nevertheless, his mind concerning me remains unchanged, and who can turn him from his purposes? Whatever he wants to do, he does.

Read: Job 23:1-27:23

Job continues to defend himself to his friends and resolutely stands on his innocence. His friends are convinced that Job is being judged for some secret sin that he will not confess. They want him to confess this sin so that he can be justified before God. Job's friends do not believe that Job is innocent and Job does not believe that he is guilty. It is because of these differing perspectives that we have this book. Often our own viewpoints of God and the things of our lives follow the same kinds of thought processes as what is going on here with Job and his friends.

In chapter 23 of our reading today, Job makes some great statements about God. He wants to have a face-to-face meeting with God so that he can present his case to God. Then Job goes on to say that it is not possible to do that because he can't get to God. Even though God is working all around Him, Job can't see Him and can't go to where He is. Then Job makes the statement in our verse today. He recognizes the futility of doing that anyway; God isn't going to change His mind. Job's desire to meet with God is based on him trying to change God's mind about the circumstances of his life. Job's viewpoint is based on doing what he can to alleviate the pain that is in his life. One of the reasons why Job was allowed to be tested by Satan was so that you and I would be able to see God more clearly. Through one man's suffering, millions of people have been able to see God with more clarity.

God is God and nothing that we think, say, or do is going to change the fact that He is supremely in control of everything. Just because we are uncomfortable doesn't mean that what is happening to us is wrong and that God should change it. We have no idea what God might be doing through our trials and tribulations that may impact another person's life or maybe like Job's, millions of others.

While we are in the midst of difficult situations and everything seems hopeless it is almost impossible to look at the situation from the viewpoint of how it is going to help others or even how God might be working to help us. The life of Joseph is a great example of a man in whose life God used trials and tribulations to save his family and blessed him in the process. It might have been hard or even impossible for Joseph to see that while he was sitting in that Egyptian prison.

Regardless of what your trial is, there is an example in the Bible of how God worked in circumstances that were similar. Job was focused on his problems and changing God's mind even though he knew that God doesn't change His mind. We need to focus on trying to understand the mind of God so that we might change our minds to be more like Christ's. Jesus, teach us to think like You.

AUGUST 28 || JOB 30:20

I cry to you, O God, but you don't answer me. I stand before you, and you don't bother to look.

Read: Job 28:1-30:31

Job in his anguish cries out to God and feels that his prayers are being ignored by God. Job has lost virtually everything in his life. His children have been killed and all of his possessions and wealth have been taken away. Then to top it all off, Satan inflicts him with boils all over his body. Most of us could not even imagine the pain that he is experiencing at this time; both physical and emotional. In his pain and suffering Job cries out to God and wants Him to answer.

In our pain and suffering we do the same thing; we cry out to God and expect Him to answer us and to do it right now. God does not owe us an answer. If He does answer us it is because of His love for us and because of His amazing grace. God's timing is also a function of His grace and His will. He determines when we get an answer to our prayers, not us. God calls us to be persistent in our prayers. That means that we are to keep praying until He answers us; however long that takes.

In our pain and suffering, the only thing that we can see is our circumstances. It is very difficult to see past the things that are going on in our lives. Job only knows that he needs relief from the circumstances of his life and so he speaks what his heart is feeling. Sadly, his friends do not do a very good job of encouraging him; quite the contrary, they tend to discourage him with their insistence upon his guilt.

What Job needs to know in his pain and suffering is that God always answers the prayers of His children. The answer may not come in the time that he wants or in the way that he wants but it always comes. Job needs to know that God is always watching over him. There is never a moment when the eyes of God are not on His children. The Bible promises that God will never leave us or forsake us. That is a promise and God keeps every one of His promises. Just because you can't hear God or see Him doesn't mean that He is not there and not painfully aware of every detail of your life.

In our pain and suffering we desire God's attention the way that we should always desire it. We only cry out to God in our suffering and trials. We should be crying out to God every time we sense that His presence is not strong with us. That happens when we get distracted from God; not Him getting distracted from us. We can get distracted so easily by the many things that are going on in our lives. We can get distracted by prosperity and success. Hobbies and pleasure can also be a source of distraction. Just the everyday things of life can be a distraction from our relationship with God. God's desire for all of us is that we would crave His presence all the time. It is His desire that we would recognize quickly when we have wandered from His immediate presence and cry out to return to Him. Jesus, teach us to crave Your presence in our lives every moment.

Rick Lancaster / PLANTERS PERSPECTIVE

AUGUST 29 || JOB 33:14

But God speaks again and again, though people do not recognize it.

Read: Job 31:1-33:33

Elihu is an interesting character in the account of Job. He is not listed among Job's three friends when they are introduced in chapter two; he just shows up here in chapter 32. When God rebukes Job's friends, no mention is given to Elihu. Those kinds of things have always fascinated me; not because there is some deep theological truth to be found in that, I just want more of the story than is told in the scriptures. Then I remember that if God didn't think it important enough to record than I don't need to know it.

Elihu goes on for six straight chapters proclaiming the incredible attributes of God. It is a wonderful picture of God that Elihu paints and worthy of greater study. The verse that caught my attention this morning was the one above. One of Job's greatest complaints against God is that God won't talk to him about what is going on in Job's life. Job wants to talk to God so that he can present his case to God and ask God why things are the way that they are. Job feels that God is ignoring Him.

Elihu tells Job and us that this is not true. God is speaking; we just don't recognize it when He does. Why is it that we would not hear God when He speaks to us? In Job's case he was allowing his pain and suffering to block God's voice. When we focus our eyes on our circumstances it is virtually impossible to hear God's voice. We must, no matter how difficult it might be, take our eyes off of the trials of our lives and turn our ears toward God; then we will hear Him.

Another reason why we may not hear God's voice even though He is talking to us on a regular basis is because we have not learned to recognize His voice. It is possible to hear and recognize God's voice on a regular basis. It takes desire and persistence to know God and to know what it is that He is going to talk to you about. The two main tools that we have for doing that are prayer and the Bible. The Bible is how we learn about the heart, mind, and will of God. As we learn about God we will be better able to recognize when He is speaking to us because we are going to recognize the things that He is talking about from His written Word.

It is through prayer that His voice is heard most frequently. When we pray we are opening up a channel of communication with God. And I don't mean that when we pray that God starts talking. God is always transmitting, but when we pray we turn on our receiver so that we can hear. It is always a good idea during your prayer time to take some time to just sit and listen for God. If you fill up your prayer time with you talking, you may miss something that God is saying to you. God has so much that He wants us to hear if we would just listen. If we would just learn to perceive his voice and respond there is no end to the ways that He will bless us. Jesus, teach us to perceive You and Your voice.

AUGUST 30 | | JOB 36:5

God is mighty, yet he does not despise anyone! He is mighty in both power and understanding.

Read: Job 34:1-36:33

Elihu continues his speech to Job and his 'friends'. And here he changes his topic to the wisdom and understanding of God. And in speaking of God's understanding, Elihu describes God as mighty in strength. God's understanding and wisdom are some of the things that make Him mighty in strength.

But one of the incredible things about God is that even though His power, might, strength, wisdom, and understanding are far beyond that of mortal man, He despises no one. When we think of the word despise we think specifically of hatred. To despise someone is to view them as inferior or not worthy of notice.

And God, even though He is so far above man, does not think him unworthy of notice. God does not treat man as inferior. God does not despise anyone. And God wants us to have that same attitude in our lives. God does not want us to despise anyone.

As God works in your life, your ministry, and your church, He is going to bring people into your life. And He does that so that you will minister to them. And we need to resist the temptation to think that it is a distraction. It is very possible that God brought this person to you because you were exactly the right person to help them. It could also be that God wants to use them to minister to you in some way.

Jesus had some very harsh words for the Pharisees. They thought that they were more righteous than other people. Their attitude separated them from the people that they should have been serving. God doesn't call us to be better than other people; He calls us to serve other people. To do that you must have the same attitudes that God has. God, the Father, and Jesus set the examples that we are to follow.

God wants us to have greater knowledge and wisdom, but He doesn't want us to use that knowledge and wisdom as a wedge between us and other people. He wants us to use it as a tool to serve others. And to truly serve others you have to love them and you have to think that they are worthy of being served.

There is no one in this universe that God doesn't love. He does not despise anyone. He calls you to do likewise and to love others by using the gifts of wisdom and knowledge to build them up and not tear them down. If you ever get too big to serve God's people, you might be too big for God to use for anything. Jesus, help us to stay humble.

Rick Lancaster | PLANTERS PERSPECTIVE

AUGUST 31 || JOB 38:2

Who is this that questions my wisdom with such ignorant words?

Read: Job 37:1-39:30

Job has been laying out his case before God and Job's 'friends' have been trying to get Job to see what they think that they see. God responds to Job from the whirlwind, not with answers but with questions. Why didn't God answer Job's questions? Because Job's questions were based out of his ignorance of God and the ways of God!

Like the toddler asking questions about why things happen the way that they do, there comes a point as a parent that we tell them: 'Because I said so!' Or, 'that's just the way that it is!' The toddler's mind cannot possibly understand why things are the way that they are until their mind gains an understanding of the world around them.

God's ways and thoughts are so much higher than us that we are barely equivalent to the toddler. There is no way that we can understand God's ways or thoughts. There is no way that we can totally or completely understand why things happen the way that they do. And so that leaves us with a choice. Either we whine and complain and question God. Or we can totally and completely trust Him.

Everyone, at some point in your life, ministry, or church, will come to a place where you are tempted to question God. God, why did you allow this to happen? God, I thought you said... God, why didn't you... And when that temptation comes, resist it! The problem is not with God, it is with you. Your understanding is incomplete. And because your understanding is not complete, you cannot understand the reasons for what is happening.

Our response to God in these kinds of circumstances is not to question God, but to go to Him and beg Him for His mercy and grace. Pray that He will increase our understanding and help us to understand His purposes in whatever is going on. Believe God when He says that He will never leave us nor forsake us. Believe Him when He says that he has a plan and a purpose for your life.

It all comes down to trust and faith. Do you trust God? Do you believe God? Not just with your life, but with your ministry, and church as well? If you are questioning God, you are doing so from a position of ignorance. Before you ask God any questions, you answer the ones that He asked Job. Jesus, help us to rest in the truth that we know almost nothing compared to you and that you have our lives in your hands.

SEPTEMBER

SEPTEMBER 1 | | JOB 40:2

"Do you still want to argue with the Almighty? You are God's critic, but do you have the answers?"

Read: Job 40:1-42:17

All throughout today's reading God has unleashed a barrage of questions to Job. Each of these questions was a description of the omnipotence, the unlimited power, of God. God then tells Job to answer the questions. Basically God is saying to Job: "If you can answer these questions than you can be My critic!' This is a great lesson for all of us to learn.

God created everything and made everything the way that it is through His power and by His own design. At no point did He consult man because man could not counsel God. There is nothing that man knows that God does not know. The inverse is not true; there is very much that God knows that man does not know. For us to criticize God is arrogance or ignorance or both.

It is another of the great mysteries of God's great grace that He even allows us to criticize Him. God knows that we are ignorant of all His ways and power and so just like a parent that ignores the things that a small child says, God ignores many of the foolish things that His children say. I am very thankful for that because I can look back on my life and see that I have said some incredibly foolish and ignorant things. One of the things that God desires in our relationship with Him is that we would grow in knowledge of who He is and His ways. God wants us to be less ignorant about Him every day. As we grow in our knowledge of God, we are less prone to foolishly criticize God for the things that He does or allows to happen in our lives. Unfortunately, we often have to get a lecture from God to learn the lessons that help us to understand Him better.

Job is being lectured at by God because Job wanted to defend Himself before God. He wanted to present his case before God and tell God that what had happened to him was not right. Too many of us do exactly the same thing with God when things aren't the way that we want them to be. God would say to you the same thing that He said to Job: "Who do you think you are?"

It is not our place to question God the way that Job did in this book. It is appropriate for us to ask God to reveal Himself more fully to us. When your circumstances are difficult don't question God as to why it is happening, ask God to reveal to you how He is trying to help you to know Him more through these circumstances. It is even OK to ask God to change your circumstances so that they are more in your favor; just as long as you know that God doesn't have to change your circumstances just because you asked. Part of trusting God is knowing that He is in complete control of everything; even in your most difficult circumstances. Everything that happens in your life is an opportunity to know God better. The better we know God, the less likely we are to question the things that happen in our lives. Jesus, help us to learn quickly.

SEPTEMBER 2 || ECCLESIASTES 2:24

So I decided there is nothing better than to enjoy food and drink and to find satisfaction in work. Then I realized that this pleasure is from the hand of God.

Read: Ecclesiastes 1:1-3:22

As we read the book of Ecclesiastes we can come away with a great sense of futility in everything that we are doing. This somewhat dark book was written by Solomon near the end of his life. It is difficult to ascertain what his spiritual condition was when he wrote this book but it is believed that he had returned to the Lord by this time. This book has an incredible wealth of things to teach us about the way that we view the world around us and the things that we do.

It especially addresses our motivations and reasons for doing the things that we are doing. It helps us to look upon our own lives and test to see what is driving us; what is motivating us to do the things that we are doing. Most of the book refers to the negative point of view and shows us the attitudes and motivations that are wrong. And this is why this book tends to be misunderstood and avoided.

There is a reason why we exist on this planet. There is a reason why God created us. And it is our responsibility to discover what that reason is and what our purpose is and then live a life that fulfills that reason and purpose. The things that are important to us are the things that we are living for. In our text we see three different things that people tend to live for. Throughout today's reading Solomon addresses all three.

Some are motivated by food or the satisfaction of their bodies. Others are motivated by drink or the distraction of their minds. And others are motivated by work or a sense of accomplishment and achievement. Solomon addresses each individually and says that each as a motivation for life is vanity, foolishness, or vapor. But in our verse for today Solomon says; "there is nothing better than to enjoy" those things that he earlier says are foolishness.

God gave us those things so that we could enjoy them. They become foolishness and vanity when we allow them to be the motivation of our life. Too often we take the things that God gave us to enjoy and allow them to become the center of our lives. We can get to a place that we worship these things through the way that we handle them and allow them to control our lives.

We can get to the same place within the ministry or the church. We can allow this thing that God has set up to minister to others to be something that we worship. We can allow ourselves to be so consumed by the ministry or the church that we can lose sight of the God that they represent. Jesus, help us to worship You and enjoy the things you gave us

Rick Lancaster / PLANTERS PERSPECTIVE

SEPTEMBER 3 || ECCLESIASTES 4:12

A person standing alone can be attacked and defeated, but two can stand back-to-back and conquer. Three are even better, for a triple-braided cord is not easily broken.

Read: Ecclesiastes 4:1-6:12

This is a pretty familiar verse, especially for weddings. It calls people to stand together and therefore become stronger. This verse applies to so much more than just marriage; it applies in every area of life. In the Christian world we call this fellowship. Our problem is that we limit this thing we call fellowship to things like potlucks and bowling. It is so much more than that.

There is a saying that most of us have heard, "There is strength in numbers." And that is true spiritually also. While all we need in this world is Jesus, He doesn't want us to be in isolation from others. In Genesis 2 He said, "It is not good that man should be alone." The reason why it is not good is because alone we are vulnerable to attack. Those attacks come from many fronts; they come from our own desires, from a sinful world system, and from our enemy, Satan.

Fellowship is, on the surface, Christians gathering together to have fun. That is a great reason to do it but it can't be the only reason for it. A greater and more important reason for fellowship is to develop relationships with other Christians. It is through these relationships that the strength of numbers is seen.

Solomon in our verse for the day says that two together can conquer the enemy that attacks them. They can do that because they both defend the back of the other. Our weakest point is the part of our lives that we can't see. By inviting people to be a closer part of your life, you are inviting them to stand at your back and defend you. This invitation comes with a responsibility. If you invite them to watch your back, you in turn have an obligation to watch theirs.

In my own life I have come to realize that no one person can do this for me. Solomon went on to say that three is better than two. I know that certain people are better equipped to help me in some areas that others are not. I now actively seek out people that I can establish and develop fellowship relationships with so that we both can become stronger. Each of those people is stronger on a particular front than I am and I may have a strength that they need.

None of us 'need' anyone but God. But God in His wisdom designed us with a need to be in fellowship with other people. Our sinful natures might limit us to the fun part of fellowship. God would have us stand back-to-back with our fellow Christians and be victorious in whatever battle comes to us or them. Jesus, teach us how to be vigilant and faithful.

SEPTEMBER 4 || ECCLESIASTES 8:15

So I recommend having fun, because there is nothing better for people to do in this world than to eat, drink, and enjoy life. That way they will experience some happiness along with all the hard work God gives them.

Read: Ecclesiastes 7:1-9:18

As you read through the book of Ecclesiastes you can get a sense of hopelessness in Solomon. We need to remember the state that he is in when he wrote this book. Solomon has turned away from the God and has been worshipping the gods and idols of his many wives. And for all of his wisdom, Solomon had no knowledge of heaven or eternal life. You can tell as he writes that this life is all that he knows and therefore it colors his whole way of thinking. This is a beautiful picture of how most of the world views this life; they are trying to make the most of this life because they have no knowledge about the next one.

Today's verse is a picture of the futility and hopelessness that most people view the world. To them there is nothing beyond the grave and so you might as well enjoy this life as much as you can. This has created the mindset of consumerism and short-term thinking. The world views life from the standpoint that you need to enjoy it while you can because there is no tomorrow.

This verse can also be viewed from God's perspective; which is how God would like us to see it. Solomon suggests that the best way to go through life is to do those things that you enjoy. He reminds us that God is going to give us hard work to do and there is no way to avoid that but we should also try to enjoy the life that we have. Solomon's basis for this conclusion is wrong but his conclusion is correct; God does want to us to enjoy this life along with the hard work that He is going to give us.

The big difference is the motivation. The world is motivated to enjoy this life because that is all that they have. As Christians our motivation for enjoying this life is because that is what God wants us to do while we wait for eternity in heaven to begin. For the world, the search for enjoyment is desperate and often futile. For the Christian it is a choice that we make as we go through this life; we can choose to enjoy it.

This is an area that most Christians need to grow in their spiritual life; understanding that enjoying the life that God has given us is a choice. Too often we think that enjoyment is natural. We usually will base our enjoyment upon the circumstances of our life. God's desire is that we would look past our circumstances and choose to enjoy as much of this life as we can. Just because things are hard doesn't mean that we can't have fun. It takes a great amount of strength and faith to look beyond the pain and trials of this life and trust God enough to enjoy life despite our circumstances. Choose today to start having fun regardless of the circumstances of your life. Live this life to its fullest as you wait for the next life. Jesus did; and so should we. Jesus, the life you gave us was meant to be fun; help us to choose that life even when life gets hard.

Rick Lancaster / PLANTERS PERSPECTIVE

SEPTEMBER 5 || ECCLESIASTES 12:11

A wise teacher's words spur students to action and emphasize important truths. The collected sayings of the wise are like guidance from a shepherd.

Read: Ecclesiastes 10:1-12:14

As the book of Ecclesiastes comes to a close, Solomon reminds us of the purpose and objective of the book and ultimately of his life. God had blessed Solomon with incredible wisdom. His wisdom was greater than that of anyone that had lived. And Solomon knew as his life was drawing to a close that his purpose in life was to share that wisdom with others.

Here in our verse for the day Solomon tells us that the wise teacher's words will create a reaction within those that hear them. They will also deal with important truths. How important that is for us as we strive to build godly homes, ministries, or churches. God's desire for all of His children is that they be conformed into the image of His son Jesus. The only way that can happen is if people change from the way that they are to the way they should be. And the only way they can do that is if people teach them how to do that.

As we teach those people that God has placed around us, we must stick to the important things and teach in such a way as to show them the way to change to be like Jesus. If we aren't doing that, then we are not being wise teachers. It has been said: "Major in the majors and minor in the minors". We must not allow ourselves to get caught up in the insignificant issues of the day but must stick with the issues of eternity.

Our verse for today ends by reminding us that these wise sayings will guide us like a shepherd. They will keep us from danger and lead us to safety. They will nourish our souls and fill us with the good things of God. They will mend our wounds and heal us when we are sick. They will lead us back when we have gone astray. Within the word of God resides all that we need for life and happiness.

Whether or not you have the position of teacher or shepherd, if you are in a family, ministry, or church, you have a responsibility to share the wise sayings of scripture with those around you. You do that through your words and your actions. God calls all of His children to share His truths with others and to live out those truths in their lives. Our lives should be living examples and illustrations of the truths of God.

Look around you! Are the words that you are speaking and the behaviors of your life spurring people to action? Are they moving to become more like Jesus? Jesus, teach us to teach them to love You and to be like You.

SEPTEMBER 6 || SONG OF SONGS 2:2

Young Man: "Yes, compared to other women, my beloved is like a lily among thorns."

Read: Song of Songs 1:1-4:16

Song of Songs or Song of Solomon is one of the most beautiful and poetic books in the Bible. This song written by Solomon describes the way that he feels about a woman that he has fallen in love with. There is also a great picture of Christ and His church found in this beautiful song. Open your heart and let the Spirit speak to you of the Love that Jesus has for you.

As you read through Song of Songs it might be difficult to pull out a verse that speaks of leadership or ministry but in today's verse we find something that many people might not normally think about. In Solomon's love song he compares his lover's beauty to everyone else's and finds no equal. In this is a great truth that all of us need to embrace.

A long time ago I was taught to view my wife as the most beautiful woman that I could imagine; not that I would change the way she looks, but that the way she looks is perfect to me. This way of thinking would also be described as contentment but it is much more than that. By thinking of my wife in this way, I am satisfied in her and have no desire beyond her. This keeps me from being tempted by other women, no other woman even compares to my wife.

This applies not just to our relationships with our spouses but in every area of our lives. It applies in your home and possessions and jobs and hobbies. It applies also in your ministry or church. We can sometimes become disenchanted with something about the ministry or church that we are involved in. When that happens we start looking around to see what else is out there and we start comparing it to where we are. Because of our disenchantment we will see the other thing as better than where we are. When we go ahead and jump to the new thing we often find that it really wasn't better after all. Then we start looking again and begin a life-long cycle that leaves us empty and unfulfilled.

Where you are and what you are doing is where God has placed you. When He is ready to move you on to something else, He will. Until then you should be working to develop an attitude in your heart that says that what you are doing and where you are doesn't compare to anywhere else. This doesn't mean that if you are in a really bad situation that God wants you to stay there; it means that you stay and are satisfied where you are until God wants to move you, not because you don't like it or it is hard.

By having this attitude of satisfied contentment, you will sense a kind of joy and peace that you may not have felt before. It brings a freedom that allows you to truly enjoy life instead of always looking for the next thing that you think will make you happy. Trust God to move you when He wants to and enjoy what he has already provided; that is the fulfilled life. Jesus, help us to be happy with what You have given us.

Rick Lancaster / PLANTERS PERSPECTIVE

SEPTEMBER 7 || SONG OF SONGS 8:6

Place me like a seal over your heart, or like a seal on your arm. For love is as strong as death, and its jealousy is as enduring as the grave. Love flashes like fire, the brightest kind of flame.

Read: Song of Songs 5:1-8:14

Here is one of the most beautiful pieces of text in all of scripture. Solomon writes this love story to describe the way that he feels about his young bride. His description of her is wonderful and romantic. It is difficult to come away from this text without feelings of love stirring deep within you.

When I first read this book I wondered why it was in the Bible. Then God revealed something to me that has radically changed the way that I think of my wife. Solomon was describing the way that he viewed his young wife. There is no way of knowing what she looked like but Solomon saw her the way that he describes her in this book.

In our verse for today the young woman asks the man to place her as a seal over his heart. A seal was used to close a letter and keep it that way until the person that it was addressed to opened it. A seal was also used to let the reader know who sent the letter. By placing her as a seal over his heart he was sealing his heart from all others.

God's plan for my marriage is that there is only one woman that He has chosen for me. And I get to choose how I view her. I can choose to view her as the perfect wife for me or I can choose to see her imperfections. Years ago I determined in my heart to view my wife as the perfect woman for me. And in my heart I view her just as the young man in our text for today views his lover. I have placed her as a seal over my heart; only she can open it. It was a decision and a choice that has kept me faithful and in love.

As Christians we are described as the bride of Christ. As a man this is a little difficult to embrace, but embrace it we must. Christ asks us to place Him as a seal over our hearts. Only Christ should have a position higher in our hearts than our spouses. And no one else should have a position higher than your spouse. It is your choice to make; Christ first, spouse second, and all others after.

God sees us as a beautiful masterpiece of His creation. We need to view our spouses the same way. Stop looking at flaws and start looking at them through the eyes of Christ. He gave His life for them and He thinks they are beautiful. Read Solomon's Song of Songs again and picture you and your spouse as the two main characters in this story. Let the descriptions of the characters be descriptions of you and your spouse. Jesus, help us to choose to put a seal over our hearts that only You and our spouse can open.

SEPTEMBER 8 || ISAIAH 2:17

The arrogance of all people will be brought low. Their pride will lie in the dust. The LORD alone will be exalted!

Read: Isaiah 1:1-2:22

There is something about arrogant and prideful people that will usually annoy us. Their arrogance is often very irritating and we are repelled by their actions or behaviors. We feel that way about arrogant and prideful people because that's the way that God feels about them. Few things seem to bug God like arrogance and pride.

Arrogance and pride come as a result of someone thinking too highly of themselves and then attempting to exalt themselves over others; sometimes even over God. Such is the case of the prophecies that God gives to Isaiah. Israel, Judah and all the other nations that Isaiah speaks prophecies against have all acted arrogantly. Israel has acted as though they are special because God chose them from among all the nations. They allowed this to cause them to act in some very foolish ways, believing that God would protect them no matter what they did.

At other times the nation of Israel acted as though they did not need God. This is also arrogant and prideful. To say that you don't need God is to attempt to exalt yourself to a position that is equal with Him. That is something that God will not tolerate.

None of us would actually say these things but it is our actions that tell what is in our hearts. Our actions tell God and the world what we believe and who we are worshipping. When we are exalting ourselves, we are building altars to ourselves and telling God that we don't need Him.

There is a warning that all of us need to understand and heed. If we don't humble ourselves, God will do it for us. God will not tolerate arrogance or pride in His people forever; He will act to break us of those nasty habits. And if necessary He will break us down until we are literally in the dust on our faces at His feet. He will humble us because He alone deserves exaltation but also because He loves us. When we are arrogant and prideful we are out of the intimate fellowship that God created us to be in.

It is much better to humble ourselves then to wait until God does it. When we wait for God to humble us, it is always so much more painful. It is like your children when they have done something wrong. If they come to us before we come to them we will usually lessen the consequences that we give them. If we have to 'catch them', the consequences are always more severe. God doesn't want to spank us but He will if we won't do what we need to. Humble yourself before God. His word says that if we will do that, He will exalt us. Jesus, help us to humble ourselves and exalt You.

Rick Lancaster / PLANTERS PERSPECTIVE

SEPTEMBER 9 || ISAIAH 3:12

Children oppress my people, and women rule over them. O my people, can't you see what fools your rulers are? They are leading you down a pretty garden path to destruction.

Read: Isaiah 3:1-5:30

One of the most difficult ministries in the world is the ministry of counseling. People will come to you when their lives are falling apart or when they are surrounded by enemies and ask you for help. Often they are looking for a magic solution to their problem that includes little or no change on their part. Usually they come when the situation is desperate and the damage is great.

An even harder ministry is the ministry of prophet. The ministry of prophet is to speak forth the word of God. Isaiah was a prophet who spoke forth God's word in a powerful way. He relayed from God to the nation of Israel the things that God wanted them to know about. Some of those things involved future events and some involved their lives at that time. In today's verse we see a combination of the two.

Some of the hardest people in the world to reach are the ones that don't think anything is wrong. Life is a 'garden path' and everything is going great. As a preacher, they often sit in front of me on Sunday mornings. The expression, 'fat, dumb, and happy' applies to them. Everything is going well in their lives and therefore they don't need to make any changes in their lives.

What is interesting to me about this verse is that it is directed to followers, not to leaders. God often had His prophets give messages to the leaders of the people. Here He is speaking to the people themselves and wants them to wake up from their stupor and examine the path that they are on.

There is a balance that we must walk as Christian believers that at times is going to bring us to difficult decisions. God expects us to respect and follow the leaders that he has appointed to lead us. But He doesn't expect nor want us to follow them blindly. He wants us to examine the path that our leaders are leading us down and He expects us to act when that path is leading us to destruction.

It is how we act that determines what type of a follower we are going to be. All throughout Scripture we see examples of people that confronted their leaders. Some of those examples are terrible, others bring glory to God. There is not room in this devotional to describe just how to do that. The point is that we as followers must not get too comfortable on the 'garden path' and lose sight of where we are going. Examine yourself and examine the path that you are on and then seek the Lord and His direction on how to respond. If you see signs of destruction further down the path, seek counsel on the best way to proceed. God expects us to know where we are headed. Jesus, teach us to keep our eyes on the path ahead of us.

SEPTEMBER 10 || ISAIAH 6:8

Then I heard the Lord asking, "Whom should I send as a messenger to my people? Who will go for us?" And I said, "LORD, I'll go! Send me."

Read: Isaiah 6:1-7:25

In chapter six of Isaiah we have this fascinating account of the vision that Isaiah has of the Lord. This chapter is a great study for anyone that wants to develop a heart of service to the Lord. In this chapter are several great images of how we should respond to the Lord. In the verse we are looking at today we have the attitude of a servant willing to go where the Master wants to send them.

The Lord asks the questions "Whom shall I send?" and "Who will go?" Both of these questions could very easily be stated as commands. God doesn't have to ask us to do anything; He could command us to do everything. But that is not the relationship that He wants to have with us. God is looking for those that are willing to go.

Isaiah's response is: "I'll go! Send me." Isaiah's heart was willing to go wherever the Lord might choose to send him. Would that be your response? If God said that there was someplace that He needed to send someone to, would you raise your hand and say "I'll go! Send me."?

One of the ways that you can check your heart in this is to think of some place that you would not be willing to go. As you see the news of different peoples and places, are there any that you wouldn't go to? If there are then you are not where Isaiah was. Don't be afraid to do this, God isn't going to send you someplace that is out of His grace and ability to keep you just because you tell God that you would go if He asked you.

God cares more about a willing heart than he does about great ability. Often our own abilities lead us to limit what we think God will do through us. We might even try to tell God how and where He should be using us. Isaiah didn't ask God where he was to be sent and he didn't ask what people he was to go to. Isaiah told God that he was willing and ready.

We also need to be willing and ready. Until you are willing and ready to go anywhere that God might choose to send you then you aren't really God's. He wants all of you and when He has all of you then you are ready to be used to do great things for God. Until then, He will keep working on you to prepare you for the great work that He is planning for you. Your role is to open your heart to Him and allow Him to get you to the place where you can say as Isaiah did: "I'll go! Send me." Jesus, help us to have the courage to go where You lead with willing and ready hearts.

SEPTEMBER 11 || ISAIAH 9:1

Nevertheless, that time of darkness and despair will not go on forever. The land of Zebulun and Naphtali will soon be humbled, but there will be a time in the future when Galilee of the Gentiles, which lies along the road that runs between the Jordan and the sea, will be filled with glory.

Read: Isaiah 8:1-9:21

Isaiah has been speaking strong words against the nation of Israel and Judah. He is one of the many prophets that God sent to try to get the nation of Israel to turn from their rebellion and idolatry and turn back to Him. Isaiah spoke the things that the Lord showed him were going to happen. Then, here in our verse for the day he gives them some hope for the future. They were going to be humbled; specifically they were going to be overthrown 'soon' and they would be taken away as captives to a foreign land. In a future time the land that was theirs was going to once again be filled with glory.

This prophecy was filled literally by Jesus when He walked, taught, and worked many miracles in the area of Galilee. Their rebellion would some day end and God would reveal His glory to them again. Sadly, when it did happen many people chose not to see it and rejected God once again when they rejected Jesus.

There are times when we or someone around us will deliberately walk away from what it is that God wants us to do. Because God is righteous and holy, He must discipline us and if necessary He will also punish us. But we can take hope in the knowledge that God won't punish us forever. God's grace is never-ending and He will always be working to draw us back to Himself.

Even the punishment that He brings into our lives is for the purpose of turning our hearts back to Him. The sooner that we realize this, the quicker the punishment will end. We must be careful not to do what the Israelites did and blame God for our circumstances. God is righteous and perfect; the things that He causes or allows in our lives are to work out His righteousness and holiness within us.

The darkness and despair that we might be experiencing now will not go on forever. And we get to choose when it will end. We need just repent and turn our hearts back to God. We need to allow the Holy Spirit to humble us and our hearts. Don't fight what God wants to do in your life; it only makes it harder. There are two ways to do everything in life; your way which is the hard way and leads to darkness and despair. Or you can do it God's way which leads to gladness and light and His glory and blessings.

There is a road that runs through your life which other people see and walk upon with you. What will they see there; darkness and despair or the glory of God? The choice is yours to make. Choosing your way means that you walk alone; choosing God's way means you walk with God. Jesus, teach us to walk in Your light.

SEPTEMBER 12 || ISAIAH 10:15

Can the ax boast greater power than the person who uses it? Is the saw greater than the person who saws? Can a whip strike unless a hand is moving it? Can a cane walk by itself?

Read: Isaiah 10:1-11:16

God is describing how He is going to use the king of Assyria to punish His people for disobedience and rebellion. He then goes on to say that He is going to then punish the king of Assyria because of his pride and arrogance. It was God who gave the Assyrian king his power and it was the Lord who gave him the victory over His people. Isaiah accuses the Assyrian king of boasting of his power to overcome the people of God.

Isaiah then asks the rhetorical questions above. The answer is the same in all four questions; 'No!' The point is simple, the king of Assyria may boast of his great power and accomplishments but it is God that used him as a simple tool to accomplish His will in the world and in the lives of His Chosen People.

There is an important lesson in this for modern-day Christians, especially those that are leading families, ministries, or churches. Don't look upon the things that God is doing through you as 'your accomplishments'. This devotional is close to the 600th one that I have written. It would be very easy to be impressed with myself for having accomplished something like this. Then I remind myself that I am not the writer, but only the conduit through whom the Holy Spirit has chosen to flow to produce this devotional.

If it ever becomes something that might be considered great, it is only because God has chosen to do so. I am simply the pen that God chose to write it. Without His hand holding the pen, it would never have happened. I am a tool in the hand of the Master.

It is this understanding that positions us to be of even greater use to God. When we understand and acknowledge that He is in control and is controlling everything we are then in a position to be used to an even greater degree. Our next choice must be to let Him use us when He wants to and in the way that he wants to. A pen cannot tell the person holding it what to write.

Nothing will remove you from a place of usefulness to God like pride and boasting. God resists the proud and boasting is stealing God's glory. Instead we should have humble hearts before God and men. I have a goal of writing one of these devotionals for every chapter in the Bible, all 1,189 of them. It will only be possible if I keep my heart right before the Lord and remember who is actually doing the writing.

Whatever you do in this life, whether it is great or small is because God has used you to do it. Give Him the glory and rejoice that He chose to use you. Jesus, help us to be willing tools in the hand of the Master.

SEPTEMBER 13 | | ISAIAH 14:26

I have a plan for the whole earth, for my mighty power reaches throughout the world.

Read: Isaiah 12:1-14:32

Most of the world does not acknowledge God. There are also people that are rebellious toward God. Most of the world believes that they are in some way in control of the world around them. Today's verse counters that belief; God is the one who is in control. God's power has no limits; either in amount or breadth.

Our verse also tells us that God has a plan for the whole earth. We might sometimes think that God's plan extends to just those that believe in Him. That is not the case; even those that don't believe in God or are rebellious to God are a part of His plan for the whole earth. No one or nothing is outside of God's plan.

Too often we might be tempted to disregard someone because they are in obvious rebellion to God and we can see no way that God would be able to use them. That is a limited view of the power, grace, and mercy of God. God can and does use anyone or anything that He desires to accomplish His will and plans. The Bible has many examples of how He uses godless people and nations to punish His wayward children. The Bible also describes how God uses nature and the things of this world to accomplish His plans.

We need to expand our view of the power of God. God used the Assyrians to expel the nation of Israel from the Promised Land because of their unfaithfulness. God used ravens to feed Elijah. He used a great fish to get Jonah where he needed to be. God one time used some annoying little insects to move me to be in a position to minister to someone that needed to hear from God. There is nothing that is outside of God's power and control to accomplish His plans in the world.

If we would look at this world with our spiritual eyes open we would see so much more of His power at work all around us. Even in the small, seemingly insignificant, things God is in the midst with His infinitely amazing power. When you look for His power and you see it at work, it will build your faith. As your faith increases you are better able to see His mighty plan being accomplished in the world.

It can be hard with all of the bad things going on in the world to see that but by faith we must look to see it. God knows what is going on everywhere and He sees everything and His power is at work to cause things to happen in the world. And in the midst of all that we see around us we need to rest in the knowledge that His ways are not our ways. What we see as something that needs God's attention is probably a part of God's plan to accomplish something else; possibly within you or through you. Look at the world around you with the awe and wonder of a small child seeing Disneyland for the first time. It is a marvelous place filled with the power and glory of God. Jesus, open our eyes.

SEPTEMBER 14 || ISAIAH 17:7

Then at last the people will think of their Creator and have respect for the Holy One of Israel.

Read: Isaiah 15:1-18:7

In our verse for the day Isaiah gives us an explanation as to why God sends punishment into our lives when we rebel against Him. He wants us to think about Him and respect Him. This is a beautiful picture of God and the way that He would like us to relate to Him. It is found in the two descriptions of God and our response to those descriptions.

First, we are told that God is our Creator. For us to truly interact with God the way that He desires we need to begin with an understanding that He created us. Not only did He create us but He determined exactly how we are going to turn out. He has a master plan that determines the ideal manner in which we develop and grow and function in this world that God created.

Our response to that knowledge is that it should cause us to think about God. If we spent more time thinking about the God that created us we would think less about ourselves and our circumstances. We would also be less likely to sin because we are focused on our Great Creator instead of the things that we want or could be doing. This doesn't mean that we should run away to some retreat and become a monk or something. It means that we should allow everything in this world to cause us to think about God. The sunrise, the birds chirping, the song on the radio, a child's smile, everything should cause us to think about our Creator.

Second, we are told in our verse that God is the Holy One of Israel. Holiness describes who and what God is. Holiness is the absolute absence of sin. God is absolutely perfect. He never makes mistakes and He never does anything that is wrong. He is also in complete control over all of His creation. Because He is holy, that means that everything that happens has happened according to His perfect plan. Free will comes into play here but the main thing we need to understand is that what God does is perfect.

Our response to God's holiness is to respect Him and His ways. To show respect is to indicate through our actions that we believe that what God has done or is doing is right. This can be hard when our circumstances are unfavorable but those are the times when we need to do it the most. Because God's ways are perfect we need to behave as if we believe that what God has allowed in our lives are the perfect circumstances to accomplish His plan. When we try to take the matter into our own hands we are being disrespectful of God. We need to trust God and believe that what is going on is for His purposes. Trust in Him and respect His ways. Jesus, teach us to love and respect you.

SEPTEMBER 15 || ISAIAH 19:13

The wise men from Zoan are fools, and those from Memphis are deluded. The leaders of Egypt have ruined the land with their foolish counsel.

Read: Isaiah 19:1-21:17

Isaiah is prophesying about Egypt. Egypt as a nation had been one of the richest and most powerful nations in the world. Few nations could compare to the things that they had accomplished. One of the things that they prided themselves on was their wisdom. They did have a lot to be proud of. Things like the pyramids are still marvels of engineering and construction. But with all of their great accomplishments, they confused intelligence for wisdom.

Wisdom is a very precious thing. The Bible teaches us that we should search it out like we would gold or precious stones. Where we go to look will determine how successful we are at finding wisdom. If we go to the wrong source what we may find is knowledge but knowledge alone is not enough to produce wisdom. In fact, history has proven countless times that knowledge by itself will usually lead to foolish decisions.

There is only one source of wisdom and that is God. He is the source of both wisdom and knowledge. Amazingly we will gladly receive knowledge from Him and then reject wisdom from Him. That is the height of foolishness. It is sad when someone is foolish due to ignorance. But it can be disastrous when someone claiming to be wise makes foolish decisions.

The leaders of Egypt sought wisdom from every source they could find. They relied heavily upon 'wise' men to counsel them and to make their decisions. Often these men would be the descendants of men that had proven themselves wise in the past. This became a position of great influence and people desired the position not because they wanted to share the wisdom they had but because they wanted the power that came with the position.

The Bible teaches us to get the counsel of others before we make decisions. As leaders in God's families, ministries, and churches we must be looking to the right source of that counsel. Wisdom comes from God and so we need to be seeking people that have a relationship with God for our counsel. Seeking counsel from ungodly sources can be disastrous. While the secular world has an incredible wealth of knowledge, we must not let that replace the counsel of God's word and those of God that have been given the gift of wisdom.

The world seeks counsel from people that they hope are wiser than they are. But no matter how 'wise' someone in the world is, they cannot know the mind of God. And without knowing the mind of God, the 'wisest' of counselors may lead you to do the opposite of what God would tell you to do, and that would be disastrous. Jesus, teach us to seek You where we can find all wisdom and knowledge.

SEPTEMBER 16 || ISAIAH 22:13

But instead, you dance and play; you slaughter sacrificial animals, feast on meat, and drink wine. "Let's eat, drink, and be merry," you say. "What's the difference, for tomorrow we die."

Read: Isaiah 22:1-24:23

God is calling the city of Jerusalem to repent. Through the prophet Isaiah He has proclaimed the judgments that are about to befall this city that God chose as His own special place for the people to worship Him. These judgments are coming because the people have turned away from God and are worshipping idols and have stopped trusting God. One prophet was sent after another to warn the people of Israel and to tell them what they needed to do so that these judgments would not come to them.

Today's verse is a sad testimony to the way that most people respond to God's call to repentance and right living. In spite of God's warning of judgment, and His promise of blessings for obedience, they would rather suffer death than forsake their sins. That is so hard to sit by and watch this happen in people's lives. As a pastor it is sometimes necessary to tell people that their sins are separating them from their God and that if they continue, His judgment is likely to fall upon them. Rather than change they will continue in their sin and resign themselves to the fate that awaits them. How pathetic is that? God promises a life that is filled with His blessings and provision and protection. His grace and mercy are poured out without limit on those that are His children. But rather than experience God's blessing some people will actually choose to receive God's judgment.

It is difficult to convince people that they are choosing judgment, but that is exactly what they are doing. The people of Isaiah's day knew that God had said that He was going to judge them for their sins because they wouldn't turn back to Him. If they had repented and turned back to God, He would have relented from sending His judgment upon them. Instead they chose to focus on their sins and live a life of hopelessness.

It is not God's desire to judge anyone. He created us so that we would be in fellowship with Him and worship Him. In His perfect holiness He must judge those that deviate from that original design. It is His amazing grace that causes Him to be as patient as He is; He doesn't want any of His creation to be lost. If we don't respond to His many attempts to bring us back to Him, we leave Him with no option but to judge us.

Jesus came to this earth so that we would have a direct connection back to the Father for instant access to Him for everything in our lives. The Holy Spirit actively reminds us of the reason why we were created and shows us when we wander away from that design. When we reject the leading of the Spirit to be right with God we are rejecting the work that Jesus did on the cross and give the Father no option but to remove His hand of blessing from our lives and ultimately to judge us for our choice. Jesus, teach us to repent at the first sign that we have wandered off of the path.

Rick Lancaster | PLANTERS PERSPECTIVE

SEPTEMBER 17 || ISAIAH 26:12

LORD, you will grant us peace, for all we have accomplished is really from you.

Read: Isaiah 25:1-28:13

Our verse for the day is found in a song of praise and thanksgiving for God's salvation. A day is coming in which the nation of Israel will sing this song because God has restored them to their place as His special people. Until that day this song is a testimony of what God has done for all those that have turned to Him for salvation through His Son Jesus Christ.

The verse for the day says that God will grant us peace. Too often we look to other people or things to find peace in our lives. The only true source of peace is God. The only way to achieve true peace in your life is to look to Jesus and trust in Him alone. The only kind of peace that the things of the world can provide is weak and temporary compared to the peace that God provides. In Philippians we are told that there is a peace that surpasses understanding; that is the peace of God.

One of the evidences of your relationship with God is peace; it is one of the fruits of the Holy Spirit. When we are at peace with God, He produces peace in our lives. This is the time that we need to be the most careful as Christians, when we have peace in our lives. For some reason when we have peace in our lives we tend to take our eyes off of God and start to focus on ourselves. We can even begin to take credit for creating the peace in our lives.

We need to do as Isaiah suggests; we need to recognize how it is that we have accomplished all that we have. Everything that we have and everything we have done has been done by God. Any success that we have is a result of God working in our lives. Any things that we have acquired are a result of His blessing our lives. Any skills or abilities that we have are a result of His empowering us to do what He wants us to.

To achieve and maintain peace in our lives, we need to fully embrace the knowledge that without God we are nothing and can do nothing. This goes against our sinful tendencies and against what the world teaches us to believe. It requires that we humble our hearts before the Lord and acknowledge that He is Master of everything in our lives.

There would be so much more peace and success in our lives if we would just surrender to this truth and stop trying to find peace and success through the world. It is also a truth that the further that we surrender to this truth, the more peace and success we experience in our lives. In my own life, marriage, family, and church I am trying desperately to daily achieve new levels of surrender in all those areas I might experience new levels of peace and success. God is looking to bless His people; all we have to do is let Him by surrendering to the truth that He is God. Jesus, thank you for all that You do for us every day.

SEPTEMBER 18 || ISAIAH 30:10

They tell the prophets, "Shut up! We don't want any more of your reports." They say, "Don't tell us the truth. Tell us nice things. Tell us lies."

Read: Isaiah 28:14-30:11

Isaiah is given a message by God to give to the nation of Judah. The message is as timeless as it is tragic. It portrays a side of human nature that makes me sick to my stomach and hurts my heart. The fact is that most people don't want to hear the truth. Most people would rather hear a lie that makes them feel good than hear the truth that might convict them.

This was given to Judah as a warning. God wanted them to know that if they preferred the lie to the truth that He would let them have what they wanted. God also warned them of the consequences of that choice. He compared that kind of a desire to living near a wall that was weak and was about to collapse. If you hate the truth and resist God's attempts to bring you to righteousness, He will allow the wall of lies to collapse upon you.

As a pastor I have frequently run into people just like God is describing in today's verse. They can see the wall of lies collapsing around them and they want me to tell them something that is going to make them feel better about themselves or about their situation. Instead, I tell them to move away from the wall. I tell them to admit that they are living close to the lie or I will tell them to look for the sin in their lives. That is not what they want, they prefer the lie.

As leaders of families, ministries, or churches we will all face people like this. What we need to do is to resist the temptation to give them what they want. They want to hear 'nice things' and we will be tempted to tell them things that are in fact lies or possibly worse, half-truths. We don't want them to leave or we don't want them to think less of us. Resist that temptation! This is where people first learn to compromise and it is a pathway that only leads to pain, suffering, and destruction. The people that God has called you to lead (everyone is called to lead someone) need you to tell them the truth. They may not want you to but they need you to tell them the things that they don't want to hear.

As we mature in the Lord, we learn that the truth is always the right answer for every situation. We also learn how to tell the truth in a way that expresses the meekness, gentleness, and love of Christ. We are not doing anyone a favor by making them feel good about themselves. They need to know the truth that will set them free from whatever bondage is present in their lives. If God has placed them in your lives and given you the opportunity to tell them the truth, then God is expecting you to do just that. In fact, He will ask you about it when He sees you in heaven. Sometimes that hard thing is exactly what they need to hear; let them hear it. Jesus, teach us to love and tell the truth!

Rick Lancaster / PLANTERS PERSPECTIVE

SEPTEMBER 19 || ISAIAH 31:7

I know the glorious day will come when every one of you will throw away the gold idols and silver images that your sinful hands have made.

Read: Isaiah 30:12-33:9

God can foresee a day when we will choose to throw away all of the idols that we have made. Most people that read this will probably say that they don't have any idols in their lives to throw away. There might actually be some that don't, but probably not. Most people probably have more idols in their lives than they are even aware of. Anything that takes any place in your life that Jesus should have is an idol and God is not happy about it. But God knows that some day we will throw them all away and our worship of Him will be pure and undefiled.

In our verse for the day we are told that gold idols and silver images were made by our own hands. These things that we are worshipping were made by our hands. To worship something is to give it some power to control and provide for your life. I don't think we understand just how foolish it is to think that something that we made with our own hands can take care of us or provide for us. We will sometimes give control of our lives to something that has no power other than what we have given it.

Not only did we make these things with our hands but we made them with our sinful hands. That means that the things that we can make with our own hands can be no more holy or righteous than we are. The things that we make with our own hands can have no more power than we do. Something that is imperfect cannot make something that is perfect. The only way that we can make anything with our hands that is of any value in our lives or the lives of others is to remove the idols of gold and silver from our lives and let Jesus take His rightful place in our hearts.

To throw these idols away we might need to literally remove things from our lives that distract us from God. That is not what is required if you can simply eliminate its importance from your life. It has to be OK with you if God wanted to remove it; your relationship with Him should be the most important thing to you. It must be more important to you than the things you have or your position or fame or any such thing. If Jesus is the most important thing in your life then there is nothing that God will deny you. It is when our things possess us that we become entangled in them and our sinful hands fashion them into idols for our worship.

God can see a day when each of us will throw away our idols and worship Him the way that we should. Today we should be striving towards achieving that level of worship by systematically asking God to reveal in our lives anything that hinders our walk with Him and then taking radical steps to discard them from our lives. Jesus, help us to take out the trash.

SEPTEMBER 20 || ISAIAH 35:3

With this news, strengthen those who have tired hands, and encourage those who have weak knees.

Read: Isaiah 33:10-36:22

In this chapter of Isaiah, the prophet, speaks about the future glory of Zion. God has a special plan and blessing for the nation of Israel and its capital Jerusalem that at some future date will be made to be glorious again. But what does that have to do with us? These promises are specific for the nation of Israel and those that are not of Israel will not partake of them. They give the nation of Israel hope of a future salvation and the abundant blessings of God.

We, as Christians, also have the hope of salvation and promises of blessing. We have the hope of eternal life and the blessings of an abundant life while we wait for His return. We also have the gospel message that promises, to anyone that will receive it, the same things for them. Jesus Christ came that everyone would not have to be eternally separated from God. God gave us this good news to share with others.

Our verse for the day tells us how that good news can help others. First we are told that this good news will strengthen those who have tired hands. This speaks of the things that we do with our lives. People all around us are tired. They are tired because they are doing everything they can to get by in this world. The problem is that they are trying to do it without God or without His help. It is possible for us to do that for a while but there comes a time when we all get tired. We must surrender our will to God and let Him do for us what we can't do. We need to stop trying so hard and start letting God be God in our lives. Part of the abundant life that Jesus promised is rest from our labors.

Second, we are told that this good news will encourage those that have weak knees. The word 'encourage' means 'to fill with courage'. This world does a great job of creating fear in the minds and hearts of people. When we are afraid of what the world thinks or what it might do or what could happen we are showing a lack of faith in the God that is in complete control over everything. If we will just get to know the good news as it is revealed in God's Word, it will cast out all fear.

What we do and what we think are the ways that God is revealed to the world around us. The good news of Jesus Christ is given so that we can have strength and be fearless. The good news is also given to us so that we can share it with others because they are weak and afraid. To not share the good news with others is to deprive them of hope and peace. Some day all of us will stand before God and give account for how we shared the good news with others. The gospel of Jesus Christ is a precious gift that is more valuable when you give it away. That doesn't mean that you need to preach at them; just love God and love others, God will do the rest. Jesus, teach us to be generous givers of the precious gift of Your good news.

Rick Lancaster / PLANTERS PERSPECTIVE

SEPTEMBER 21 | | ISAIAH 37:4

But perhaps the LORD your God has heard the Assyrian representative defying the living God and will punish him for his words. Oh, pray for those of us who are left!

Read: Isaiah 37:1-38:22

Isaiah is relating in our reading for today about the time that the king of Assyria came to attack Israel. He sent a representative to Jerusalem to let King Hezekiah know that he was coming and that surrender was their only option. In his message he spoke boastfully about his prior conflicts and said that Israel's God was no match for his gods. Hezekiah's response is to go to the temple and cry out to the LORD for help.

What caught my attention in today's verse was the word 'perhaps'. With a casual reading of the verse you might think that Hezekiah is saying, 'maybe God will hear him'. I don't believe that is the correct interpretation. God hears everything; nothing escapes his gaze or ears. There is no question that the LORD heard the boastful words of the Assyrian representative. The word 'perhaps' would be better placed with God's possible response to the representative. I believe that what is being said here is, 'perhaps God will punish him for his words.'

That is where we sometimes struggle with God. Our sense of justice expects God to punish evildoers quickly and decisively. This is especially true when we are truly doing our best to be right with God and do the right things with those around us. We feel that in our righteousness that God should act immediately to defend His name and our cause.

In His sovereignty, he doesn't always do that. Sometimes He does nothing, at least from our perspective. But then that is our problem. We can only see what God is doing from our perspective. God's ways are so far above our ways! Our perspective is limited by our limitations as humans. Only God can see everything, everywhere, and at all times.

From our limited perspective we expect God to work in a certain way within our circumstances. Perhaps He will but there is also a chance that He won't. He is always at work and in control of all situations and circumstances and His way of dealing with your particular circumstance might be radically different than what you might want or expect.

It wasn't long after this that the angel of the LORD descended upon the camp of the Assyrians and killed 185,000 in the night. The king took his army and left Israel and was soon after killed by two of his sons. We get no word in Scripture about what happened to the representative. That means that it is not important for us to know what happened to him. God did what he wanted to do and that should be enough for us.

Trust God to act on your behalf within your circumstances. And trust God enough to not be concerned about how He intends to do it or about the results. Those are all His responsibilities. Jesus, help us to pray and then leave it for You to handle.

SEPTEMBER 22 || ISAIAH 41:4

Who has done such mighty deeds, directing the affairs of the human race as each new generation marches by? It is I, the LORD, the First and the Last. I alone am He."

Read: Isaiah 39:1-41:16

Every generation that marches by seems to think that it has some supreme control over its destiny and actions. God reminds us that is not the case. In this century we have taken to naming the different generations that come onto the scene; baby-boomers, baby-busters, generation X, etc. Each one of these generations seems to have its own unique signature on history. What today's verse tells us is that each new generation that marches by still has the fingerprints of God all over it.

Most people find it difficult to think outside of their generation. Often when we look to the next generations we see things that offend us or confuse us. We often forget that the previous generation did the same thing as they looked at our generation. As leaders of families, ministries, or churches this can be a very challenging thing to overcome. There are many groups, books, and seminars available to teach us how to minister to the 'other' generations. The question is; do we really need all of them?

In our verse for the day we are told that the Lord is directing the affairs of the human race. That means that we need not get all consumed in studying the different generations but instead studying how God might want to work in this new generation. Where we usually will get twisted up is forgetting that God works differently in each new generation. Too often we take the model that worked for our generation and try to apply it to the next generation, or worse, to the one after that. The way that God works in the life of my children will not be the same as the way that He worked in the life of my grandparents. The reason for that is that the world has changed dramatically.

While the world has changed, God has not. Our verse for the day reminds us that the Lord is the First and the Last. This speaks of His eternal existence and His immutability (He never changes). As each generation marches by God directs them in ways that are appropriate for that generation. If that were not the case then there would be no need by God to recognize the passing of generations.

For us to be effective at leading our families, ministries, or churches we must always be looking to God to direct our affairs. There is a temptation to depend upon the ministry models that have been established to direct how we minister to people. These models are tools that were developed to minister to a certain group of people for a pre-determined period of time. Ministries and churches often suffer because tools are being used that are no longer effective. The best thing to do with a tool that is no longer effective is throw it out and find one that is effective. We must be more concerned about following the direction of our Lord, than we are about pleasing the older generation. Jesus, help us to follow directions.

SEPTEMBER 23 || ISAIAH 42:20

You see and understand what is right but refuse to act upon it. You hear, but you don't really listen.

Read: Isaiah 41:17-43:13

The prophet Isaiah is speaking a prophecy against the nation of Israel. The Lord spoke through Isaiah to tell them in no uncertain terms that He did not approve of their continued rejection of Almighty God as their God. They persisted in turning to worthless idols rather than to the One True God.

Often as we read texts such as this one today, we can't relate to how it might apply to us. What does Israel's turning from the Lord to idols have to do with modern-day Christians? Quite a bit more than you might think! Not much has changed in the last 2,500 years as it relates to the way people respond to God. We may not be Jews, God's Chosen People, but we are God's children. As such we do many of the same things that the Jews did. Many of the warnings and exhortations to the Jews apply directly to the 21st Century Christian.

Today's verse tells us that the Jews were guilty of not paying attention to God. They knew about Him but they did not listen to Him or do what He told them to do. They had the Law given to them by Moses to teach them how to live with God in fellowship and communion. They had the prophets to help them understand the world around them and to point them back to God whenever they wandered away from Him.

Even though this verse was written more than two thousand years ago it could easily be spoken to many of the Christians that sit in churches today. For years they have heard the truth about God and how He wants to work in our lives. Sermon after sermon has described to them the life that Jesus died to give them. Message after message has instructed them in the pathway to the abundant life that Jesus promised to His people. And just like the Hebrews of Isaiah's time they refuse to act upon what they know.

This was very frustrating to Isaiah. He knew that the Jews were headed for disaster because they refused to do what God wanted them to do; because they refused to go where He wanted them to go. As a pastor, I can feel that same frustration as I preach week after week knowing that many people are there because a sense of obligation and not so they can know Christ.

Going to church is meaningless if you are not going to meet with Jesus. Showing up on Sunday will not please God if you do not come with a heart to please God in your worship. Attending services is a waste of time if you have no desire to serve God. God has no interest in people filling churches; He wants churches filled with people that are coming to be filled with His Spirit. Don't come so that you can say you did; come so that you can do what He tells you to do. Jesus, give us Your heart of obedience.

PLANTERS PERSPECTIVE / *A Devotional*

SEPTEMBER 24 || ISAIAH 44:20

The poor, deluded fool feeds on ashes. He is trusting something that can give him no help at all. Yet he cannot bring himself to ask, "Is this thing, this idol that I'm holding in my hand, a lie?"

Read: Isaiah 43:14-45:10

It is sometimes amazing to see the things that people will hang on to in their lives even though they are harmful to them. Isaiah is trying to teach the people the foolishness of idolatry. He is trying to help them to understand that it makes no sense to fashion an idol with your own hands and then worship it as a god. In our verse for the day, Isaiah grieves as he tells them that this poor person is deluded and they are trying to sustain themselves with something that can provide no nourishment at all.

Not only that but the person that worships idols doesn't even have the sense to look at the thing that they are worshipping and question whether or not it is worthy of their worship. To worship anything other than God is to worship something that cannot give you what you think that it can. So by worshipping an idol, you are in fact worshipping a lie.

The Bible teaches that God is a jealous God and will not tolerate His children worshipping anyone or anything other than Him. One of the reasons for this is because He knows that idol worship is useless; it is a waste of a person's life. Idols cannot give us the things that we would go to them to provide us; only God can.

Idol worship is still prevalent in many countries around the world. We are not free from it in this country either. Even within some denominations of the church we find things that resemble idol worship. The non-denominational churches are not free from this matter either. Some will create programs or buildings that can take on the form of idols. Sadly, some pastors and ministry leaders will also allow themselves to become idols to their congregations. It is all foolishness and those that are following that path are feeding on nothing and are blindly wandering down a path of destruction.

As leaders of families, ministries, and churches we need to be actively looking for the idols in our lives and around us and breaking them down. There is only one thing that should ever be worshipped and that is Jesus Christ. We need to be looking for those things in the lives of those people that we are called to lead and teach them to break down those idols as well.

Idols are anything that we allow into our lives that attempt to act as a replacement for God in our lives, families, ministries, or churches. They might be hard to spot and they will always be protected by very foolish emotions and unreasonable justifications. When we trust in something or someone to provide for us what only God can, we are worshipping idols. Of course God will use people and things to provide for us, but who are we trusting in; God or the person or thing? Jesus, teach us to see through our own foolishness to see the idols in our lives as we feed on the richness of Your word.

Rick Lancaster / PLANTERS PERSPECTIVE

SEPTEMBER 25 || ISAIAH 47:6

For I was angry with my chosen people and began their punishment by letting them fall into your hands. But you, Babylon, showed them no mercy. You have forced even the elderly to carry heavy burdens.

Read: Isaiah 45:11-48:11

The Lord gives Isaiah another prophecy against the nation of Babylon. This verse is rich in spiritual application. God was angry because the nation of Israel rejected Him, their God and Savior to chase after false idols. God is displeased when we choose anything or anyone over Him. After all He has done for us, He expects us to worship only Him. If we refuse, we should expect to experience His displeasure.

This verse also tells us that God punishes His people when they are disobedient or rebellious. We like to believe that God only punishes 'bad people'. Compared to God, we are all bad people and deserve far more punishment that we get. It is God's incredible mercy that keeps Him from giving us all the punishment we deserve.

We also learn that God punishes the nations that mistreat His people. Over and over prophets of God spoke of the destruction of the nation of Babylon. The nation of Babylon was destroyed just as the Lord predicted. Babylon also represents the evil world system that we see today and includes all false religion. The book of Revelation speaks of the ultimate fate of this world system; total destruction.

What was of particular interest to me was that God told the nation of Babylon that he had began the punishment of His people by allowing them to fall into the hands of their enemies, the Babylonians. God is saying clearly that the reason why Babylon was able to defeat the Jews was because God allowed them to. God had withdrawn His hand of protection from His Chosen People.

There is a tremendous lesson in that for all of us whenever we find ourselves in the hands of our enemies; God has allowed them to prevail over us. Any time the enemy has victory in our lives we must understand that it was allowed by the Lord. Until the Lord withdraws His protective hand from us, it is impossible for the enemy to prevail in our lives. Our enemy can take no ground that the Lord hasn't given him permission to take.

Israel was being punished for disobedience and rebellion. That is one of the primary reasons why God withdraws His hand of protection but it is not the only reason. Sometimes He will allow an enemy to gain ground so that we will draw nearer to the Lord and grow in our faith. It may also be to prove our faith.

Our response should be the same regardless of why we think the enemy is prevailing; run to the Lord and humbly seek His presence more fully. Do all that you can to obey God completely and trust Him with your whole being. Ultimately your enemy cannot prevail against you if you will seek God in this way. God always protects His faithful people. Jesus, help us to run to You whenever we see the enemy on our borders.

SEPTEMBER 26 || ISAIAH 49:4

I replied, "But my work all seems so useless! I have spent my strength for nothing and to no purpose at all. Yet I leave it all in the LORD's hand; I will trust God for my reward."

Read: Isaiah 48:12-50:11

Isaiah takes a look around at the ministry that he is doing and is very disappointed with what he sees. He feels that all of his efforts have been useless and have been a waste of his strength and energy. Anyone that gets involved in ministry of any kind for any length of time is going to find themselves feeling the same way that Isaiah does here in our verse for the day. We might wonder why we are doing the things that we are doing and even question whether or not God cares about what we are doing.

There are lots of reasons why this happens. We might not see anyone responding to the work that we are doing. Sometimes people don't appreciate the things that we are doing for them. We might feel very lonely because no one seems to care how much we are doing for the Lord. We might even be persecuted for the work that we do for the Lord. This and so many more things can cause us to be very frustrated with the way things are going in ministry. These times are going to come and we so we shouldn't be surprised when we find ourselves whining and complaining to God. It is our response to that realization that is important.

God doesn't want us to grumble and complain. When we do we are showing a lack of faith in the God that allows things to happen in your life and has the ability to do something about it. Everything that goes on in the universe is under God's control. To grumble and complain about anything is to forget who God is.

Isaiah ends our verse for the day by saying that he is going to leave all of his concerns in the hands of the Lord. He doesn't see that his work is useful for himself or for anyone else. But, in obedience he continues the work and trusts God to reward him for his efforts. Most faithful servants desire no more than to know that their master is happy. I believe that is the reward that Isaiah was looking for.

The key is leaving all of our cares and concerns about the things that we do for God in His hands. Only the Lord can recognize whether or not what we are doing is useful or not. We are not in a position to judge the fruitfulness of our labors. God assigned us the work that He did and only asks that we would be faithful to it. If you are faithful but don't see any fruit right away just leave it in the Lord's hands and trust Him for your reward. It is right to look for fruit; that is one of the ways that we know that we are where God wants us to be. Sometimes the fruit is very slow to mature. At those times we just need to trust the Lord and wait on Him. For 2,500 years Isaiah's ministry has been bearing fruit. Jesus, help us to wait patiently for your reward.

Rick Lancaster / PLANTERS PERSPECTIVE

SEPTEMBER 27 || ISAIAH 53:6

All of us have strayed away like sheep. We have left God's paths to follow our own. Yet the LORD laid on him the guilt and sins of us all.

Read: Isaiah 51:1-53:12

Few chapters in the Old Testament speak more powerfully about Jesus than does this chapter in Isaiah. It is a marvelous picture of our Lord and what he did for us. In our verse for the day it says that we have strayed away just like sheep. It says that all have strayed. This should remind us that what Jesus did on the cross, He did for me and for you. It was personal! If you have been walking with the Lord for some time there is a tendency to forget that we were once lost sheep. We need regular reminders that we were rescued from the wasteland and restored to a right place with the Good Shepherd.

We are also told that we have left God's paths. We do that a lot more often than we should, which is never. Every time we do something because we want to rather than because the Lord leads us to, we are wandering off of His path for our lives. For some people when they find themselves just a little off the path they rush back to the Shepherd. Others wander far away and the Shepherd has to come find them. Thankfully for all of us, it doesn't matter how far we wander, the Shepherd is always looking to restore us back into His flock.

God calls it sin when we wander from His path to follow our own ways. Don't harden your heart when you hear something like that. Instead, repent and ask Him to forgive you. That instantly restores you back into the flock of God. It may not eliminate the consequences, because God's justice requires that the natural consequences be paid. What we don't have to experience is the penalty of that wandering.

When we sin, we disqualify ourselves from heaven because only the pure, righteous, and holy are allowed to go there. But because of God's amazing grace He made a way for us to enter into eternal life in spite of our wandering hearts. That way was Jesus Christ. When Jesus went to the cross God laid the sins of the whole world on His shoulders. Christ bore the burden of our sins onto the cross. Because of what Jesus did, we have the privilege of spending all of eternity with Him.

There will be times again in the future when we will all wander from the path. Our love of God and appreciation for what Jesus did for us ought to cause us to do it less and less frequently and it should also cause us to recognize it when it happens. And when we recognize it we need to immediately humble our hearts before Jesus and ask Him to forgive us. His amazing grace is also what He employs to forgive us of all the future times that we will wander. The more that you grow to understand how amazing God's grace is the closer you will desire to be to the Shepherd that watches over your soul. Jesus, teach us to stay close to You and to rush back to Your loving arms when we wander.

SEPTEMBER 28 || ISAIAH 55:8

"My thoughts are completely different from yours," says the LORD. "And my ways are far beyond anything you could imagine.

Read: Isaiah 54:1-57:14

God doesn't think like we do. There is no way that our minds can think like God's can. All of human intelligence combined does not impress God because He is far beyond the best that man will ever be. Many people live out their lives trying to prove how smart they are compared to other people. One glimpse of the mind of God would let them know that they don't know that much.

As we go through this life, we need to keep this truth in our hearts. There will be times when we don't understand what is going in our lives. There will be times when things are not going the way that we planned them. Some of these times we will be struggling just to keep our heads above water. It is at these times that we must understand that God's mind is so much greater than ours.

One of the other attributes about God's mind that comforts me is that he is outside of time. He does not view time as one day after another. God sees time like we would look at a picture. He can look anywhere in time that He chooses to. It is also stated that He can see all of it at once. Our finite, temporal minds cannot fathom that; it is way beyond us.

The Bible also teaches that God thinks about me a lot. He thought about me before time. He thought about me before I was born. He thought about me while I was in my mother's womb. He thinks about me now. He also has a plan for my life in the future. God's thoughts of me are too great for me to count.

Put all that together with the fact that God loves me with an infinite, never-ending love and I am filled with a great sense of awe and peace. God knows me and loves me. God knows everything that is going on in and around my life. God knows how it is all going to turn out and how things are going to turn out for me. What an incredible thing that is to know. I don't need to know what God knows to know that God knows what is best for me.

Trusting God means that we don't need an answer to the 'Why' questions of our life. We might ask them because we can't understand our God's thoughts and ways but we don't need Him to answer them. I am so thankful that God's ways are far above my ways. I want a God that can handle all of those things that are going to come into my life that I can't understand. Only a God bigger, smarter, and stronger than me or anything that this world can throw at me is big enough for me. Jesus, thank you for being a big God!

Rick Lancaster | PLANTERS PERSPECTIVE

SEPTEMBER 29 || ISAIAH 59:1

Listen! The LORD is not too weak to save you, and he is not becoming deaf. He can hear you when you call.

Read: Isaiah 57:15-59:21

There are times when it seems like God is so far away that He cannot save us from the attacks of our enemies and the assaults of the world. We feel like we could scream at the top of our lungs and He would not hear us because He has moved so far from us. Isaiah teaches the people of Israel and us that God hasn't moved; we have. In the verses that follow our verse for the day, Isaiah tells us that it is our sins that create a separation between God and us. God is immovable; nothing can move Him. We, on the other hand, are moved by many things; not the least of which is sin.

There is no place that we could possibly go that God's hand could not reach us to save us. God's strength and abilities far exceed the combined weaknesses of every person that has ever lived. God could rescue every living soul from any kind of danger instantaneously and simultaneously; His arm has no limits. Only our sin prevents us from being rescued by Him.

No matter how far we have wandered there is no distance that is so far that God can't hear us when we pray. God's ears are always tuned in to His children and He can hear and respond to every prayer spoken by every person alive without even breaking a sweat.

In those times when God seems so far away the first thing that we need to do is to examine our hearts to make sure there is no unconfessed sin there. If there is we just need to confess it and repent from it. God will forgive us and the distance that we feel will be reduced or eliminated immediately.

There will also be times when we feel a distance from God that is not associated with sin. God will sometimes withdraw from us to test our hearts to see if we will remain faithful to Him. It is at those times when it can be the most difficult and it is in those times that we need to hold onto a verse like today's. There is no place that I can get to that God is not right there to rescue me if He wills to. There is no place where my voice is so faint that He can't hear me even if He doesn't respond to me right away.

There is never a moment when I am out of sight or hearing of my loving Father in heaven. That gives me great comfort because there are times when He is out of my sight and hearing either because I have wandered or He is testing me. All I need to do is test my heart and keep my eyes on Jesus. If I do that I know that this time will pass and I will once again find myself walking hand-in-hand with my Savior. Jesus, remind us often about how close you really are.

SEPTEMBER 30 || ISAIAH 62:1

Because I love Zion, because my heart yearns for Jerusalem, I cannot remain silent. I will not stop praying for her until her righteousness shines like the dawn, and her salvation blazes like a burning torch.

Read: Isaiah 60:1-62:5

Isaiah reveals his heart in today's verse. Throughout this book he has spoken prophecies against the nation of Israel and the city of Jerusalem. But it is not in his heart that he wants to see the things that he spoke about come to pass. He loves Israel and the city of Jerusalem. Because of that love Isaiah feels compelled to speak out and to pray.

Isaiah's goal is not to condemn the nation of Israel or any other nation for that matter, but to warn them away from the danger that they are heading toward. God has given Isaiah visions of the future and told Isaiah to tell the people what he has seen. God doesn't want to destroy anyone and so He warns them of the danger that they cannot see. It is God's desire that everyone would heed His warnings and respond in a way that takes away the need for judgment and punishment.

Isaiah goes on to say that he is praying for Zion and Jerusalem. Even while he is speaking out judgments and warnings, he is praying. Prayer is one of the signs of a person that has the love of God in their hearts. Prayer aligns our heart to the heart of God and releases His power in the universe around us.

Isaiah is praying for two things in particular; righteousness and salvation. Righteousness is rightness with God. Isaiah wants the nation of Israel to be so right with God that their behavior lights up the whole world around them. That is precisely what results from righteousness with God. We usually think that righteousness is a very personal thing; it is all about me and my relationship with God. It is never that simple. Your righteousness is a tool that God uses to reveal Himself to other people through your life.

What does your life reveal about the nature, character, and abilities of God? What does your righteousness reveal about the holiness of God? What does your faith reveal about the faithfulness of God? You can be certain of one thing; your righteousness is revealing what you believe to be true of God. It was Isaiah's prayer that his people's righteousness would be so bright that it would rival the brightness of the dawning sun.

Isaiah was also praying for the salvation of Zion and Jerusalem. This was likely a literal salvation from her enemies. Isaiah was praying that God would rescue Zion and Jerusalem from her enemies. That salvation was to blaze like a torch. A torch brings light to the darkness. It is also a symbol of hope and guidance.

If you are reading this you are probably already saved. Your salvation should be a beacon for others, to draw them to salvation. Is your life guiding others to Christ? Can they see the hope of eternity in your eyes? They should! You remain on this earth to be a bright beacon in the darkness of this world to the lost and dying. Jesus, I pray that they will all let their light burn ever brighter.

Rick Lancaster / PLANTERS PERSPECTIVE

OCTOBER

OCTOBER 1 || ISAIAH 64:4

For since the world began, no ear has heard, and no eye has seen a God like you, who works for those who wait for him!

Read: Isaiah 62:6-65:25

As we come to the end of the book of Isaiah, he speaks to us about the final judgment that will befall those that do not turn to God. Isaiah also speaks about the salvation and restoration of those that do trust in God. And in our verse for the day Isaiah compares God to all the other gods that people vainly worship. Since the beginning of this earth, no one has seen or heard of a God like the Lord Almighty.

The characteristic that Isaiah points to as proof of what a Great God the Lord is, He works. No other god actually does anything like God. They can't because they aren't God. Some people worship nature, which follows its own course without respect to what man is doing or wants. Some people worship creations of their own hands which is the ultimate in vanity and futility. And some worship demons whose sole desire is to destroy those that are worshipping them. Only the Lord Almighty 'works for' those that worship Him.

We are told in our verse for today that God works for those that 'wait for Him'. Waiting is something many of us struggle with. Because we can't see God and can't see what He is doing or know what He is thinking it can be very hard to wait. It can be like waiting for a repairman to come fix your computer. You know something is not correct but you don't know how to fix it. You've called the repairman but you don't know when he is coming. What do you do until he shows up?

Often we will try to fix the problem ourselves while we wait. That usually doesn't work and will often make the situation worse. The same thing is true of our lives. God will work in our lives but we must wait for Him to show up to fix what is wrong in our lives. If we try to fix it ourselves we are likely just to mess our lives up that much more.

If I am waiting for my computer to be fixed, what I need to do is work on everything that I can do that doesn't require the computer. I need to stay busy; I can't just sit at my desk staring at the broken computer. People will often become frozen because something is wrong in their lives. They will sit and stare at their problem until it goes away. That is useless and wasteful. Get busy doing what you can until the repairman, God, shows up to fix what is wrong.

Waiting on the Lord is not about sitting around wallowing in the muck and mire of your problem. Focus on the things that you can do and don't worry about the things that you can't do. If you can't do them, worrying about them won't get them done. Waiting on the Lord is about trusting God enough to take your eyes off of your problem and focusing on the things that God wants you to do. Jesus, help us to stay busy while we wait for You.

Rick Lancaster / PLANTERS PERSPECTIVE

OCTOBER 2 || ISAIAH 66:1

This is what the LORD says: "Heaven is my throne, and the earth is my footstool. Could you ever build me a temple as good as that? Could you build a dwelling place for me?"

Read: Isaiah 66:1-24

In today's verse we see the immensity of God alluded to. Nothing can contain Him. No structure could ever be big enough for Him to live in. All of creation is not large enough for Him to dwell in. Even David said as he built the temple for God that it was inadequate to house God. It seems kind of foolish for us to think that we can build something for God but that is exactly what we do; especially when it comes to church buildings.

As some point as we lead ministries and churches our minds turn to buildings and other structures. We get it in our minds that we will build this beautiful edifice that will glorify God. I believe that God would have us to look at buildings differently than that. A building is a tool; it is something we use as long as it is useful and then we replace it with another that is more useful.

If we would do that there would be much simpler church buildings constructed with a greater focus on use than upon looks. God doesn't care how big your building is or how beautiful it is if people aren't being drawn to His son within it. The purpose of the buildings that we build should be to help people get to know Jesus. You don't need a huge elaborate building to do that.

As Jesus was leaving the last time before He was crucified His disciples were pointing to how amazing the temple was and I can imagine Jesus shrugging His shoulders before He told them that soon this temple that they were so impressed with was going to be torn down. In Israel today you can still see where the stones of the temple were pushed off of the temple mount and created craters in the sidewalk around it.

No building that we build today is likely even to be around in 100 years. Don't build to impress God or men; it is a waste of time and the resources that God gave you to grow the kingdom. We should strive to build buildings that are pleasing but not extravagant. Our buildings should be simple and humble like our Lord was during His ministry upon the earth.

Build buildings that will build people in their relationship with Jesus. Anything else is likely to be arrogance and vanity. You can't build a building that will impress God so build one that will make it easier for people to draw near to God. God is impressed by churches that reach the lost for Jesus Christ. Jesus, help us to see our buildings as tools that you want to use only as long as they are useful.

OCTOBER 3 || JEREMIAH 1:5

"I knew you before I formed you in your mother's womb. Before you were born I set you apart and appointed you as my spokesman to the world."

Read: Jeremiah 1:1-2:30

Jeremiah was called to be a Prophet of the Lord at a young age; probably late teens or early twenties. In the New King James Version Jeremiah complains to God regarding his appointment by saying: "I cannot speak, for I am a youth." Jeremiah knew that God was calling him to a very difficult ministry. It was a ministry that Jeremiah did not feel qualified to do. People associate wisdom with age. Jeremiah knew that people would have a difficult time receiving the message from him because of his youthfulness.

That didn't matter! God had a plan and that plan included Jeremiah being a Prophet at a very young age. God's plan had been set before Jeremiah had even been conceived. God knew that He had called Jeremiah to this impossible ministry. God even knew what results Jeremiah would have in this ministry.

It gives me great comfort and strength to know that God knew me even before I was formed in my mother's womb. It gives me great confidence to know that God had a plan to set me aside and appoint me to the ministry that He called me to. It was no accident or mistake that I am doing what I am doing. It is all a part God's great plan for my life.

There are going to be times in ministry when it is hard. And there are going to be times when it is impossible. Jeremiah was often threatened and even attacked. But God had told Jeremiah this is the plan that I have for you and I am going to protect you and help you to accomplish My will. It will be hard in ministry and sometimes you may wonder if you are doing the right things or you may wonder if you are having any kind of an impact for God. It is not your place to wonder about those things; it is God's.

God is responsible for the results of the ministry that you do; not you. You are responsible to do what God set you apart and appointed you to do. If you catch yourself wondering about what you are doing, that is a sign that you need to get your focus back on God and what He appointed you to do. You do your part and then trust God to do His.

God doesn't call us to do great things for Him. He only calls us to do what He told us to do. He does the great things! Whether your ministry is easy or hard is up to God. Whether your ministry is ultra-successful or seems like a failure is up to God. The only thing that we can do and are responsible for is doing what we were created for, set apart for, and appointed to do. Everything else is God's. Jesus, thank you that I am not responsible for the results of the things that you have called me to do for You.

Rick Lancaster / PLANTERS PERSPECTIVE

OCTOBER 4 | | JEREMIAH 3:15

And I will give you leaders after my own heart, who will guide you with knowledge and understanding.

Read: Jeremiah 2:31-4:18

Most of Jeremiah's prophecies were centered on the unfaithfulness of Judah and Israel and on God's faithfulness to them. As you read through the book of Jeremiah, you will see one prophecy after another beseeching the Israelites to return to their God and to forsake their worship of idols. The book is filled with descriptions of the curses that were going to befall the Israelites if they did not respond. It was also filled with promises of the blessings that God would pour out on them if they would repent from their disobedience.

One such promise is found here in our text for today. God promised to give them leaders that would be able to guide them. They already had leaders that were guiding them. Any leader, by the very nature of the fact that they are a leader guides those that they lead. The question is where they are leading them to. Throughout the books of Kings and Chronicles we see how the king influences the people either toward God or away from Him.

God's promise here in our text is that the leaders that He would provide would lead with knowledge and understanding. The knowledge that these leaders have is of God and of His plan for His people. This knowledge is God-breathed, meaning that we can seek after it, but God has to provide it. This is also true of understanding how to use the knowledge to move people toward God; it must come from God.

Our text for today gives what might be the single most important characteristic of a leader of God's people. Whether you are a leader of a family, Bible study, ministry, church, or corporation having this characteristic will enable you to be an effective leader. God told the Israelites that He would give them "leaders after my own heart".

This word 'after' describes the active seeking or pursuing of something. God is telling the Israelites that these leaders would be actively seeking to know and understand the heart of God. And even more than that, they are actively working to conform their own heart into the same shape as that of God's.

As leaders it is not enough just to lead people; we must be leading them somewhere. And as leaders 'set apart and appointed' from before the foundation of time to lead God's people, we must lead them to God. To do that our hearts must be soft and pliable so that the Master Craftsman can shape our hearts to look like His. We do that by seeking to know God in a deep and personal way and by seeking to understand His plan for His people. Jesus, change my heart to be like Yours.

OCTOBER 5 | | JEREMIAH 5:25

Your wickedness has deprived you of these wonderful blessings. Your sin has robbed you of all these good things.

Read: Jeremiah 4:19-6:15

God had promised the nation of Israel tremendous blessings. He promised to be their God and provide them with an abundant life filled with all the good things that He had created for them. There was only one requirement placed upon them and that was that they were to obey God in everything. God is challenging the people of the nation of Israel here and asking them why they are choosing the path they are on. In our verse for the day God lets them know what the consequences are of their choice.

When we are experiencing tough times and we are not being blessed by the Lord we will often point to bad luck or even to the actions of someone else. We seldom look into the mirror and ask the questions that God was asking the nation of Israel. If we did we would have a much different outlook regarding our circumstances and we would experience a significantly more blessed life.

God doesn't withhold his blessings from His obedient children. When we follow the path that He has laid out for us, we can count on the Lord to provide and protect all along the way. God desires to bless us and asks only that we would obey Him and worship Him. God doesn't ask so much of us that we would suffer to obey Him. In fact, what little suffering or sacrifice that we experience as a result of being obedient is usually insignificant in comparison to His blessings for obedience.

Jeremiah went on to tell the nation of Israel that their disobedience and disrespect was going to cost them dearly. God promised to send invaders into the land of Israel to cause them great suffering. As God's creation we are given two choices; obey God and be blessed or disobey God and suffer. God has that right because He created us for His good pleasure. One of our problems is that we mistakenly believe that we are in charge of our own destiny. The sooner we realize that we are not in control and that God is the better off we will be.

God has prepared a banquet table of blessings and promises. They are ours for the taking. We simply need to come to that table through obedience and worship. When we choose to disobey or divide our worship with something or someone else we are forfeiting those blessings. In many respects we are telling God that we choose not to be blessed by Him. Of course we won't say it that way but that is exactly what we are doing.

We can easily return to the table of God's blessings through repentance and seeking His forgiveness of our wickedness and sinfulness. God's blessings are endless and the life He means for us to live is abundant. Jesus, help us to get to the table of Your blessings.

Rick Lancaster | PLANTERS PERSPECTIVE

OCTOBER 6 | | JEREMIAH 7:27

Tell them all this, but do not expect them to listen. Shout out your warnings, but do not expect them to respond.

Read: Jeremiah 6:16-8:7

It is difficult to imagine how difficult the ministry of Jeremiah must have been. It is reported that Jeremiah had no visible success within his time of ministry. Not a single person is believed to have responded to the ministry of this man of God. Here in our verse for the day the Lord tells Jeremiah that is exactly what is going to happen; no one will listen and no one will respond.

As a pastor, one of the great encouragements of my life is to see the ministry that I am doing result in the fruit of lives that are changed for God. There are times in my ministry that I wonder if I am having any impact at all in the world. God is always faithful at those times to send someone to me to remind me that God is working through me to reach His children.

Jeremiah lived in a time and place that the people's hearts were hard toward God. They didn't want to hear from God and they had no intention of responding to Him even if they did hear from Him. He was in the most difficult ministry of all; proclaiming the gospel to people that don't want to hear it and don't feel they need it.

Nothing has changed in the world in the last 2,500 years. There are still people that have no desire to hear from God. There are still people that want nothing to do with God or the things of God. Those people are all around us. Some might even be in your own family. They can even be in your church! What should we do with those people in our lives? The very same thing that Jeremiah was told to do; tell them what God wants them to know.

God would tell you the same thing He told Jeremiah, keep telling them the truth. They aren't going to listen and they aren't going to respond but you keep warning them and telling them the truth. We can never fully know the effect we are having on others. Even though it appears that they are not listening or responding, we can't know what is going on in their hearts. The seeds that we plant in their lives may take a long time to sprout and there may not be fruit until long after they are gone from our lives.

God is calling us to be faithful to Him and to the ministry that He has given us. Whether or not we get to see any fruit from that ministry is wholly up to God. We will be evaluated based on our obedience to God's call on our lives, not based on the fruit that we produce. The fruit is God's responsibility, obedience is ours. Jesus, help us to faithfully obey You regardless of the results that we see around us.

OCTOBER 7 || JEREMIAH 8:11

They offer superficial treatments for my people's mortal wound. They give assurances of peace when all is war.

Read: Jeremiah 8:8-9:26

The prophet Jeremiah speaks this prophecy toward the scribes and priests of the nation of Israel. These were the men that were to be teaching the people how to fear and worship God and yet they were misleading them with false assurances. They were treating this mortal wound that they had with a band-aid. The mortal sin that the people were suffering from was idolatry. They had turned away from God and His ways and were following the ways of the wicked nations around them.

The image that I see in this is that the people have cancer and the scribes and priests are giving them aspirin to make them feel better. It might make them feel better but it is doing nothing to heal them of the disease that they have. To be healed they need dramatic, immediate, and strong action. God is warning them that they are close to death; if they don't do something soon it will be too late.

We still see a lot of this in the church. From the teaching to the counseling; people are being given aspirin when they need surgery or radiation. They are just given band-aids when they need amputation. People don't need to feel good, they need to see God. The only way that people can see God is if they deal with the cancer and other diseases that are ravaging their lives. They need to receive radical treatment so that they can be healed.

As leaders of families, ministries, and churches we need to be careful that we are not giving out band-aids and aspirin to our people. We should always, in love, be telling the people the truth about where they stand with God. Sometimes that means saying something that is hard and hurts deeply. Just as a surgeon is not afraid to cause pain to see healing take place in a patient's life, we should not be afraid to use the loving scalpel of truth to remove a soul-threatening disease from someone's life.

In fact, as leaders we will stand before God and give an accounting of how we have done that very thing. We might even try to justify our actions by saying that we didn't want to hurt them. But by our negligence we are allowing them to suffer more than a little pain that might draw them to healing.

This is where the Holy Spirit is so critical in our lives. We should strive to be gentle and meek with those that God has called us to lead. But there comes a time when we need to inflict the pain of truth strongly into a person's life. This is only possible if we are practiced at speaking the truth no matter what the circumstances. We should never hold the truth back from someone that needs to hear it. Their very soul may hang in the balance. Jesus, give us the words of truth to speak and the love to speak them.

Rick Lancaster / PLANTERS PERSPECTIVE

OCTOBER 8 || JEREMIAH 10:21

The shepherds of my people have lost their senses. They no longer follow the LORD or ask what He wants of them. Therefore, they fail completely, and their flocks are scattered.

Read: Jeremiah 10:1-11:23

Jeremiah is speaking out against the leaders of the nation of Israel. God often relates to the leaders of His people as shepherds. The responsibility of the shepherd is to protect, nurture, and care for the flock so that it is strong, healthy, and productive. A shepherd usually does not own the flock that he is watching over. A shepherd is assigned to the flock by the owner of the flock. As a servant of the owner, the shepherd must stay in contact with the owner to determine his desires for the flock.

Jeremiah is telling the leaders of Israel that they have become senseless. What they are doing doesn't make sense. The way that they are leading the flock of God's people is foolish and harmful. The verse gives two proofs that the shepherd/leaders are senseless, disobedience and disrespect. It also gives us the impending result of their senseless leading, utter failure and the flock will be scattered.

These shepherds are not following the Lord and therefore their actions are senseless. Obedience to God's commands is not an option for a leader of God's people, at least for a leader that has some desire to be successful in God's eyes. If we are leaders of the people of God, then we must recognize that they are His flock and we have been entrusted to care for them. To do that successfully, we need to follow carefully the directions that He has given for that work. If we do not obey God, then our activities, regardless how energetic or imaginative, are senseless and doomed to fail utterly. Only obedience to God can result in success with God.

These leader/shepherds also did not ask God what he expects of them. This is pride, arrogance, and disrespect toward God. The flock is His. The shepherd/leaders are His. Only God has the right to determine where that flock is going and what it will do. To fail to go to the Lord and ask Him for direction is a sure way to fail at the work of leading God's people. We get our direction from the Lord primarily through prayer and the Word of God. It is disrespectful to try to lead God's people if you don't regularly come to Him and ask for His guidance and direction.

Jeremiah also warns them and us what will happen if we fail to respond to this warning, our flock will be scattered. This is one of the things that drives me to draw ever closer to the Lord in my daily life and in my leadership of my family and church. The idea that my failure in this area could result in my family or church suffering is more than I can accept. Nothing could give me more pain than if my sin caused God's people to be scattered out of His presence. Take your responsibility as shepherd of God's people seriously, even if your flock consists only of your family. Obey God and seek Him daily. Jesus, teach us to shepherd like You do.

OCTOBER 9 || JEREMIAH 12:5

Then the LORD replied to me, "If racing against mere men makes you tired, how will you race against horses? If you stumble and fall on open ground, what will you do in the thickets near the Jordan?"

Read: Jeremiah 12:1-14:10

Jeremiah has been whining and complaining to God about what he sees in the world around him. The wicked people seem to be prospering and don't seem to care about what God thinks about their evil behavior. Jeremiah wants to see justice; He wants God to punish the wicked people around him.

Based on the Lord's response in our verse today we can deduce that Jeremiah was feeling like quitting his ministry for the Lord. He was experiencing what we commonly call 'ministry burnout'. Ministering to uncaring, rebellious people had left him tired and depressed. It is interesting to me that God doesn't encourage Jeremiah, but instead challenges him.

The Lord asks Jeremiah some questions that cause him to examine himself. It seems as though the Lord is telling Jeremiah that the things that he sees going on around him will in fact get worse than they are now. The Lord asks Jeremiah how he is going to do things in the future, if he is burned-out now.

Ministry burn-out is a fact-of-life. At some point in your life in ministry it is going to get so hard that you just want to lie down and quit. You will be tired of ministering to people that are uncaring and rebellious. Or they will betray you and attack you or your character. The thought of another day of ministry will depress you.

Jeremiah was a prophet. His ministry was to relate to the nations around him the word of the Lord as it was given to him. Immediately after our verse for the day God gives Jeremiah more things to say to the nations. God gives him more work to do. There is no sense in the text that God gave Jeremiah any time to get over his burn-out.

The prophet Jeremiah had taken his eyes off of the work that God had given him to do and he was looking at his circumstances. He was looking at the results of his labors rather than at the Lord of his labors. Any time we take our eyes off of the Lord, we are eventually going to find ourselves tired and depressed. The only solution is to get your eyes back on the Lord and get back to the work that He gave you.

Ministry burn-out is a fact-of-life. This is true because we are weak creatures that are too often distracted away from our source of strength and endurance and focus on the injustices of the world. If we keep our eyes on the Lord and obey Him implicitly, then we will not burn out in ministry. When you begin to feel tired and depressed, refocus on the Lord and ask Him to remind you of the work that he assigned to you. Jesus, help us to only do what You want us to do.

Rick Lancaster / PLANTERS PERSPECTIVE

OCTOBER 10 || JEREMIAH 16:13

So I will throw you out of this land and send you into a foreign land where you and your ancestors have never been. There you can worship idols all you like — and I will grant you no favors.

Read: Jeremiah 14:11-16:15

God is telling Jeremiah to make some pretty harsh predictions to the people of the nation of Israel. God is telling Jeremiah that he has already removed His hand of protection and peace from them and that they should not expect grace or mercy from Him either. The reason is because they have turned away from God and worshipped other gods. These idols are worshipped to satisfy their own evil desires and it sickens God. The Jews are God's chosen people and He views their actions as adultery.

In our verse for the day God tells them what the consequences are for their adulterous activities; to be driven out of the Promised Land. This is the land that God promised to Abraham and his descendants forever. God is driving them out because they have defiled the good land with their evil practices. God tells them that if that is the life they want, they can have it but not in the land that He promised to bless them in.

God goes on to tell them that He will grant them no favors while they are in the land of their exile. He was not going to help them in any way while they were in their backslidden state. The nation of Israel had experienced the protecting hand of God for hundreds of years. It is unlikely that they truly understood the magnitude of what was about to happen to them. They believed that they were safe and secure in the land and that God wasn't going to let anything bad happen to them.

We can't live anyway that we desire and expect God to bless and protect us. God promised us a life that is rich and full. That life is found in and lived in Jesus Christ. As we abide in Christ, we experience the life that Christ died to give; a good and blessed life. Our problem is that we are just like the Israelites, once we are safe and secure in the land of promise we begin to think we can live any way we choose. This ultimately leads to us not following God and following after other things instead. God calls that idolatry and adultery.

Because of God's great and infinite love for us He will try repeatedly to get us to repent of those things and return to Him. If we resist and continue to live our lives for ourselves and in our own way, God will slowly begin to withdraw His hand of protection and blessing from us. If we still don't respond He will send an enemy into our lives to attack or torment us. His desire is that we would realize our need for Him and dependence upon Him and turn back to Him. If that doesn't work, He will drive us out of the life He promised us and turn us over to our fleshly lusts. He stills hopes that we will realize our error and return to Him. All this is avoided by a life lived in close communion with Christ. Jesus, help us to stay close to You.

OCTOBER 11 || JEREMIAH 17:8

They are like trees planted along a riverbank, with roots that reach deep into the water. Such trees are not bothered by the heat or worried by long months of drought. Their leaves stay green, and they never stop producing fruit.

Read: Jeremiah 16:16-18:23

Today's verse is one of the thousands of promises found in God's Word. It is a promise that God's people will be able to endure all of the difficult circumstances of life. Even more than that, it promises that they will prosper during the difficult circumstances of life. It doesn't say that they won't be touched by those things but that they will be secure and fruitful during those times.

This is one of the many conditional promises found in the Bible. The preceding verse calls God's people blessed if they trust in the Lord and put their hope and confidence in Him. This means to us that we can be successful and fruitful in the midst of great difficulties by trusting God and putting our hope and confidence in Him.

I found it interesting that the very next verse after today's verse speaks about the wickedness of our hearts and that we shouldn't trust the things of our heart. This speaks to our feelings and emotions. We can't trust our feelings and emotions because they lie to us about what is going on in the world around us.

The preceding and following verses are bookends to our verse for the day. What are we trusting in, God or our feelings and emotions? Where is our hope and confidence, in the Lord or in our heart? Your heart is fickle and unreliable. Only God is worthy of trust. Only the Lord is someone in whom we can depend upon regardless of the situation or circumstances.

It is a great encouragement to me that I don't have to depend upon my own heart and what I feel or know. It gives me great confidence to know that God has offered to me all that I need, simply through trusting Him. And then on top of that He promises me that I will be fruitful even in the times of drought or famine. When the world around me is experiencing difficult times, my trust in the Lord will sustain me and cause me to be fruitful.

Promises like this should cause us to examine our lives and evaluate whether or not we see this promise being fulfilled in our lives. If not, we should be asking God to reveal to us any areas where we are not doing our part to meet His conditions for fulfillment. God is faithful; He will always do His part if we do our part. If one of His promises to us is not being fulfilled in our lives it means we are probably not meeting the condition for fulfillment. The solution is simple, humble your heart before the Lord and do what He says. And then you will experience the fullness of His promises. Jesus, help us to appropriate all Your promises.

OCTOBER 12 || JEREMIAH 20:9

And I can't stop! If I say I'll never mention the Lord or speak in his name, his word burns in my heart like a fire. It's like a fire in my bones! I am weary of holding it in!

Read: Jeremiah 19:1-21:14

Jeremiah had the incredibly difficult ministry of prophesying the impending judgment that was about to befall Jerusalem and Judah. The Babylonians are about to lay siege to Jerusalem and many of the people will be killed and many more will go into exile to Babylon.

In our reading for today Jeremiah is complaining to God about the ministry that he has been given. No one is listening and everyone is turning against him. It is difficult to say whether anyone responded to Jeremiah's messages or not. No one seemed to believe him, at least until the army of Babylon was camped outside the gates of the city.

Even though Jeremiah was complaining and felt as though he was wasting his time he knew that he had to continue doing what he had been told to do by God. He had to speak the truth whether people were going to listen or not. Jeremiah felt compelled to speak out what God was saying to him. He describes this compulsion as a fire burning in his heart and in his bones. He also says that if he tries to hold it in, meaning to not speak, that he becomes weary.

The truth is the truth! And it doesn't matter that a lot of people don't want to hear it. In fact most people don't want to know what it is that God wants to tell them. But it doesn't change the fact that God wants His messengers to faithfully proclaim the truth with every breath that they take.

If you try to hold it in, it will burn inside of you until you cannot hold it any longer. God doesn't want you to hold onto it; He wants you to give it to those that it was intended for. The role of the messenger is to carry the message to whom it is intended and to give it to him. To withhold the message is to be disobedient and unfaithful.

Jeremiah's complaint to God is that he is being mistreated and persecuted because he is doing what God told him to do. And in our verse he says that even though this is happening he can't stop obeying God. Jeremiah knows that he must obey. God has not promised him great success and He doesn't promise us that we will be successful in the ministry that He has called us to. He didn't call us to be successful; He called us to be faithful. Only God can define what success is in your ministry. It is believed that Jeremiah saw no response to his messages; not a single person responded. And yet God considered Jeremiah to be a faithful servant. You be faithful, even if it looks like nothing is happening. Jesus, help us to speak the truth in love without hesitation.

OCTOBER 13 || JEREMIAH 22:4

If you obey me, there will always be a descendant of David sitting on the throne here in Jerusalem. The king will ride through the palace gates in chariots and on horses, with his parade of officials and subjects.

Read: Jeremiah 22:1-23:20

David had been king of Israel about four hundred years before the time of Jeremiah's prophecies. God had promised David that one of his descendants would sit on the throne forever. But this was a conditional promise and the condition was that the kings of Israel had to obey God. Jeremiah is repeating this conditional promise to Jehoiakim, a descendant of David, who has been made king by the king of Babylon.

With this conditional promise was also a promise of blessing. God promised to bless Jehoiakim so that he would be wealthy and powerful. All he had to do was his part; he had to obey God. The scriptures tell us that he did not do his part and suffered the consequences of his disobedience.

God desires to bless us and to fill our lives with all the good things that He has created just for us. Our problem is that we will often try to get the blessing before we do the obedience. Jehoiakim went about chasing after the good things of life and paid no attention to being obedient to God. Babylon will, before very long, come and take from Jehoiakim all of those things that he was chasing after.

As we lead our families, ministries, and churches we can be tempted to take a shortcut to God's promises and blessings. Too often we will jump ahead to the blessing that God promised without paying our sacrifice of obedience. What we need to understand is that when we sacrifice obedience, we are also sacrificing blessing.

It is very simple, if you want God's blessings and to see His promises fulfilled you must first be obedient. If you try to shortcut the process you are being disobedient and God will not bless you.

We live in a society that views sacrifice as something that only people of certain professions do; like firemen, policemen, and the military. Jesus told us that the only way that we could keep our life was to give it. Only through sacrifice, can you truly be obedient to God. Your obedience will cost you something, probably not your life but it will cost some portion of it.

If you desire to see God's promises being fulfilled and His blessings pouring out in abundance into your family, ministry, and church you must make a sacrifice of obedience to His Word. Only through sacrificial, unconditional obedience should you expect to receive the fullness of God's blessings. Jesus, help us to give it up so that we can go up.

Rick Lancaster | PLANTERS PERSPECTIVE

OCTOBER 14 || JEREMIAH 23:29

"Does not my word burn like fire?" says the LORD. "Is it not like a mighty hammer that smashes a rock to pieces?"

Read: Jeremiah 23:21-25:38

In our reading today, the Lord is rebuking the false prophets that were present in Jeremiah's time. A false prophet is someone that says they have a message from the Lord but do not. The motive for giving a false prophecy is to cause someone to follow them rather than the Lord. This could be an issue of pride, greed, lust, or just plain wickedness.

The Lord challenges His 'true messengers' to speak forth every word that He gives them. God's Word is true and righteous. In Hebrews we are told that the Word of God is living and powerful. God spoke to the prophets of Jeremiah's day with messages of righteousness. The false prophets gave messages appease people and to advance their own cause or position.

In the verse that precedes today's God says that there is a difference between the words of the true and false prophets. The difference is described in the form of two questions. In the first the Lord asks, 'Does not my word burn like fire?' Fire is a picture of judgment and purification. To the wicked, God's word speaks of impending judgment and a warning to turn from sin and to God. To the righteous fire speaks of purification. God's word instructs the righteous how to be more righteous.

The second difference between the words of the true and false prophets is that the true word 'Is...like a mighty hammer that smashes a rock to pieces.' To the unbeliever the Word of God will smash down the defenses they place to keep God out of their lives. God doesn't want us to use His Word like a hammer, beating people into submission. God's Word offered humbly, gently, and with love is a hammer. Once in a person's life it will smash the rocks that block the way to salvation.

In a believer's life God's Word acts as a hammer to break down the fortresses that we have allowed to exist in our lives. All of us have areas of unbelief or sin in our lives that God wants to work out of us. Some of those things are behind great walls of habit, fear, insecurity, or distrust that prevents us from surrendering that area fully to God. Only His Word has the power to break through to give us freedom from that bondage.

As modern believers God has given all of His word in the Bible. One of the last things that Jesus said to His disciples was that they should be 'witnesses' of Him to the rest of the world. As a believer you have been given a message to give to the world around you. That message found in the words of Scripture has the power to change your life and the lives of all those you come into contact with. Be a 'true messenger' and use it to bring people to their Savior. Jesus, teach us to cherish Your Word.

PLANTERS PERSPECTIVE / *A Devotional*

OCTOBER 15 || JEREMIAH 27:13

Why do you insist on dying—you and your people? Why should you choose war, famine, and disease, which the Lord will bring against every nation that refuses to submit to Babylon's king?

Read: Jeremiah 26:1-27:22

God is about to punish the nation of Israel because they have been rebellious and turned away from the One True God to worship worthless idols. To punish them He is going to send Babylon to conquer them and take them away into captivity for a period of time. The false prophets have been telling King Zedikiah of Judah that Babylon will never come. Jeremiah is trying to warn them not to resist God's punishment.

In today's text Jeremiah warns that any nation that resists God's punishment will experience war, famine, and disease. God is saying you are better off to take the punishment than if you were to resist it. God is giving them a choice between life and death. By choosing life they will live out their lives in Babylon. While this is not the life that they would choose for themselves, it is better than the alternative.

They will be choosing the alternative when they resist God's punishment for their disobedience. By resisting they are choosing death through war, famine, and disease. Two simple choices; God's way or your way, life or death. There is no third option.

It is God's desire that He would never have to punish His children. Most parents have no desire to punish their children. The Bible teaches that God chastises or punishes those that he loves. When God spanks His children, it is proof that He loves us. God's chastisement is meant to cause us to repent from our sinful ways and then draw near to Him as we should.

Getting a spanking from God is never going to be fun. But it is proof that God still loves us and wants us to be in close intimate fellowship with Him. But that fellowship is always going to be on God's terms and not ours. The Bible teaches us that God is a jealous God; He will not share us with another 'god'. If we allow anything to enter our life that takes His place in our lives, we are opening ourselves up to receive His punishment. God will always warn us first and give us a chance to repent, just like He did to the Israelites through the prophets. If we refuse to listen, we are choosing God's punishment.

As uncomfortable as God's punishment might be, it is far better than resisting and experiencing the consequences. Our best response when we suspect that we might be experiencing the punishment of God is humbly repent of any sins that we know about in our lives and ask Him for forgiveness and mercy. And then we need to trust God with whatever happens next in our lives, even if it means a long trip to Babylon. Jesus, teach us follow closely and repent quickly.

Rick Lancaster / PLANTERS PERSPECTIVE

OCTOBER 16 || JEREMIAH 29:7

And work for the peace and prosperity of Babylon. Pray to the LORD for that city where you are held captive, for if Babylon has peace, so will you."

Read: Jeremiah 28:1-29:32

Jeremiah is still in Jerusalem after King Nebuchadnezzar of Babylon has taken much of the population into exile in Babylon. Jeremiah writes to the exiles there and tells them to settle down and live as normal a life as they can because they are going to be there for seventy years. He tells them to have children and to find wives for their sons. This would probably been a bit of a blow to them because they were probably thinking that it would only last a little while.

Then Jeremiah speaking under the inspiration of God tells them to start to pray for the peace of Babylon. This is probably not what the exiles thought they should be praying at that time. They were probably praying that God would send a deliverer to rescue them; not that their captor would have peace.

God had a plan and that plan included the exiles living in the land of Babylon for seventy years. Their prayers were not going to change that part of the plan. But their prayers could change how things went for them as they lived there. They couldn't change the duration of their time in Babylon but they could change the quality of time that they would be there.

God's plans are firm! When He says He is going to do something, our prayers are not likely to change that. Of course there are accounts in scripture of God changing His plans when a people (Nineveh) or a person (King Hezekiah) responds correctly. But for the most part, God's plans will be carried out exactly the way that He said they would.

Our prayers are often directed at changing our circumstances in a very personal and specific way. The problem is that often our prayers are an attempt to get God to change His plan. God is not likely to change His plan just because you don't like it or because it makes your life uncomfortable. God may be calling you to pray for the people or situation that is making you uncomfortable. God might bless you by blessing them first.

This goes against our human nature; to pray for a blessing on those that oppress us or persecute us. But that is exactly what Jeremiah was told to tell the exiles. He was told to tell them to pray that their oppressors would be blessed. There is another aspect of this that it is important for us to see. The exiles played a role in getting peace for Babylon. By telling the exiles to pray for Babylon, God was telling them that He wasn't likely to bring peace unless they did pray for it. Could it be that God has told you to pray for peace and blessings for those that are oppressing you? Could He be waiting for you to start praying so that He can bring peace and blessings into your life by bringing peace and blessings into theirs? Jesus, help us to pray for peace in the Babylon in our lives.

OCTOBER 17 || JEREMIAH 31:18

I have heard Israel saying, 'You disciplined me severely, but I deserved it. I was like a calf that needed to be trained for the yoke and plow. Turn me again to you and restore me, for you alone are the Lord my God.'

Read: Jeremiah 30:1-31:26

The nation of Israel had been conquered and much of the population taken into exile. God allowed this for a purpose; He was training His people to follow Him and Him alone. The people had been guilty of idol worship and were following any pagan practice that appealed to them. God had warned continuously that if they did not stop that He was going to drive them from the land. God used the Babylonians, a fierce and vicious people to fulfill this warning.

Today's verse is a prophesy of a time when the nation of Israel will turn away from the idols that they have been worshipping and turn back to God. They will acknowledge that God had to discipline them so that they would be trained to follow God. Throughout much of today's reading are the prophesies about the punishment that God inflicted upon Babylon. How can we tell the difference between God's discipline and His punishment?

As with most things about God, it is a matter of the heart. The nation of Israel knew the God of Abraham, Isaac, and Jacob. They had just taken their eyes off of Him and turned them to worthless, lifeless idols. The Babylonians did not know God, nor did they desire to. The Babylonians were a proud and arrogant people. God disciplines His children and punishes those that will not turn back to Him.

There will probably be times in all of our lives when we are being disobedient or rebellious against God. If we are, we will feel God's hand heavy upon us. It is at times like that, that we might feel that God is punishing us. Punishment is the act of inflicting pain as a result of some offense. Discipline is the act of inflicting pain for the purpose of correction. Scripture is quite clear; God punishes those that will not turn to Him and disciplines those that will.

When we feel God's hand heavy upon us we need to turn to Him and ask Him to reveal where we may be disobedient or rebellious. We need to ask God to reveal to us how He is trying to train us to follow Him more closely. If God is disciplining you it is a sign that He loves you. Allow His discipline to draw you closer to Him. We cannot fight God's discipline; but must embrace it as the training that we need so that we can be more like His Son Jesus.

God doesn't want to discipline us. He would much rather we never wander from the path that He desires us to walk. But we like sheep have gone astray. We will wander and God will correct us. Welcome His correction and respond quickly to it. Jesus, help us to respond more quickly to Your staff so that You don't need to use the rod.

Rick Lancaster | PLANTERS PERSPECTIVE

OCTOBER 18 || JEREMIAH 32:17

O Sovereign LORD! You have made the heavens and earth by your great power. Nothing is too hard for you!

Read: Jeremiah 31:27-32:44

Jeremiah has been imprisoned by King Zedekiah because he keeps telling the king and the people that Nebuchadnezzar is going to come and destroy Jerusalem. Rather than listening to what God is saying through Jeremiah, King Zedekiah tries to shut him up by locking him up. The things that Jeremiah said were going to happen are happening. King Nebuchadnezzar of Babylon is there with his army and they have laid siege to Jerusalem.

Jeremiah is in a tough spot. He is in prison for doing what God told him to do and there is a vicious army outside the gates of the city that are going to do what God said they were going to do. This is a dark time for Jeremiah and the people of Israel. Jeremiah's response to his circumstances is perfect; he glorifies God!

Jeremiah doesn't look at his circumstances and throw a pity party. Instead, he rejoices in who God is, what He has done, and what he can do. In our verse for today, Jeremiah begins by acknowledging that God is sovereign. That means that God is in charge. Being sovereign, God has the right to do whatever he wants, when He wants, and however He wants. Jeremiah knows that God has the right to destroy the city of Jerusalem and everyone in it because He is sovereign. Jeremiah acknowledges that even his circumstances are within God's sovereignty. Jeremiah then states as a fact that God has created the heavens and the earth by His power. God has done amazing things in all of our lives and He wants us to remember those things; especially when things are tough. When your circumstances are hard and spinning out of your control, remember that God created everything that you can see and He created you.

Jeremiah makes a statement at the end of this verse that is very powerful; "Nothing is too hard for You!" There is nothing that is too hard for God. No matter how hard our circumstances may become; they are not too hard for God. There is absolutely nothing that God can't do within the tough situations of our life. There is no limit to how much God can do to help us to deal with the hard things in our life. There is end to His power to act on our behalf to change our circumstances.

Jeremiah's circumstances were tough, but he knew that they were not too tough for God. Jeremiah knew that God was powerful enough to get him out of prison and to cause King Nebuchadnezzar to leave Jerusalem alone. However big your problem is; God is bigger! However hard your situation is; God is stronger! However desperate your circumstances seem to you; God is still sovereign and still in control. In the midst of your trial and circumstances, praise God for who He is, what He has done, and what He can do for you. Jesus, help us to see You through our circumstances.

OCTOBER 19 || JEREMIAH 34:16

But now you have shrugged off your oath and defiled my name by taking back the men and women you had freed, making them slaves once again.

Read: Jeremiah 33:1-34:22

The topic of slavery is one that our western sensibilities struggle with. The word evokes some very strong images in our minds. In the culture of Jeremiah's time it was as natural as day-care is for our children today. It was often used to take care of people that couldn't take care of themselves. A person would place themselves into the care of another person. They would lose their freedom but they would gain the security of the homeowner.

God's plan for the Hebrews was that He didn't want them taking advantage of their Hebrew brethren and so He established laws limiting slavery. All Hebrew slaves were to be freed to go and start their own lives after they had served for six years. The Hebrew slave was then given the choice to go or to stay. If he chose to stay, it would be for the rest of his or her life.

King Zedekiah for some reason decided to free all the Hebrew slaves that were in Judah and made an oath before God to treat their Hebrew brethren the way that they should. This obviously pleased God. But the leaders and the people went back on their oath and took the men and women back into slavery that they had freed.

It is probably difficult for us to picture what it would have been like for those people that had freed their slaves. Those slaves would likely have done all the work of the house and field and flocks. They would have taken care of everything that needed to be done. With those slaves gone it would have been very difficult for them to live their normal life. To do what God had called them to do and what they had committed to God to do was going to be hard. Your life is no different than that of the Hebrew homeowners. As your relationship with Jesus grows and matures there are going to come times when God is going to call you to make some kind of a commitment to Him. Fulfilling that commitment might even cost you something or be uncomfortable. It might mean a time of inconvenience or require an adjustment of your lifestyle.

The Hebrew homeowners shrugged off their oath to God and He didn't like it. God wants to bless us more than we can imagine. The only way that we can hope to receive all that God has promised us is to answer when He calls and keep our commitments to Him. Our temporary times of difficulty or inconvenience are nothing compared to the times of refreshing that God wants to give us. Don't run from your commitments to God just because it gets hard. Run to God and let Him help you keep your commitments. Jesus, help us to count our oaths to You as precious and worth keeping.

Rick Lancaster / PLANTERS PERSPECTIVE

OCTOBER 20 || JEREMIAH 36:24

Neither the king nor his officials showed any signs of fear or repentance at what they heard.

Read: Jeremiah 35:1-36:32

Jeremiah received a word from God which Jeremiah had written on a scroll. Jeremiah then sent his servant Baruch to the Temple to read this scroll to the people. In this scroll were all the prophecies that God had given to Jeremiah concerning Israel and its people. God's plan was that maybe the people would respond and turn away from their sins and turn back to God. One of the king's officials heard what Jeremiah had written on the scroll and so he had the scroll taken to the king. But before he did, he warned Jeremiah's servant to hide and that Jeremiah should hide as well. The king responded to hearing the words that God had spoken through Jeremiah by first burning up the scroll and then ordering that Jeremiah be arrested.

God's desire was that the words on the scroll would bring conviction to the hearts of the people and to that of the king and his officials. God wanted them to fear Him and to repent of their sins. His desire was to heal the land of the sin of idolatry that had so permeated the nation of Israel. But instead of conviction, the king felt contempt for the message and the messenger. King Jehoiakim would suffer the consequences of his faithlessness and sin by being killed and being left unburied.

Two of the most important character traits that God desires in His people, especially His leaders are fear of God and repentance. God wants us to have a reverential awe and respect for who He is, what He has done, and what he can do. He also wants us to have hearts that are so tuned into His that we repent or turn away from our sin as soon as we realize that we have sinned against God.

King David was an imperfect man. He made some huge mistakes in his life; adultry, murder, and lying just to name a few. And yet the Bible refers to him as "A man after God's own heart". King David had a deep respect and fear of God and he was quick to repent when confronted with his sins. That is what God desired of King Jehoiakim and his officials. Because they did not respond that way God judged them and the nation of Israel and very soon they would be taken away into captivity in Babylon.

God knows that his people cannot be perfect. If they could have been perfect He wouldn't have had to send His Son as a sacrifice for their sins. He wants His people, especially those that have been called to lead to fear Him always and to repent of their sins quickly. If there are Babylonians knocking on your door, it might be time to take a hard look at your heart. Do you hold God in the reverence, awe, and respect that He deserves? Have you repented of all sin that you know about in your life? Jesus, teach us to fear You and help us to repent from anything that separates us from You.

OCTOBER 21 || JEREMIAH 38:15

Jeremiah said, "If I tell you the truth, you will kill me. And if I give you advice, you won't listen to me anyway."

Read: Jeremiah 37:1-38:28

Jeremiah has been going through some very difficult things. God has been giving him some hard messages to relay to the king of Israel and to the people. That message is that God is sending the Babylonian army to conquer the nation of Israel because they have once again turned away from the One True God to worship worthless idols. Jeremiah has been telling the people that it will go much better for them if they surrender to the king of Babylon. If they do not, he has warned them that they will be killed and the city of Jerusalem will be burned to the ground.

The leaders object to Jeremiah's prophecies and first have him thrown into prison. Jeremiah continues to speak forth the prophecy and so the leaders convince the king that Jeremiah needs to die. He gives them permission to do what they want and they throw him into a cistern. He is rescued from the cistern but then placed back into prison. All this is happening because Jeremiah is telling them the truth about what God is going to do.

King Zedekiah decides he wants to talk with Jeremiah and brings him out of the prison to the temple. Zedekiah wants to hear what the Lord has to say about the trouble that they are facing. He wants to know if he is going to survive the siege of the Babylonian army. Zedekiah commands Jeremiah to tell the truth. Every time Jeremiah does that he gets into more trouble and you might think that at some point he might give up and cave in to the pressure of his circumstances. But as a man of God, he knows that he can't.

Instead Jeremiah tells Zedekiah that responding to the king's request is a waste of his time. What boldness! Jeremiah knows that Zedekiah doesn't really what to hear the truth, he wants to hear something that will make him feel better about his circumstances without having to face the fact that he is in rebellion against God.

People have not changed much since Jeremiah's time. They still don't really want to hear the truth even though they act as though they do. They come to church in the hopes that they will hear something that will make them feel better, or to find a 'magic pill' to solve all their problems. Even if we give them advice, they will not listen or follow it.

The king promises not to kill Jeremiah. Personally, I don't believe that Jeremiah was really concerned about whether he would kill him or not. Jeremiah was determined to tell him the truth regardless of the consequences or outcome. The message did not change, surrender to the Babylonians or suffer the consequences. Zedekiah didn't listen and everything Jeremiah prophesied came to pass and Zedekiah was made to watch as his sons were killed and then his eyes were gouged out. Even though they won't listen, we need to tell people the truth regardless of what it might cost us. Jesus, teach us to value the truth over our comfort or safety.

Rick Lancaster / PLANTERS PERSPECTIVE

OCTOBER 22 || JEREMIAH 39:18

Because you trusted me, I will preserve your life and keep you safe. I, the LORD, have spoken!

Read: Jeremiah 39:1-41:18

Jeremiah gives a word of prophecy to Ebed-melech the Ethiopian. Ebed-melech is only mentioned here in our verse for the day and in the previous chapter of Jeremiah. Jeremiah had been imprisoned in a dungeon that had waist-high mud in it. Ebed-melech went to King Zedekiah and asked the king to save Jeremiah from the dungeon. Zedekiah sent Ebed-melech to save Jeremiah.

Ebed-melech was a eunuch in King Zedekiah's court. What his role was is not mentioned in scripture. There is no mention as to why He did what he did to rescue Jeremiah. He was Ethiopian which means he wasn't a Hebrew; one of the children of God. And yet, because of his actions in chapter 38 of Jeremiah God sends Jeremiah a message to give him.

The king of Babylon is about to sack the city of Jerusalem and destroy it and kill many of its people. Those that aren't killed will be sent into exile with the exception of the very poorest people. Ebed-melech had a right to be afraid. As a part of the court, there was a good chance that he would be killed immediately. So God sends him this word of hope and encouragement.

Jeremiah was ministering to a nation of people that did not want to hear what he had to say. All God wanted them to do was to repent from their sins and turn back to him. But they wanted to go their own way, regardless what God said. Jeremiah's was a tough ministry! It must have encouraged Jeremiah to receive this message for the Ethiopian eunuch. It would have told him that someone believes; someone is trusting God. This foreigner had more faith than most of the Chosen People of God.

There may be times in life and in ministry when you feel like you are in chains in a dungeon in mud up to your waist. And you might be wondering if anything that you are doing is making a difference. Trust that God is preparing an Ethiopian eunuch to come and rescue you and it is very likely that something that you did or said influenced them to trust God enough to do it.

God told Ebed-melech that because he had trusted God that he was going to rescue him from the impending doom. He had trusted God and rescued Jeremiah and now God was going to rescue him. God's actions almost always follow our actions. To see God rescue us, we must first trust Him to do so. Do your part and then trust God to do His part. Jesus, in You we trust!

OCTOBER 23 | | JEREMIAH 42:6

Whether we like it or not, we will obey the LORD our God to whom we send you with our plea. For if we obey him, everything will turn out well for us.

Read: Jeremiah 42:1-44:23

The Babylonians have taken many people from Israel into exile in Babylon and left a few in Israel to maintain the land. Some of the leaders of the army and other leaders come to Jeremiah and ask him to speak to the Lord for them. They had it in their mind to flee to Egypt and they wanted God to bless their plan to do what they wanted to.

They then tell Jeremiah that no matter what God says that they will do it, even if they don't like what they hear God telling them to do. As you read the text of what God tells Jeremiah to tell the people you can tell that their hearts were not right when they asked Jeremiah to speak to God. God tells them that He knows what they are thinking and tells them that their plan is not going to work. He then lays out what is going to happen to them if they go ahead with their plan anyway. If they do what they are thinking even though God is telling them not to, they will find that destruction will follow them wherever they go. In chapter 43 of Jeremiah the true heart of the people is revealed as they refuse to listen to what Jeremiah is saying on behalf of God. They accuse him of lying and they go ahead to do what they had wanted to do anyway. This is after they committed to do it whether they liked God's answer or not.

When we go to God there are going to be times when the things that He tells us are not what we want to hear. He is going to tell us to do things that will make us uncomfortable or that cause us to make some kind of a sacrifice. The leaders of the people knew the truth; they knew that they needed to do it whether they liked God's plan or not. They also knew the most important part of this truth; that everything would go well for them if they would obey God. What they didn't want to believe was that the opposite truth was also true; if they disobeyed, everything would not go well for them.

God rightfully expects us to obey Him. This is especially true when we go to God and ask Him for direction and guidance. If you go to God for something, it must be with the understanding that whatever He tells you, you will do. That is the only way that you can expect God to cause things to go well for you. Otherwise, you are asking God to bless your plan whether or not He agrees with it. That is never going to happen.

Whether you like it or not, God's plan for you includes things going well for you. But to see that happen, you must obey the things that He tells you to do. If you decide to do your plan after God has told you not to, understand that things will not go well for you. You may not believe that now, but you will. If you go to God, be prepared to do whatever He tells you to whether you like what it is or not. Only then will it go well with you. Jesus, help us to come to you often and teach us to obey you every time.

Rick Lancaster | PLANTERS PERSPECTIVE

OCTOBER 24 || JEREMIAH 45:5

Are you seeking great things for yourself? Don't do it! I will bring great disaster upon all these people; but I will give you your life as a reward wherever you go. I, the LORD, have spoken!

Read: Jeremiah 44:24-47:7

Chapter 45 of Jeremiah is written to encourage Baruch, Jeremiah's scribe. Baruch was responsible for recording all the things that Jeremiah received from the Lord. It is easy to understand why Baruch might be discouraged. Jeremiah's prophesies speak of the impending destruction of Jerusalem and the enslaving of God's people. It is easy to imagine these kinds of prophesies creating a sense of fear and dread in the heart and mind of Baruch.

Few things are as depressing in ministry as knowing that God's judgment is going to fall upon someone and knowing there is nothing you can do to stop it. As a pastor, I am regularly faced with people that have made some very bad choices. They come to me and want me to help them fix their lives and make all the bad things stop. Often I have to share with them that it is some sin in their lives that is causing the problems and for the consequences to stop they need to change.

That is not what people want to hear. They want you to pray a special prayer that erases the consequences without and inconvenience in their lives. They want me to give them a pill that changes everything or wave a magic wand over their lives to transport them to some fairy tale life that only exists in their imaginations. When I tell them the truth they are usually less than enthusiastic about what the solution to their situation is. They often leave with no intention of doing the things that God wants them to do.

It is very frustrating to watch this happen day after day. Thankfully, God brings some into our ministries that hear the truth, apply it to their lives, and experience the blessings of obedience to God. They are the exceptions, most don't really care what God wants or thinks. As a pastor I know what their disobedience is going to cost them and it hurts my heart to see them insist upon doing things their own way. Baruch was overwhelmed and exhausted by what he perceived to be a hopeless situation.

As ministers of truth we can believe that we are going to be God's tools to do great things for Christ. We single-handedly will change the world for Jesus Christ. After a while we realize that just because we are armed with the truth of God and empowered with the Spirit of God people will change only as much as they want to. And often that is excruciatingly short of where God desires them to be. When we come to that realization it can make us weary and we feel overwhelmed.

God promised to give Baruch his life as a reward for his faithful service. We are called to be faithful, nothing more, nothing less. Be faithful and He will reward you with a life that only He can give you. Jesus, help us to stay the course.

OCTOBER 25 || JEREMIAH 49:11

But I will protect the orphans who remain among you. Your widows, too, can depend on me for help.

Read: Jeremiah 48:1-49:22

Jeremiah is speaking out a prophecy against the nation of Edom. Because of their sins against the people of God, He is planning to destroy them as a nation. The fact that God would do something like that bothers many people. They wonder why a loving God would destroy people. What they are failing to understand is that God never destroys anyone that has not had an opportunity to turn to Him but has rejected Him. God wants all people to be His people and to rest under His loving care and protection. But those that reject Him and oppose Him fall under His judgment.

We can't fully understand why God does what he does because we are not capable of thinking like God. Instead of trying to understand we can rest in our knowledge of His character toward His people and those that He cares for. Today's verse is an example of that.

Even though God intends to destroy the nation of Edom from the face of the earth, He promises to take care of the widows and orphans of Edom. God's love, compassion, and grace towards the helpless is a source of great hope. The Bible doesn't tell us how God was going to keep this promise but we need only rest in the fact of God's faithfulness to believe that it is true.

Because we live in a world that is filled with war, violence, famine, and disease there will always be orphans and widows that need God's protection and care. It is God's desire that His protection and care are provided through His people. God blesses His people to be a blessing to others. As a nation that has been greatly blessed by God, we have an obligation to be a blessing to the orphans and widows of the world.

We can't reach them all, nor does God expect us to. We just need to do what we can. God will take care of the rest of them. We might think that we don't need to do anything, God has promised to do it, so I don't have to think about it. We need to be careful not to allow that thought to stop us from trying to do something. There is always a chance that God has chosen you to be the method that He desires to use to keep that promise to them.

God is faithful! He has promised to take care of the orphans and widows, and He will! If He intends for you to be a part of that and you do nothing, they will still be taken care of somehow but you will miss out on being used by God and you will lose the blessing that He intended to give you. You don't have to sell everything you own and give it to the poor. Be sensitive to the Spirit's leading and do what He tells you. It is usually something simple and easy. Let Him use you to do the amazing. Jesus, show us how to care for the orphans and widows.

Rick Lancaster / PLANTERS PERSPECTIVE

OCTOBER 26 || JEREMIAH 50:6

My people have been lost sheep. Their shepherds have led them astray and turned them loose in the mountains. They have lost their way and can't remember how to get back to the fold.

Read: Jeremiah 49:23-50:46

Jeremiah is speaking to the people of Israel about what is going to happen in the near future. He has already told them that they are going to be led away into captivity in Babylon. In the verses just before this one Jeremiah told them that their captivity would end by Babylon being overthrown and utterly destroyed. At that time they will head back toward the land that God promised to their ancestors.

Today's verse is a sad commentary about the spiritual condition of the people and about the sin of their leaders. The Bible often refers to God's people as sheep and their leaders as shepherds. It is a great picture of the roles that leaders serve to the body of God's people, shepherds entrusted with the care and raising of His flock.

Israel's leaders had led the people astray. When we first read something like this we might think that they did it on purpose. While that might be the case occasionally, it is more likely that a much more subtle event took place. Rather than deliberately leading others astray they more likely were led astray themselves first. And because they were leaders they were followed by those they were leading.

It is a tremendous responsibility to be a leader among God's people. You are called to shepherd a part of God's flock. As sheep they need someone to lead them back to the fold because they may not remember how to get back there themselves. The fold represents a place of safety and rest. It is the shepherd's responsibility to get the flock to the fold. Israel's leaders were guilty of leading the people astray and then abandoning them in the mountains where they became prey of wild animals.

The people that God has entrusted to your leadership may not know how to protect themselves from the enemies that surround them and seek to devour them. They need someone to lead them and guide them back to the place of safety and rest. It is up to the shepherd/leaders to bring their people to the place of ultimate safety and rest, Jesus Christ.

Your flock might be as small as your family or as large as a ministry or church. To ensure they don't get led astray you need to stay close to the Good Shepherd, Jesus Christ. Do that and your flock will be safe and rested in the fold of God's perfect love and care. Take your responsibility seriously because God does. Jesus, help us to stay close to You.

OCTOBER 27 || JEREMIAH 51:17

Compared to him all people are foolish and have no knowledge at all! They make idols, but the idols will disgrace their makers, for they are frauds. They have no life or power in them.

Read: Jeremiah 51:1-53

Our verse for the day is found within a prophecy of the overthrow and destruction of Babylon by the Medes. In the midst of this prophecy the prophet Jeremiah breaks out in declaration of God's attributes. It is as though Jeremiah is suddenly overtaken with a sense of awe and wonder about how great God is. This is a natural thing for someone that is being used by God. When we are serving and God's Spirit is working in us or through us, we will break out in praise or adoration of God. It is almost as if we can't help ourselves, we must say something about how amazing God is or we will burst.

After seeing how great God is, Jeremiah turns back to examine mankind and declares to us what he sees in today's verse. Compared to God all men are foolish and have no knowledge. Mankind seems to take great pride in its accomplishments. We marvel at the feats of people that are greater than we are in one area of life or another. We are enthralled with the abilities of great athletes, artists, or musicians. We stand in awe of the enormous things that men have built.

This verse is proven true when we promote these things of man to a place of worship in our lives. We attribute to them some life or power that we think they might give to us, only to be disgraced because they have no life or power and all the energy that we put into worshipping them is wasted and useless.

We might think that we are immune from idol worship in modern America but we are actually guiltier of it than many of the less civilized countries of the world. We disguise our idol worship with Madison Avenue and Wall Street but we still foolishly worship things that have no life or power. We know this is true because when we are in our greatest need they have nothing to offer us.

Only God is worthy of our worship. Only Jesus can give life. Only the Holy Spirit can provide the power we need to this life well. If we give any of the worship that should go to God to an idol we will be disgraced and we will find ourselves empty and powerless.

The more that I get to know God, the more I realize how little I actually know about Him. The more I grow in my knowledge of God, the more I realize how much greater He is than I am. As I look at the things that God has done, the things of man begin to pale in comparison. It is ultimate foolishness to worship anything that man could make rather than worshipping the God that made man. Jesus, show us those things that we have put in Your rightful place in our hearts and minds.

Rick Lancaster / PLANTERS PERSPECTIVE

OCTOBER 28 || JEREMIAH 52:10

There at Riblah, the king of Babylon made Zedekiah watch as all his sons were killed; they also killed all the other leaders of Judah.

Read: Jeremiah 51:54-52-34

Leaders of families, ministries, and churches can learn a lot about the consequences of disobedience to God from the life of King Zedekiah. The nation of Israel had turned away from worshipping the One True God again. God warned them to turn back and His warnings fell on deaf ears. He had warned them that if they did not turn back to Him that He would kick them out of the Promised Land. The prophet Jeremiah had told Zedekiah that God intended to turn them over to the king of Babylon. He then instructed them not to resist the punishment of God.

King Zedekiah refused to submit to God's punishment, and in so doing he was being disobedient to God. The result of his disobedience was that the city of Jerusalem was destroyed and he was captured. In our verse today, we are told that he was then taken to the king of Babylon and made to watch as his sons were killed. Then all the leaders of Judah were killed and finally Zedekiah's eyes were gouged out.

God's punishment for rebellion was that the people would be exiled to Babylon where they would have lived out their lives. It is true that they were exiles but they would at least have been alive. Instead, because of Zedekiah's stubbornness, they endured a siege that caused many to die of starvation before the Babylonians finally broke through and then killed most of the people of Jerusalem.

To be a child of God implies that we will obey God. As Christians, obedience shouldn't be an option, it is expected of us. As leaders of God's people, we are under even stricter obligations to obey. As a believer the consequences for disobedience are the withdrawing of God's hand of blessing. The consequences are often concentrated within my own life. As a leader, the consequences have much broader reach than just my life.

Zedekiah's rebellion and disobedience cost him his sons, his leaders, his city, and ultimately his eyes. He lived out the rest of his life in a prison in Babylon. This should give any true leader of God's people reason to pause and examine their lives. Are you ignoring the clear warnings of God? Are you willfully disobeying His commands? If you are, you are putting not only yourself at risk but your family, your ministry, your church, and maybe even your life.

Not only that, but it is a terrible witness of Jesus Christ. When we insist on making God punish us, we are ruining any testimony we may have had with the rest of the world. If this speaks to your heart, then humble yourself before God before it is too late. There is more at stake then just you, and if you really care about other people you won't hesitate to respond to God's call to repent. Jesus, teach us to respond immediately to Your call.

PLANTERS PERSPECTIVE | *A Devotional*

OCTOBER 29 || LAMENTATIONS 2:14

Your "prophets" have said so many foolish things, false to the core. They did not try to hold you back from exile by pointing out your sins. Instead, they painted false pictures, filling you with false hope.

Read: Lamentations 1:1-2:22

Jeremiah wrote the book of Lamentations to record what he and others were feeling during one of the darkest hours of Israel's history. God had given them the land of Canaan; the Promised Land. He told them that it was theirs for all time and that He would drive all the enemies from the land from before them. All they had to do was worship Him only and obey His voice. When God promised all these things to Israel He also warned them. He told them that if they did not obey Him and turned away from Him that He would drive the children of Israel from the 'good land' that He gave them. The Israelites did exactly what God told them not to do and they joined themselves to the nations around them and turned away from God.

God then sent people, His Prophets, to warn the Hebrews that they were in danger. These men were given messages from God telling the people that their God was angry with them and calling them to come back to true worship of the one and only True God. The people didn't like the messages that these men of God were giving. Other men seeing an opportunity for themselves started sharing 'messages' of their own creation that spoke of prosperity and safety. These men were doing it because it caused them to be seen as 'prophets'. They were successful because their messages made people happy.

God didn't want to send the Hebrews into exile and so He sent His prophets to warn them away from the danger. The people didn't want the truth, they wanted messages that made them feel good. God had blessed the children of Israel tremendously and He wanted to continue to do that. But to be blessed they had to obey Him. Because they wouldn't obey and preferred to hear from the false prophets, God was left with no other option than to do what He said He was going to do; drive them from the land.

As people chosen by God to lead families, ministries, and churches, our responsibility is much the same as the prophets of old. There are people all around us that God is preparing to judge because they won't turn from their sinful lives to worship Him with their whole hearts, soul, mind, and strength. The false prophets of our text told people that everything was okay while the walls around them were collapsing. People must be told the truth so that they can choose God's blessing or His judgment. As God's spokespersons, we should never tell someone that things are okay when we know that God is not happy. Jesus, help us to warn those around us so that they don't have to be judged.

Rick Lancaster / PLANTERS PERSPECTIVE

OCTOBER 30 || LAMENTATIONS 3:25

The LORD is wonderfully good to those who wait for him and seek him.

Read: Lamentations 3:1-66

The book of Lamentations is a record of the sorrow and grief that Jeremiah and the people of Israel were experiencing after having been exiled from the land that God had promised to their ancestors. This was a result of their rebellion and disobedience to God's command to worship Him as the only True God. Instead they turned from God to worship the gods of the people of Canaan; worthless idols that could not help them or save them.

Lamentations is an expression of the pain that they are feeling as a people over the consequences of their sins. There are many sad descriptions of what they are feeling. There are also some wonderful expressions of the character and attributes of God within this dark book. Such is the case with our verse for the day.

The prophet Jeremiah states that the Lord is 'wonderfully good'. That is a remarkable statement considering their circumstances. The king of Babylon has conquered the nation of Judah and taken away most of its people in exile to Babylon. God's goodness is not dependent upon our circumstances. God is always good because the very nature of God is good. Just because my circumstances are bad, it doesn't mean that God is bad. God is always good.

Jeremiah then says that God directs His goodness toward people. This goodness of God is directed to people under two conditions; those who wait for Him and those who seek him. At first glance these two conditions almost appear to be contradictory. Waiting implies inaction, while seeking implies action. Since there are no contradictions in Scripture, the problem must be in definition.

Waiting on the Lord is an active thing. It means that we trust God to complete His will in our lives and we are actively doing the things that He has instructed us to do. We are not trying to force our will upon our circumstances are striving to escape them. Waiting on the Lord means that we trust that God is in control and that He is going to act on our behalf.

Seeking the Lord happens more in our hearts than it does in our actions. It involves allowing the Holy Spirit to work within our heart and mind to conform us into the image of Jesus. The activity of seeking the Lord is to do those things that assist in this process, like prayer and Bible reading and study.

As we wait on Him and seek Him we will see the goodness of God. This verse is a proclamation of one of the attributes of the Lord. We can rest in it and trust our life to it. If we are not sensing the goodness of God, we simply must keep waiting and keep seeking. His word is absolutely true and He is faithful to keep His word. Jesus, help us to wait and teach us to seek You daily.

OCTOBER 31 || LAMENTATIONS 5:19

But LORD, you remain the same forever! Your throne continues from generation to generation.

Read: Lamentations 4:1-5:22

The book of Lamentations is a sad song of what Jeremiah saw as Jerusalem was being destroyed by the Babylonians. His home had been destroyed. His family and friends were either killed or sent away into exile. The words that are recorded of Jeremiah's lamenting are probably insufficient to express the pain in his heart as he saw his beloved Jerusalem fall to the enemy invaders. Jeremiah's whole world is turned upside down. Everything that he had was gone and everyone that he knew had been taken away. And even the things that weren't taken away or destroyed were changed by the Babylonian army. Everything was changing and it made Jeremiah sad to see it happening to the city where God said that He would dwell among men.

Then here in our verse for the day Jeremiah breaks out in praise to God. Even though his whole world was changing and that it would never be the same again for him or the nation of Israel; he knew that God is eternally unchanging. No matter who is in power in the world; God is on the throne of the universe and there is nothing in heaven or on earth that is going to change that. Jeremiah was a voice of righteousness in the land of Israel and the Hebrews ignored him and persecuted him. And even though he served God faithfully; he suffered right along with all the others that God was punishing. God protected him from being killed during this time but God did not exclude him from the suffering.

Sometimes we believe that because we are being faithful to God that we will be excluded from all pain and suffering. Nothing could be further from the truth. And if you are in a church or ministry that teaches that, than you need to be warned because the only people that are excluded from pain and suffering in this world are the people that have left this world to be with Jesus. Everyone else will experience some amounts of pain and suffering as God continues to form and shape our characters. Those that are faithfully following and serving God may be excluded from some of the harsher elements of that process but they will experience some part of it.

God's plan for our lives requires that we experience some of those things. Because we are in a fallen world; God will be judging the unrepentant and punishing the rebellious. Unfortunately, that means that we get to experience some of the consequences of that divine work. But God is still on the throne! Jesus, help us to see through our circumstances so that we can know what You are working on in us.

Rick Lancaster / PLANTERS PERSPECTIVE

NOVEMBER

NOVEMBER 1 || EZEKIEL 2:5

And whether they listen or not—for remember, they are rebels—at least they will know they have had a prophet among them.

Read: Ezekiel 1:1-3:15

In our reading for today Ezekiel receives his first vision from God and his commission or call from God. Ezekiel was called by God to be a prophet to the people of Judah that had been taken into exile in Babylon. There are some interesting things about the way Ezekiel is called and his ministry. First his calling to be a prophet of God is preceded by a vision of some angelic beings and the glory of God. This sets the tone for many of Ezekiel's later prophecies.

Second, Ezekiel is given a scroll to eat that contains prophecies and funeral songs. Once he eats it he is given the specifics of his call. It is simple; tell the people what I have told you. God's instructions to Ezekiel are very simple; tell the people what I have put inside of you. But then God tells Ezekiel that the people probably aren't going to listen to him.

God gives Ezekiel virtually the same mission that He gave to Jeremiah. Ezekiel was to minister to the people of Judah that were in exile in Babylon and God told him that they were a stubborn and hard-hearted people. God is telling Ezekiel in advance that his ministry is going to be to a people that didn't want to hear what God had to say and it was very likely that they would hate him for doing it.

We also see God's purpose for doing it in our verse for the day. God wanted the people to know that a prophet of God had been among them. Ezekiel's ministry was to proclaim to the people what was going to happen to them in the future. And when those future events took place the people would think back to Ezekiel and realize that he had been telling them what God said. God's purpose was to show them their stubborn and hard-hearted ways in the hope that they would repent and turn back to Him.

God will usually pick who it is that we are to minister to. And while everyone would rather minister to those that will respond correctly, that is not always going to be the case. Sometimes we will be tasked to be an Ezekiel or Jeremiah. We might be a lone voice crying out in the wilderness of stubbornness and hard hearts. That doesn't change the fact that God called you to that wilderness and has a purpose in it. Both Ezekiel and Jeremiah had powerful ministries that lasted long after they were gone. Just because you don't see any fruit doesn't change your responsibility to be faithful to God.

God has a plan that you are given a part in. And no matter how microscopically small your part is, it is still part of God's plan to save the entire world. None of us can possibly know how our small acts of ministry might be used by God to fulfill His great plan. Jesus, help us to be faithful even while surrounded by a stubborn and hard-hearted world.

Rick Lancaster / PLANTERS PERSPECTIVE

NOVEMBER 2 || EZEKIEL 3:18

If I warn the wicked, saying, 'You are under the penalty of death,' but you fail to deliver the warning, they will die in their sins. And I will hold you responsible, demanding your blood for theirs.

Read: Ezekiel 3:16-6:14

Ezekiel's call from God is further defined in today's reading. God has appointed Ezekiel to be a watchman for the nation of Israel. God is going to send warnings to the nation and to individual people and it is Ezekiel's responsibility to pass those warnings along to the people immediately. God then tells Ezekiel that he will be held responsible if those warnings do not get passed to their intended recipients. In fact, if Ezekiel failed to deliver the warning God said that it would be Ezekiel's blood that He would claim as a penalty.

Ezekiel was given the incredibly difficult task of warning some very powerful people and nations about the impending judgment of God. He was telling kings to surrender their nations to King Nebuchadnezzar or else they would be destroyed. He was to speak against the prophets that were speaking lies in God's name. He was one man trying to warn the world that God was not going to stand by and watch His children disobey Him any longer.

How many of us have been asked to do anything remotely as difficult as that? And yet we hesitate or even refuse to confront a Christian couple that is living together before they are married. Who are we afraid of? You can be sure it is not God! If we had a healthy fear of God, then we would not hesitate to confront the sin that is in front of us.

As leaders of families, ministries, and churches we have a God-given responsibility to warn those in our care of dangers that are around them. We have an obligation before God to warn the flock that has been entrusted to us of the things that are likely to harm them or their relationship with God. If we don't, then we must understand that we will stand before God some day and give an account for the warnings that He gave to us that we did not give to others.

Out of a real love for God and for others we should be willing and ready to share the warnings that God gives us for others. God told Ezekiel that some would respond and some would not. It was God's desire that these warnings would prevent some people from falling away from God completely. It was not Ezekiel's responsibility to determine who would or would not respond. His responsibility was to say what God told him to say. If our hearts are motivated by a love for God and for others, than we should not hesitate to share God's warnings with others. It would be better to embarrass them for a moment than for them to experience the consequences that are likely to result from their sins. If you love them, then tell them the truth. Jesus, give us the love and the boldness to speak the truth into people's lives.

NOVEMBER 3 || EZEKIEL 9:11

Then the man in linen clothing, who carried the writer's case, reported back and said, "I have finished the work you gave me to do."

Read: Ezekiel 7:1-9:11

Ezekiel speaks about the destruction that is going to befall Jerusalem and the nation of Israel pretty soon in today's reading. God is angry because the people continue to worship idols even after He has sent prophets to warn them repeatedly. They have refused to hear what God is trying to tell them.

Ezekiel then sees a vision of six men that God sends into the city of Jerusalem, starting in the Temple, to kill everyone that is worshipping the worthless idols. One of these men is sent out ahead of the others to place a mark on the head of everyone that is saddened by all of the sin that they see. It would appear from the text that this man did not play a role in the passing of judgment but was tasked to protect those that were still loyal to God.

It is my belief that this is the role that God wants each of us to play in the world today. Too often we act like one of the five with our battle clubs out to execute God's judgment upon this wicked and sinful world. That is not our role. Our role is to precede the five men and do everything that we can to find and mark all those that will believe in Jesus.

One of the interesting things about this text is that it would appear that the man with the writing case also had a weapon. And though he carried it, it does not appear that he used it. This is inferred because he returns before the other five do. This man was armed and had the ability to execute judgment upon the wicked but that was not his task, nor his responsibility.

As we lead the families, ministries, and churches that God has entrusted to us, we need to follow this man's example. God has given us the ability and equipped us to do many things but He has not called us to do them all. We have got to be so careful to focus only on those things that God has called us to do. There may be things that God has given you incredible gifts and abilities to do that He is not asking you to do.

When this man returns to the Lord he tells Him: "I have finished the work you gave me to do." What a powerful statement! God assigns the work and we are responsible to complete it. We don't need to think up things to do for God. We just need to do the work that He assigned to us. And we need to stay at it until it is finished. Jesus, on the cross said; "It is finished!" He had completed the work assigned to Him.

Even our ability to complete the work is a gift from God. The Bible teaches that God is faithful to complete the work that He started in us. But as in all things with God, we must do our part. Our part is to do what we have been assigned and to do it until we can report back to God and say: "I have completed the work you gave me to do." Jesus, help us to stick to the task that you gave us to do for You.

Rick Lancaster / PLANTERS PERSPECTIVE

NOVEMBER 4 || EZEKIEL 11:5

Then the Spirit of the LORD came upon me, and he told me to say, "This is what the LORD says to the people of Israel: Is that what you are saying? Yes, I know it is, for I know every thought that comes into your minds."

Read: Ezekiel 10:1-11:25

There is a part of us that believes that our minds are a private place that only we know what happens there. We believe that we can hide things there from God. Our verse for the day tells us something much different. There is nothing in our minds that is hidden from God's holy gaze.

In a strange way this is comforting to me. I have a desire as a man trying to be a true Christ-follower to be holy. But the truth is that I daily miss the mark of perfection that God desires for me to hit. Through Christ's blood I have forgiveness for all the sins that I commit, but God expects me to come in repentance of those sins and seek reconciliation. Knowing that I can't hide my sins from God makes it easier for me to come to Him whenever I need to.

The more intimately we are acquainted with this concept of God's absolute omniscience, the more we are willing to accept the purifying work of the Holy Spirit in our minds. Of course, this assumes that I agree with God that some of the things that come into my mind are sinful, ungodly, or impure. God is a gentleman; He will not force His purity upon us.

This is one of the reasons why a daily exposure to the written word of God is so important. It is within the pages of the Bible that we find truth. It is the truth of God revealed in Scripture that God desires to use as our guide to holiness. Without a regular feeding of God's words of life, we will mentally starve our minds of the very thing it needs to survive spiritually.

This is also why it is so important that we control what we do allow to come into our minds. The old computer saying, 'Garbage in, garbage out!" applies to our minds as much as to computers. If we do not do anything to filter the things that come into our minds than we will not be able to do anything about what comes out in our lives. If you put enough garbage into your life, you can be assured garbage will come out.

It also comforts me to know that God knows not just the thoughts that come into my mind but also from where those thoughts came. The enemy is quite good at inserting thoughts into my mind. I don't understand how he does it, but I know that he does. Some of those thoughts can be very disturbing and disgusting. God does not judge me for my thoughts; it is what I do with my thoughts that determine my relationship with God. We are told to capture our thoughts and bring them under submission to the obedience of Christ. Humble your heart and mind before God and allow the Holy Spirit to help you to do that. Jesus, thank you that You know me so well and love me anyway.

NOVEMBER 5 || EZEKIEL 12:2

Son of man, you live among rebels who could see the truth if they wanted to, but they don't want to. They could hear me if they would listen, but they won't listen because they are rebellious.

Read: Ezekiel 12:1-14:11

Ezekiel is given this word from the Lord in one of the many visions that he received. In this series of visions God is telling Ezekiel to speak out against the children of Israel that are leading His people astray through false prophecies and lies. These false prophets are telling the people that they have nothing to worry about, that there is going to be peace in Jerusalem.

The problem with this is that God was planning to judge Jerusalem and all of Israel for its continued idol worship. God had told the nation of Israel to drive out all of the Canaanites from the land of Israel when they first entered it. He told them to do that because if they didn't the children of Israel would quickly begin worshipping the gods of the Canaanites. But the children of Israel didn't drive them out and they did just what God said that they would do; they began doing the same evil and wicked things that God was angry with the Canaanites for doing.

These false prophets were telling the people not to worry; everything was going to be okay. Everything wasn't going to be okay; in fact it was about to get very bad. In the reading for today you can make a case that it is the fault of the false prophets for leading the people astray; and they do deserve a measure of responsibility. But our verse for the day says something else. The people also bear some responsibility for their actions.

God is not hard to find. God wants everyone to find Him. Anyone that wants to find Him will find Him. Our verse for the day tells us that the people of Israel were being rebellious. They could have done the right things but they didn't want to. They could have seen and heard from God but that is not what they wanted. They didn't want to hear that they were doing something wrong; they wanted to hear that everything would be all right.

As leaders of God's people, whether it is a family, ministry, or church, there are going to be times when you need to tell the flock entrusted to you things that they don't want to hear. Ezekiel was told by God to tell the people exactly what He said. He wasn't told to tell them what would make them feel good. We have the responsibility to show them God so that they can see Him. We have the responsibility to speak for God as He directs us to speak for Him so that they can hear from God. It is then the people's responsibility to not rebel against God. It is their responsibility to see and hear from God. It is our responsibility to show and speak. It is their responsibility to see and hear. To do that we also, as leaders, need to be seeing and hearing God. If we rebel and refuse to see and hear God, so will the people that God has given us to care for. Jesus, help us to humble ourselves before You and to see You clearly and hear from You often.

Rick Lancaster / PLANTERS PERSPECTIVE

NOVEMBER 6 || EZEKIEL 15:2

Son of man, how does a grapevine compare to a tree? Is a vine's wood as useful as the wood of a tree?

Read: Ezekiel 14:12-16:41

In this short chapter the prophet Ezekiel gives a message to the people of the nation of Israel. This is a tragic and terrifying message. In essence, the Lord is proclaiming their soon destruction. The Lord tells them that He is going to be tenacious and thorough about making the land desolate.

The reason for this harsh attitude of God is because the people of God have been unfaithful to their God. The Lord had made many promises to the nation of Israel about His care and protection of them. The only condition that God put on them is that they would stay away from the false gods and idols of the land and worship Him alone.

What struck me about today's verse was the comparison that God makes between the wood of a vine and a tree in relation to his people. The Lord makes the connection between usefulness and faithfulness. The Lord goes on to say that the people of Jerusalem have become useless because of their unfaithfulness.

We were all created for a purpose that God established before the foundation of the earth. As our Creator, God has the right to determine what our purpose is in this universe. We all have the general purpose of being created to worship and glorify God. Then God also has assigned us more specific purposes for accomplishing His will on this earth and for the furthering of His kingdom.

The people of Jerusalem had wandered from their general purpose; to worship God and glorify Him as the Only True God. Because they had done that, they were described as useless. They were so useless that they weren't even very good for burning. But they were to be burned just as rubbish is piled up and burned; not for a purpose but just to be disposed of.

It is difficult for me to imagine being useless to God. He created me, He knows everything about me, He takes care of me, and He loves me with an unfathomable love. The idea that I could become useless to Him is difficult to comprehend. This verse, and many others like it, makes it very clear that God expects us to be what we were created to be; God-worshippers. If we are not, then we are wasting our lives and will accomplish nothing useful in the eyes of God.

On the other hand, if I do worship God and live to glorify Him, then my life is useful to Him. I may not see just how useful it is but I can rest in the knowledge that God only asks me to be faithful so that I can be useful. God is looking for men and women that will be faithful to Him so that He can show Himself to be strong on their behalf. Jesus, help us to be faithful to You and Your plan for our lives.

NOVEMBER 7 || EZEKIEL 17:18

For the king of Israel broke his treaty after swearing to obey; therefore, he will not escape.

Read: Ezekiel 16:42-17:24

This message is given to Ezekiel about King Zedekiah of Israel. Zedekiah was made king of Israel by the king of Babylon after he had conquered Jerusalem the first time. The Babylonians took many people into captivity in Babylon but left people in Israel to maintain the land and send tribute money to Babylon. We are going to see in the next few days' reading that Zedekiah rebels against King Nebuchadnezzar. To become king, Zedekiah had to swear to be loyal to Nebuchadnezzar. In this way the nation of Israel was able to maintain its identity.

This message from Ezekiel is telling Zedekiah that God is going to be angry with him for rebelling against Babylon. At first reading we might wonder why God is angry with Zedekiah for trying to be freed from the oppression of this wicked nation. There are a couple of reasons why God is angry about this. First, God was the one that prepared Babylon to come and punish Israel for its sins of idolatry. God had repeatedly warned the leaders and people not to worship any other God than Him but they resolutely refused to listen to Him. God told them very specifically that if they did not stop this evil and wicked practice that He was going to drive them from the land. Babylon was the tool that God used to fulfill His promise of punishment to the nation of Israel. By rebelling against Nebuchadnezzar, Zedekiah was actually rebelling against God.

Second, Zedekiah had made an agreement with Nebuchadnezzar to be loyal to him. God was upset because Zedekiah was breaking that covenant which he had sworn in the name of the Lord. God had selected Zedekiah to protect the remnant of people in Israel from being completely destroyed by setting him up as king. By breaking the covenant that he had made, Zedekiah was putting the whole nation at risk. In fact, we will see that many people will lose their lives and many more will be taken into exile by King Nebuchadnezzar as a result of Zedekiah's unfaithfulness.

While at first it might seem difficult to see how this might relate to you or your ministry, it does. God is going to allow or cause you to enter into agreements, contracts, or covenants with people or organizations in the world. We must be faithful to those agreements. We can't decide that we don't have to fulfill it just because they aren't Christians. If you make an agreement to do something or to pay something, you made that agreement not only with them but with God. You no longer have the option of rebelling against that commitment. And if you do chose to rebel, understand that God will be angry.

Being a person of integrity sometimes means fulfilling agreements or commitments that are not in our best interest. Whatever it might cost to be a person of integrity is nothing compared to what it would cost to rebel against God. Jesus, teach us integrity.

Rick Lancaster / PLANTERS PERSPECTIVE

NOVEMBER 8 || EZEKIEL 18:24

However, if righteous people turn to sinful ways and start acting like other sinners, should they be allowed to live? No, of course not! All their previous goodness will be forgotten, and they will die for their sins.

Read: Ezekiel 18:1-19:14

Ezekiel has been teaching the people of Israel about how God's justice works. This is a fascinating chapter to study to become better acquainted with this sometimes challenging topic. People have often associated death with the judgment of God. And while God will take someone's life as an act of judgment for their sins, we cannot determine that all deaths are an act of God judging that person's sins.

What fascinates me about today's verse is the thought that we can't depend upon our past righteousness to guarantee God's approval of our lives. This reminds us of the people that think they have 'spiritual fire insurance'. They believe because they said a prayer or did some good spiritual thing that they are saved from hell. They then go on to live the same life they were living before without a backward glance toward what God might want from them. These people may or may not have ever been saved but might believe that they are safe. They are deluded and have been misled.

Some are indeed saved and yet believe that their relationship with God permits them to dabble in a few areas of sin. They assume that God will forgive them and so they do not resist the temptations to sin. This is taking God's grace for granted and is blasphemy. God's grace is a gift that He gives to those He wills and withholds from those that He wills. To take God's grace for granted is like playing Russian Roulette with a fully loaded pistol; you are going to get blasted.

Righteousness is not an event it is a lifestyle. To live a righteous life, we must be continually climbing toward the Lord. Because of sin in our hearts and in the world, the minute we stop climbing we start sliding back down toward the life we used to live. That is where we get the term back-sliding. All we have to do to start back-sliding is stop seeking God's righteousness and His kingdom.

It might shock some people to hear that God might kill a righteous person to keep them from sinning. It shocks them because they see life as more important than righteousness. God sees things differently than we do. He can look at our whole lives and see where the pathway that we are on leads to. And because He has given us the freedom to choose between good and evil, He knows that we may choose to take a pathway that leads to greater evil. In His love and mercy, He might strike us dead to prevent that from happening. Your life doesn't end at death. We live on for all eternity. God views the righteousness of our lives as far more valuable than the physical aspect of our lives.

Living a life of daily pursuing righteousness and avoiding sin does not guarantee a long life but it certainly places you where God's amazing grace can be released into your life with great abundance. Jesus, help us to keep climbing up to You.

NOVEMBER 9 || EZEKIEL 20:39

As for you, O people of Israel, this is what the Sovereign LORD says: If you insist, go right ahead and worship your idols, but then don't turn around and bring gifts to me. Such desecration of my holy name must stop!

Read: Ezekiel 20:1-49

One of the things that God continually chastised the nation of Israel about was their worshipping of idols. Of all the sins that God spoke to them about, this was the one that He was the most upset about. Time and time again, God commanded them to worship Him alone. There are many occasions that God was close to destroying them completely because of their unfaithfulness to Him.

God is the only true and living God. All the idols that the Israelites were worshipping were lifeless and unable to do anything for them. These images of wood and stone were utterly useless and God said that by worshipping these things the people also became useless.

Before we judge the Israelites too severely, we need to understand that we are often just like them. It is amazing how quickly we can allow something to take God's place in our lives. Worship is hard-wired into our DNA. We will worship someone or something. The question is not, if we will worship, but what we will worship. God made it very clear on numerous occasions that their only choice was Him; the True and Living God.

In our verse for today, God tells the Israelites to choose. He wants them to choose between worshipping their worthless idols and Him. God is perfect and holy. When we come to Him it must be with the attitude that He is the absolute ruler of the universe and that He alone is worthy of our worship. By worshipping idols that can do nothing and then coming to God, the Israelites were either trying to elevate their worthless idols to the level of God or worse, bringing God down to the level of the worthless idols.

God will not be mocked and He will not allow us to share His place in our lives with anything or anyone else. He will give you the choice. And in today's reading it was said several times that by choosing God, you were choosing life. It was also very clear that by choosing to worship the worthless idols that they were choosing death; both physically and spiritually.

We need to search our hearts and try to determine if we have allowed someone or something to be set up as an idol in our lives. What is it that we care more about than God? What is it that we will sacrifice our life to besides God? What is it that we will sacrifice our time with God for? If there is anything or anyone in your life that you would not give up for God, then you may be at risk of choosing it or them over God. It is unlikely that God is going to ask us to give up those things that are precious to us but He doesn't want them to be more precious than our relationship with Him. Jesus, help us to sweep all the worthless idols from our lives so that our hearts can be pure before you.

Rick Lancaster / PLANTERS PERSPECTIVE

NOVEMBER 10 || EZEKIEL 22:30

I looked for someone who might rebuild the wall of righteousness that guards the land. I searched for someone to stand in the gap in the wall so I wouldn't have to destroy the land, but I found no one.

Read: Ezekiel 21:1-22:31

God is about to unleash His fury upon the nation to Israel for their unfaithfulness to Him. In our text for today, Ezekiel also speaks for God about their adulterous behaviors with the pagan nations around them. By the end of our reading for today, King Nebuchadnezzar comes and lays siege to Jerusalem and conquers it.

God is looking for someone! God is looking for someone with eyes to see the spiritual condition around them. Righteousness is a wall that protects us from the enemies that surround us and from God's judgment of sin. God is looking for someone that can see that this wall has gaps in it. God doesn't want them to just see it, He wants them to stand in the gaps of that wall and do something about it.

If you had a fortified city and there was a gap in the wall, it meant that your enemy could come into your city and defeat you. Righteousness is the wall that defends your life, family, ministry, church, or organization. If there is a gap in that wall, the enemy WILL attack you there. To defend a city with a gap in its wall you would send your best warriors to defend that section of the wall. In the spiritual battle we do this through prayer. If there is a gap in the wall of righteousness in your life, family, or ministry then start praying. The battle is often won or lost in prayer or lack of prayer. While prayer will stave off the attacks that will come, the longer that the gap remains in the wall the greater the likelihood that the enemy is going to break through and defeat you. The wall of righteousness must be repaired. That is accomplished through the Word of God and a closer walk with Jesus.

In Ezekiel's time God was looking for someone that would stand in the gap and repair the wall of righteousness for Jerusalem and the nation of Israel. God was looking for one person that would lead Israel back to Him and to His righteousness. He found no one. He is still looking for people that will lead their families, ministries, and churches back to Him. We live in a world that is set upon leading us to destruction. God wants men and women to stand in the gap and pray for their organizations and countries so that they might defend them from the enemies that are set on destroying them. One person might be all that God is looking for to prevent His Righteous Anger from being poured out.

You could be that one person that God is looking for to stand in the gap and protect those around you. You might be the one person that God is looking for to help to rebuild the wall of righteousness in some person's life or in some organization or even in your country. Will you stand in the gap? Jesus, help us to stand and to rebuild.

NOVEMBER 11 || EZEKIEL 23:35

And because you have forgotten me and turned your back on me, says the Sovereign LORD, you must bear the consequences of all your lewdness and prostitution.

Read: Ezekiel 23:1-49

In this chapter Ezekiel uses a graphic and powerful word picture to describe the way God feels about the way the cities of Samaria and Jerusalem have acted toward God. Samaria is the capital of the ten tribes of Israel that broke away from Judah after King Solomon died. Jerusalem is the capital of the two tribes of Judah and Benjamin. Ezekiel describes these two cities as sisters that have become prostitutes, selling their love to anyone that came along.

What caught my attention in this verse was the reference to the consequences that they were going to experience. It is strange to me how often I am confronted by people that are surprised that they must experience the consequences of their sins. It is often because they fail to see the connection between their sins and the consequences that naturally follow.

Some people also wrongly believe that forgiveness takes away the consequences of sin. The Bible nowhere teaches that principle. Forgiveness does take away the penalty of sin but it doesn't necessarily take away the consequences. God, in His sovereignty, can take away the consequences of our sins. In my experience and what I see in Scripture is that God often uses our consequences to teach us about sin. Some people respond better to the lessons taught through consequences than they ever will through God's love and grace.

In today's verse Ezekiel tells both Samaria and Jerusalem that they are going to experience all the consequences for all of their sins. The reason they were going to experience the full measure of their consequences is because they had forgotten their God and turned away from Him.

We are all going to sin. As true Christ-followers that thought should repulse us and cause our hearts to hurt. As disciples of Jesus we should be growing in holiness as we allow the Holy Spirit to conform us into the image of Jesus. However, we are still sinners saved by grace and there is still a chance that we are going to sin. How we respond when we become aware of our sin makes all the difference in the world.

Repentance and humility are keys to a life that is pleasing to God. When we become aware of our sin God desires that we would humble our heart before Him and turn away from our sin and turn back to Him more fully. God may or may not dismiss the consequences of those sins, but I am certain that He will pour out His amazing grace upon you within those consequences. Jesus, help us to turn to You quickly.

Rick Lancaster / PLANTERS PERSPECTIVE

NOVEMBER 12 || EZEKIEL 26:12

They will plunder all your riches and merchandise and break down your walls. They will destroy your lovely homes and dump your stones and timbers and even your dust into the sea.

Read: Ezekiel 24:1-26:21

This chapter of Ezekiel is a terrifying prophecy against the city of Tyre. Ezekiel foretells the utter destruction of this once great city. As predicted King Nebuchadnezzar came and wiped Tyre from the face of the earth. At one point in the attack the people of Tyre escaped to an island off the coast. King Nebuchadnezzar then built a road using all the materials of the destroyed city, including all the stones, timbers, and dust. He eventually reached the island and massacred everyone on the island.

This judgment fell upon the city of Tyre because they had rejoiced in the fall of Jerusalem. God had punished His people by allowing them to be taken away into captivity. His desire was that they would learn the hard lesson taught by severe consequences not to turn away from Him to worthless idols.

God warned Tyre of impending judgment. God had a reason for warning them. In the book of Jonah we are told of another city that God had passed judgment upon; the city of Nineveh. God sent the prophet Jonah to the city of Nineveh to inform them that God was planning to utterly destroy them because of their wickedness. The king and everyone else in the city took the warning seriously and humbled themselves before God and repented. Because they did, God relented and did not destroy Nineveh.

God does not have to warn someone that He intends to destroy them for their wickedness. God created them and because He is God He is well within His rights to destroy those that do not live up to their Creator's standards of holiness and righteousness. But God is also full of grace and mercy. It brings God no joy to destroy the wicked. It is His desire that all would come to follow Him and love Him.

The people of Nineveh humbled themselves and repented and so God relented. Tyre did not repent and so God kept His word and utterly destroyed it, exactly as the Bible said would happen. God's warnings are intended to cause people to repent so that God does not have to utterly destroy them.

The Bible is filled with God's warnings to His people and to the rest of the world. We need to take those warnings seriously. If we become aware of a warning that applies to our lives or some thing in our lives, we need to immediately humbles ourselves before the Almighty God and ask Him to forgive us. In His amazing grace He will forgive us every time. Jesus, teach us to take Your Word seriously.

NOVEMBER 13 || EZEKIEL 28:3

You regard yourself as wiser than Daniel and think no secret is hidden from you.

Read: Ezekiel 27:1-28:26

Today's reading is mostly about the city of Tyre. It was one of the most influential cities of the time. They possessed great wealth and power. And as is usually the case, their great success led them to become proud. And God's word is quite clear about how he feels about pride. Tyre was not only prideful about their great accomplishments but also about their great wisdom. They believed they knew more than anyone else in the world. This kind of belief can lead to great arrogance and other very harmful attitudes. Once you start believing that you are wise, you begin viewing others in relation to your wisdom and you begin to put others down.

God resists the proud and He confounds the wise. Tyre was completely and utterly destroyed by King Nebuchadnezzar. All of their success, wealth, and wisdom got them nowhere. With everything they had, they were missing the one thing that would have saved them; a relationship with God.

The times that we live in today are not that much different than they were in the days of Ezekiel. There are still people, organizations, and countries that are experiencing great wealth and success. There are people that believe that they are wiser than anyone around them. There are people and organizations that believe their wealth and wisdom will protect them. There are countries that believe that they are invincible. Without God, these people, organizations, and countries will experience the same fate as Tyre. While there may not be a King Nebuchadnezzar marching on their gates, God is preparing someone or something to humble and confound them.

Churches and ministries are not immune from this disease. Some believe that because they represent God, that they can behave the same way that Tyre was with arrogance and pride. God will not hesitate to humble a church or ministry leader that behaves in this manner. We cannot even begin to believe that because we are in the church that we are immune to this kind of correction.

God is looking for strong leaders that are humble and meek. He wants His leaders to be people that know that without God they would have nothing and that compared to God they know nothing. Only this type of attitude and behavior can assure God's protection and provision. The moment we look to ourselves for anything that we do or have is the moment that God stops being able to work fully in our lives, ministries, and churches. God doesn't need us but He wants to use us to reach out to the whole world to reveal Jesus to the lost. Staying humble and meek opens the door to our heart for Him to do that. Jesus, teach us to know nothing except You and to need nothing but You.

Rick Lancaster / PLANTERS PERSPECTIVE

NOVEMBER 14 || EZEKIEL 29:20

Yes, I have given him the land of Egypt as a reward for his work, says the Sovereign LORD, because he was working for me when he destroyed Tyre.

Read: Ezekiel 29:1-30:26

This is likely one of those Scriptures that some people wonder about. First it says that the pagan king Nebuchadnezzar was working for God when he destroyed the city of Tyre. And then it says that God rewarded him for that work by giving him the land of Egypt. Both of these things might be hard for some people to understand or accept about God.

God used King Nebuchadnezzar of Assyria as a tool or weapon to do His work in the world. God is sovereign. That means that there is nothing or no one that is outside of His control. God had judged the city of Tyre because of their wicked rejoicing over the fall of Jerusalem. God then influenced King Nebuchadnezzar to destroy it. We know that God influenced him to do it, though we don't know how.

When we think of God destroying a city for wickedness we will usually think of Sodom and Gomorrah. God supernaturally reached down from heaven and destroyed it. While God can and does operate in the supernatural, He usually does His work within this world using natural people and things.

King Nebuchadnezzar was then rewarded for his work. In his destruction of the city of Tyre they worked very hard and received no spoil for their efforts. There were some spoils taken but the effort was so great that those spoils were consumed before the victory was won. The taking of Tyre cost more than the spoil they collected. God rewarded this pagan king for obedience to God's influence. It is highly unlikely that King Nebuchadnezzar realized he was being used by God but God rewarded him anyways.

As you meditate upon this it may change the way that you view the world around you. Daily on the news we see one conflict after another. We also see wicked people prospering. It can all be very confusing and disturbing. There appears to be no sense to it and no justice. What we can't see is the sovereign hand of God at work. Of course much of it is the wickedness of man at work but some of it is God's supernatural influence over the natural world. Often we will not be able to determine which it is.

God can and does influence people in this world to accomplish His will. He even influences the wicked people of this world to carry out His plan. And yes, He will even reward them when they submit to His influence. This does not change their wickedness into good and it does not change their destiny. They are simply tools or weapons in the hand of Sovereign God. It can be very confusing trying to sort out what God is doing in the world around us. Simply accept the fact that He is Sovereign and that His plan and will are being done in the world around us. Jesus, help us to rest in the knowledge that You are in control.

PLANTERS PERSPECTIVE / *A Devotional*

NOVEMBER 15 || EZEKIEL 32:17

On March 17, during the twelfth year, another message came to me from the LORD.

Read: Ezekiel 31:1-32:32

Ezekiel is given another message that describes what is going to happen to Egypt and other godless nations. The Lord instructs Ezekiel to weep for these nations because they are going to be sent to the world below. It grieves the Lord's heart that anyone would refuse to choose His love and grace and instead choose to be separated from Him forever.

In today's verse Ezekiel is given 'another' message. It occurred to me as I was reading that there is a reason why the Lord gave Ezekiel 'another' message; it was because he was faithful with the first message. In fact, Ezekiel had received many messages from the Lord because he had been faithful to speak forth the messages that the Lord was giving to him.

God wants to speak to all of us and I believe that He desires to give messages to us that are intended for other people. I don't necessarily mean that He will use us like He did Ezekiel but I can say for certain that there are people all around you that the Lord wants to get a message to and there is a good chance that He wants to use you to do it. All around you are people that need to hear from God that do not want to or know how to listen for His voice.

It is an amazing and somewhat frightening thing to think that the God of the universe might want to use me to get a message to one of His creations. God doesn't need us; He could get these messages to people without us but He chooses people like you and me to speak on His behalf to the people around us that are heading down the wrong path. He wants them to know that it grieves His heart that they are going the way that they are. His goal in giving you a message for others is that they would turn around and follow a path that leads to fellowship with Christ and life.

What an amazing privilege it is to be used by God to help people come to know Jesus and experience eternal life. And the radical thing about that is that He can and desires to use anyone. No one is beyond the range of God to use as one of His special messengers. God can use absolutely anyone to give someone a message of God's love, or hope, or peace, or joy, or encouragement. It doesn't require training or special education; it only requires the presence of the Holy Spirit in your life.

Ezekiel was given many messages and some of them were spectacular. Because Ezekiel was faithful to give the messages he was given, he was given 'another' one. I like that! I would like to receive another message from the Lord and so I will be faithful to share the one He has already given me. How about you? Jesus, help us to share with others.

NOVEMBER 16 | | EZEKIEL 33:8

If I announce that some wicked people are sure to die and you fail to warn them about changing their ways, then they will die in their sins, but I will hold you responsible for their deaths.

Read: Ezekiel 33:1-34:31

Ezekiel was given the responsibility to be a watchman for the nation of Israel. His role was to tell the people of the danger that was approaching. That danger was God's judgment of their sins. And in our verse for the day God drops a very heavy burden upon Ezekiel. God tells him that if he fails to fulfill his role to warn the people of the danger that he, Ezekiel, will be responsible for their deaths. God also tells Ezekiel that if he warns them and they choose not to respond that he is not responsible for their deaths.

As Christians, God is going to speak to us about other people also. He wants us to warn them about the danger that they are in. And there is a reason why God puts this huge responsibility on us. That reason is because God loves people. The reading for today says that God takes no joy in the death of a sinner. There is no pleasure for God when the wicked die. God's desire is that they would repent and turn back to Him.

Our reading tells us that if the wicked repent, their sins will not be counted against them and, if the righteous turn away from God their righteous deeds will be forgotten. God wants everyone to love Him like He loves them. When we don't, He must punish and judge us because God is just. Only by repenting can we hope to escape judgment and punishment.

Because God loves us so much He will send warnings. He will let us know that He is displeased with our lives and that He wants us to change. He will warn us of the impending judgment and give us an opportunity to repent. He will always give us the choice of repenting or living in our sin. That is one of the incredible things about God. He will let you choose. If you experience the judgment or punishment of God it is because that is what you chose. Don't blame God for your choices.

As Christians and as leaders of families, ministries, or churches God is calling each of us to be watchmen over His people. He wants us to warn people of the danger that they are in. He wants us to help Him to show them that they need to repent so that they might not suffer the pain and suffering that will always accompany sin and rebellion. But even in that you get to choose. You are allowed to choose whether or not you will obey God and warn those that are headed for disaster. Can you imagine standing before God and finding out someone wasn't in heaven because you failed to warn them? If we had any idea how bad it would be to be eternally separated from God we would not hesitate even for a moment to warn them. Jesus, help us to boldly and in love warn those that need to be warned.

NOVEMBER 17 || EZEKIEL 36:26

And I will give you a new heart with new and right desires, and I will put a new spirit in you. I will take out your stony heart of sin and give you a new, obedient heart.

Read: Ezekiel 35:1-36:38

God is speaking to the people of Israel in this prophecy given through Ezekiel. Because of their sins and rebellion God's reputation with the surrounding nations has been tarnished. Because the people of Israel turned away from God He sent them into exile just as He said that He would. Then the other nations started speaking out against God saying He wasn't able to take care of them in the land that He gave them.

To protect His reputation God was planning to bring His people back into the land. He wanted them to understand that it had nothing to do with their worthiness but His reputation in the rest of the world. I think we sometimes forget that it is God that causes the world to revolve and not us. We forget that God is the One that holds all things together. We exist because of God and for God's purposes.

The people of Israel forgot about their God and started living in the ways of the world around them. This angered God and caused Him to send them into exile so that they might remember their God and return to Him. God knew that they someday would do that and then made them this amazing promise in our verse for the day.

God promised to change their hearts. Sin has a terrible effect upon the human heart. The more that we allow sin to exist in our lives the harder our heart becomes toward God and other people. If not changed, our hearts can become as hard as stone. This means that they are not sensitive to God or spiritual things.

This verse tells us the changing of human hearts is the work of God. Often people struggle with their own hearts or the hearts of others in the vain hope of changing them to soft, obedient hearts. No amount of human effort can change the human heart. Only the Spirit of God has the power to replace a heart of stone with a new, obedient heart.

If you know someone that has a heart of stone, you need to love, pray, and trust. Love them as much as you are able to. Pray that God would reach down from heaven and replace that heart of stone. Then, you trust God to do what He will do. Keep loving, praying, and trusting until God works.

If it is your heart that needs to change, you need to simply surrender to His will in your life. Don't fight the work of the Spirit in your heart. The sooner you submit to the heart surgery that needs to happen, the sooner you will be able to live the promised life of Christ. Jesus, give us Your heart.

Rick Lancaster / PLANTERS PERSPECTIVE

NOVEMBER 18 || EZEKIEL 37:12

Now give them this message from the Sovereign LORD: O my people, I will open your graves of exile and cause you to rise again. Then I will bring you back to the land of Israel.

Read: Ezekiel 37:1-38:23

God gives a message of encouragement to Ezekiel to give to the people of Israel. God had kept His threat to punish the children of Israel for turning away from Him. God had told them that if they turned to worship other gods other than the One and True God that He would drive them from the good land that He had given them. They did exactly what God told them not to do. And so God did exactly what He said He was going to do.

God used the king of Babylon to punish the children of Israel. This was after He had warned them on numerous occasions that He was going to do it. He even told them that He was going to use King Nebuchadnezzar to drive them out of the land that He had told them that they could have forever. Some might look at this situation and say that God was going back on His word. He had told the children of Israel that the Promise Land would be theirs forever. So why was He kicking them out of the land? His promise of an eternal homeland was a conditional promise; there was a part that the children of Israel played in keeping the land forever. That condition was that God was to be their only God. Because of their unfaithfulness, God was forced to keep His threat to them because of His faithfulness.

Even in the midst of punishing the nation of Israel for its unfaithfulness, God makes another promise to the His chosen people. He promises to bring them back to the land that He had promised them to keep forever. All they have to do to see this promise fulfilled is the same thing that they needed to do in the first place; worship only God. To see God bring them back from exile, all they had to do was repent from their sin of idolatry and turn back to God.

God is so faithful and full of grace and mercy. No matter how far we wander from Him, He is waiting for us to return to Him so that He can fulfill all the promises that He made to us. No matter what we might have done in our lives, He stands ready to forgive the repentant heart and bring any and all of us back from whatever exile we forced Him to send us to. God's grace and mercy are endless and difficult to fully comprehend. We don't need to understand; we just need to accept it and do it.

If you have wandered away from the intimate fellowship with God that He desires to have with you; just repent and turn back to Him and He will bring you back from wherever He exiled you to and into the incredible life that He desires you to have. Don't wait and don't fight. The sooner that you give in to God, the sooner you will be experiencing the life that Jesus came to give you. It all begins with repentance. Humble yourself before God and ask Him to forgive you and then watch Him begin to work in your life. Jesus, help us to ache when we are absent from your present.

NOVEMBER 19 || EZEKIEL 39:18

Eat the flesh of mighty men and drink the blood of princes as though they were rams, lambs, goats, and fat young bulls of Bashan.

Read: Ezekiel 39:1-40:27

In this prophecy a great enemy of Israel will come from the north. This enemy, Gog, is believed by many to be some form of the Russian Empire. God will convince them to attack Israel and in the process of the attack God will utterly wipe out their entire army. Most believe this to be a future event. Its purpose is to declare the power of God to an unbelieving world. God will supernaturally protect the nation of Israel from an overwhelming attack.

In today's verse God has called the birds and wild animals to come to a sacrificial feast. This great enemy of Israel and God will suffer such a great defeat that it will take months to bury all the dead. God will send birds and animals in great numbers to eat the flesh of all the fallen enemies of God. This will be a horrific scene that hopefully will take place after the Rapture of God's church.

Some might read a verse like this and wonder what it says to us today. The obvious thing is that God can and will protect His people from their enemies. It also tells us that no enemy is so overwhelming that God can't utterly defeat them. It also tells us that the mighty men and princes of this world are not as great and mighty as we might see them to be.

In this verse they are compared to sacrificial animals. In the sacrificial system of Israel the animals were sacrificed to God. Usually only a small portion was burned in the fire. The rest was eaten by the priests or by the people making the sacrifice. In this sacrificial feast mentioned here the animals are the ones doing the eating. It is backwards of what is normal.

We should not be too concerned about what the rest of the world thinks or is doing. We need to stay focused on what the Lord would direct us to do. This is especially true if we are called to lead in families, ministries, or churches. Let God take care of the world. Let God deal with the mighty men and princes that might be lining up and preparing to attack you. You focus on the things that God has set before you.

Just remember when you feel overwhelmed by the pressures of the world that Jesus has overcome the world. Remember this account today; that God can supernaturally act on your behalf and rescue you in a way that shocks the whole world. Trust Him and Him alone to be your strength. Hold fast to His truth. Walk daily in His ways and let His Holy Spirit direct your path. Jesus, help us to look for Your hand upon all things around us.

Rick Lancaster | PLANTERS PERSPECTIVE

NOVEMBER 20 || EZEKIEL 41:22

There was an altar made of wood, 3 ½ feet square and 5 ¼ feet high. Its corners, base, and sides were all made of wood. "This," the man told me, "is the table that stands in the LORD's presence."

Read: Ezekiel 40:28-41:26

Ezekiel is given a vision that takes him on a tour of the temple. At this time in history there was no temple. Solomon's temple had been destroyed. So this vision is looking to the future. Some believe that this points to the temple that existed at the time of Christ. Others believe it looks even further forward to a time when Jesus has set up His kingdom.

Our verse for the day describes an altar that appears to be the altar of incense. On this altar the priest would offer up incense and prayers for the atonement of the people. Incense is often used in Scripture as an illustration of prayer. Prayer is said to rise up to heaven like incense. The prayers of the righteous are also described as sweet-smelling like incense.

When we pray we are making a sacrifice or an offering up to God. Many people view prayer as a way to get things from God but it is in fact a time when we should be giving to God. To truly pray we need to give God our will, our mind, and our heart. We should be giving Him adoration, respect, and honor. It is perfectly correct to ask God for what we need or want, but those requests should follow us giving to God what He deserves.

What struck me about this verse was that this table stands in the Lord's presence. When we pray we are entering into the Lord's presence. We are stepping up to a table that He is already standing at. I believe our prayers will be more passionate and powerful as we embrace this image and understand its significance more deeply. When we pray we are standing in the very presence of God.

Our prayers do not have to travel through a trillion miles of wires or airwaves to reach God. They do not travel through a switchboard or router to get to a server in heaven. When we bow our hearts before God we are ushered directly into His presence. As the words leave our hearts they go directly to the ears of the Almighty God that is Creator of all that we know or see.

Prayer should be an intimate conversation between you and your loving Father. Don't let the fact that He is in heaven cause you to wonder if He can hear you. He can hear you because you have come up to His altar of prayer. Pray as though He is right there because He is. Not only is He right there but He loves to hear from His children. It brings Him joy when we come to His table to talk with Him. Jesus, teach us to pray like You are standing right there with us.

NOVEMBER 21 || EZEKIEL 42:14

When the priests leave the Holy Place, they must not go directly to the outer courtyard. They must first take off the clothes they wore while ministering because these clothes were holy. They must put on other clothes before entering the parts of the building complex open to the public.

Read: Ezekiel 42:1-43:27

Ezekiel is given a very detailed vision of the temple of God. Later in our reading Ezekiel is told that this vision is given so that he can tell it to the people of Israel and so that they will be ashamed about their idolatry. The Lord tells Ezekiel that the primary law of the temple is holiness. The people of Israel had forgotten this and had stopped treating the things of God as holy.

In our verse for the day Ezekiel is told about the rooms that the priests will use to eat the sacrifices that were offered by the people. A portion of those sacrifices were given to the priests as their food. The Law of Moses required that these offerings be eaten in a holy place. These rooms were also used to store the various offerings that weren't being eaten at that time. All of these things and places were considered holy. Even the clothes they were wearing were considered holy.

There are some aspects about the Mosaic sacrificial system that I envy. There was a clear-cut delineation between what was holy and what was unclean. As modern Christians we do not have the Law to guide our understanding of what is holy and what is not. As Christians we are under the law of grace; we are saved because of the grace of God and our faith in Jesus, not because of adherence to a set of rules and regulations.

Just because we don't have clear-cut descriptions of what is clean and what is unholy doesn't mean that we don't have to concern ourselves with it. We also need to be very careful to stay away from unholy things. And when we do come in contact with them we need the cleansing of the Word of God and God's forgiveness to purify us.

The Israelites were where they were at this time in history because they had forgotten this and God chastised them and punished them. They are His chosen people; we should not think that He won't do the same thing to us. God expects us to keep holy things holy and to stay away from things that will make us unholy in His sight.

The Israelites were called to keep themselves pure and so are we. They had clear-cut instructions on how to do that. We have the Word of God and His Holy Spirit. We need to let these guide us to holiness and purity. God promised to bless His people and that they would be a blessing but that was only as long as they kept themselves holy. We also can be blessed and be a blessing to others only as long as we keep ourselves holy. Jesus, teach us to keep Your holy things holy.

Rick Lancaster / PLANTERS PERSPECTIVE

NOVEMBER 22 || EZEKIEL 44:8

You have not kept the laws I gave you concerning these sacred rituals, for you have hired foreigners to take charge of my sanctuary.

Read: Ezekiel 44:1-45:12

God is having Ezekiel remind the nation of Israel about the way that He told them that He wanted to be worshipped. God had given the Israelites very clear and extensive instructions on how He wanted to temple worship to take place. Over time the Israelites started to treat these instructions nonchalantly. These rituals became so common that the Israelites started to bring in foreigners to do the work for them. What a powerful warning is found in this for all of us.

God had given them clear directions on how to perform the various rituals that He commanded them to keep. God didn't change His mind later. To God these rituals were as important as the first day that He gave them to the Israelites. What changed were the hearts of the people. The longer that they did these rituals the less meaningful they became; they became commonplace and mundane. At the same time the people that were responsible for conducting these rituals began to think of themselves as important. The more important they thought themselves to be, the more mundane became the rituals that they were performing.

As modern evangelical Christians we do not have the same types of rituals that the Israelites did. They had very specific ways of worshipping God. We are given much more freedom in the manner that we come to worship God. We do have some rituals like communion and baptism but most things that we do are not dictated explicitly by God. I believe that puts us at even greater risk of falling into the same trap that the Israelites did. Because we don't have clear, distinct direction from God on how we should worship Him that we are at greater risk of making our worship mundane and common.

God deserves our very best and He deserves that we treat every aspect of our worship of Him with reverence and awe. Every aspect of our lives which we do as an act of worship toward God (which should be every part of your life) should be approached as something holy. How you dress when you go to church or to your Bible study should show your reverence and awe of God. That doesn't mean you need to wear some special kind of clothes but you should ask yourself if God would be pleased with what you are wearing. When you tithe it is an act of worship; do it with joy and gladness. Prayerfully ask God to direct you in all those kinds of things.

Treat the things of God as holy because they are. God is not happy when we treat His things as common and mundane. If God has called you to serve Him in any way (which He has) then you should treat that as a holy privilege and thank Him for it by serving faithfully and diligently. God's blessings are often a product of our obedience. Don't get tired of doing those good things that He gave you do to. Jesus, teach us to serve.

NOVEMBER 23 || EZEKIEL 45:17

The prince will be required to provide offerings that are given at the religious festivals, the new moon celebrations, the Sabbath days, and all other similar occasions. He will provide the sin offerings, burnt offerings, grain offerings, drink offering, and peace offerings to make reconciliation for the people of Israel.

Read: Ezekiel 45:13-46:24

Ezekiel's vision of the future of the nation of Israel includes this description of the role of the prince. Depending upon your interpretation of this vision this prince is either a literal prince over the people of Israel or it is the Prince of Peace Jesus. Because of the nature of the things that are going on it seems to make better sense that this is a literal prince, a leader for the nation of Israel.

This prince is to provide for the various offerings that are required in the Law of Moses. The purpose of those offerings is for the reconciliation of the people. The Law of Moses instructed people they could be reconciled to God. They needed to be reconciled because they just like everyone else committed sins that separated them from their God. These various offerings were meant to atone for their sins and bring them back into fellowship with a righteous and holy God.

The prince has the role of leading the people in this act of worship. He was to make sure that everything that was needed for these offerings was available to them. The prince had the responsibility of leading people toward reconciliation with God.

As Christians, there is no longer a need for these offerings because the ultimate offering was made at the cross of Jesus Christ. His sacrifice was the perfect offering to take away our sins. Even though our sins are forgiven they still work to separate us from a righteous and holy God. We do not need to bring offerings to God to be reconciled. Instead we need to bring ourselves as a living sacrifice.

As leaders of families, ministries, or churches we must lead people to the altar of God. We need to teach them through our lives and words what it means to be a living sacrifice to God. It is up to us to provide what they need so that they can be reconciled to their God. Many of those that we lead will never find their way there without help. If God has called you to lead, even if it is only in your family or a small group of people in your church or at your work, they need you to lead them to God.

The prince was called to provide in all areas that the people were to called to make offerings to God. The same applies to us as leaders. In all areas of life and ministry, you need to be finding ways to lead those that follow you to the altar of God's grace and mercy. If you are not sure how to do that then you find someone to lead you and teach you. Jesus, teach us to lead them to You.

NOVEMBER 24 || EZEKIEL 48:11

This area is set aside for the ordained priests, the descendants of Zadok who obeyed me and did not go astray when the people of Israel and the rest of the Levites did.

Read: Ezekiel 47:1-48:35

As the Lord is describing to Ezekiel how the land should be divided out to the tribes He tells Ezekiel to give a special piece of land to the descendants of Zadok. These descendants have the distinction of having been faithful to God even when all of their fellow countrymen had turned to idolatry. Because of their faithfulness they were given the distinct privilege of ministering before God in the temple. No one else was allowed to do it.

These descendants of Zadok were no better or more holy than the other Israelites. What made them different was their faithfulness to God. What makes this especially important is the fact that they did this while the rest of the nation practiced idolatry all around them.

We live in a world where idolatry is increasingly prevalent. In the US it is not the kind that the Israelites were practicing but it is idolatry none the less. Instead of worshipping stone and wood idols, we are worshipping idols of money, position, possessions, or power. We may not sacrifice animals to these idols but we sacrifice our relationships and lives to them.

God calls us to turn away from all of those idols and worship only Him. That can be incredibly difficult because everyone around us is likely worshipping those idols. To go against the flow of everyone around you takes great courage and an unflinching faith that God is in control. God's desire is that we would be faithful to His call on our lives regardless of what the rest of the world is doing.

What Zadok and his descendants experienced from their faithfulness was a special place in the kingdom of God. One of the things that struck me in this text was that Ezekiel is talking to the descendants of Zadok. We leave a spiritual legacy behind for all of those that follow after us. When we are faithful to God's call and instructions, our descendants, both physical and spiritual will reap rewards and blessings. Of course, they also need to be faithful otherwise they risk losing the blessings and breaking the chain of reward.

Whatever the world does around you, just be faithful to God and He will look down upon you and smile. You may receive a reward in this lifetime and you may not but your descendants will likely reap a harvest of blessings and rewards from your faithfulness. The only way to do that is to keep your eyes on Jesus. Don't spend too much of your time looking at what everyone else is doing; you concentrate on what God is calling you to do. Jesus, help us to be faithful.

NOVEMBER 25 || DANIEL 1:8

But Daniel made up his mind not to defile himself by eating the food and wine given to them by the king. He asked the chief official for permission to eat other things instead.

Read: Daniel 1:1-2:23

King Nebuchadnezzar came with his army and besieged Jerusalem and conquered it. In addition to the precious items from the Temple of God he also brought back many prisoners of the people of Israel. Nebuchadnezzar ordered that the 'strong, healthy, good looking' young men of the captives be brought to his palace. They were to undergo a three-year training process to determine if some of them would be fit to become advisors in his royal court.

Daniel was one of the four young men named that were selected to be a part of this process. The king assigned to them the best of the food and wine that was served to him as their ration. Daniel made up his mind not to eat that food and wine because he felt that it would defile him. He then asked for permission to eat something else.

Daniel was a Jew and had been raised under the strict dietary rules of the Law of Moses. God gave to Moses to give to the nation of Israel very strict instructions as to the things they could and could not eat. These dietary laws were meant to result in the Jews being a separated people. They were meant to be different from the world around them. The dietary laws were just one of the ways that God wanted to use to cause the Hebrews to be a people that stood out from the rest of the world.

Daniel could have easily justified in his own mind that he was a prisoner exiled from his homeland. He could have easily convinced himself that he really didn't have a choice. Daniel is showing great faith in God and resolve of character to make a choice like this. This is even more remarkable when we remember that Daniel was a teenager at this time.

In many respects we are just like Daniel. This world that we live in is not our home. As Christians we are citizens of heaven. We are just passing through this world as we wait for our graduation to heaven. The world is also trying to 'train' us to be like it is. And just like Daniel, we are daily being offered things that will defile us.

We are called to be a separated people. Unlike the Jews we do not have the Law as a guideline. Instead we look upon the New Testament as our guide and we depend upon the Holy Spirit to teach us about holiness and separation from the things of the world.

It all begins with a single choice, much like the one that Daniel made in our verse for the day. We must choose not to be defiled by the world around us. Even if we never fully attain it our goal must be absolute holiness and righteousness. If we don't set that as our goal, then we have no hope of even approaching it. Choose not to be defiled by the world around you. Jesus, help us to choose daily to be undefiled.

Rick Lancaster / PLANTERS PERSPECTIVE

NOVEMBER 26 || DANIEL 2:30

And it is not because I am wiser than any living person that I know the secret of your dream, but because God wanted you to understand what you were thinking about.

Read: Daniel 2:24-3:30

King Nebuchadnezzar has a dream that he doesn't understand and so he calls for all of his wise men and commands that they tell him the meaning of the dream. The wise men logically ask Nebuchadnezzar to tell them what the dream was so that they can interpret it. Nebuchadnezzar refuses to tell them and insists that they tell him what his dream was and then give the interpretation or they will be killed.

Daniel is one of Nebuchadnezzar's wise men. For some reason he is not present when this exchange is taking place. The king is furious and gives orders to have all the wise men executed. That was probably not the wisest decision that he could make but it does open the door for God to prove His power and wisdom to the king and to us.

Daniel hears about the decree to kill all the wise men and sends a message to the king to hold off until he has enquired of the Lord. Daniel is brought before the king and he asks Daniel if he can interpret the dream. Daniel's reply was, 'No!' He then explained to Nebuchadnezzar that only God could perform a miracle like that.

At that moment Daniel had an opportunity to promote himself and bring glory to himself by claiming credit for the interpretation he was about to give. Instead, Daniel pointed the pagan king Nebuchadnezzar to the Almighty God. In our verse Daniel tells the king that the reason why he is able to interpret this dream is not because he is wiser than anyone else. He is able to interpret this dream because God wanted Nebuchadnezzar to understand what the dream meant.

This is true humility! Daniel is claiming no credit for this ability and is giving all the glory to God. All of us will find ourselves in similar kinds of places. God will desire to reveal Himself and His power and attributes to others and He will be looking for someone to be the vessel of that display. Daniel is telling the king to take his eyes off of the vessel and put them on the source of the power. We need to do the same thing as we experience Almighty God at work within us.

Nebuchadnezzar acknowledged God's power as a result of this miracle. God also elevated Daniel to a position of high authority within the kingdom of Babylon. If we will just humble ourselves before God and give Him all the glory that is due Him, we can be pretty sure that God will do similar things for us. God may not make you Vice President but he will give you grace in other areas of your life. Don't take credit for the things that God is doing in your life or in the world around you, point everyone to God and His power. Jesus, help us to turn everyone's eyes to You.

NOVEMBER 27 || DANIEL 4:30

As he looked out across the city, he said, 'Just look at this great city of Babylon! I, by my own mighty power, have built this beautiful city as my royal residence and as an expression of my royal splendor.'

Read: Daniel 4:1-37

Babylon is said to have one of the most spectacular cities ever constructed. It was a wondrous thing to behold. King Nebuchadnezzar was very successful at his campaigns of conquest and was a prolific builder. Daniel chapter four is fascinating because much of it appears to be written from the perspective of King Nebuchadnezzar, a pagan king; it is as though he is narrating this chapter.

Early in the chapter God had warned him in a dream that something pretty dramatic was going to happen. Daniel interpreted the dream and told Nebuchadnezzar that his kingdom was going to be torn away from him and he would be driven mad and driven from the kingdom that he had built to live like an animal for seven years. This vision was fulfilled twelve months later and was triggered by Nebuchadnezzar's statement in our verse for the day.

The king looked out over the incredible city that he had built and then allowed his pride to express itself. God had determined to make an example of Nebuchadnezzar to the rest of the world. God used this seven year event to prove to the whole world that He is in complete control over everything including the pagan kings and kingdoms of the world.

As Christians, especially Christian leaders, we cannot exclude ourselves from the lesson that God is teaching here. Nebuchadnezzar's pride and arrogance was the trigger to this event. As leaders of families, ministries, or churches we can find ourselves also standing on the roof of some impressive structure or inside some amazing organization or in a place where our efforts are being recognized. What we do at that moment will determine how the rest of our life may play out.

God put Nebuchadnezzar on a seven year time-out. God will not hesitate to do that to any of the rest of us as well. If we begin to look around at the things that God is doing and begin to believe in our hearts that we are responsible for it happening we can be assured that God is preparing a grassy field for us to hang out in until we figure out who is really in charge.

We can avoid that ever happening by just humbling our hearts before God. Few sins anger God like the sin of pride. The Bible is rich with warnings and exhortations against pride. It is also filled with promises for those that practice the opposite of pride, humility. Humble your heart before the Creator of the universe before He does it for you. Jesus, help us to recognize that everything in our lives is as a direct result of You working on our behalf.

Rick Lancaster | PLANTERS PERSPECTIVE

NOVEMBER 28 || DANIEL 5:17

Daniel answered the king, "Keep your gifts or give them to someone else, but I will tell you what the writing means."

Read: Daniel 5:1-31

King Belshazzer of the Babylonians decided to throw a big party and during that party he had the holy vessels, gold and silver cups, from the temple in Jerusalem brought out so that his nobles could drink from them. Right in the middle of the party a hand appears and writes something on the wall. The king gets pretty freaked out about this and so he calls in all of his wisest men to determine what it means. He promised to these men great rewards if they would just tell him what the words meant. None of them could. The queen mother tells the king that there is a man that probably can interpret the writing on the wall.

Daniel is brought before the king and the king tells him that if he will interpret the writing that he will reward him including a promotion to the third highest ruler in the land. In our verse for the day Daniel tells the king that he can keep his gifts. It is very possible that Daniel knew what was about to transpire that very night and that the rewards would be meaningless once Belshazzer was killed and Darius became king.

But there is another principle that we as Christians should take careful heed of. Daniel had a gift from God to interpret things like the hand writing on the wall of Belshazzer's banquet hall. Daniel knew that it was not appropriate to 'sell' that gift. Belshazzer offered to pay Daniel to use the gift that God had given Daniel freely. God has also given each of us gifts that He expects us to use for His glory and to proclaim His name just as Daniel did.

Daniel responded and told the king that the rewards were not necessary and that he was going to do what the king asked anyway. We should be just as willing to share the gifts of God with others as Daniel was. Because of his obedience to the king and to God all of the king's nobles and his guests saw the power of God at work. Daniel was willing to serve God even if there wasn't a reward.

The story continues that Belshazzer did in fact reward Daniel with all that he said that he would. Belshazzer was killed that very night and his kingdom was conquered by the Medes and the Persians so it is difficult to know how long Daniel got to keep his reward. In Daniel's heart he had already determined to serve God regardless if there was a reward or not. Could you say the same thing about your service to the Lord? If there was absolutely no reward of any kind, would you continue to serve? If no one ever said thank you, would you continue to do what you are doing now? If no one appreciates you or if they take advantage of you, will you still serve? Daniel did! Jesus did! You should! Jesus, help us to look upon You as our reward.

NOVEMBER 29 || DANIEL 6:4

Then the other administrators and princes began searching for some fault in the way Daniel was handling his affairs, but they couldn't find anything to criticize. He was faithful and honest and always responsible.

Read: Daniel 6:1-28

King Darius plans to reorganize his kingdom. It is quite large and so he divides it into 120 provinces and assigns a prince over each of them. He then assigns three men to oversee the 120 princes. These three men would report directly to King Darius. It was a good system to control a large territory without getting too bogged down with dealing with individual provinces. Daniel was one of the three men overseeing the princes. He quickly proved himself to be the most capable of all and so the king planned to put Daniel in charge of the whole kingdom.

All the other guys didn't like the idea that Daniel was going to be in charge of everything and so they started to watch him very carefully to find some kind of fault or flaw in his character. They could find nothing to criticize about Daniel or the way that he handled his affairs. The way that these evil guys described Daniel is the way that I want unbelievers to view me; faithful and honest and always responsible.

Daniel is working in an environment that is about as difficult as you can possibly find and still maintain his integrity. He is working closely with a pagan king. He is very likely being exposed to all of the evil and wickedness that went on around the royal chambers of the king. He is also dealing with all of the politics and intrigue that goes on in a position like his. The temptations to compromise his faith and integrity must have been tremendous and yet his accusers can find nothing to charge him with. Instead they must fabricate a scenario that will trap Daniel.

If people look into your life and examine your character, would they describe it like these men described Daniel? Is your character such that people have to contrive and scheme to accuse you? Your circumstances are probably far less tempting than Daniel's were. God would call you to a Daniel level of faith. Trust God to the point that you can work in any environment while maintaining your integrity and character.

God blessed Daniel in very real and practical ways as a result of his faith and integrity. God wants to bless you as well. Stand up for the truth and refuse to compromise your integrity. It might result in some discomfort and trials as the world fights against what you are doing but you can rest assured that if you are being obedient to God that He will protect and provide for you. King Darius knew of Daniel's integrity and was sad when he discovered that he had passed a law that would cause Daniel harm. Not only did God protect Daniel but He also dealt very harshly with his enemies. Trust God; let Him be your defender and strong tower. You just do what is right! Jesus, teach us to be like You.

Rick Lancaster / PLANTERS PERSPECTIVE

NOVEMBER 30 || DANIEL 7:10

And a river of fire flowed from his presence. Millions of angels ministered to him, and a hundred million stood to attend him. Then the court began its session, and the books were opened.

Read: Daniel 7:1-28

Daniel has received a vision that describes to us the events that will take place during the End Times. This chapter is one of the keys for understanding the events that will take place at the end of Satan's reign upon the earth. A little further in this chapter is a description of Jesus Christ taking back authority, honor and royal power over all the earth.

Today's verse in context concerns the ultimate judgment facing the Antichrist. What I found interesting (as if you have any trouble finding something interesting in a chapter like this) was the reference to angels. The Bible paints a fascinating picture of these supernatural creations of God. Unfortunately, the Bible does not give us a clear picture of what they look like, their abilities, or their roles. The descriptions we do have indicate these creatures are fantastic and powerful

Two groups are mentioned in today's verse. The first group of angels is ministering to God. The word 'ministering' can also mean 'serving'. Millions of angels are busy ministering to God. There is no clear description of what these angels are doing. Elsewhere we see angelic beings around the throne worshipping God.

It is the second group that most fascinates me; a hundred million angels standing by the throne of God to attend Him. The word 'angel' is literally translated as 'messenger'. Throughout Scripture we see angels fulfilling this specific role of delivering messages to people from God. It is this role of messenger that makes this image so amazing to me.

God is a God of order and economy. He is not wasteful and things seem to flow with a sense of balance and symmetry. God would have one hundred million angels standing by because that is how many He needs to accomplish the task that He is doing.

People will sometimes wonder if God really does still give messages to His people. I believe emphatically that the answer is 'yes'. In fact, I believe that is probably the primary role of these one hundred million angels. I believe that they stand there waiting for God to give them messages for His people. And because there are one hundred million of these angels, I believe that God is keeping them busy and they are making frequent trips to the earth to give God's messages to His people.

When we pray we should see in our minds eye God calling over an angel with the reply to our prayer. That doesn't mean that every prayer gets answered the way that we want it to be but every prayer is answered. It also comforts me to know that I cannot pray so much that God would run out of angels to bring me answers. Jesus, teach us to pray confidently.

DECEMBER

DECEMBER 1 || DANIEL 8:12

But the army of heaven was restrained from destroying him for this sin. As a result, sacrilege was committed against the Temple ceremonies, and the truth was overthrown. The horn succeeded in everything it did.

Read: Daniel 8:1-27

Daniel is given a vision of the near future. He sees the overthrow of the Medo-Persian Empire by the Greek Alexander the Great. After Alexander's pre-mature death the Greek Empire is divided into four sections ruled by four generals. The 'little horn' of our text for today is likely Antiochus IV Epiphanes. One of the things that Epiphanes did was to cause the Temple worship to cease and replaced with all sorts of terrible forms of pagan worship.

In our verse for the day we are told that the army of heaven was restrained from destroying him. That creates a fascinating picture of heaven. It is as though the armies of heaven are looking down upon the earth and when they see this evil taking place, their immediate response is to come down and destroy the offender. Their zeal for the holiness of God's Temple burns hot within them.

They are restrained from destroying this terribly wicked man. It is fairly obvious in the text that there is a significant battle taking place between the forces of evil and the armies of God. For some reason God restrains them. A couple of things can be learned from this. First, if they had not been restrained, the armies of God would have destroyed this evil man and his evil forces. We should never assume that just because God doesn't do something that He can't do it. There is nothing that God can't do.

The second thing is much harder to understand, regardless how long you have walked with the Lord. He will allow some evil people to continue in the world and even allow them to prosper. The 'horn' in our verse for the day succeeded in everything it did. We will probably not fully understand why God allows that until we get to heaven.

God does allow the darkness of evil to continue and even to succeed in driving out the light of His truth from the world. One of the reasons why He does this is so that His light will shine that much brighter from those that cling to the truth. We might look around the world today and see what seems to be a similar scenario of the darkness and evil succeeding in this world. As carriers of the light of God's truth we need to shine brightly to all those around us.

While the times that we live in are getting darker by the day, they are not even a shadow of what the end-times are going to be like. Even the terrible things that Epiphanes did will pale in comparison. We don't know when those terrible times might start, and thankfully as believers we will not be made to endure them, but those that are left behind will have to endure evil that is unrestrained in this world. It is up to us to shine as brightly as we can so that those that we love know the truth. Jesus, help us to get rid of anything that blocks Your light from our lives.

DECEMBER 2 || DANIEL 10:12

Then he said, "Don't be afraid, Daniel. Since the first day you began to pray for understanding and to humble yourself before your God, your request has been heard in heaven. I have come in answer to your prayer."

Read: Daniel 9:1-11:1

Daniel had received a vision that troubled him greatly. He began to pray and ask God to give understanding of what the vision meant. It took three weeks for the answer to come to Daniel and it came in a spectacular way; an angel delivered it to him. Daniel is overwhelmed by this appearance and needs to be strengthened by him.

There are some tremendous truths to be found in this verse and text. Daniel was told that God had heard his prayer from the first moment that he had begun to pray. When God doesn't answer our prayers right away I believe that we sometimes think that we need to keep praying our prayers because we think that God didn't hear us the first time. Or we might think that God didn't understand what we were praying for. God doesn't need us to repeat ourselves, He doesn't need us to speak louder, He doesn't need us to maintain a certain posture while praying; God hears our prayers.

We are taught in scripture to keep coming to God with our prayers. That is not so that we will change God's mind or so that He will hear us but so that we will be changed and we will hear His voice. Persistence in prayer is not a lack of faith but proof of it and also the conduit to hearing from God.

One of the keys to getting a response from God to your prayers is also found in this verse; Daniel humbled himself before God. Daniel didn't understand the vision that he had received from God. He admitted that to God and asked God to give him understanding. Few things will set your prayer life on fire like humility. It is our pride and selfishness that often hinders our prayers from being answered.

It takes humility to admit that you don't know something or that you need help. It takes faith to believe that God is able to bring understanding and is able to give us what we are looking for. It takes both humility and faith to see our prayers being answered. In Daniel's case we see it also takes patience. Daniel waited three weeks to receive the answer to his prayers. The answer to his prayers was being blocked by one of Satan's princes. For Daniel to receive his answer God had to send reinforcements to assist this angel.

If you have been waiting a long time for your prayers to be answered, be encouraged by this verse. Be persistent; keep praying. Do what you can to make sure that you are praying according to God's will by comparing your request to God's Word. Then, check your heart and make certain that you have humbled yourself before God and that you believe that God hears you and will answer your prayer. Jesus, help us to wait.

Rick Lancaster / PLANTERS PERSPECTIVE

DECEMBER 3 || DANIEL 11:32

He will flatter those who have violated the covenant and win them over to his side. But the people who know their God will be strong and resist him.

Read: Daniel 11:2-35

Many of Daniel's prophecies are similar to this one, they will have dual fulfillment. This is one of those cases. In today's reading we see an event described that was fulfilled about two hundred years later by Antiochus Epiphanes. Then Jesus referred to the same prophecy as a future event, pointing to an event that is expected to take place during the Tribulation Period.

Today's reading speaks of a man that will through subtlety and diplomacy take power and will deceive many to follow him. He is the same person as the 'little horn' from Daniel 8. He will even convince some to forsake their covenant relationship with God to join his side. It is very likely that this is referring to Jews during the Tribulation period. Some of them will be deceived into turning away from God to follow the Antichrist. There are many that believe that the False Prophet of Revelation is one of these deceived Jews.

In our verse for the day we are told that some will not be deceived. These are the ones that 'know their God'. There is a powerful lesson in this for all of us. We live in a culture and society that puts little importance on the truth or God. Much of the influences in our lives are meant to deceive us and draw us away from knowing our God.

Nothing in this world could be more important than knowing God intimately and as completely as is humanly possible. While we can never know God in His infinite fullness, we can know Him as He has revealed Himself in His Word and in His Son Jesus. To stand up against the onslaught of daily influences to turn from God, we must daily seek to know Him more fully.

The key to resisting the enemy and standing strong in the face of ceaseless attacks we need to know our God. It is not necessary to develop a battle plan of defense, simply get to know the Lord and trust Him to be your strong fortress. We don't need to launch a strategic attack against our enemy. We need to rest in the strength of our Almighty God and allow Him to fight the battles of this life.

As we get to know our God better and better, we may also find ourselves recruited to get into some part of the battle as one of His soldiers. Until He recruits you, you focus on getting to know Him. Eventually everyone will be called, but we need to know Him intimately enough to recognize His voice when He calls. Too many people try to stand on their own strength and abilities. They take getting to know God as seriously as they do studying a menu before ordering a meal. They get to know just enough to place an order and then forget the rest. They are the ones that will be deceived and will turn away at the first invitation by our cunning enemy. Jesus, teach us everything there is to know about You.

PLANTERS PERSPECTIVE / *A Devotional*

DECEMBER 4 || DANIEL 12:3

Those who are wise will shine as bright as the sky, and those who turn many to righteousness will shine like stars forever.

Read: Daniel 11:36-12:13

Like today's reading, many of Daniel's prophecies speak of the end-times. This particular prophecy appears to speak of the Great Tribulation to come just before Christ returns to set up His kingdom. This prophecy is probably meant for the Jews specifically. Sadly, most Jews do not accept that Jesus was nor is the Messiah. This means that when Jesus comes to take His church out prior to the Tribulation that they will be left behind to endure the seven wraths of God's wrath being poured out on a Christ-rejecting world.

During that time two-thirds of the Jews will die during the many disasters that will befall the earth. But because the Jews are the Chosen People of God many will also experience divine protection. There are also 144,000 that will be sealed for the purpose of sharing the truth with the whole world. During the Tribulation many Jews will come to understand that Jesus is in fact who He said that He was and they will accept Him as their Messiah. It is these that Daniel is referring to.

While I believe this prophecy is meant for the Jews of the Tribulation, there is a message for Christians as well. God is pleased when we do what He wants us to do. Our obedience to His will is the gateway to His blessings in our life. Nothing pleases Him more than when we speak to others about His Son Jesus Christ. That is especially true when we are speaking to others that do not know Jesus or have turned away from Him.

There is a sense in our verse for the day that when we get to heaven we are going to be able to identify those people that have been active at sharing God's truths with others. Somehow they will stand out from all the others in heaven. They will stand out like stars in the night sky.

It is hard for me to separate my sinful nature from that picture. I like the idea of standing out in heaven. But I also know that once I get to heaven I won't really care if I stand out or not. My attention will be focused on the throne and upon He who sits upon it. The Bible speaks in many places about rewards and similar things in heaven. We have to be careful that we don't get so caught up in the idea of positions, and treasures, and rewards that we forget that we do all those things for Jesus.

Everything we do for God must be motivated out of our love for Jesus. As sinful creatures that can sometimes be very difficult. This is especially true if God gives you a level of success in the ministry that He has entrusted to you. The more successful we are, the more vulnerable we are to disqualifying sins. As leaders, we have an even greater need to keep our eyes on Jesus and our heart pure toward Him and His work on the earth. The hope of rewards in heaven should be an encouragement in the hard times but never the reason why we serve. Jesus, help us to want You more than anything in this life or in heaven.

Rick Lancaster / PLANTERS PERSPECTIVE

DECEMBER 5 || HOSEA 3:1

Then the LORD said to me, "Go and get your wife again. Bring her back to you and love her, even though she loves adultery. For the LORD still loves Israel even though the people have turned to other gods, offering them choice gifts."

Read: Hosea 1:1-3:5

The prophet Hosea was sent to give the nation of Israel a message from God that was intended to shame them into returning to the Lord. They had turned away from Him and were worshipping worthless idols and God painted a picture of that in the book of Hosea as prostitution. As far as God is concerned anyone that turns away from the Lord is acting as a prostitute, selling their affection to someone that they are not married to.

God created us to be His; no one else's. We are His special possession; whether we want to be or not. When we reject His love by rejecting His Son we are playing the harlot and committing adultery against God. A person with a hard heart doesn't really care about that but those with a heart that is sensitive to God will be offended by that thought. That is good; it shows that there is hope for our restoration to a right relationship with our Lord.

Playing the prostitute doesn't always mean that we have turned totally away from the Lord. It can also mean that we have just split our affection between God and something else. Only God can be the Lord of our lives; He must have the premier position in our lives. There are many things in my life that are important to me; my wife, my children, my church, my friends, my home, and many other things. All of these things take a distant second to God in my life. If any of those are elevated to a place equal or higher than God then I am committing spiritual adultery against God.

The cool thing about God is that no matter how unfaithful we are, He is always faithful. No matter how long or in what ways I might wander from the Lord, He is always faithful to take me back and to cleanse me of my adultery through repentance and forgiveness.

The book of Hosea is targeted at the entire nation of Israel but it calls out the leaders of the nations as the cause of the prostitution in Israel. As leaders of our families, ministries, and churches we must never forget that our sins will affect the lives of those we have been called to lead. If we sin, then there is a high probability that they are going to sin as well. Where we lead, they will follow. If we lead them into sin like idolatry, we must realize that we will give an accounting for that before the Lord.

In a message that I heard recently it was said that the most important thing that a pastor needed to have for his church was his own personal holiness. To lead others toward holiness, we must first be holy. In our verse for the day we are reminded that God is faithful and loves us even when we have been unfaithful. Jesus, give the ability to stay close to you.

DECEMBER 6 || HOSEA 4:6

My people are being destroyed because they do not know me. It is all your fault, you priests, for you yourselves refuse to know me. Now I refuse to recognize you as my priests. Since you have forgotten the laws of your God, I will forget to bless your children.

Read: Hosea 4:1-5:15

The prophecies of Hosea are given in a time when the nation of Israel has almost entirely turned away from the Lord. Within this book is some very difficult imagery that is meant to shock and upset the people. God desires that they will be shocked back into a right relationship with Him.

The nation of Israel had been chosen to be the unique object of God's love and grace. No other nation experienced as intimate a relationship with God as did the Israelites. No other nation was promised God's protection and blessing like the Jews were. All God expected in return was that they worship Him alone. Time and again, they rejected God's desires and worshipped false gods.

The result of turning away from God was that they did not know God. This lack of knowledge was destroying them. Not knowing God has severe impact upon every aspect of our lives. It is not just a physical destruction, but in all aspects of our lives. An ignorance of God will destroy us emotionally, relational, professionally, and of course, spiritually.

In our verse the prophet Hosea proclaims for God that the priests were to blame for this. They had the responsibility to teach people about God. Their problem was that they really didn't know God themselves. And it wasn't because they couldn't know God; it was because they refused to. The priests had access to everything that they needed to know God better than anyone else. The one thing they lacked was a fear of the Lord. It didn't bother them that God would be upset if they didn't try to know their One True God.

The consequence of this attitude on the part of the priests was that God was going to refuse to accept them as His priests. As Christians we are a part of the priesthood of Christ. That means that all of us are called to help others get to know Christ. If you are involved in any kind of leadership in your life, family, or ministry then this responsibility is magnified. We will all stand before God some day and give an account of how well we fulfilled this calling to make Christ known to others. The text reminds us that we must know him ourselves first.

God takes this seriously. So seriously that it comes with a severe consequence. He tells the priests that because they have forgotten His laws He will forget to bless their children. As a parent of three children, I want my children to be blessed. One of the ways that I can make sure that they are is to come to know God intimately and then teach others to know Him, including my children. Jesus, teach us to know You.

Rick Lancaster | PLANTERS PERSPECTIVE

DECEMBER 7 || HOSEA 9:8

The prophet is a watchman for my God over Israel, yet traps are laid in front of him wherever he goes. He faces hostility even in the house of God.

Read: Hosea 6:1-9:17

In the Old Testament, the office of prophet was a very important thing. This person had the mighty role of speaking to the people the things that God wanted them to know. You didn't ask for the job and you couldn't be trained to do it. God selected the people that He wanted to be prophets. When God spoke to a prophet, he was expected to tell the intended recipients exactly what God said. There are also many accounts of people going to the prophets and asking them to inquire of the Lord for something that was going on in their lives.

The office of prophet no longer exists in the church. However, the spiritual gift of prophecy does. God still speaks to individuals and requires them to share His message with others. God is still using people to be watchmen over His people. The difference now is it is not just Israel but for all that would believe. God has chosen certain people to be His representatives to watch over and guard His people.

In the church today that is anyone that has assumed a role within a ministry or church, especially a leadership role. Within a ministry or church, your responsibility is not to do a certain job but to minister to the body as the Lord would direct. This will be accomplished through a series of tasks and activities but the objective is to do ministry, not just do the tasks and activities. Part of that ministry is to be a watchman over the flock of God. And as you are doing that ministry He is going to speak to you about things that he wants you to share with those that you come into contact with. And when He does we must be sure to share those things.

We must be very careful with this responsibility. Often we can think we are hearing from God when we are actually hearing from our flesh. We know we are hearing from God, when what we are saying lines up with the word of God. Also, what we say should draw people to God and should be edifying in nature. We must know that what we are saying is the truth. The problem is that many people don't want to hear the truth. They would much rather live their lives the way that they want to, not the way that God wants them to. And to protect themselves from the truth they will attack those that tell the truth. We might like to believe that within the church this doesn't happen but it does all too frequently.

Don't be surprised when someone within your ministry or church is hostile when faced with what God wants to say. It happened in the Old Testament to the prophets and it happened to Jesus. Why should you be any different? Jesus, help us to share the truth in love and to love those that are hostile toward your truth.

DECEMBER 8 || HOSEA 10:1

How prosperous Israel is—a luxuriant vine loaded with fruit! But the more wealth the people got, the more they poured it on the altars of their foreign gods. The richer the harvests they brought in, the more beautiful the statues and idols they built.

Read: Hosea 10:1-14:9

God had blessed the nation of Israel tremendously. This tiny little nation was incredibly prosperous. We see the same condition in the nation of Israel today. It is a lush and prosperous nation. Through the prophet Hosea the Lord tried to show the nation of Israel how they had allowed their prosperity to draw them away from God rather than toward Him. There is also a warning for everyone that is a believer in Jesus Christ.

One of the greatest dangers that a Christian can face in this life is success and prosperity. Most people look at a statement like that and shake their head and say that I am nuts. Most people believe that success and prosperity are the answer to all of their problems. The problem is that when we live our lives seeking success and prosperity, we find it to be a very elusive goal. We are never successful or prosperous enough.

We as modern Christians in America don't really have a very good picture of what it means to pour out an offering onto an altar. In many parts of the world you will see altars all over with offerings poured out on them. In America we have different kinds of altars. They are expensive cars and RVs, clothes, and jewelry. It is cosmetic surgery and beauty salons. Not that any of these things are evil in themselves unless they become a place of worship of our success and prosperity.

One of obvious places where this is seen is in the buildings that we construct. What do our homes, ministry buildings, and churches communicate about God? Are they places where the grace, mercy, blessings, and love of God are manifested? Or are they places of opulent testimony of OUR success and prosperity? The exact same building could be one or the other and the determining factor is found in your heart. Is it a place where the glory of God is seen or is it a place where your glory is seen?

Before we begin to pour the wealth, whether great or small, that God gives us onto anything that might be viewed as an altar we need to be very sure that it is an altar that God would have us to build. Don't waste the blessings of God building something that doesn't bring glory to God. If you do it, is a waste and He will not bless it.

If you are going to build a home; build it so that it can be used to bless God's people. If you are going to construct a building for ministry, build it so that it can minister to His people. If you are going to build a church; do it so that the lost sheep of God's flock are drawn into it. Do that and God will be glorified and He will continue to prosper you so that you can continue the work. Jesus, teach us to handle success and prosperity as we would a venomous snake.

Rick Lancaster / PLANTERS PERSPECTIVE

DECEMBER 9 || JOEL 1:9

There is no grain or wine to offer at the Temple of the LORD. The Priests are mourning because there are no offerings. Listen to the weeping of these ministers of the LORD!

Read: Joel 1:1-3:21

The prophecies of Joel tend to focus on a period of time known as the Day of the Lord. The Jews knew this to be a time when God pours out His righteous judgment on a sinful world. Joel describes in terrifying detail a time when God's wrath is poured out on the world that He created.

In today's reading Joel describes the effects of this time of judgment as a time when all crops are ruined by an invading army of locusts. This army was going to utterly ruin everything. The result is seen in our verse for the day. The priests are weeping because there is nothing available to use for offerings in the Temple.

It seems from the text that the priests are upset because they can't make the daily offerings. I am certain that this is a part of what is going on but it is not all. What is not obvious from this text is that this meant that the priests weren't getting anything to eat either. The sacrificial system was an elaborate set of sacrifices and offerings to continually remind the people of their desperate need for God's provision and protection.

Very few of the offerings were burned up completely. Most of them included a portion of the offering to be burned up on the altar and in some cases the offering was waved before the altar and none of it was burned up. Everything that was not burned up was given to the priests as their food. If there was nothing to offer to the Lord, then there was nothing for them to eat. This then meant that they needed to work to provide food for themselves and for their families.

The role of the priests was to minister before the Lord and to the people. It was the priests that were responsible for teaching the people about God. The more they were required to work to provide for themselves the less they were able to teach the people about God. The less the people knew about God, the more likely they were to turn away from the Lord. All of these reasons combined were the reasons why the priests wept.

As a minister myself, I can empathize with the priests of Joel's time. If I was not able to serve God in the way that I was called it would be a tremendous burden to my heart. I am blessed that the ministry that I serve is able to provide for my family's needs. With the current economic conditions that may not always be the case. We can't say for certain that we are in the last days but the signs certainly cause us to believe that the time of Christ's return could be soon. Joel's prophecy was meant to cause people to want to turn their hearts more fully to the Lord. God calls all His people to give for the work of the ministry of Jesus. As the last days approach, don't forget to do your part to keep that work going by providing for the 'priests' that God has called to teach you about Jesus. Jesus, help us to help those that You have called to be ministers.

DECEMBER 10 || AMOS 1:1

This message was given to Amos, a shepherd from the town of Tekoa in Judah. He received this message in visions two years before the earthquake, when Uzziah was king of Judah and Jeroboam II, the son of Jehoash, was king of Israel.

Read: Amos 1:1-3:15

Amos was given a message from God to give to the nations of Judah and Israel to warn them of the impending destruction that was coming because of their disobedience. That is the grace of God at work. God had already told them that if they didn't follow Him and obey Him that He was going to destroy them and expel them from the land that He had promised and given them. No further warning was necessary; God would have been in His rights to simply destroy them. But that doesn't work within God's amazing grace. He wants everyone to repent of their sins and get into a right relationship with Him. Because of His grace, he will be patient and He will send warnings to turn us back to Him.

Amos was a shepherd; that's what caught my attention this morning. It seems that God had an unusual love for shepherds. I find that interesting because we often hear teachers say that shepherds were despised as one of the lowest trades there was. It just goes to show you how different man and God are; things that we despise, God loves.

The role of the shepherd is one that I have come to appreciate and cherish. In my own life and ministry I have come to see myself more as a shepherd than anything else. So much of scripture points to the role and nature of a shepherd; especially of God's people. It has become my goal to be a shepherd and to use as my model all the examples of shepherds in the Bible. Amos is one such example. Amos spoke out against the idolatry that was ruining the nations of Israel and Judah. He also spoke out against the other nations around Israel.

As a shepherd of the flock we need to speak out against the sin that is all around us. Amos was not concerned about whether or not he offended people or made them angry. God gave him a word to share and he did boldly. My responsibility as a shepherd of God's people is to do the same thing; as He gives me a word for someone or the church, I am to give it to them the same way that He gives it to me. God has perfect knowledge and He knows just the right words and methods to reach His sheep. We should never add to the things He gives us for His people nor should we ever change it in any way.

Amos is a good example of a shepherd but the perfect example is Jesus Christ, the Good Shepherd. He also spoke forth the things of God that people needed to hear. As He shared His style of presentation was different for the person and situation that He was in. To the innocent He was gentle and loving. To the seeking, He was instructive. To the proud and arrogant, He was firm and unyielding. Jesus, teach us to be shepherds of Your flock.

Rick Lancaster / PLANTERS PERSPECTIVE

DECEMBER 11 || AMOS 4:6

"I brought hunger to every city and famine to every town. But still you wouldn't return to me," says the LORD.

Read: Amos 4:1-6:14

Today's reading is one that might cause some people to question whether God is truly a loving God. In chapter four of Amos, the Lord says that He has brought hunger, famine, drought, blight, plagues, and destruction to the cities and towns of the land. Amos is speaking to God's people. God is doing all these terrible things to His own people. God is causing His own people to suffer. Why in the world would He do such a thing?

The answer is found in our verse for the day. The Lord says, 'But still you wouldn't return to me.' This is the first of five times that this phrase is repeated exactly. The reason all these things were happening to God's people is because they wouldn't come to Him and worship him as their God.

One might say that this seems a bit harsh. We need to keep in mind that God has consistently warned them that if they turned away from Him that all these things would come upon them. This started with Moses while they were in the wilderness. In Deuteronomy 28 Moses laid out very clearly that God would bless them in their obedience and curse them if they were disobedient. God is being faithful to His word. He has also been faithful to send prophets that spoke to the people warning them from their sinful practices and exhorting them to return to God.

What struck me about this text was that there were probably people within those cities that did return to the Lord. God has always maintained a remnant within his people. And even though they were doing what they could to follow the Lord they still had to experience the suffering of the unrepentant people around them.

This has really struck me as I see all that has transpired this year (2008). The weakened economy has had dramatic consequences throughout the entire world. We have seen people losing their homes and jobs at record rates. As a result marriages are struggling and failing which carries its own severe consequences. The upcoming year does not bring with it any promises of that getting any better. Some 'experts' suggest that we may not have seen the worst of it yet. People in the church are not immune to these difficult times. In fact, they are experiencing them at the same rate as those that are outside the church.

God's goal is still the same; He wants all of His people to return to Him. As Christians we are just as likely to turn away from God as the Israelites of Amos' time. Returning to Him doesn't guarantee relief from the difficult times God is allowing in the world around us. He certainly could and if it is His will He will. All we can do is seek Him with our whole heart, soul, mind, and strength and trust Him with everything. Then we need to pray that our country would return to Him and worship Him as their God. Jesus, help us to help Your people return to You.

DECEMBER 12 || AMOS 8:11

"The time is surely coming," says the Sovereign LORD, "when I will send a famine on the land—not a famine of bread or water but of hearing the words of the LORD.

Read: Amos 7:1-9:15

Amos had the difficult task of prophesying judgment upon the nations of Israel and Judah. They had turned away from God and had rejected all of the warnings of the prophets that God had sent before Amos. In today's verse we see that God is about to create a famine that will fall upon the land of Israel and Judah. This is not the usual famine that wipes out all the crops so that there is no food to eat. This famine is a withdrawal of the ability to hear the words of the Lord.

This is virtually impossible for the modern day Christian to conceive of. The words of the Lord are very easy to hear with television, radio, and the internet; not to mention churches on nearly every corner. We have no lack of the words of the Lord filling our ears. But even with all of that there is something of a famine in our land for the words of the Lord as well. It is not that the words of the Lord are not here but that people are not hearing them.

People can hear or watch some of the best preachers in the world twenty-four hours a day and seven days a week. But if the words that they are speaking are not having an effect which results in a change in that person's life then they are not hearing those words and they are in a spiritual famine. Usually this famine is self-inflicted and is a result of a lack of faith; they simply don't believe enough to allow the Holy Spirit to make changes in their lives. Too many people now view the teachings that they are exposed to as entertainment.

God desires that we would tune our ears in to His voice. To do that, we need to humble ourselves and ask Him to speak to us. We shouldn't listen to preachers to be entertained but we should be earnestly seeking a word from the Lord that will help us to make the changes that are necessary in our lives to be more like Christ. Jesus said that we need to feed upon every word that proceeds from God. We need to develop a hunger for the word of God and to do that we need to deny ourselves some of the things that we use to fill ourselves with.

If we don't seek the words of the Lord we might find ourselves in a spiritual famine. We can take steps that ensure that we are getting a steady diet of God's word. As we continue feeding upon His word we become more attuned to His voice as He is speaking to us. As we hear His words, we need to obey them and allow the Holy Spirit to make those changes that God wants to make. As we allow each of those changes we are better prepared to hear God's voice. Jesus, help us to hunger for a regular diet of Your word.

Rick Lancaster | PLANTERS PERSPECTIVE

DECEMBER 13 || OBADIAH 4

Though you soar as high as eagles and build your nest among the stars, I will bring you crashing down. I, the LORD, have spoken.

Read: Obadiah 1-21

With only 21 verses, Obadiah is one of the shortest books in the Bible. It is primarily a prophecy of judgment against the land of Edom but it also includes a prophecy of blessing for the people of God. In this prophecy against Edom God is telling them that they will be treated the way that they treated the people of Israel.

Edom was not the only nation to treat the people of God badly and so we need to pause and ask the question why God is singling them out here. A little later in the text God explains why; it is because the Edomites and the Israelites are close relatives. In fact, their ancestry can be traced back to two brothers, the two sons of Isaac, Jacob and Esau. Esau was also called Edom and was the father of the people of Edom. Jacob was renamed by God as Israel and was the father of the Israelites. Both the Edomites and the Israelites could race their ancestry back to Abraham.

When the nation of Israel was taken away into exile, the Edomites gloated over their misfortune and even helped their enemies to capture them. God considered that a great evil and promises to punish them for it. In our verse for the day God is telling them that there is nowhere that they can hide from His vengeance. No matter how powerful or great they might become, God is going to bring them crashing down.

This would have come as an encouragement to the people of Israel. God promised to punish the people that had so unfairly treated them. That should also be a great encouragement to us. People are going to treat you unfairly; that you can be absolutely certain of. This is especially true if you seek to follow God with your whole life.

What we are tempted to do is to take matters into our own hands and execute vengeance upon those that have attacked us or mistreated us. The problem with that is then God won't act to avenge you. If you take matters into your own hands, God will not interfere. If you think about that logically you will understand why God tells us to leave vengeance with Him. Who do you think is better equipped to execute perfect and total justice, you or God? God, of course! And in case you don't already know this, He doesn't need your help.

Our problem is that we don't know if, when, or how God is going to deal with the people that mistreat us or offend us. This is another of those areas in life where God wants us to trust Him completely. Trusting Him with those that have attacked us means letting go of all the hurt they have caused us and expecting God to do His part. It means that we will be okay with whatever He chooses to do, even if we never know what it is that He does or is going to do. It means being okay even if it looks like God is not doing anything about it. He is, we just don't see it. Jesus, teach us to trust You.

DECEMBER 14 | | JONAH 1:3

But Jonah got up and went in the opposite direction in order to get away from the LORD. He went down to the seacoast, to the port of Joppa, where he found a ship leaving for Tarshish. He bought a ticket and went on board, hoping that by going to the west he could escape from the LORD.

Read: Jonah 1:1-4:1

The account of Jonah is one that most children learn at a very young age. Even as adults we love the imagery of this fascinating account of the reluctant prophet. Jonah receives a message from the Lord for the people of the wicked city of Nineveh. Jonah then does something very peculiar, he tries to run away from God. To us that sounds very odd.

It makes more sense once we understand a little more about the culture of the day that he was in. In Jonah's time most of the pagan cultures had gods that were related to the areas in which they lived. Once you leave the area of the gods you would be outside of their area of influence. They also believed that if you wanted to have your god come with you on your trip you had to carry them with you. They would literally carry their idols with them to ensure that their gods were coming with them.

As Jonah was getting onto that ship he thought he was leaving the area that God lived in and therefore was leaving His area of influence. As modern, New Testament believers we know that there is no place that is outside of God's influence. Jonah was trying to get away from the Lord, when there is no place that he could have gone to be away from God. We look at his actions and see them as very foolish. His foolish behavior is rooted in his ignorance of one of God's attributes.

When we are ignorant of any of God's attributes or character we can easily find ourselves in the same kind of place as Jonah. We start making decisions out of our ignorance of God that end up being very foolish and carry some consequence that we would rather not experience. Jonah ended up in Nineveh like God wanted but he had to spend three days in the belly of the great fish and then spewed out on the beach smelling like the inside of a fish.

One of the many lessons that we can learn from Jonah is that we must come to know God intimately if we want to make good decisions. Jonah wasted his money and time buying the ticket and getting on the boat. Too many waste much of their life because they do not make any attempt to know God. They then end up doing foolish things that are a complete waste.

All wisdom and knowledge is found in and through God, especially as He manifested Himself through His Son Jesus Christ. If you want to be known for wisdom and knowledge then come to know Jesus more and more. Your life will grow to be more productive and fruitful. You will waste less of your life and make fewer foolish decisions. Jesus, help us to grow in our knowledge of You.

Rick Lancaster | PLANTERS PERSPECTIVE

DECEMBER 15 || MICAH 1:5

And why is this happening? Because of the sins and rebellion of Israel and Judah. Who is to blame for Israel's rebellion? Samaria, its capital city! Where is the center of idolatry in Judah? In Jerusalem, its capital!

Read: Micah 1:1-4:13

Micah is one of the pre-exile prophets that God sent to tell Israel and Judah that He was through with their continuing idolatry and unfaithfulness. God had proven to them very clearly that He was God and proven Himself faithful in providing them with the land that He promised to Abraham and his descendants. All God asked for in return is they worship Him alone and they stay away from the pagan idols of the nations around them. Because they would not heed the warnings of the prophets, God is now sending prophets to forecast their destruction.

God was giving them one last chance to repent and turn back to Him before He executed judgment. This is reminiscent of Jonah and his warning to Nineveh. If Israel and Judah had repented and turned back to God at this point God would have spared them just like He did the city of Nineveh.

What caught my attention in today's verse was where God placed the blame for the sins of the nation of Israel and Judah; their capitals, Samaria and Jerusalem. This struck me because this is inferring that the true source of the problem in the nations of Israel and Judah was to be found in their leaders. God was blaming the leaders of the nations for the sins that the people were committing.

The Bible teaches that each of us will stand before God and give account for the things that we have or have not done in our lives. This verse also lets us know that as leaders we will stand before God and give an accounting of the things that others did because of us. This should put a whole different complexion on your responsibility as a leader of your family, ministry, or church. This should cause us to examine the things that those that we are leading are doing and asking God if we are doing things that are leading them to sin.

Some people are going to sin regardless what we do. What we need to be concerned about is that we are not teaching people to sin as the leaders of Israel and Judah were doing. The people did what they saw their leaders doing, and the people around us will do the same thing. What we teach the people must line up with the way that we live our lives and our lives must line up with the word of God and His will for our lives. If we live in that way, we will be able to stand before God with a clear conscience. We can also rest in the knowledge that God's judgment will not fall upon us or our families, ministries, or churches because we are leading people to Christ and not away from Him. Jesus, help us to examine ourselves and the fruit of the ministries that you have entrusted to us.

DECEMBER 16 || MICAH 6:3

O my people, what have I done to make you turn from me? Tell me why your patience is exhausted! Answer me!

Read: Micah 5:1-7:20

In today's text God confronts the nation of Israel to defend themselves as in a court case. In some respects God is suing them because of their behavior towards Him. God's complaint against Israel is that they have breached their contract with Him. He wants to know why they have done this. God wants the Israelites to explain to Him what He has done that has caused them to behave this way.

The nation of Israel were the chosen people of God; His special possession. He made a covenant with their ancestors to be their God and they were to be His people. In the terms of that contract God promised to give them everything they needed and to protect them from their enemies. The Israelites part of those terms is that they were to worship only God and nothing or no one else. The nation of Israel had turned away from God to worship idols and God wants to know why.

As Christians we also have been chosen by God to be His special possession; not in the same way as the nation of Israel but with the same terms. We are to worship only God and in return He promises to provide for us and protect us. If we wander away from the covenant that He made with us then we should expect the same question from God. God wants to now why we would do that. These questions are meant to cause us to examine ourselves. We need to look deep within our hearts and question why we would turn away from God. Before you say you would never turn away remember that Peter told Jesus that He would never forsake the Lord and then did. Never be so prideful that you think that you cannot fall in this area.

One of the demands that the Lord makes in His case against the people is an explanation as to why their patience has been exhausted. They had been waiting for something to happen in their lives and because it didn't they turned to other gods to try to cause it to happen. This is something that we need to be on our guard about as well. There are probably things in all of our lives that God is not acting upon in the timing we desire and there may be a temptation to take the matter into your own hands. Be careful; to do that is to turn away from God.

The most difficult lesson we probably need to learn in our lives is patience. Waiting for the Lord to act in our lives may be the most difficult thing we have to do. We live in a culture that is able to give us what we want almost instantly. This has created in many people an attitude of impatience toward God. The Bible teaches that those who wait on God will not be disappointed. The inverse is also true; if you don't wait on the Lord you will be disappointed. Jesus, help us to wait patiently for You to act.

Rick Lancaster / PLANTERS PERSPECTIVE

DECEMBER 17 || NAHUM 1:3

The LORD is slow to get angry, but his power is great, and he never lets the guilty go unpunished. He displays his power in the whirlwind and the storm. The billowing clouds are the dust beneath his feet.

Read: Nahum 1:1-3:19

The first chapter of the book of Nahum is a study in contrasts of the character of God. He is described as a jealous God that angrily deals with His enemies. He is also described as a good God, a strong refuge for His people. A study of the character of God will reveal many great contrasts. You will also find that those contrasts are very consistently applied to certain groups of people. God's anger is only applied to His enemies. God is always a refuge to those who trust in Him. His character is sure; we can depend upon God to behave in accordance with His character without fail.

One of God's traits that we all ought to be very thankful for is that God is slow to get angry. God has established a standard that He expects His creation to meet. The problem is no one can meet this standard on our own merits or abilities. God doesn't get angry the first time we fail to meet His standard. He patiently waits for us to turn to Him for help. He waits with a patience that is beyond human comprehension. And all the while He is waiting, He continues to pour out His love and kindness upon us.

Our verse for the day goes on to say that His power is great and that he punishes the guilty. God is patient and He will wait a very long time for us to repent and turn to Him. But that doesn't mean He won't punish us. This verse is directed at unbelievers, telling them that God will punish them for their guilt. As believers we have this verse as a source of encouragement. It can be very discouraging to see unbelievers mocking God or persecuting us because of our faith. This verse should provide encouragement that God is waiting for just the right time to punish them.

But even in that we need to acknowledge God's love and grace. He is waiting in the hopes they will repent and turn to Him for salvation. If they do, their guilt is washed away by the blood of Jesus' sacrifice on the cross. They might not get punished for their sins against you before they were saved. If we have the heart of God, that will be okay with us. Once saved the old things pass away and all things are made new.

It is fair to pray for God to punish the guilty because His word says that He never lets the guilty go unpunished. It is not okay to ask God to punish the redeemed. Remember, if you want God to punish a believer for some mistake that they made, God will use that same standard for you. You are asking God to punish you along the same lines as you are asking Him to punish others. Of course God is God and He will do as He wills but we are warned in Scripture to be careful how we pray. We should pray with the same heart as Jesus. We learn how to do that as we grow in our knowledge of Jesus as He is revealed in Scripture. Jesus, give us the desire to grow in our knowledge of You.

DECEMBER 18 || HABAKKUK 1:11

They sweep past like the wind and are gone. But they are deeply guilty, for their own strength is their god.

Read: Habakkuk 1:1-3:19

The prophecy of Habakkuk has to do primarily with God using the nation of Babylon to punish the nation of Israel because they turned away for the True and Living God to worship worthless idols. The Israelites were living just like the pagan nations all around them and this made God angry. And so God used the pagan nation of Babylon to punish His people.

The nation of Babylon was a strong and vicious nation. The Bible likens them to wild animals in the way that they terrorized the peoples that they conquered. They showed no mercy and they showed no pity. And for a time they were unstoppable. One of the reasons they were so powerful was that God wanted to use them to get His people to turn back to Him. In our text for today, God proclaims that the nation of Babylon is deeply guilty. Their guilt comes not from the way they were treating others but because of their hearts. The Babylonians were worshipping their strength. This world we live in today is not that different than it was 2,600 years ago, people still are worshipping their strength.

National pride can easily turn into the worship of strength. Personal or corporate success can lead to a type of worship of strength. The people we tend to admire and sometimes idolize are those that exhibit some strength we do not have. We have got to be so careful not to put people up on pedestals, they don't belong there; only God does. Their strength, power, ability, or success comes from God. He is the only one worthy of our worship.

In our ministries and churches, we must be careful about this as well. We pray that God will make our ministries strong and successful. Our challenge is that once it does, we will begin to look at the strengths as the reason why the church or ministry is strong. What a dangerous trap we can fall into. The very thing that we pray for and God desires to do can be a snare that causes us to stumble.

The success of your family, ministry, or church will not be measured by how big, strong, or powerful it is. It will be measured by how well you keep Christ at the core. If Christ ever moves out of the center of your family, ministry, or church and something else is what people see at the center, then you should be warned that God may be preparing a Babylon to come and get your attention. Jesus, help us to see any strength, success, power, or influence we have as another reason to worship You and You alone.

Rick Lancaster / PLANTERS PERSPECTIVE

DECEMBER 19 || ZEPHANIAH 3:9

On that day I will purify the lips of the people, so that everyone will be able to worship the LORD together.

Read: Zephaniah 1:1-3:20

The prophet Zephaniah is given a vision of what lies ahead for the nation of Israel. In that vision God describes His disappointment regarding the way His chosen people are behaving toward each other. God's desire is that His people would be a special people; a holy people. The word 'holy' means 'set apart'. Too often we interpret this to mean we are to be perfect. For us a better word might be 'different'. God's people should be different from the rest of the world. That is what God is upset about with His people; they are just like the rest of the world.

It is not difficult to imagine that He has the same complaint about His people today. It is often difficult to tell the difference between the people of the church and the people of the world. The behaviors and attitudes of those in the church reflect those of the world. That should not be so!

Zephaniah is describing a future day when God will purify the lips of all the people so that they can worship the Lord together. It occurred to me as I was reading this that if God will cause this to happen in the future, it would please Him if His church was attempting to accomplish it before He comes. God wants all of His people to worship Him together. God wants united worship within the Church. I am not suggesting the different denominations and church organizations should be disbanded. The One-World church is not scheduled until after we are raptured. I am suggested that we stop fighting over territory and semantics and attempt to worship God together.

We should be working toward building relationships with other groups of like mind to find ways to worship God together. We all have our own styles and doctrines but the God we worship is One. There is enough common ground between us to provide opportunity to fellowship and worship. Obviously, there are some groups that we should avoid because they are apostate or heretical.

Even as I write this I know it is very difficult. People are suspicious of other groups and will defend their territory tenaciously. Personally, I believe that is a lack of trust in God's plan and ability to build His church. My only concern is that we pursue God's will in all things of the church and leave the actual building of it to Him.

Some day we will all worship the Lord together. The Lord will need to purify our lips first but it is going to happen. I would rather that He do that now in my life so that I can enjoy the fruits of that worship today. Let's stop quibbling over spiritual pedigrees and meaningless details and worship our Lord. Jesus, purify my lips.

DECEMBER 20 || HAGGAI 2:4

But now take courage, Zerubbabel, says the Lord. Take courage, Jeshua son of Jehozadak, the high priest. Take courage, all you people still left in the land, says the LORD. Take courage and work, for I am with you, says the LORD Almighty.

Read: Haggai 1:1-2:23

Zerubbabel and the remnant of the Israelites that have returned from the exile look at the temple as it is being rebuilt and weep because it is much poorer than they remember. God sends them a word of encouragement through the prophet Haggai. They needed this word because they were working very hard and yet the work was not resulting in something as nice as what had been before. The leaders and people were discouraged.

As we go about the work the Lord has for us to do we also can get discouraged. Sometimes it seems like all the work we are doing is resulting in something far less than we think it should. Sometimes it even seems like we are wasting our time. We might even wonder if we would be better off leaving this work to do something else. Don't be too hasty; God might have a word for you in this verse.

God told the Israelites to take courage. You might wonder what this verse might have to do with discouragement; it has everything to do with it. To be discouraged is to lack courage. Courage is the ability to act regardless of external circumstances. We usually relate courage with fear or danger; we say someone is courageous when they do something despite the danger around them. Courage is the ability to do anything despite whatever circumstances surround us. The Israelites lacked courage because the work was not producing the results that they wanted. I am certain that many of us can relate to that in our lives, marriages, families, at work, or in our ministries or churches. You also lack courage, are discouraged because of what you see as lacking. The Lord told the Israelites to 'take courage' which is what caught my attention in this verse. The idea of taking implies that you don't have something and you need to go somewhere else to obtain it.

The Lord goes on to tell them, in addition to taking courage they should continue to work. Just because we are discouraged doesn't give us reason to quit trying, to quit working. Too often we run from the things that discourage us rather than doing what the Lord is directing the Israelites to do; take courage and work. The Lord then tells the Israelites how and why they should do this; 'I am with you'. As long as God is with us we have a ready source of all the courage we should ever need. We need to go to Him and 'take' the courage we need to deal with whatever circumstances come our way. Then we just need to keep at the work He assigned to us regardless of how we think it is turning out. The results are not your responsibility; they are God's. Your responsibility is to take courage and work. Jesus, help us to come to You for what we need.

Rick Lancaster | PLANTERS PERSPECTIVE

DECEMBER 21 || ZECHARIAH 1:3

Therefore, say to the people, "This is what the LORD Almighty says: Return to me, and I will return to you, says the LORD Almighty."

Read: Zechariah 1:1-21

The book of Zechariah was written after the exile. The people had begun to return and the second Temple had been started but not finished. Zechariah's prophecies are filled with fascinating imagery that points to a future time when the Messiah will restore the glory of the city of Jerusalem. The book was written to encourage and exhort the people of God to hold fast to their faith.

The book opens with a clear exhortation to return to God. As we read an exhortation such as this we need to keep in mind that it wouldn't have been written if they hadn't turned away from God. Turning away from the Lord and returning to Him are a common theme throughout much of the Old Testament. If anyone struggles with believing in the base sinfulness of man he just needs to read the Old Testament and keep track of the number of times it is recorded that God's people turned away from Him after He supernaturally rescued them from their enemies.

In our verse for the day we see the system God uses to restore His people. He expects them to return to Him. It is then that God will return to them. God's word clearly teaches that God will never leave nor forsake His people. So the idea of God returning to His people must mean something other than a physical return. It relates to His activity in the lives of His people.

God will never leave us nor forsake us. But if we rebel and turn away from Him He will withdraw His hand of blessing, provision, and protection from us. All we have is from God and all we will receive will come from God. Every circumstance that has come into our lives has been directed by the Lord. Without God's hand of protection and provision the things that come into our lives will be seen as curses rather than blessings. But God's purpose remains true; he desires that we would return to Him. He will use whatever method He must to see that happen. He will even allow terrible things to happen if that is what it is going to take to get you to return to Him.

God doesn't want that to happen. He would much rather we would always want to be His people and would seek Him with our every breath. God wants to pour out blessings in our lives that are so great we have to share them with others. He wants to provide for our every need. He wants to protect us from every enemy. But if we insist on having our own way and not following His way, we leave Him with no choice but to withdraw from us. God's love for us is so great that if we will humble ourselves and return, He will never reject us. If you find yourself feeling distant from God, simply return to Him and you can expect Him to return to you. Jesus, help us to run to You.

DECEMBER 22 || ZECHARIAH 3:2

And the LORD said to Satan, "I, the LORD, reject your accusations, Satan. Yes, the LORD, who has chosen Jerusalem, rebukes you. This man is like a burning stick that has been snatched from a fire."

Read: Zechariah 2:1-3:10

Zechariah is given a vision of things going on in the spiritual world. In this vision he sees Jeshua, the high priest, standing before the angel of the Lord. Right beside Jeshua is Satan accusing him of many things. This is a familiar scene. The Bible teaches us that Satan is the accuser of the brethren. That means that he is constantly bringing charges against God's people to God.

We also know that Satan is a liar and the father of lies. What is not clear based on Scripture is whether or not he lies in the presence of God. We do know that it is impossible to lie to God; He knows everything, all the time. It would seem to me that God wouldn't permit him to lie in His presence.

What this means is that when Satan accuses us, it is about things that are true. Satan accuses us before God of sins that we have committed. I believe that is what is going on here. That is evidenced later by the fact that his clothes are filthy. The angel of the Lord instructs others standing around to remove the filthy clothes and replace them with clean ones. This is a picture of God's grace specifically in the area of forgiveness. God's forgiveness cleanses us of the filth of our sins.

Jeshua is the high priest and represents the priestly order. Just because Jeshua was the high priest doesn't make him automatically righteous and holy. He was just as much a sinner as anyone else. And just like everyone else Jeshua needed God's grace.

The Lord says to Satan, 'I reject your accusations.' It doesn't say that they are not true but that He rejects them. This is one of those incredible truths about our relationship with the Lord. He knows that we are sinners and he knows that we sin. He also has Satan standing there in His presence accusing us at every opportunity. But rather than being disappointed or upset, he rejects those accusations.

For us as Christians this is because of the finished work of Jesus Christ on the cross. Jesus paid the price for every sin and wrong thing we have ever done or will do once for all time. I would think it must be very frustrating to Satan that his accusations are regularly rejected by Jesus. But for us it means we never need to concern ourselves about whether or not Jesus will accept us. That doesn't give us a license to sin. God hates our sins and wants us to repent or turn away from them. But having done that, our relationship to God is open and free. Satan is a powerful enemy and a tenacious accuser of Christians but his accusations are rejected by the Lover and Savior of our souls. Jesus, thank You for knowing us and loving us anyway.

Rick Lancaster / PLANTER'S PERSPECTIVE

DECEMBER 23 || ZECHARIAH 4:10

Do not despise these small beginnings, for the LORD rejoices to see the work begin, to see the plumb line in Zerubbael's hand. For these seven lamps represent the eyes of the LORD that search all around the world.

Read: Zechariah 4:1-5:11

As you begin any work the Lord sets before you, meditate on this verse. The prophet Zechariah gives this message from the Lord to Zerubbabel as he is rebuilding the temple in Jerusalem. The work is going slowly and so God sends a word to Zerubbabel and the people to encourage them.

God's eyes go throughout the whole earth and when He sees His people working on the projects that He has set before them, it pleases Him. This verse asks us the question, if God is pleased how can we be displeased? God hasn't asked us to build Him a huge temple, He has asked us to build a marriage, family, ministry, or church.

As we look at the work that is going on we should respond as God does. Today's verse says that God rejoices to see the work happening. That should be our exact response, to rejoice at what the Lord is doing in our midst, no matter how small.

The old people of Zerubbabel's time wept as they saw the temple being built because it was so much less than what they thought it should be. Let us not suffer from that same sin of thinking we know better than God. The parable of the mustard seed reminds us that small things in the kingdom of God can grow to be great. And First Corinthians reminds us that God uses the humble things and the despised things and the small things to do His work.

Let us rejoice in the things that God has done! Let us celebrate as each stone is laid in this house of worship that we are building for Him! Let us faithfully and diligently keep at the work until it is completed to glory and pleasure of God. Jesus, help us to keep our eyes on You as we do the work You have given us.

DECEMBER 24 || ZECHARIAH 7:13

Since they refused to listen when I called to them, I would not listen when they called to me, says the LORD Almighty.

Read: Zechariah 6:1-7:14

One of the most important tools that we have as we do a work for God is prayer. It is the lifeblood of any ministry or work. Whether this ministry succeeds or fails; flourishes or languishes will depend greatly on our diligence in prayer. Here in Zechariah we see a great truth about prayer. None of our prayers matter if we are not listening to what God is saying. God is always speaking to us. We have got to develop the spiritual ears to hear His voice.

God speaks to us during our prayers times. It will often come as an impression or what seems like a random thought. But if we have a heart that seeks to please Him we will be able to discern His voice. God also speaks to us through His Word, the Bible. Before you read, pray and ask God to speak to you through His Word. God's Word is alive, active, and powerful. When we read, it should be with an expectancy that God is going to act through it. God speaks through people. In Zechariah 7:13 God is rebuking the people of Israel for not listening to the prophets that He had sent to guide them back to a right relationship with Him. There are a couple of lessons here for us in this text.

First, be careful not to reject the message because of the messenger. Often we will look at someone and determine that they could not be speaking for God because of something we see in their life. God can and does use the unlikeliest people to do His work. Look at me if you need proof of that. Have a heart to hear God, regardless of the messenger and you will.

Second, we are called to be messengers of God's will. What do people see when they look into your life. Do they see a life that is a testimony of what God is doing? Or are they likely to reject the message because the messenger is not believable? As messengers, we need to try to be a reflection of the Person that is sending the message.

Are you listening to God? If you want to know that God is listening to you, you must first be listening to Him. And when you hear His voice, be ready to obey. For it is through obedience that God's power, provision, and blessings flow. Jesus, open our ears to hear Your voice clearly.

Rick Lancaster | PLANTERS PERSPECTIVE

DECEMBER 25 || ZECHARIAH 8:6

This is what the LORD Almighty says: All this may seem impossible to you now, a small and discouraged remnant of God's people. But do you think this is impossible for me, the LORD Almighty?

Read: Zechariah 8:1-23

Zechariah speaks this word of encouragement to the people of Jerusalem. They are discouraged because their beautiful city still lies mostly in ruins. The task of rebuilding is overwhelming because there are many fewer people than once lived in the city. There don't seem to be enough people to get the work done. To them it all seems impossible.

The Lord encourages them by telling them that it is not impossible for Him to do. He uses His name 'Lord Almighty' to remind them that He is all-powerful. There is nothing that God cannot accomplish if He wishes to. God allows 'impossible' things to come into our lives so that we will turn to Him for help. It is as God operates in the impossible things that he shines the most brightly to an unbelieving world.

There are times in life and ministry when it seems like the work is impossible or there are too few people to accomplish what is needed to be done. Instead of being discouraged, we should take courage from the Lord Almighty and then look for Him to act on our behalf.

As we approach the end of one year and look forward to another, we might not see a bright or easy time ahead of us. There may be difficult things coming in the year or years to come. As we approach the return of Jesus, that will become increasingly true. This should not be a source of discouragement. Instead, it should cause us to more resolutely fix our eyes upward for our redemption is nearer today than ever before.

If you look around at your circumstances and see impossible circumstances or you feel like you are the only ones still left to do the work, keep in mind that you and the Lord make a majority. In the book of Philippians we are told that in Christ we can do all things. That includes impossible things.

One of the lessons that you learn early on in ministry is that no matter how much ministry you do there will always be more ministry than you can do. Ministry never ends. The needs of people will always exceed the people that are available to meet those needs. As someone called to minister to people, that can be very discouraging. All around me are the ruins of lives of people that the world is trying to destroy. I have learned that God only expects me to do as much as I can. Once I have done all that I can, He expects me to leave the rest for Him to handle. The same is true for you. All God expects you to do is your part. Everything else is His responsibility. That brings me great comfort and peace. Jesus, teach us to do our part and then trust the rest to You.

DECEMBER 26 || ZECHARIAH 9:12

Come back to the place of safety, all you prisoners, for there is yet hope! I promise this very day that I will repay you two mercies for each of your woes!

Read: Zechariah 9:1-17

Today's reading is an incredible section of scripture. It is rich in prophecy about the first and second coming of Christ. In the midst of today's reading is this promise that we find in the verse that we are looking at today. We should all make a habit of looking for and noting the promises that God makes in scripture. Some of those promises were made specifically for the nation of Israel and they don't apply beyond them but a great many of them apply to anyone that will believe in and trust God.

Our verse for today is one such promise. It is intended for everyone and is intended to be believed and lived by anyone that desires it. The promise is a precious gift that we need to treasure but it also needs to be shared. Just like almost every other gift that God gives us, He wants us to share it with others.

Zechariah is speaking to people that understand what it means to be in captivity. Many of the people that would have heard this message first hand had experienced captivity in Babylon. And while they were not physically in prison they knew that they were not free. They had been exiled to Babylon by King Nebuchadnezzar.

This is a promise of hope! God has promised to the prisoners that every woe that they have experienced will be repaid with two mercies. What a beautiful thing that is! That means that God sees each and every struggle or trial that goes on in my life. Not only does He see them but He also keeps a record of them. And that record is kept so that God can counter them with twice as many mercies. That means that for each of these tough times that God has allowed into our lives He is going to bless us twice as much in areas we don't deserve.

We live in a world that has very creative ways of taking people into captivity. There are people all around us that are prisoners. They are prisoners to some kind of sin or idolatry. Many of these are sins of the flesh but more people are prisoners of sins of the mind than of the flesh. Many of them do not even know that they are prisoners. What they do know is that their lives are not what they are supposed to be. They need a place of safety and hope. And that is where we come in. We may have already experienced the truth of this promise and now God wants us to share it with others. As leaders of families, ministries, or churches it is our responsibility to get this truth out to those that need it so desperately. They need to know there is hope and they need someone to tell them how to get it. Jesus, help us to be the ones that share this promise of safety and hope with others.

DECEMBER 27 || ZECHARIAH 10:2B

So my people are wandering like lost sheep, without a shepherd to protect and guide them.

Read: Zechariah 10:1-11:17

The Bible often refers to people as sheep and for good reason. Much of the way we behave is very similar to sheep. And one of the most obvious ways is in matter of shepherds. Without a shepherd, sheep will wander wherever they want to, with little or thought about where they are going or what dangers may lay ahead. People are just the same, without someone to lead them, they will wander through life with little or no thought of what is ahead.

Here in Zechariah 10, God is rebuking the leaders of the people because they are not leading the people toward God. He is challenging their motives and warning them against their sin. If God is calling you out of the pew and into any ministry, He is calling you to be a shepherd. And as anyone assumes a role of shepherd, they must begin a daily process of heart-checks. Daily we must examine our heart, our motives, even our desires for leadership. We must daily allow the Holy Spirit to reshape our heart to that of a shepherd. We must regularly ask ourselves: 'Am I here to serve the people or are the people here to serve me'. Our desires must be sacrificed so that the needs of the flock can be attended to.

God is looking for shepherds, because the people His Son came and died for are like sheep, wandering around lost and helpless. And God takes it very seriously when one of His shepherds is not tending the flock that has been entrusted to them. It can be a terrifying thing to think about. God will judge you for how well you tended the flock He asks you to watch over.

However, you can be comforted by the fact that He will only judge you for what you were to do. Not for what the flock does. Your responsibility is to lead the flock to Christ. It is their responsibility to follow. God will not judge you because the flock uses their free will to do what they want to, that's just how sheep are. You do your part and let God do the rest!

Lead the flock God has entrusted to you. You do this best by being a good follower. You imitate Christ first and then you lead that flock to do the same thing. Jesus, teach us to follow so that we might lead!

DECEMBER 28 || ZECHARIAH 12:7

The LORD will give victory to the rest of Judah first, before Jerusalem, so that the people of Jerusalem and the royal line of David will not have greater honor than the rest of Judah.

Read: Zechariah 12:1-13:9

The prophet Zechariah is speaking about a time that could very well be now or the near future. It speaks of Judah standing against the enemies that come against it victoriously. As we watch the events unfolding in Israel, it should amaze us as this tiny little nation stands against nations all around that seek to annihilate it.

Jerusalem is the center of the world as far as the Jew is concerned. That is where God said He had chosen to dwell with His people. Jerusalem is where His temple was and where it will be rebuilt in the Tribulation. Jerusalem will be the focus of much attention in the end-times. And yet, for a time, it is not completely controlled by the nation of Israel.

As important as the city of Jerusalem is to the Jew, it is not going to be given undue honor over the tribe of Judah. There is a fascinating study in this as it relates to the Jew. It also gives us a picture of our faith that we should not overlook. God gives honor in ways that are different than the ways that we do as imperfect humans.

We look upon great men and women and give them honor based on a human set of standards. We often evaluate them by comparing them to ourselves. These evaluations can be based on personal experience or on the person's reputation. And often those evaluations are based on wrong or incomplete information. Or we might even be using an evaluation system created by the world system.

Where this might have the greatest application in our lives is in our roles as leaders of families, ministries, or churches. There is a real temptation to believe that, because of our role, we deserve greater honor than someone else. This is a dangerous temptation that finds its source in pride.

God determines who is to be honored and when they will be honored. True selflessness will desire that others are honored before self. That fights against every bit of popular thought and against our own selfish desires. Unrestrained we will seek to be honored by everyone around us, even those that deserve more honor than us. If not controlled, this can even corrupt our hearts to the point of attempting to dishonor others so that we can get more honors. Let God decide if and when you are to be honored. Rejoice with those that God chooses to honor. Honor those that God has shown to be worthy of honor. Live a life that is worthy of honor and then trust God to honor you in whatever way He chooses. Jesus, help us to honor You by being honorable.

Rick Lancaster / PLANTERS PERSPECTIVE

DECEMBER 29 || ZECHARIAH 14:6-7

On that day the sources of light will no longer shine, yet there will be continuous day! Only the LORD knows how this could happen! There will be no normal day and night, for at evening time it will still be light.

Read: Zechariah 14:1-21

As Zechariah prepares to close his book of prophecies he does with a chapter that is both mysterious and encouraging, especially to the nation of Israel. In these last prophecies of Zechariah we see the Lord assuming total control and dominion over the earth and the peoples of all nations.

One of many fascinating things about these prophecies is found in our verses for the day. We are told that the normal passing of days ceases. It will always be daytime, there will be no night, no darkness. There is an obvious inference to an overwhelming presence of holiness and absence of sin but there is something else that needs to seen.

This prophecy is meant to be taken literally. A time is coming when the sun, moon, and stars will cease to shine and the world will be illuminated by another source. In Revelation 21 we are told what that other source is; it is the presence of God and the Lamb.

For reasons only God knows, Zechariah wasn't allowed to see that truth. Instead he marveled at this amazing thing. The human mind and body are so attuned to the passing of days by the rotation of the earth around the sun that when we cannot sense it, we become restless and uneasy. Zechariah's mind was struggling to understand how this could be possible. This was a great mystery to Zechariah and his book captures his amazement and faith.

Even though he couldn't understand how this was possible he knew that God did understand. He acknowledges that his ignorance didn't prove that God didn't exist but that his ignorance proved God's greatness. People often view the things they don't understand as proof of God's inability to be God. Prideful, they believe God should explain to them everything that is going on in their life and in the world around them.

This is especially true during difficult circumstances. Something bad or difficult happens and we don't understand why. They are a mystery to us. We then go arrogantly to God and demand that He explain what He is doing. God owes us nothing, including an explanation of why He has allowed something to happen in our lives that we don't like or that makes us uncomfortable. Our response should be like Zechariah, 'Only God knows'. Instead of objecting to the mysteries of life and the world around us, we should rejoice in God's greatness and majesty. We may not understand but God does and that should strengthen and encourage us as we walk through the mysteries of life. Jesus, thank You for the mystery of Your life and work.

DECEMBER 30 || MALACHI 2:5

The purpose of my covenant with the Levites was to bring life and peace, and this is what I gave them. This called for reverence from them, and they greatly revered Me and stood in awe of My name.

Read: Malachi 1:1-2:17

God chose the Levites from among the other tribes of Israel to be very special. They were to be the ones that led the people in worship. Their job was to teach the people about God and how to worship Him. They were to make sure worship was done in a way that showed God the respect and honor that He deserved.

They received no inheritance with their brother tribes when the Promised Land was distributed. Their inheritance was the Lord. Their reward for being used by God was God. As Christians, the Levitical system seems to have little or nothing to do with us, but as you study the role of the Levitical priests, we start to see some connections.

As you study the Levites you learn that different groups had different responsibilities in the tabernacle and ultimately the temple. Each group cared for a specific part of the tabernacle or temple. Some groups were responsible for setting up, some for tearing down, some for praise and worship, some for handling the sacrifices and offerings, and some for teaching the people. Does any of that sound familiar?

As part of a church plant or any new ministry, many of the same functions that took place in the tabernacle are taking place in your ministry, except the sacrificing of animals, I hope. And your role within that ministry is like that of the priest of the tabernacle. In fact the New Testament tells us that Jesus is our High Priest and that we are all 'a holy priesthood'. All of us have been grafted into this role of priest. Within the Levitical priesthood there were only two divisions, the High Priest (only one) and all the rest of the priests.

Our High Priest is Jesus Christ and all of the rest of us have the responsibility as His priests to help the congregation to worship God. Whether you are a pastor, ministry leader, volunteer, or toilet cleaner; you are a part of that priesthood. Our verse for today tells us that as priests in God's church, we are all part of a covenant with God. And within the terms of that covenant we are entitled to life and peace, that's God's part. Our part is reverence and awe. Reverence is to show honor and respect. Awe is an overwhelming feeling of reverence or admiration. Jesus, help us to live our lives in a way that shows You and the rest of the world that we revere you and stand in awe of Your name.

Rick Lancaster / PLANTERS PERSPECTIVE

DECEMBER 31 || MALACHI 3:16

Then those who feared the Lord spoke with each other, and the LORD listened to what they said. In his presence, a scroll of remembrance was written to record the names of those who feared him and loved to think about him.

Read: Malachi 3:1-4:6

Every time we think about God He knows it and it pleases Him so much that He has it written down in a book of remembrance. That is an incredible thought, both terrifying and wonderful. It is terrifying because I know some of the thoughts that pass through my head. They make me sick! What must they do to God? This truth that God knows my thoughts makes me desire to, "renew my mind" as Romans 12:2 tells us to with greater passion.

But it is also a wonderful thing that God loves it when my thoughts are on Him. We all know how it makes us feel when someone says to us 'I was thinking of you'. It usually brings us joy. Let's not forget that we were created in God's image. Many of the things that bring us joy are the same things that bring Him joy. He is a person after all, not an entity without feelings.

This can also be a very convicting verse. How often do I think about God during the day? Do I only think about Him when I need something from Him? And when I do think about Him, what am I thinking?

This is especially true in this day when the world has conspired to fill every waking moment with something that is not of God. But even the things of God can be used to prevent us from thinking about Him. It is a very common trap that people fall into, getting so busy doing things for God that they forget to spend time with God.

As we get involved in some work for the Lord, the enemy will use various devices to try to knock us out of the game. A pastor friend of mine is fond of saying: "If the Devil can't get you to take your foot off of the gas, he will get you to push it all the way to the floor." He will cause you to get so busy doing things for God that you stop doing them with God.

As we think about God, it is His chance to speak to us and to help us in whatever work He has set before us. We must take the time to spend time with God, even if it means doing fewer things for God. Years ago I heard a comment on this verse that I have adopted as my own: "If there is an angel in heaven writing down every time I think about God, then I am going to try to give that angel writer's cramp". Jesus, help us to think about You more and more every day. Help us to put our time with You higher than anything else in our day. Help us to have "the mind of Christ."

PASTOR RICK LANCASTER

Favorite Scripture: John 15:13 "Greater love has no one than this, than to lay down one's life for his friends.

My testimony is that of the power of a praying wife. Kelly and I were married in 1981. Kelly has been a Christian since she was a young child. I had gone to Sunday school, but have no recollection of meeting Jesus there. My life before Christ can best be described as one based on self-confidence and self-reliance. I seemed to succeed at everything I tried. I did well in the military and well in my job. This left me with the attitude that I didn't need God. Kelly prayed for me and witnessed to me for 16 years. A major job change put me into a place where I had a great amount of time to think and reflect. It seemed important to me to find out what it was that Kelly believed in. I was traveling a lot and, thanks to the Gideon's, I started finding some answers in the Bibles in hotel rooms. There came a point that I realized that my attitude toward God was based on my ignorance of who He is and what Jesus has done for me.

In October 2004, God called my family and me out of Revival Christian Fellowship to plant a church in the French Valley area of Murrieta, California. With us came a small group of faithful friends that have grown to be more like part of our family.

In starting Core Christian Fellowship, God impressed upon me the desire to help the people of our community to build strong healthy families. I am looking forward to serving the Lord by serving the families of this area for as long as the Lord wills or as long as He tarries.

Rick Lancaster is Senior Pastor of Core Christian Fellowship in Murrieta, CA. Rick has published a wide range of articles and devotional materials aimed at drawing Christians into a deeper faith with Jesus.

He and his wife Kelly have three children and they live in Southern California.

For more from Rick Lancaster visit www.corechristian.com

PLANTERS PERSPECTIVE / *A Devotional*

www.ingramcontent.com/pod-product-compliance
Lightning Source LLC
LaVergne TN
LVHW041606070426
835507LV00008B/153